PORTUGAL
MADEIRA THE AZORES

DISCARD

Turismo de Lisboa

Editorial Director   Cynthia Clayton Ochterbeck

THE GREEN GUIDE PORTUGAL MADEIRA THE AZORES

Editor	Alison Coupe
Principal Writer	Peter D. Smith
Production Manager	Natasha G. George
Cartography	Alain Baldet, Peter Wrenn
Photo Editor	Yoshimi Kanazawa
Proofreader	Jonathan P. Gilbert, Rachel Mills
Layout & Design	John Higginbottom, Natasha G. George
Cover Design	Ute Weber, Laurent Muller

Contact Us:

The Green Guide
Michelin Maps and Guides
One Parkway South
Greenville, SC 29615
USA
www.michelintravel.com
michelin.guides@us.michelin.com

Michelin Maps and Guides
Hannay House
39 Clarendon Road
Watford, Herts WD17 1JA
UK
☎ (01923) 205 240
www.ViaMichelin.com
travelpubsales@uk.michelin.com

Special Sales:

For information regarding bulk sales,
customized editions and premium sales,
please contact our Customer Service
Departments:
USA   1-800-432-6277
UK   (01923) 205 240
Canada 1-800-361-8236

Note to the Reader

One Team…
A Commitment to Quality

There's just one reason our team is dedicated to producing quality travel publications—you, our reader.

Throughout our guides we offer **practical information**, **touring tips** and **suggestions** for finding the best places for a break.

Michelin driving tours help you hit the highlights and quickly absorb the best of the region. Our descriptive **walking tours** make you your own guide, armed with directions, maps and expert information.

We scout out the attractions, classify them with **star ratings**, and describe in detail what you will find when you visit them.

Michelin maps featured throughout the guide offer vibrant, detailed and easy-to-follow outlines of everything from close-up museum plans to international maps.

Places to stay and eat are always a big part of travel, so we research **hotels and restaurants** that we think convey the essence of the destination and arrange them by geographic area and price. We walk you through the best shopping districts and point you towards the host of entertainment and recreation possibilities available.

We **test**, **retest**, **check and recheck** to make sure that our guidebooks are truly just that: a personalized guide to help you make the most of your visit. And if you still want a speaking guide, we list local tour guides who will lead you on all the boat, bus, guided, historical, culinary, and other tours you shouldn't miss.

In short, we remove the guesswork involved with travel. After all, we want you to enjoy exploring with Michelin as much as we do.

The Michelin Green Guide Team

PLANNING YOUR TRIP

INTRODUCTION TO PORTUGAL

©Pictures Colour Library

CONTENTS

DISCOVERING PORTUGAL

Associação Turismo do Algarve

MADEIRA AND THE AZORES

©Vera Bogaerts/iStockphoto.com

HOW TO USE THIS GUIDE

PLANNING YOUR TRIP

The blue-tabbed PLANNING YOUR TRIP section at the front of the guide gives you **ideas for your trip** and **practical information** to help you organize it. You'll find tours, a host of breaks in the great outdoors, a calendar of events, information on shopping, sightseeing, kids' activities and more.

INTRODUCTION

The orange-tabbed INTRODUCTION section explores **Nature** and the Sea. The **History** section spans ancient Armor through today. The **Art and Culture** section covers architecture, art, literature, language, traditions and folklore, while the **Country Today** delves into modern Portugal.

DISCOVERING

The green-tabbed DISCOVERING section features Portugal's Principal Sights, arranged alphabetically and by region,

featuring the most interesting local **Sights**, **Walking Tours**, nearby **Excursions**, and detailed **Driving Tours**.

⧉Contact information, ⬢admission charges, ⦵hours of operation, and a host of other **visitor information** is given wherever possible. Admission prices shown are normally for a single adult.

STAR RATINGS★★★

Michelin has given star ratings for more than 100 years. If you're pressed for time, we recommend you visit the ★★★, or ★★ sights first:

★★★　Highly recommended
★★　　Recommended
★　　　Interesting

Address Books - Where to Stay, Eat and more...

WHERE TO STAY

We've made a selection of hotels and arranged them within the cities by price category to fit all budgets (&see the Legend on the cover flap for an explanation of the price categories). For the most part, we've selected accommodations based on their unique regional quality, their regional feel, as it were. So, unless the individual hotel embodies local ambience, it's rare that we include chain properties, which typically have their own imprint.
&See the back of the guide for an index of where hotels featured throughout the guide can be found.

WHERE TO EAT

We thought you'd like to know the popular eating spots in Brittany. So, we selected restaurants that capture the regional experience—those that have a unique regional flavor (&see the Legend on the cover flap for an explanation of the price categories). We're not rating the quality of the food per se; as we did with the hotels, we selected restaurants for many towns and villages, categorized by price to appeal to all wallets. &See the back of the guide for an index of where restaurants featured throughout the guide can be found.

MAPS

- **Principal Sights maps** on the cover.
- Detailed maps for **major cities** and **villages**, including **driving tour maps** and larger-scale maps for **walking tours**.

All maps in this guide are oriented north, unless otherwise indicated by a directional arrow. The term "Local Map" refers to a map within the chapter or Tourism Region. A complete list of the maps found in the guide appears at the back of this book, as well as a comprehensive index and list of restaurants and accommodations.

See the map Legend at the back of the guide for an explanation of map symbols.

> ### A Bit of Advice
> Green advice boxes found in this guide contain practical tips and handy information relevant to the sight in the Discovering section.

ORIENT PANELS

Vital statistics are given for each principal sight in the DISCOVERING section:

- **Information:** Tourist Office/Sight contact details.
- **Orient Yourself:** Geographic location of the sight with reference to surrounding boroughs, towns and roads.
- **Parking:** Where to park.
- **Don't Miss:** Unmissable things to do.
- **Organising Your Time:** Tips on organising your stay; what to see first, how long to spend, crowd avoidance, market days and more.
- **Especially for Kids:** Sights of particular interest to children.
- **Also See:** Nearby PRINCIPAL SIGHTS featured elsewhere in the guide.

SYMBOLS

Spa	**Spa Facilities**		**Wheelchair Accessible**
Kids	**Interesting for Children**		**Tours**
	Also See		**On-site Parking**
	Tourist Information		**Directions**
	Hours of Operation		**Hikes**
	Periods of Closure		**On-site eating Facilities**
	Closed to the Public		**Breakfast Included**
	Entry Fees		**A Bit of Advice**
	Credit Cards not Accepted		**Warning**

Contact - Addresses, phone numbers, opening hours and prices published in this guide are accurate at the time of press. We welcome corrections and suggestions that may assist us in preparing the next edition. Please send your comments to:

UK
Michelin Maps and Guides
Hannay House
39 Clarendon Road
Watford, Herts WD17 1JA
travelpubsales@uk.michelin.com
www.michelin.co.uk

USA
Michelin Maps and Guides
Editorial Department
P.O. Box 19001
Greenville, SC 29602-9001
michelin.guides@us.michelin.com
www.michelintravel.com

Driving tours

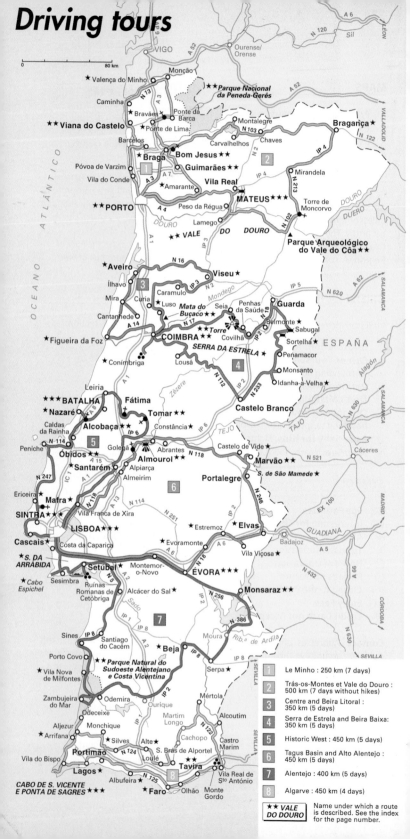

Legend / Route index:

1. Le Minho : 250 km (7 days)
2. Trás-os-Montes et Vale do Douro : 500 km (7 days without hikes)
3. Centre and Beira Litoral : 350 km (5 days)
4. Serra de Estrela and Beira Baixa: 350 km (5 days)
5. Historic West : 450 km (5 days)
6. Tagus Basin and Alto Alentejo : 450 km (5 days)
7. Alentejo : 400 km (5 days)
8. Algarve : 450 km (4 days)

★★ **VALE DO DOURO** Name under which a route is described. See the index for the page number.

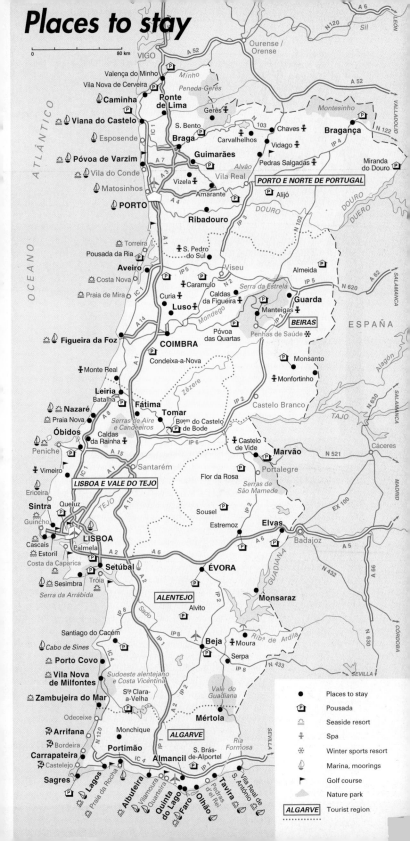

Places to stay

A window in the Alfama, Lisbon
B.Brillion/MICHELIN

MICHELIN DRIVING TOURS

Local Driving Tours

Listed below are sights within the *Discovering Portugal and Madeira* sections of the guide, where you can find local driving tours.

PORTUGAL
- ALGARVE
- CARAMULO
- CASTELO BRANCO
- RIO CÁVADO
- VALE DO DOURO
- SERRA DA ESTRELA
- PALMELA
- PINHEL
- SERRA DO SÃO MAMEDE
- SERRA DE SINTRA

MADEIRA AND THE AZORES
- MADEIRA: FUNCHAL
- MADEIRA: EAST COAST
- MADEIRA: TOUR OF THE ISLAND
- MADEIRA: SOUTHWEST COAST
- THE AZORES: SÃO MIGUEL
- THE AZORES: TERCEIRA
- THE AZORES: FAIAL
- THE AZORES: PICO
- THE AZORES: SÃO JORGE
- THE AZORES: FLORES

WHEN AND WHERE TO GO

When to Go

Portugal has a relatively mild climate. However, the best time to visit the country depends on the region you wish to visit: the north is cooler than the south, and particularly in the mountains where winter can be harsh.

In mid-summer the temperatures can rise pretty high (40°C/104°F) especially on the Algarve and in the interior making it uncomfortable to those unaccustomed to such heat. For a tour of the whole country, spring or autumn are the best seasons.

SPRING

Spring is the best time to visit the south of the country if you wish to avoid the heat of summer and the masses who flock to the beaches of the Algarve. It is also the season when the flowers, which adorn so many houses, come into full bloom and the countryside is green. Surfers will love Spring on the blustery west coast. Late March and April (depending on the date of Easter) offer the added attractions of Holy Week festivities, especially in Braga.

Landscape of Moura region in Alentejo

H. Champollion/MICHELIN

SUMMER

The summer months are hot and dry in land, but in the coastal areas the heat is tempered by sea breezes. The northern coast (the Costa Verde) can have a few days of rain in mid-summer. Many *romarias*, festivals, feast days and sporting events take place during the summer months (&see *Calendar of Events*) and, of course, it's the best time to head for the beaches. Average sea temperatures are as follows: 16–19°C/61–66°F on the west coast; 21–23°C/70–73°F on the Algarve coast. Average summer temperatures for major towns and cities are: Porto – 20°C; Lisbon – 26°C; Évora – 29°C; Faro – 28°C.

AUTUMN

In the north with the chestnut trees and vineyards, the countryside takes on some lovely tints. The Douro and Dão valleys with their many vineyards become a hive of activity during the grape harvest (mid-September to mid-October). Autumn is also the ideal time to visit the Minho and Trás-os-Montes regions. Average temperatures in these two regions are 13°C/55°F and 8°C/45°F respectively (between October and December).

WINTER

Winter is a pleasant season to visit the Algarve coast, where swimming is possible from March to November (sea temperature: 17°C; air temperature: 18°C), the Costa de Estoril (sea temperature: 16°C; air temperature: 17°C), and, above all, Madeira and the Azores (sea and air temperature: 21°C), where winters are mild and sunny, though the odd day of drizzle is possible. The Algarve is transformed at the end of January when the almond trees start to blossom.
In winter, between January and March, skiers flock to the winter sports centres in the Serra da Estrela. Golfers can visit Portugal at almost any time of the year, particularly in the south where the winters are warm and often

Boats at Sagres port

R. Mattes/MICHELIN

sunny. Around Lisbon, too, virtually the whole year is good for golf though around Porto winters can be a little chilly.

Where to Go

There is so much to do in Portugal – cities, palaces and other monuments, the culture trail, the vineyards, the beaches; surfing, paragliding, skydiving and golf for the sports-minded; shopping, museums, whale and dolphin watching, hiking the mountains, cycling, horse riding… and always the wonderful Portuguese food and wine – not forgetting port-tasting in and around Porto.

Lisbon, Portugal's capital, has more museums and monuments than anywhere else and is ideal if you wish to get to know the cultural life of the country. Nearby, as a bonus, you will find the palaces of Sintra, Mafra and Queluz, all of them easily reached on a day trip and all well worth a visit. On the outskirts of Lisbon itself is the historically important centre of Belém, with its monastery, tower and museums (&see *BELÉM*).

For sun-worshippers the Algarve in summer is hard to beat. By day there are water sports, sailing excursions, deep-sea fishing expeditions, diving and skydiving, or you could just soak up the sun on one of the glorious beaches or tiny coves. After dark the entire coast comes alive with bars, restaurants and clubs catering for the evening pleasures of thousands of fun-loving visitors.

For something different try Madeira or the Azores. The Azores are quiet, well away from the madding crowd. Volcanic, friendly and laid back, these islands, some of them hardly ever visited, are a haven or peace almost halfway across the Atlantic, on the main yacht route between Europe and the Caribbean. Diving, whale watching, walking and relaxing are the order of the day. Madeira is covered in flowers, has the highest mountain in Portugal (Pico Ruivo) – perfect for hiking – and plenty of other walks. Madeira has many botanical gardens where you'll find exotic plants from around the world. February or early March is a wonderful time to visit, especially if you can catch Carnaval – or go to the flower festival later in the year. Sports enthusiasts will find the best paragliding on Madeira, some excellent golf (and a course on nearby Porto Santo), together with diving, sea-kayaking and cave-walking.

SHORT BREAKS

Short breaks are very popular and a couple of areas of Portugal are just made for this. It is easy and relatively inexpensive to reach both Porto and Lisbon for a weekend.

Porto
Porto is a good place to get to know Portugal. It's a lively, hard-working city, but once the offices close the inhabitants know how to enjoy themselves.
The city itself has many monuments and museums; there is port-tasting in the great port lodges in Vila Nova de Gaia, just across the river Douro, where you can learn about port and get to enjoy some special samples. The Ribeira river-front area has excellent nightlife where you can join in the open-air party that seems to progress from one bar to the other all evening.

Lisbon
Lisbon makes a wonderful destination for a long weekend. With its glittering array of designer shops and boutiques you can spend almost an entire weekend of shopping, particularly as many of the shopping malls stay open until 11pm. The Avenida de Liberdade has the high-quality names but for something different there's the flea-market in Alfama on Saturday mornings. For culture-vultures Lisbon has more museums and monuments than you could count – don't miss Belém with its famous tower, the Monument to the Discoveries; the world-famous Gulbenkian Museum, home to one of

Sea kayaking in Funchal, Madeira

DRT Madeira

Europe's greatest art collections; the Park of Nations, built for Expo98 but now housing the world's second-largest aquarium, several water gardens, a knowledge centre, a theatre, casino and a huge shopping centre – all connected by an overhead cable car. And with a Lisbon Card (*see LISBOA*) you get free transport and free or reduced entry to most museums, art galleries and other attractions – many of which are free anyway on Sunday mornings.

A. Cassaigne/MICHELIN

Colourful houses on Cais da Ribeira, Porto

Ideas for Your Visit

FOOTBALL

Football fans frequently pop across to Lisbon just for a weekend during the season to watch Benfica or Sporting Lisbon. Getting tickets is easy (about €35–50) and with cheap flights and hotels, a weekend of football in Lisbon can work out less expensive than going to watch a top London team! The evening entertainment is fun, too, especially in the Bairro Alto district or along the river-front in the old dockyards, now converted into glitzy bars and clubs.

RIVER CRUISING

Perhaps the most relaxed way to visit Portugal for a week of pre-arranged travel would be a Douro Valley river cruise. Lie back and indulge in all you want to eat and drink as you cruise along the glorious river Douro between steep hillsides lined with vineyards, soaking up the sun as you go or even having a work-out in the on-board fitness centre.

HORSE RIDING

For something more active you might wish to consider a one-week horse riding expedition through the coastal and inland Alentejo, south of Lisbon. Some competence in the saddle is required.

SPAS

In the UK many people think of spas as being something you do in the inner-city – more of the health-club type of thing. These exist in Portugal of course, but many of the Portuguese spas are natural spas, most of them dating back to Roman times. "Taking the waters" was popular a century ago and is now back in fashion. For ailments of many sorts, from intestinal to pulmonary, liver problems, arthritis or just because you want a detox, one of the natural spas in Portugal could be the ideal place for a few days' R and R.

RELIGION

Being a predominantly Catholic country, Portugal has its fair share of churches, cathedrals and other sacred monuments, as well as quite a few museums dedicated to sacred art. Almost every village has its religious festivals to honour a Saint. Semana Santa, the week leading up to Easter, is observed seriously in several places, none more so than in Braga, the 'spiritual' capital of Portugal.

Another important aspect of religious life in Portugal is the pilgrimage to Fátima, the site of an apparition of the Virgin Mary in 1917. Thousands of pilgrims flock to this site each month, and whether you join in or not, the spectacle is impressive. The dates in May and October are the most important (*see Calendar of Events*).

KNOW BEFORE YOU GO

Useful Websites

www.visitportugal.pt
The official Portugese Tourism website with a wealth of well-presented information on everything from themed itineraries to upcoming events to where to stay and eat.

www.portugal.org/tourism
An excellent source of basic information and details are handily laid out on a region-by-region basis.

www.portugal-live.net
A good website for those looking for hotels in particular, plus lots of information on tourist sights.

www.portugal.com
A commercial site through which you can make reservations for restaurants and hotels; good suggestions for holiday programmes.

Tourist Offices

PORTUGUESE NATIONAL TOURIST OFFICES

London:
11 Belgrave Square, London, SW1X 8PP; ☎0845 355 12 12; fax (020) 7201 6633; www.portugaloffice. org.uk; www.visitportugal.com.

New York:
590 Fifth Avenue, 4th floor, New York NY 10036-4704, ☎(212)-354-44-03/4; fax (212)-764-61-37; www.portugal.org.

Toronto:
60 Bloor Street West, Suite 1005, Toronto, Ontario M4W 3B8, ☎(416)-921-73-76; fax (416)-921-13-15.

Dublin:
54 Dawson Street, Dublin 2; ☎(01) 670 91 33; (01) 670 91 34; fax (01) 670 9141.

LOCAL TOURIST OFFICES

♦ **ICEP** (Investimentos, Comércio e Turismo de Portugal). Posto de Turismo – Praça dos Restauradores, Palácio Foz, Lisboa. ☎213 46 33 14/213 46 36 43

♦ **Direcção Geral de Turismo**, Avenida António Augusto de Aguiar, 86, 1050 Lisboa; ☎213 57 50 86; and Praça Dom João I, 25-4°, 4000 Porto; ☎222 00 58 05.

Tourist Information Centres –
All Portuguese towns have a Tourist Information centre, known as Posto or Comissão de Turismo or simply Turismo, marked on Michelin town plans with an 🄸. The addresses of individual Tourist Offices are listed in the introductions to the Principal Sights.

International Visitors

PORTUGUESE EMBASSIES AND CONSULATES

♦ **Portuguese Embassy, London:** ☎(020) 7235 5331.
♦ **Portuguese Consulate, London:** ☎(020) 7581 8722.
♦ **Honorary Consulate, Manchester:** ☎(0161) 228 3116.
♦ **Portuguese Consulate, Washington DC:** ☎(202) 332 3007.
Consulates in Boston, Chicago, Houston, Los Angeles, Miami, New Orleans, New York and San Francisco.

FOREIGN EMBASSIES AND CONSULATES IN PORTUGAL

♦ **British Embassy:** Rua São Bernardo, 33, 1249-082 Lisboa; ☎213 96 11 91.

- **British Consulates:** Rua São Bernardo, 33, 1249-082 Lisboa; ☎213 92 41 59.
  Avenida da Boa Vista, 4100-120 Porto; ☎226 18 47 89
  Quinta do Bom Jesus, Rua das Almas 23, Pico da Pedra, 9600 Ribeira, Grande, Açores; ☎296 49 81 15.
  Apartado 417, 9000 Funchal, Madeira; ☎291 22 01 61.
- **American Embassy:** Avenida das Forças Armadas, 1600-081 Lisboa; ☎217 27 33 00.
- **American Consulates:** Honorary Consul in Madeira and the Azores.
- **Canadian Embassy:** Avenida da Liberdade, 200-3, 1269-121 Lisboa; ☎213 47 48 92.
- **Canadian Consulates:** Avenida da Liberdaade 198-200, 3rd Floor, 1269-121 Lisboa; ☎213 164 600; fax 213 164 693.
- **Embassy of Ireland:** Rua da Imprensa à Estrela 1-4°, 1200-684 Lisboa; ☎213 92 94 40.

Entry Requirements

Because Portugal is part of the European Union, holders of any EU **passport** do not need **visas** to enter Portugal, although visas may be necessary for some Commonwealth visitors and for those planning a stay of more than three months. For anyone travelling by air or sea some form of photo identification is necessary. The most widely accepted form of identification is a **passport**.
US citizens should obtain the booklet *Your Trip Abroad*, which provides useful information on visa requirements, customs regulations, medical care, etc. for international travellers. Apply to the Superintendent of Documents, PO Box 371954 Pittsburgh, PA 15250-7954. ☎202 512 1800. http://travel.state.gov/travel/tips/tips_1232.html.

EU Duty-Free Allowances	
Spirits (whisky, gin, vodka, etc.)	10l/2.6gal
Fortified wines (vermouth, port, etc.)	20l/5.3gal
Wine (not more than 60 sparkling)	90l/23.7gal
Beer	110l/29gal
Cigarettes	3 200
Cigarillos	400
Cigars	200
Smoking tobacco	3kg/6.6lb

Customs Regulations

UK citizens can apply for a Customs guide for travellers: http://customs.hmrc.gov.uk. The US Customs Service offers a publication *Know Before You Go* for US citizens: for the office nearest you, consult the phone book, Federal Government, US Treasury (www.customs.ustreas.gov). The table above shows duty-free allowances for EU citizens. For non-EU citizens, contact your country's consulate or embassy.

Health

The **European Health Insurance Card** (EHIC), which replaced the old **E111 form**, entitles the holder to free or reduced-cost urgent treatment in case of an accident or unexpected illness in EU countries. Valid for between three and five years this card should be presented to the relevant medical services before treatment, as not all treatments are available without charge. The card can be obtained from the NHS, Newcastle-upon-Tyne, either by post (forms available at Post Offices), by phone ☎0845 606 2030, or online at: www.ehic.org.uk.
Other **medical insurance** is advisable. Since medical insurance is not always valid outside the United States, American travellers are advised to take out supplementary medical insurance with specific overseas coverage.

Chemists *(farmácias)* or pharmacists are open weekdays 9am to 1pm and 3pm to 7pm, Saturdays 9am to 1pm.

Accessibility

Many of the sights and places listed in this guide are accessible to people with special needs and their helpers. Sights marked with the ♿ symbol have wheelchair access but it is advisable to telephone prior to your visit to re-check.

Though a late starter in adapting its infrastructure to accommodate people with special needs, Portugal's main airports and train stations have ramps and lifts. However, other public transport, such as the metro and buses, does not cater for those in wheelchairs. Newer trams in Lisbon are slowly becoming more wheelchair friendly, but the old yellow type have no facilities.

Access is improving, though, as Portugal signed up for the European 'City and People with Disabilities' initiative. Towns subscribed to this include Beja, Évora, Maia, Seixa, Faro, Lisbon and Leiria. **Holiday Care** (www.holiday-care.org.uk) has further information, particularly about accommodation.

GETTING THERE AND GETTING AROUND

By Plane

Various airlines operate regular services to the international airports in Portugal (Lisbon, Porto , Faro and Funchal). Contact airlines and travel agents for information and timetables. **British Airways** and **TAP Air Portugal** operate daily flights from London to Lisbon (2hr), Porto (1hr 45min) and Faro (2hr 30min). There are also many budget flights between the UK and Portugal, including services by **Monarch, easyJet** and **Ryanair**. Flights to the Azores operate via Lisbon. There are several direct flights between London and Funchal (Madeira).

- **TAP Portugal:** ☎ 0845 601 0932; www.flytap.com
- **British Airways:** ☎ 0870 55 111 55; www.britishairways.com
- **Monarch:** www.flymonarch.com
- **easyJet:** www.easyjet.com
- **Ryaniar:** www.ryanair.com

TAP Air Portugal, United and Continental operate daily flights from New York to Lisbon (6hr 30min). There are numerous connecting flights from many other major American cities.

TAP ticket office – 3rd floor, 608 Fifth Avenue, New York 10020, ☎ (212) 969 5775 or toll-free for information and reservations, ☎ 800 221 7370.

Internal flights

TAP Air Portugal operates flights from Lisbon and Porto to Madeira (Funchal) and from Lisbon to the Azores (Ponta Delgado on São Miguel). Local airlines operate inter-island flights in the Azores. Internal flights are the most practical way of travelling from the north to south.

Major airports – Lisbon, Porto, Faro, Funchal and Porto Santo (on Madeira); Ponta Delgada, Santa Maria and Terceira (in the Azores).
Journey times: Lisbon – Porto: 45min; Lisbon – Faro: 40min; Lisbon – Funchal: 1hr 40min; Lisbon – Ponta Delgada: 1hr 50min.

- ◆ **TAP Air Portugal**: Praça do Marquês do Pombal, 3A, Lisboa; ☎ 213 17 91 60; www.flytap.com.
- ◆ **Portugália**: AerPorto de Lisboa; ☎ 218 40 89 99; www.flypga.com.

Boarding on a ferry in Lisbon

♦ **SATA**: Air Açores; ☎296 28 23 11
www.sata.pt.

By Ship

There are no direct ferry services between Great Britain and Portugal. However, there are overnight car-ferry services between Plymouth and Santander (Spain) and from Portsmouth to Bilbao (Spain) two to three times a week; journey time: 24hr. Distances from Santander are 960km/596.5mi to Lisbon, 800km/497mi to Porto and 1 280km/795mi to the Algarve.

Across the Channel then on through France and Spain

Although a long journey by road, it is possible to use the Channel Tunnel or cross-Channel services and then drive. The distance to Lisbon by road when you have landed from the car ferry or taken the Channel Tunnel is about 2 100km/1 305mi. The most direct route is via Paris, Bordeaux, Irun and then either San Sebastián or Valladolid or Burgos, Salamanca, Vilar Formoso and Coimbra to Lisbon.

By Train

It is possible to travel to Portugal from the UK by train (through France and Spain), although it is a long trip and possibly more expensive than flying, albeit a most pleasant way to travel. Details from:

🚃 **Rail Europe**: ☎0870 584 8848;
www.raileurope.com
🚃 **Eurostar**: ☎0875 186 186;
www.eurostar.com
🚃 **Eurotunnel**: ☎08705 353 353;
www.eurotunnel.com
🚃 **European Rail**:
☎(020) 7387 0444;
www.europeanrail.com

PORTUGUESE RAILWAYS

Caminhos de Ferro Portugueses (CP) has a rail network linking major cities and an inter-city service. The *rápidos* or express trains are fast. The *directos* or inter-city trains are slower, make more stops and have both first and second class compartments.
There is a tourist pass which is valid on the entire rail network for a period of 7, 14 or 21 days. For further information ☎218 88 40 25; www.cp.pt.

By Coach/Bus

Fairly regular coach services to Portugal are operated from London (Victoria Coach Station) by **Eurolines**, a consortium of coach operators in conjunction with National Express. To the main destinations they operate year-round but other cities are served only on a seasonal basis. The journey takes a couple of days. For details contact your nearest National Express Office or Agent.

Porto station decorated with azulejos

BY COACH

Portugal's national coach network (Rodoviária Nacional) is extensive and covers all parts of the country. For information, contact: Rodoviária Nacional, Avenida Duque d'Avila 12 – 1000-140 Lisboa; ☎213 57 77 15. www.rede-expressas.pt (in Portuguese only).

By Car

DOCUMENTS

Nationals of EU countries require a national **driving licence**; nationals of non-EU countries require an **international driving licence**.
For the vehicle it is necessary to have the registration papers (log-book) and a national identification plate of the approved size.
An International Insurance Certificate (Green Card) is compulsory. Third party insurance is also compulsory in Portugal. Special breakdown and get-you-home packages are a good idea (AA, Five Star RAC, National Breakdown, Europ-Assistance). Members of the American Automobile Association should obtain the brochure "Offices to Serve You Abroad".
If the driver of the vehicle is not accompanied by the owner, he or she should have written permission from the owner to drive in Portugal.

DRIVING REGULATIONS

- The minimum driving age is 17.
- Traffic drives on the right.
- It is compulsory for the front-seat passengers to wear seat belts.
- The drink-driving rules in Portugal are very strict: one small beer can put you over the limit.
  Be very careful.

The rules of the road are the same in Portugal as in other continental countries and Portugal uses the international road sign system.
The Portuguese road network includes over 500km/370mi of motorways.

Tolls are payable on most motorways and bridges.
Maximum speed limits are:
- 120kph/75mph on motorways (auto-estrada);
- 90kph/56mph on dual carriageways (estrada com faixas de rodagem separades);
- 90kph/56mph on other roads;
- 50kph/31mph in built-up areas.

BREAKDOWN SERVICE

The Portuguese Automobile Club (Automóvel Club de Portugal), Rua Rosa Araújo 24, Lisboa 1200, ☎213 18 01 00, offers members of equivalent foreign organisations medical, legal and breakdown assistance.

PETROL/GASOLINE

Diesel and unleaded petrol (gasolina sem chumbo) are generally available throughout the country. Credit cards are accepted in most petrol stations, but visitors are strongly advised to have other means of payment with them. Petrol stations are generally open from 7am–midnight, although some open 24hr a day.

CAR RENTAL

The major car rental firms have offices in all large towns. Cars may be hired from airports, main stations and large hotels. The minimum age to qualify for car rental is 21 though insurance is higher for under-25s.
When renting a car be very careful where you park and don't trust anyone who tries to direct you to "private parking". Illegally parked cars are often towed and it will cost €120 to get it back, plus the parking fine. Major car hire companies include:

Avis	☎213 46 26 76	www.avis.com
Hertz	☎213 81 24 30/ 36	www.hertz.com
Europcar	☎219 40 77 90	www.europcar.com

ROUTE PLANNING

Available on the Internet, this service offers various routes to drivers, distances between towns and cities, as well as details of restaurants and bars at **www.ViaMichelin.com**.

Maps and plans – Michelin map 733 at a 1:1 000 000 scale covers the whole of the Iberian Peninsula, as does the Michelin Atlas Spain & Portugal (scale: 1:400 000). Map 733 at a 1:400 000 scale covers Portugal and includes an index and an enlarged inset map of Lisbon. Michelin plan 39 with a scale of 1:10 000 covers the city of Lisbon, with details on one-way streets, main car parks and public buildings.

WHERE TO STAY AND EAT

Where to Stay

Hotel and Restaurant recommendations are located in the Address Books throughout the *Discovering Portugal* section of this guide. For coin ranges and for a description of the symbols used in the Address Books, see the Legend on the cover flap.

HOTELS

The **Michelin Guide Spain & Portugal** guide is revised annually and is an indispensable complement to this guide, with information on hotels and restaurants including category, price, degree of comfort and setting. Towns underlined in red on the Michelin map 733 are listed in the current edition of the *Michelin Guide Spain & Portugal* with a choice of hotels and restaurants.

The Portuguese Tourist Board also publishes a list with hotel categories ranging from one-star to five-star establishments. In Portugal hotel prices are inclusive of VAT (12 per cent or 21 per cent) and the price of breakfast is almost always included in the cost of the room.

POUSADAS

The state-owned *pousadas* are marked by a "g" sign on the Places to Stay map in this guide and on the Michelin map 733. Special mention should be made of around 30 Portuguese *pousadas*, most of which are extremely comfortable, restored historic monuments (castles, palaces and monasteries) in beautiful sites or excursion centres. The *pousadas* are very popular and usually full, so it is always wise to book in advance. For further information, contact ENATUR, Avenida Santa Joana Princesa 10, 1749-090 Lisboa, ☎218 48 12 21, or the Portuguese National Tourist Office, or check the websites: www.pousadasportugal. com or www.pousadasofportugal. com.

ESTALAGEMS

These are similar types of establishments, often refurbished historic buildings, but they are privately owned.

RESIDÊNCIAS

These comfortable guest houses are almost on a par with some hotels but they do not serve meals.

PENSÕES

A *pensão* is a more modest guest house.

BED AND BREAKFAST

Again the type of accommodation on offer is varied, although the term **Turismo de Habitação (TH)** usually covers historic houses and manors. ou will alos see signs for **cuartos.** There are numerous establishments in northern Portugal but again it is necessary to book in advance. In the north, contact Associação do Turismo de Habitação, Praça da República, 4990 Ponte de Lima, ☎258 74 16 72 or 258 74 28 27.

For accommodation in rural houses apply to ANTER (Associação de Turismo no Espaço Rural), Rua 24 de Julho, 1-1° – 7000-673 Évora, ☎266 74 45 55.

CAMPING

See △ sign on Michelin map 733. In Portugal independent camping outside official sites is not allowed. The local tourist information centres can provide a list of official campsites. The official classification awards stars (1 to 4) to state-owned sites and lists private ones. The *Roteiro Campista* guide, containing details of all campsites and their location, is available from Roteiro Campista, Rua do Giestal 5, 1300-274 Lisboa, at a cost of €10.

Federação Portuguesa de Campismo, Av Coronel Eduardo Galhardo, 24D, 1170-105 Lisboa ☎218 12 68 90/1 or 218 12 69 00. www.roteirocampista.pt. When you arrive at a campsite you will be asked for your passport and for an international camping carnet, which is obligatory. You can get details on these carnets from the Fédération Internationale de Camping et Caravanning (F.I.C.C.): www.ficc.be/novo. It is advisable to book in advance for popular resorts during summer.

YOUTH HOSTELS (POUSADAS DE JUVENTUDE)

Portugal's 22 youth hostels (including two in the Azores) are open to travellers with an International Card. For further information, contact MOVIJOVEM, Pousadas de Juventude, Av. Duque de Ávila, 137, 1069-017 Lisboa, ☎213 13 88 20 or 213 52 86 21. Hostelling International/American Youth Hostel Association (☎202 783 6161) publishes the *International Hostel Guide for Europe* listing properties throughout Europe. You can get good information on all the youth hostels in Portugal from the official site: www.pousadasdejuventude.pt

Where to Eat

RESTAURANTS

The Portuguese keep fairly similar dining hours to the British and Americans. As a general rule, restaurants serve lunch from noon to 2.30pm and dinner from 7pm onwards. You will find many restaurants closed on Sunday nights, even in cities such as Lisbon (although not the Algarve in summer). A wide selection of gourmet restaurants can be found in the **Michelin Guide Spain & Portugal**. All towns with a restaurant listed in the *Michelin Guide Spain & Portugal* are underlined in red on the Michelin map 733.

A further selection of restaurants can be found in the Address Books in the *Discovering Portugal* section of this guide. *For coin categories shown for the restaurants, see the Legend on the cover flap.*

In some of the more popular restaurants, particularly in the north, two prices are written by the same item. The first price denotes a full portion *(dose)* and the second is for the half-portion *(meia dose)*. Hors-d'œuvres are often served prior to the meal (cheese, cured ham, spicy sausage, olives, tuna and croquettes) and are added to the bill. It is customary to leave a tip of about 10 per cent of the total bill unless service is included.

Whilst it is rare (apart, perhaps from parts of the Algarve where they have a huge tourist trade) to find a children's menu, you can buy half portions *(meia dose)* – or, if you are not too hungry, you can get a main dish to share.

Soups are very big news in Portugal and appear at the start of every main meal. Fish is found everywhere but has become expensive of late and inland you will find goat, kid or rabbit on menus, often stewed slowly in wine and herbs.

House wine tends to be drinkable if you don't know what else to choose. For further information on Portuguese food and wine, please consult the *Introduction* to this guide.

WHAT TO SEE AND DO

Outdoor Fun

SAILING

There is ample opportunity for sailing in Portugal with its long coastline, the Tagus estuary and inland stretches of water. Many northern European yachtsmen stop at a Portuguese port as they sail round to the Mediterranean. In season it is possible to hire boats with or without crew. Apply to the Federação Portuguesa de Vela, Doca de Belém, 1300-082 Lisboa, ☏213 64 11 52 or 213 62 02 15; www.fpvela.pt – though a better website (in English) is: www.manorhouses.com/ports.

Coastlines where sailing is possible are marked by the symbol ⚓ on the Places to Stay map in this guide and on Michelin map 733. Marinas marked on Michelin map 733 have been selected for their facilities and infrastructure. Check weather bulletins before heading out to sea.

SURFING

Surfing is very popular in Portugal, especially along the west coast where the huge Atlantic waves come crashing in, often as high as 2m/6.5ft. The World Championships are held near Ericeira and there are several surf schools all along this part of the coast, right up to Peniche. There is also very good surfing at Praia do Guincho, near Estoril, and much further south in the northern Algarve, near Carrapteira. You will find several surf schools and camps in most of these regions and there is also one (which also caters for beginners) at Sagres.

DIVING

Diving is very popular along the Algarve, in the Azores, Matosinhos near Porto where you can reach a German U-boat, and in Madeira. A full dive will cost around €40–50. The sea caves along the Algarve coast between Albufeira and Sagres are popular with scuba divers.

WATERPARKS

These are mainly located around Lisbon and in the Algarve (⚲ see ALGARVE). Further information can be obtained from tourist offices.

Diving in Madeira

DRT Madeira

BEACHES

The symbol ⚲ on Michelin map 733 and on the Places to Stay map in this guide highlights the best beaches. The Portuguese coastline is a series of beaches from north to south.

The best known are the great sandy stretches of the **Algarve**, where both the climate and sea temperature (17°C/62.6°F in winter, 23°C/73.4°F in summer) are pleasant.

The **Costa Dourada** between Cabo São Vicente and Setúbal is a more rugged coastline with tiny curves of sand at the foot of imposing cliffs and a colder and rougher sea (15°C/59°F in winter and 19°C/66.2°F in summer).

The **Costa de Lisboa** from Setúbal to Cabo da Roca includes the pleasant, well sheltered beaches of the Serra de Arrábida, the great expanse of dunes of the Costa da Caparica south of the Tagus and the very crowded beaches of Cascais and Estoril, which are popular with Lisbonites.

The **Costa de Prato**, extending from Cabo da Roca to Aveiro, has flat sandy beaches. North of Nazaré the fishermen's boats can be seen high on the beaches. The **Costa Verde** from the Douro northwards to the Spanish border has fine sandy beaches backed inland with a pleasantly green countryside.

Many of Portugal's beaches are supervised and it is important to heed the flags: red – it is forbidden to enter the sea even to paddle; yellow – no swimming; green – it is safe to paddle and swim; blue and white chequered – beach temporarily unsupervised.

FISHING

Freshwater angling

This is done mostly in the north for trout, salmon, barbel and shad (Rio Minho and the Douro) and in the numerous mountain torrents of the Serra de Estrela (carp, barbel and trout).

A fishing permit can be obtained from the Federação Portuguesa da Pesca Desportiva, Rua Sociedade Farmacêutica 56-2°, 1150-341 Lisboa, ☎213 56 31 47. Enquire at the local Tourist Information Centres for the opening dates of the fishing season.

Sea angling

In the north the catch usually includes skate, cod, dogfish and sea perch while in the south Mediterranean species such as shark, tuna and swordfish are more common.

GOLF

The best time for golf is September to November, then March to June, although Portugal's mild climate enables golfers to play year-round. The country has a wide selection of

Associação Turismo do Algarve

Gramacho Course, Pestana Golf Resort, near Carvoeiro, Algarve

courses to choose from, most of which are of championship standard. Green fees vary from about €50 to €200 and, on the Algarve at least, pre-booking is advised. Details can be found on: www.portugalvirtual/pt_golf and www.portugalgolf.pt.

Golf courses with the number of holes and their telephone numbers are listed in the *Michelin Guide Spain & Portugal* under the nearest town and are indicated on the Michelin Map 733 by the 🏌 symbol.

OTHER SPORTS

Football

The Portuguese are great football (soccer) fans. The teams with the greatest following are Porto's FC Porto (European Champions League Winners in 2004) and Lisbon's Benfica and Sporting. Tickets for matches involving the big three are not difficult to obtain except for the big derby games. Games are generally played on Sunday afternoons with highlights from most matches on television Sunday night.

Horse Riding

Horse riding is very popular in Portugal and you can find schools that will take you on a week-long trek in the saddle, particularly in the Alentejo and Algarve.

SPAS

Portugal's tradition of elegant natural spas dates from the late 19C. The country's 40 or so spas cater to people with a wide variety of ailments. The ‡ symbol on the Places to Stay map in this guide and Michelin map 733 indicates some of the more important ones.

For further information, contact the Associação das Termas de Portugal, Avenida Miguel Bombarda, 110-2°, Dt°, 1050-167 Lisboa, ☎217 94 05 74; www.supra.pt/termas-portugal.

BIRD WATCHING

Bird watching is very popular, especially in the south of the country where many migratory birds can be observed at certain times of the year. A very comprehensive website that lists when and where various species are likely to be encountered is: www.birding-in-portugal.com. You can also visit (and book holidays online with) www.limosaholidays.co.uk.

Activities for Children   Kids

In this guide, sights of particular interest to children are indicated with a Kids symbol. Some attractions may offer discount fees for children.

🕯 *For specific activities in Lisbon, see the chapter in Discovering Portugal.*

CATERING TO CHILDREN

As family life is a very important factor in Portugal you will find **hotels and restaurants** more than happy to cater for their younger visitors and although they do not offer "children's menus" (except perhaps in some parts of the Algarve where foreign tourists outnumber the local population) – you can always ask for a *"meia dose"* (half portion) which they will always be happy to provide. There are no restrictions about taking children into restaurants or bars, though you might want to use your own judgment in the case of the latter. Apart from the Algarve most restaurants do not open much before 7.30pm for dinner.

For hotels and guesthouses, too, it is easy to get an extra bed or cot (*um berço*) put in a room with no extra cost – or perhaps minimal. In other places discounts of 50 per cent are not uncommon for children.

On **public transport**, children up to five years travel free, then half price up to 12, except on the metro in Lisbon and Porto and on buses. Most museums charge half-price for children between age five to 12.

CHILDREN AND THE SUN

Sunshine in Portugal, especially in summer, is intense and you are well advised to ensure that your child has a hat, is covered sufficiently without being stifled, and has suncream applied as appropriate. Beware strong currents if swimming, especially on the west coast where there are strong undercurrents.

ENTERTAINMENT

Portugal is wonderful for entertaining children. Here is a short list places which may be fun for kids, which are described in the relevant sights in the *Discovering Portugal* section:

Oceanarium, Lisbon
Puppet Museum, Lisbon
Toy Museum, Sintra
Portugal dos Pequenitos, Coimbra.

You'll find many more activities for children throughout this guide.

Calendar of Events

Detailed calendars of events are published by the local Tourist Information Centres. The following list is a selection of the most well-known events. *Map references in parentheses (U5) are given for places not featured in this guide but referred to on Michelin map 733.*

WEEK PRECEDING SHROVE TUESDAY

Ovar (J4) — Carnival: procession of floats.
Torres Vedras (O2) — Carnival: procession of floats.
Loulé — Carnival and Almond Gatherers' Fair.

HOLY WEEK

Braga — Holy Week ceremonies and processions.

EASTER SUNDAY

Loulé — Pilgrimage in honour of Our Lady of Pity. Repeated on the following two Sundays.

29 APRIL TO 3 MAY

Barcelos — Festival of Crosses, Pottery Fair and folk dancing.

3 TO 5 MAY

Sesimbra — Festival in honour of Our Lord Jesus of the Wounds: fishermen's festival dating from the 16C. Procession on 4 May.

FIRST SUNDAY AFTER 3 MAY

Monsanto — Castle Festival.

SECOND WEEKEND IN MAY

Vila Franca do Lima — Rose Festival: Mordomias procession in which the mistress of the house bears

---

The Days of the Week

While Monday in Portuguese is the second day of the week *(segunda-feira)*, Tuesday the third *(terça-feira)*, Wednesday the fourth *(quarta-feira)*, Thursday the fifth *(quinta-feira)* and Friday the sixth *(sexta-feira)*, Sunday, the first day of the week, remains that of the Lord *(domingo)* and Saturday, the seventh, the sabbath *(sábado)*.

This denomination is believed to have originated in the 6C when São Martinho, Bishop of Braga, took the Christians to task for using the traditional calendar dating from the time of the Chaldeans and thereby dedicating each day to a pagan divinity: the Sun, the Moon, Mars, Mercury, Jupiter, Venus and Saturn.

World Heritage List

In 1972, the United Nations Educational, Scientific and Cultural Organisation (UNESCO) adopted a Convention for the preservation of cultural and natural sites. To date, more than 150 countries have signed this international agreement, which has listed over 500 sites "of outstanding universal value" on the World Heritage List. Each year, a committee of representatives from 21 countries, assisted by technical organisations (ICOMOS – International Council on Monuments and Sites; IUCN-International Union for Conservation of Nature and Natural Resources; ICCROM – International Centre for the Study of the Preservation and Restoration of Cultural Property, the Rome Centre), evaluates the proposals for new sites to be included on the list, which grows longer as new nominations are accepted and more countries sign the Convention. To be considered, a site must be nominated by the country in which it is located. The protected cultural heritage may be monuments (buildings, sculptures, archaeological structures, etc.) with unique historical, artistic or scientific features, groups of buildings (such as religious communities, ancient cities), or sites of exceptional beauty (human settlements, magnificent landscapes, places of cultural interest) which are the combined works of man and nature. Natural sites may be a testimony to the stages of the earth's geological history or to the development of human cultures and creative genius or represent significant ongoing ecological processes, contain superlative natural phenomena or provide a habitat for threatened species. Signatories of the Convention pledge to co-operate to preserve and protect these sites around the world as a common heritage to be shared by all humanity.

Some of the most well-known places which the World Heritage Committee has inscribed include: Australia's Great Barrier Reef (1981), the Canadian Rocky Mountain Parks (1984), The Great Wall of China (1987), the Statue of Liberty (1984), the Kremlin (1990), Mont-Saint-Michel and its bay (France – 1979), Durham Castle and Cathedral (1986).

In Portugal, the following have been designated as World Heritage sites:

- **Central Zone of the town of Angra do Heroísmo, Azores**
- **Mosteiro dos Jerónimos and Torre de Belém, Lisbon**
- **Mosteiro da Batalha**
- **Convento de Cristo, Tomar**
- **Historical centre of Évora**
- **Mosteiro de Santa Maria, Alcobaça**
- **Cultural landscape of Sintra**
- **Historic centre of Porto**
- **Parque Arqueológico do Vale do Côa**
- **Historic centre of Guimarães**
- **Alto Douro Wine Region**
- **Landscape of Pico Island**
- **Madeira's Laurissilva Forest**

Shopping

HANDICRAFTS

Traditional Portuguese crafts will catch your eye, and the prices are attractive, too. From the north to the south, variety is found in the choice of colours and natural materials. In Viana do Castelo, look for hand-embroidered linen and cotton (tablecloths and napkins, shirts, aprons etc) and the classic filigree jewellery in both silver and gold. Embroidered bedspreads are a good buy in Castelo

Craft shop in Monsaraz

Branco, as are the hand-made rugs from Arrailos, while many places offer ceramics (Caldas da Rainha, Coimbra etc) and pottery (Barcelos, Alentejo, Algarve). Woodworkers make decorative objects, kitchen utensils and toys, tinsmiths are famous for *almutelias*, the traditional recipients for olive oil, while glass-makers still continue their activity in Marinha Grande. *Azulejos* tiles are found everywhere, as are objects and kitchenware made of copper (including the typical *cataplana* from the Algarve).

FASHION

The best places for shopping really depend on what you are looking for. The big cities obviously have many shops, particularly Lisbon where you will find everything you want, from high-class brand-name fashion to "junk" in the flea-market. The international brand names for fashion (Luis Vuitton, Armani, Trussardi, Burberry, Hugo Boss, Longchamp and Escada) are spread along Avenida da Liberdade in the centre of Lisbon, and also in discreet intimate malls behind the renovated façades of Chiado. Chiado also has several modern Portuguese designers selling their creations, so if you want something unique this could be the place to come. All big cities have its shopping malls and in Lisbon the largest are Colombo, Galerias Monumental, Saldanha, Vasco da Gama, Amoreiras and El Corte Inglés. They are all open until 10 or even 11pm, though not always on Sundays. Most of the smaller shops close for lunch from about 12.30pm to around 2.30pm or even later but then stay open unti around 8pm. Most smaller shops are closed on Sundays and in the less-visited areas of Portugal, on Saturday afternoons as well.

MARKETS

On Saturday morning the place to be is the Feira da Ladra (translates as Thieves' Market!) on Campo de Santa Clara in Alfama, where you'll find all sorts of things you never realised you needed. Clothes, "antiques" pirated CDs and DVDs, jewellery of all descriptions, books, linens and much more. They open at 8am so the earlier you get there the better. Obviously there will be some items that are not exactly genuine but it's up to you what you buy. It pays to haggle. Be aware of the possible presence of pickpockets in the markets. Never have money waving around in your hand – it's too tempting for some people!

Lisbon and a few other towns also have street-vendors who sell a range of items, some genuine, some not. In Lisbon, especially in Bairro Alto at night, you will notice drugs being sold quite openly.

Most of the larger towns have their weekly markets, some of which are quite spectacular. Those in Évora, Loulé and Lemago are especially good. In the countryside they tend to be more agricultural with local foods as the main attraction. If you want to have a picnic or if you are staying in self-catering accommodation the markets will be the best place to buy food and wine. If you are in Lisbon you should make a point of visiting the main market (opposite the Cais deo Sodré station near the Tagus); in Funchal the main fish market and in Setúbal the main fruit and vegetable market.

Remember that when you return to the UK there are Customs regulations concerning how much you can bring back – some foodstuffs are prohibited. Check before you leave.

Sightseeing

TIMES AND CHARGES

As admission times and charges are liable to alteration, the information below is given only as a general guideline.
Opening times and other relevant information concerning all sights in the descriptive part of this guide

...ividual adults with no reduction; if no price is shown admission is free. Special conditions for both times and charges are generally granted to groups if arranged beforehand.

Opening and closing times are given, but remember that some places do not admit visitors during the last hour or half hour.

Most tours are conducted by Portuguese-speaking guides but in some cases the term "guided tours" may cover groups visiting with recorded commentaries. Some of the larger and more popular sights may offer guided tours in other languages.

For most towns the address and/or telephone number of the local Tourist Information Centre, indicated by the symbol ▯, is given below. These centres are able to help tourists find accommodation and provide information on exhibitions, performances, guided tours, market days and other items of local interest.

City tours are given regularly during the tourist season in Coimbra, Faro, Lisbon, Porto and Viana do Castelo. Ask at the Tourist Information Centre.

Books

CONTEMPORARY PORTUGAL

Karen Brown Portugal: Portugal Exceptional Places to Stay & Itineraries 2008 by Clare Brown & Nicole Franchini Karen Brown (Karen Brown's Guides 2007)

Working and Living in Portugal by Harvey Holton (Cadogan Guides 2005)

Buying a Property in Portugal by Harvey Holton/John Howell (Cadogan Guides 2003)

Complete Guide to Buying Property in Portugal by Colin Barrow (Kogan Page 2002)

Walking in Portugal by Bethen Davies/Bn Cole (Pila Pala Press 2000)

HISTORY

Portuguese Seaborne Empire by CR Boxer (Carcanet Press 1991)

Christopher Columbus and the Portuguese, 1476-1498 by Rebecca Catz (Greenwood Press 1993)

Wellington's Peninsular Victories by Michael Glover (The Windrush Press 1996)

Portugal 1715–1808 by David Francis (Tamesis Books 1976)

The Pope's Elephant by Silvio A Bedini (Carcanet Press 1997)

A Concise History of Portugal by David Birmingham (Cambridge University Press 1993)

A Companion History of Portugal by Jose Hermano Saraiva, Ian Robertson, Ursula Fonss (Carcanet Press 1997)

The Portuguese by Marion Kaplan (Penguin Books 1998)

In Search of Modern Portugal, the Revolution and its Consequences by Lawrence S Graham, Douglas Wheeler (University of Wisconsin Press 1983)

The Making of Portuguese Democracy by Kenneth Maxwell (CUP 1997)

The Journal of a Voyage to Lisbon by Henry Fielding, T Keymer (ed) (Penguin Books 1989)

They Went to Portugal Too by Rose Macaulay (Carcanet Press 1990)

Journey to Portugal: In Pursuit of Portugal's History and Culture by Jose Saramago (Harvest Books 2002)

Portugal: A Traveller's History by Harold Livermore (Boydell Press 2004)

ART AND ARCHITECTURE

The Age of the Baroque in Portugal by Jay A Levenson (ed) (National Gallery of Art 1993)

The Fires of Excellence by Miles Danby, Matthew Weinreb (Garnet Publishing 1996)

Portuguese Gardens – Helder Carita, Homem Cardoso (Antique Collectors' Club 1991)

Houses and Gardens of Portugal
  by Marcus Binney, Patrick Bowe,
  Nicolas Sapieha, Francesco Venturi
  (Rizzoli Publications 1998)
Gardens of Spain and Portugal *by*
  Barbara Segall
  (Mitchell Beazley 1999)
Landscapes of the Azores *by*
  Andreas Stieglitz
  (Sunflower Books 1992)

PROSE AND POETRY

The Lusiads *by Luiz de Camões, trans*
  WC Atkinson (Penguin Books 1952)
Selected Poems *by Fernando Pessoa,*
  J Griffin (trans)
  (Penguin Books 1996)
Always Astonished: Selected Prose
  *by Fernando Pessoa, E Honig (*trans)
  (City Lights Books 1988)
Travels in My Homeland *by Almeida*
  Garrett (Peter Owen 1986)

Films

Portugal produces many films, primarily for Portuguese-speaking peoples, primarily Brazil. Few of the films are translated into English or have sub-

Portuguese Film Festivals

Portugal hosts a number of cinema and film festivals throughout the year, such as:

Feb: **Fantasporto** (Porto);
www.fantasporto.pt

Apr: **Caminhos do Cinema
Português** (Coimbra);
www.caminhos.info

Jun: **Festróia Festival
Internacional de Cinema
de Tróia** (Setúbal); www.festroia.pt

Sept: **Lisbon Gay & Lesbian
Film Festival** (Lisbon);
www.lisbonfilmfest.org

titles, but here is a small selection of Portuguese films translated and not:

Testamento *(1997) directed by*
  Francisco Manzo
Abraham's Valley *(1993) directed by*
  Manoel de Oliveira
Dead Man's Memories *(2003) directed*
  by Markus Heltschel
O Fantasma *directed by*
  Joao Pedro Rodrigues (2000)
The Convent *(1995) directed by*
  Manoel de Oliveira

USEFUL WORDS & PHRASES

Common Words

bank; exchange	**banco; câmbio**	goodbye	**adeus**
boat	**barco**	guide	**guia**
bus; tram	**autocarro;**	halt	**paragem**
	eléctrico	I beg your pardon	**desculpe**
car	**carro**	information	**informações**
car park	**parque de esta-**	large; small	**grande;**
	cionamento		**pequeno**
chemist	**farmácia**	letter; postcard	**carta; postal**
customs	**alfândega**	letter-box	**caixa de correio**
district	**bairro**	light	**luz**
doctor	**mêdico**	madam	**minha senhora**
entrance; exit	**entrada; saída**	miss	**menina**
expensive	**caro**	at what time..?	**a que hora..?**
good afternoon	**boa tarde**	much; little	**muito; pouco**
good morning	**bom dia**	how much..?	**quanto custa..?**
		noon	**meio-dia**
		road works	**obras**

station; train	estação; comboio
street; avenue	rue; avenida
thank you	(said by a man) obrigado
	(said by a woman) obrigada
today	hoje
toll	portagem
tomorrow morning	amanhã de manhã
tomorrow evening	amanhã à tarde
to the left	à esquerda
to the right	à direita
town; quarter	cidade
where; when	onde? quando?
yes; no	sim; não
where is?	onde é..?
the road to..?	a estrada para..?
at what time..?	a que hora..?
how much..?	quanto custa..?
road works	obras
danger	perigo
prohibited	prohibido

porto	harbour, port
praia	beach
quinta	country property
sé	cathedral
século	century
solar	manor-house
tapete; tapeçaria	tapestry
tesouro	treasure; treasury
torre	tower
torre de menagem	keep
túmulo	tomb
vista	view, panorama
dirigir-se a...	apply to...
pode-se visitar?	may one visit?

Dining Vocab

Note: for more detailed restaurant terminology consult the *Michelin Guide Spain & Portugal*.

açucar	sugar
água; copo (pequeno)	water; glass (small)
almoço	breakfast
azeite	olive oil
café com leite	coffee with milk
carne	meat
cerveja	beer
conta	bill
ementa, carta	menu
fresco	cold, chilled
gelo	ice-cream; ice cube
jantar, ceia	dinner
lista	menu (à la carte)
óleo	peanut oil
pão	bread
peixe	fish
pimenta, sal	pepper, salt
prato do dia	dish of the day
sumo de fruta	fruit juice
vinho branco	white wine
vinho tinto	red wine

Sightseeing Vocab

abadia	abbey
albufeira	reservoir
andar	storey
baixa	town centre
barragem	dam
câmara municipal	town hall
capela	chapel
casa	house
castelo	castle, citadel
centro urbano	town centre
chafariz	fountain
chave	key
citânia	prehistoric city
convento	convent, monastery
mosteiro	monastery
cruz; cruzeiro	cross; calvary
escada	stairs, steps
excavações	excavations

Typical Dishes

Açorda de Mariscos	Bread soup with clams and prawns, mixed with garlic, eggs, coriander and spices
Amêijoas à Bulhão Pato	Small clams cooked in olive oil, garlic and coriander
Arroz de Marisco	Rice with clams, shrimp, mussels and coriander
Bacalhau	Cod
Cabrito	Roast goat
Caldeirada	Spicy fish and seafood stew
Caldo verde	Potato and cabbage stew
Canja de Galinha	Chicken bouillon with rice and hard egg yolks
Carne de porco à Alentajana	Diced pork in olive oil, garlic and coriander sauce, served with potatoes and small clams
Cataplana	Steamed seafood with pieces of ham
Chouriço	Smoked sausage
Cozido	Pot roast with meat, sausage and vegetables
Feijoada	Beans prepared with pork, cabbage and sausage
Gaspacho	Cold vegetable soup
Leitão assado	Grilled suckling pig, served hot or cold
Presunto	Smoked ham
Salpicão	Spicy smoked ham
Sopa à Alentajana	Garlic and bread soup, served with a poached egg and coriander
Sopa de Feijão verde	Green bean soup
Sopa de Grão	Chickpea soup
Sopa de Legumes	Vegetable soup
Sopa de Marisco	Seafood soup
Sopa de Peixe	Fish soup

BASIC INFORMATION

Business Hours

MONUMENTS, MUSEUMS AND CHURCHES

Monuments and museums are generally open from 9.30–10am to 12.30pm and then from 2pm to 6pm. Some churches are only open for Mass early in the morning or in the evening. For more detailed information, please consult the admission times and charges in the *Discovering Portugal* section. Most have free entry Sunday mornings.

SHOPS

Generally open weekdays 9am to 1pm and 3pm to 7pm (some department stores stay open during the lunch hour). Most shops are closed on Saturday afternoons and most all day Sunday. Shopping centres are the exception as they are open every day of the week from 10am to 11pm. Street markets are normally on Tuesdays, Thursdays or Saturdays and start early, about 8am.

ENTERTAINMENT

Evening performances begin about 9.30pm and *fados* at about 10.30pm. Most trendy bars and clubs do not open until 11pm. They stay open until 2am or 4pm at weekends. Many are closed Sunday night.

Communications

TELEPHONES

Phonecards are widely used and can be purchased at Telecom Portugal shops, post offices and *tabacarias*. You can...

...prepared to pay more than the going rate. For **international calls** dial: 00 + 44 for the United Kingdom; 00 + 353 for Ireland; 00 + 1 for the United States and Canada followed by the area code (omitting the first zero) and then the recipient's number.

INTERNET

Internet cafés can be found in most large towns and you'll find Wi-Fi hotspots at many places, including some hotels.

CELL/MOBILE PHONES

Coverage for most mobile phones is good in the main parts of Portugal, but in the Azores, and inland Portugal (particularly the national parks and mountains), you will be hard put to it to receive a signal. Your own network will be able to advise you which partners they use in Portugal but do not expect 100 per cent coverage.

Electricity

Electric current – 220 volts/50Hz. Plugs are two-pin. You can get adapters at most main airports, electrical stores and souvenir shops.

Emergencies

112

In an emergency, dial 112 anywhere in Portugal.

If you lose your credit card (or have it stolen) you should call the issuing office immediately. The phone numbers should be kept somewhere safe, separate from the credit card itself. Always have a copy of the numbers...

...top pockets and ladies should *never* leave a bag anywhere, especially in bars or on the floor of a restaurant.

Mail/Post

POST OFFICES (CORREIOS)

Post Offices are open weekdays from 9am to 6pm; the smaller branches may close for lunch from 12.30pm to 2.30pm. The main post offices in large towns and those in international airports have a 24hr service. The **Michelin Guide Spain & Portugal** gives the post code for every town covered. Letter boxes and phone booths are red.

Media

NEWSPAPERS

The main Portuguese newspapers are the following: *O Diário de Notícias, O Correio da Manhã,* and *O Público*. Porto has its own daily newspaper, *O Jornal de Notícias*. Weekly publications include *O Expresso*, which has the widest readership, *O Seminário, O Independente* and *O Jornal*.

RADIO

Like the UK Portugal has dozens of local radio stations, many with non-stop music. Nationwide the biggest is Antenna 1 with a good mix of golden oldies, Portuguese music and news (in Portuguese). Antenna 2 is the classical music station.

Money

Portugal is part of the Euro zone. There are no restrictions on the amount of euro currency that you may bring into the country. As of late August 2008, exchange rates were: €1= US$1.47; €1 = £0.79. See www.xe.com for the latest exchange rates. Euro notes come in denominations of €5, €10, €20, €50, €100, €200 and €500. Beware accepting notes of high value (€200 and €500) as these are a favourite of counterfeiters. Most shops and all taxis will refuse any note larger than €100.

CURRENCY EXCHANGE AND CREDIT CARDS

Banks, airports and some stations have exchange offices. Commissions vary so check before cashing.
All major credit cards (American Express, Diners Club, Visa and Master-Card) are accepted but always check in advance.
MULTIBANCO is a national network of automatic cash dispensers which accept international credit and debit cards and enable cash withdrawal 24 hours a day.
Banks are generally open Mondays to Fridays 8.30am to 3pm. These times are subject to change, especially in summer. Most banks have cash dispensers (ATMs), which accept international credit cards.
In many out-of-the-way places, particularly inland and in the north, you will find ATMs very rare and you will also find that most smaller places with accommodation do *not* accept credit cards. Take cash.

Reduced Rates

When you are travelling and visiting several museums or other places on one trip where an entry fee is payable it is always nice to be able to get a reduction.
In Lisbon, if you are staying a few days you should invest in the Lisbon Card (adult/child €15/€8 (24hr); €26/€13 (48hr); €32/€16 (72hr), which gives you free transport on bus, tram, metro and the train to Sintra, together with free or reduced entry to most museums. Remember too, that most museums in Portugal have free entry on Sunday mornings before 2pm.
If you plan on doing much shopping buy the Lisboa Shopping Card (€4 24hrs; €6 72hrs) which gives you discounts of 5–20 per cent at over 200 shops.

Smoking

Smoking in banned in many public places in Portugal, though owners of bars and restaurants may choose whether to allow smoking on their premises or not: if they do, the area must have a ventilation system installed. Smoking is not permitted on public transport.

Temperature and Measurement

Portugal uses the metric system: distances in kilometres (km), temperatures in Celsius. Roughly speaking 85°F = 30°C and in speed 48kph = 30mph; 80kph = 50mph and 112kph = 70mph.

Time

Mainland Portugal is the same as Greenwich Mean Time, although summer time is used so the time is always the same as the UK. Madeira is the same as mainland Portugal and the Azores are always 1hr behind (summer time is observed).

Tipping

The bill is usually inclusive of service charges and VAT (12–21 per cent). An extra tip can be left for special service. Ten per cent of the fare is the usual amount given to taxi drivers and about €2 per bag for hotel porters.

CONVERSION TABLES

Weights and Measures

1 kilogram (kg) 6.35 kilograms 0.45 kilograms	**2.2 pounds (lb)** 14 pounds 16 ounces (oz)	**2.2 pounds** 1 stone (st) 16 ounces	*To convert kilograms to pounds, multiply by 2.2*
1 metric ton (tn)	**1.1 tons**	**1.1 tons**	
1 litre (l) 3.79 litres 4.55 litres	**2.11 pints (pt)** 1 gallon (gal) 1.20 gallon	**1.76 pints** 0.83 gallon 1 gallon	*To convert litres to gallons, multiply by 0.26 (US) or 0.22 (UK)*
1 hectare (ha) **1 sq. kilometre (km²)**	**2.47 acres** 0.38 sq. miles (sq.mi.)	**2.47 acres** 0.38 sq. miles	*To convert hectares to acres, multiply by 2.4*
1 centimetre (cm) **1 metre (m)**	**0.39 inches (in)** 3.28 feet (ft) or 39.37 inches or 1.09 yards (yd)	**0.39 inches**	*To convert metres to feet, multiply by 3.28; for kilometres to*
1 kilometre (km)	**0.62 miles (mi)**	**0.62 miles**	*multiply by 0.*

							7
							8
	37	6	4½		42	9½	9
Shoes	38	7	5½	**Shoes**	43	10½	10
	39	8	6½		44	11½	11
	40	9	7½		45	12½	12
	41	10	8½		46	13½	13
	36	6	8		46	36	36
	38	8	10		48	38	38
Dresses	40	10	12	**Suits**	50	40	40
& suits	42	12	14		52	42	42
	44	14	16		54	44	44
	46	16	18		56	46	48
	36	06	30		37	14½	14½
	38	08	32		38	15	15
Blouses &	40	10	34	**Shirts**	39	15½	15½
sweaters	42	12	36		40	15¾	15¾
	44	14	38		41	16	16
	46	16	40		42	16½	16½

Sizes often vary depending on the designer. These equivalents are given for guidance only.

Speed

KPH	10	30	50	70	80	90	100	110	120	130
MPH	6	19	31	43	50	56	62	68	75	81

Temperature

Celsius (°C)	0°	5°	10°	15°	20°	25°	30°	40°	60°	80°	100°
Fahrenheit (°F)	32°	41°	50°	59°	68°	77°	86°	104°	140°	176°	212°

To convert Celsius into Fahrenheit, multiply °C by 9, divide by 5, and add 32.
To convert Fahrenheit into Celsius, subtract 32 from °F, multiply by 5, and divide by 9.
NB: Conversion factors on this page are approximate.

Olive Groves with
Evoramonte citadel, Alentejo

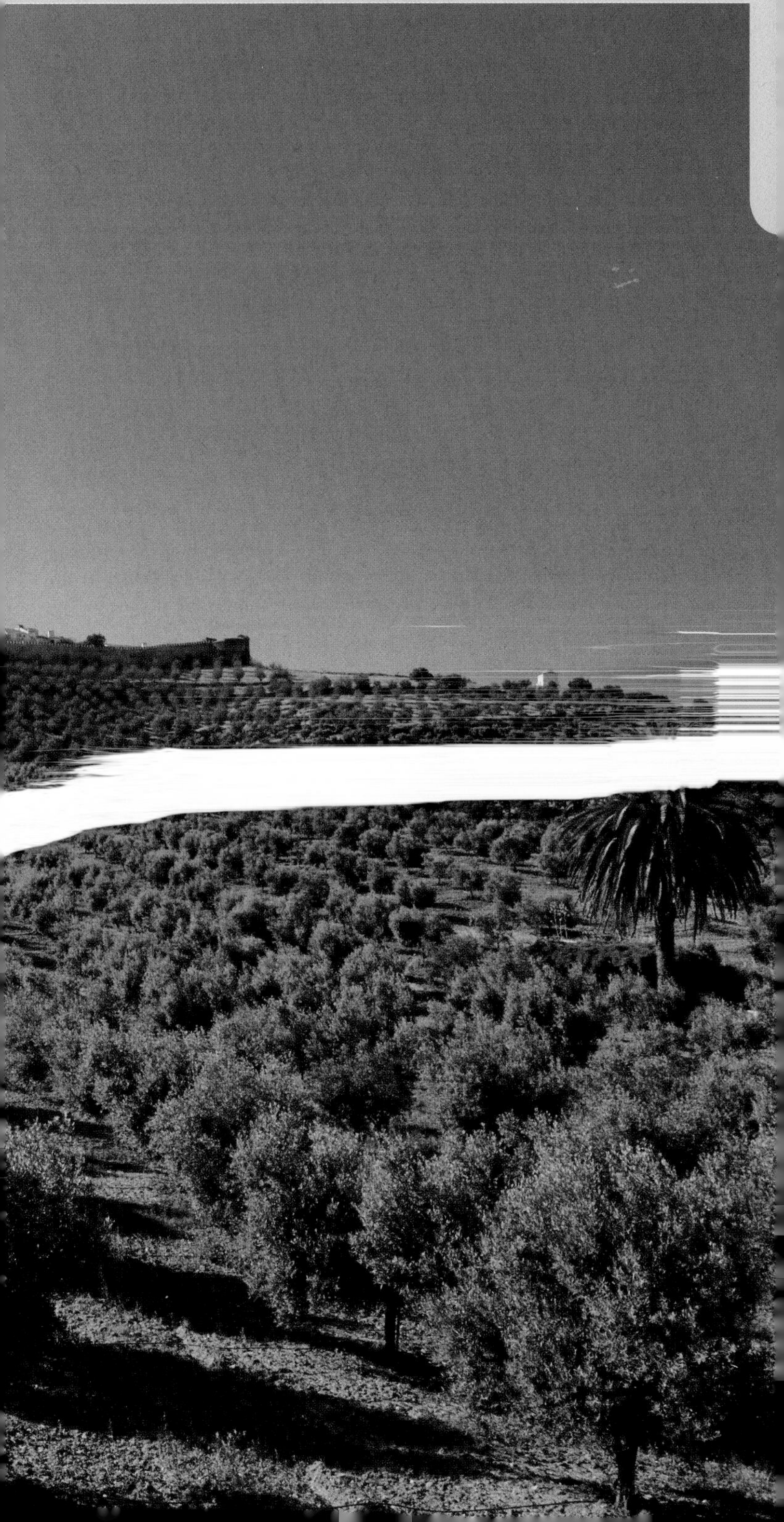

NATURE

Portugal has a wide variety of landscapes, from the mountainous north east to the flatter areas near the coast and in the south. The continental part of the country, south west of the Iberian Peninsula, occupies a relatively small area. Generally speaking, the altitude decreases from the Spanish border towards the Atlantic and from north to south; the Tagus (Tejo) divides a mountainous region in the north from an area of plateaux and plains in the south. The archipelagos of Madeira and the Azores out in the Atlantic are a distant volcanic playground, enriched by a variety of flowers, geology and history.

Geological Formation

In the Primary Era the north of Portugal was affected by Hercynian folding which resulted in the emergence of hard granite and shale mountain ranges. These were worn down in the Secondary Era to form a vast plateau out of which rose erosion resistant heights such as the Serra de São Mamede. In the Tertiary Era, the raising of the Alps and Pyrenean folding led to a brutal upheaval of the plateau, dislocating it into a series of small massifs such as the Serra do Marão and Serra da Estrela. The massifs were separated by fissures near which emerged thermal and mineral springs and, especially in the north, metal deposits. The upheavals were accompanied in some cases by eruptions of a volcanic nature which formed ranges such as the Serra de Sintra and Serra de Monchique. It was at this point that the Tagus and Sado basins were formed and the coastal plains folded into the low ranges of the Serra de Aire, Serra do Caldeirão and Serra da Arrábida. This zone of faults in the earth's crust is still subject to geological disturbance as shown in the earthquake which destroyed Lisbon in 1755 and even more recent tremors.

The coastline became less indented in the Quaternary Era through erosion of the Estremadura and Alentejo cliffs and alluvial accumulation in the Aveiro and Sines areas.

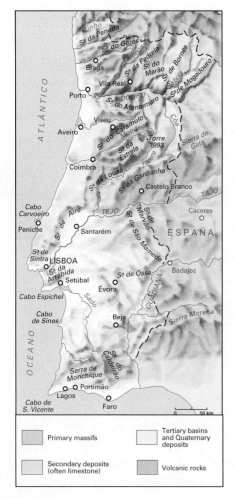

Primary massifs

Secondary deposits (often limestone)

Tertiary basins and Quaternary deposits

Volcanic rocks

Relief

The Cantabrian Cordillera extends westwards into Portugal, north of the Douro, where it takes the form of massive mountain ranges separated by heavily eroded valleys.

Between the Douro and the Tagus, the Castilian sierras extend into Portugal as particularly high relief. Monte da Torre in the Serra da Estrela is Portugal's highest mainland peak (1 993m/6 539ft). The Mondego and Zêzere valleys surround the ridge. South of the Tagus lies a plateau that drops towards the sea. Its vast horizons are barely interrupted by the minor rises of the Serra de Monchique and Serra do Caldeirão.

The 837km/520mi of coast offer incredible variety, with beaches of fine sand sheltered by rock cliffs, creeks, and promontories such as Cabo Carvoeiro, Cabo Espichel and Cabo de São Vicente. Wide estuaries are occupied by the country's main ports: Oporto on the Douro, Lisbon on the Tagus and Setúbal on the Sado. Fishing harbours like Portimão have developed in bays, or, as with Peniche and Lagos, in the protection of headlands. However, most of the coast consists of flat sandy areas sometimes lined by offshore bars as in the eastern offshore Algarve and along Ria de Aveiro.

Regions and Landscape

The areas described below correspond to the old historical provinces which closely reflect the country's natural regions. Portugal's present administrative divisions, known as districts, are also given. ◖ See Provinces and Districts map in The Country Today.

THE NORTH

The old provinces of the Minho and Douro are green and heavily cultivated while the inland regions of Trás-os-Montes, Beira Alta and Beira Baixa are bleaker and drier.

The Minho (Districts: Braga and Viana do Castelo) and the Douro (District: Porto)

The region is part of the tourist area around Oporto and Northern Portugal. The greater part of the Minho and Douro provinces consists of granite hills covered with dense vegetation. The exceptions to these are the bare summits of the Serra do Gerês, Serra do Soajo and Serra do Marão, which make up the Parque Nacional da Peneda-Gerês, and are strewn with rocky scree. The fields, enclosed by hedges and climbing vines, sometimes produce two crops a year. Vineyards, orchards and meadows contribute to the rural economy. Olive, apple and sometimes orange trees grow

Douro Valley near Pinhão

H. Champollion/MICHELIN

on the sunniest slopes. Main roads tend to follow lush river valleys like those of the Lima and the Vez. The region, with Porto (in Portuguese, Oporto) as capital, is an active one and has more than a quarter of Portugal's population.

Trás-os-Montes (Districts: Bragança and Vila Real)

Trás-os-Montes means "beyond the mountains". True to its name, this province of high plateaux relieved by rocky crests and deeply cut valleys, stretches out beyond the Serra da Marão and Serra do Gerês. The moorland plateaux, dominated by bare summits and covered with stunted vegetation, are used for sheep grazing. Remote villages merge into the landscape. The more populous river basins around Chaves, Mirandela and Bragança, with their flourishing fruit trees, vines, maize and vegetables, seem like oases in the bleak countryside.

The Alto Douro region in the south contrasts with the rest of the province by its relative fertility. The edges of the plateaux and the slopes down to the Douro and the Tua have been terraced so that olive, fig and almond trees can be grown, and particularly the famous vine that produces the grapes for port wine and *vinho verde*.

The Beira Alta (Districts: Guarda and Viseu) and Beira Baixa (District: Castelo Branco)

This region, the most mountainous in Portugal, is geographically a westward extension of the Spanish Cordillera Central. The landscape consists of a succession of raised rock masses and down-faulted basins. The mountains, of which the principal ranges are the Serra da Estrela and Serra da Lousã, have thickly wooded slopes crowned with rocky summits. Occasional reservoirs fill the sites of ancient glaciary corries or gorges hollowed out of the quartz.

The greater part of the population lives in the Mondego and Zêzere valleys. The Mondego valley, a vast eroded corridor and a main communications route, is rich arable land; with vines extending up hillsides in the vineyards of the Dâo region. The Upper Zêzere valley, known as the Cova da Beira, specialises more in livestock, wheras the main town, Covilhã, has an important wool industry.

THE CENTRE

The Beira Littoral (Districts: Coimbra and Aveiro)

This low lying region cut by many water courses corresponds approximately to the lower valleys of the Vouga, the Mondego and the Lis. There are rice fields in the irrigated areas around Soure and Aveiro. The coast consists of long straight beaches and sand dunes anchored by vast pinewoods such as Pinhal de Leiria and Pinhal do Urso, while at Aveiro, the *ria* or lagoon provides an original touch to the scenery. Inland, the cottage gardens of wheat and maize are bordered by orchards and vines. There are some beautiful forests, including Mata do Buçaco. The region's two main centres are Coimbra with its famous university and Aveiro with its *ria* and salt-pans.

Estremadura (Districts: Leiria, Lisboa and Setúbal)

In the past, this was the southern limit of the lands reconquered from the Moors, hence the name Estremadura which means extremity. Today, the region, which includes the Lisbon area, contains a third of the country's population.

Between Nazaré and Setúbal the countryside is gently undulating. Villages of single storey houses are surrounded by fields of wheat and maize. Olives, vines and fruit trees grow between clumps of pine and eucalyptus.

Along the coast, where tall cliffs and sandy beaches alternate, there are many fishing villages. The Serra de Sintra is a pleasant wooded range near Lisbon, while the Serra da Arrábida, south of the Tagus, provides shelter for small seaside resorts.

The region's activities are centred on Lisbon, the political, administrative, financial and commercial capital.

The Ribatejo (District: Santarém)

The Riba do Tejo, or banks of the Tagus, is an alluvial plain formed in the Tertiary and Quaternary Eras. On the hills along

Herd of sheep in cork plantation in Alto Alentejo

the north bank farmers cultivate olives, vines and vegetables. The terraces along the south bank grow wheat and olives. The plain is covered with rice fields, market gardens and acres of grassland for rearing horses and fighting bulls. The region, with its main centre in Santarém, is renowned for its Portuguese-style bullfights known as *touradas*.

THE SOUTH

The Alentejo (Districts: Beja, Évora and Portalegre)

The Alentejo, meaning beyond the Tagus (*Além Tejo*), covers nearly a third of Portugal. It is a vast flat plain, except for the Serra de São Mamede. There is almost no natural vegetation. However, in spite of the difficulties of irrigation, the land is seldom left fallow. The Alentejo, Portugal's granary, is also the region of the cork oak, the ilex (holm oak) and the olive tree; in addition plums are grown around Vendas Novas and Elvas, while sheep and herds of black pigs are still reared on the poorer land. The vast stretches of open countryside dotted with old villages make this one of Portugal's more attractive regions.

Traditionally, the region has been one of huge estates centred on a *monte* or large remote whitewashed farmhouse, built on a rise. The other local inhabitants live in villages of low houses with big chimneys. The situation changed after the Carnation Revolution when the land reform of July 1975 split up the estates into smaller **co-operatives**. As this has not been very successful, there has been a return to medium and large scale properties.

The coast is generally uninviting although several seaside resorts are beginning to develop. There are few harbours apart from Sines, which is well-equipped. There are no large towns; Evora with its 35 000 inhabitants acts as the regional capital but lives mainly from tourism.

The Algarve (District: Faro)

Portugal's southernmost province takes its name from the Arabic *El Gharb* meaning "west" for this was in fact the most westerly region conquered by the Moors. The Algarve, separated from the Alentejo by shale hills, is like a garden: flowers grow alongside crops and beneath fruit trees, allowing one to see geraniums, camellias and oleanders, cotton, rice and sugar cane as well as carobs, figs and almonds. Many cottage gardens are surrounded by hedges of aloes (*agaves*). The villages have brightly whitewashed houses with decorative chimneys. To the west rises a mountain range of volcanic rock, the Serra de Monchique, covered in lush vegetation. The coast is very sandy. The *Sotavento* stretch east of Faro is protected by offshore sandbanks, while the *Barlavento* section to the west consists of beaches backed by high cliffs which form an impressive promontory at Cabo de São Vicente.

Over the last few years the Algarve has undergone extensive tourist development, sometimes to the detriment of traditional activities such as fishing, canning, horticulture and the cork industry. Most of the small fishing villages have become vast seaside resorts. The main towns are Faro, Lagos and Portimão.

Parks and Reserves

There are several conservation areas in Portugal to protect the beauty of the landscape and local flora and fauna.

NATIONAL PARK

Portugal's only national park is that of **Peneda-Gerês** (72 000ha/ 177 919 acres) in the north (*see Parque Nacional da PENEDA-GERÊS*).

NATURE RESERVES

Among Portugal's specially protected areas are the nature reserves of **Montesinho** near Bragança, **Douro Internacional** in a grandiose setting of natural beauty, **Alvão** near Vila Real, and **Serra da Estrela**. Near Fátima are the nature reserves of **Serra de Aire** and **Serra dos Candeeiros**, which form a beautiful limestone landscape with many caves, **Sintra-Cascais**, nestled between the ocean and surrounding forest, **Serra da Arrábida**, **Serra de São Mamede**, the **Guadiana valley** alongside the river of the same name, **Sudoeste Alentejano and Costa Vicentina**, and **Ria Formosa** (18 400ha/45 468 acres), an ecosystem which is home to a variety of rare sea birds. All these nature reserves are in mountainous regions with the exception of the last two, situated in the Algarve, where the aim is to protect coastal areas from the harm caused by mass tourism and the rapid erosion of this coastline.

CONSERVATION AREAS

Many areas have been singled out for the protection of their flora and fauna. Among them are mountainous regions like **Serra de Malcata**, swamps such as **Paúl de Arzila** and **Paúl do Boquilobo** and river estuaries which have a particularly rich birdlife, including the **Tagus estuary**, the **Sado estuary** and **Sapal de Castro Marim-Vila Real de Santo António** in the Guadiana estuary. Dune areas, including the **São Jacinto dunes** in Ria de Aveiro and those on the **Berlenga islands** off the coast of Peniche, have also been designated as conservation areas. Most of the beauty spots in Madeira and the Azores are now classified as conservation areas (*see MADEIRA and the AZORES*).

PROTECTED LANDSCAPES

Some of Portugal's coastal areas have been declared protected landscapes to prevent uncontrolled building development. They include **Esposende** (440ha/1 087 acres) and the **Costa da Caparica** as well as a number of other listed sites around the country.

Vegetation

The diversity of plants in Portugal is a visual reminder of the contrasts in climate and types of soil found here.
The **robur** and **tauzin oak**, together with **chestnuts**, birches and maples, grow on the wet peaks over 500m/1 500ft. South of the Tagus and in the Upper Douro valley where summers are very dry, there are dense woods of **ilex** (holm oak) and **cork oak**, which grow beside heaths and moorlands sparsely covered with cistus, lavender, rosemary and thyme. Cork oaks are particularly abundant in the Alentejo. Portugal is the world's leading cork producer.
Eucalyptus mainly grows along the coast together with **maritime pines** and umbrella pines, which form vast forests beside the beaches near Leiria, Coimbra and Aveiro. Aleppo pines dominate in the Serra da Estrela. Eucalyptus and pines are being planted on ever-increasing areas of land.
Mediterranean plant species acclimatise well in the Algarve, where one may see **aloes** *(agaves)*, as well as **carob**, **almond**, **fig**, **orange** and **olive** trees.

HISTORY

Portugal was part of the Iberian Peninsula until the 11C. The earliest people were of Celtic orgin, but were overrun, in succession, by the Greeks, Carthaginians, Romans, Visigoths and in 711, the Moors, who remained in control for several centuries. Portugal's first attempt at independence came in 1065, though Spain regained control. In 1143, the country finally emerged as an independent kingdom.

Time Line.

9C–7C BC — The Greeks and the Phoenicians establish trading posts on the coasts of the Iberian Peninsula, inhabited in the west by Lusitanian tribes, originally a Celtiberian population.

3C–2C BC — The Carthaginians master the country; the Romans intervene (Second Punic War) and take over the administration of Lusitania, so named by Augustus. Viriate, chief of the Lusitanians, organises resistance and is assassinated in 139.

5C AD — The Suevi (Swabians) and Visigoths occupy most of the Iberian Peninsula.

MOORISH OCCUPATION

711 — The Moorish invasion from North Africa.

8C–9C — The Christian war of **Reconquest** of the Iberian Peninsula begins at Covadonga in Asturias, led by Pelayo in 718. By the 9C, the region of Portucale, north of the Mondego, has been liberated.

THE KINGDOM FOUNDED

In 1087, Alfonso VI, King of Castile and León, undertook the reconquest of present-day Castilla-La Mancha. He called upon several French knights, including Henry of Burgundy, descendant of the French king Hugues Capet, and his cousin Raymond of Burgundy.

When the Moors were vanquished, Alfonso offered his daughters in marriage to the princes. Urraca, heir to the throne, married Raymond; Tareja (Teresa) bought the county of Portucale, which stretched between the Minho and Douro rivers, as her dowry to **Henry of Burgundy** in 1095. Henry thus became Count of Portugal.

Henry died in 1114; Queen Tareja became regent pending the coming of age of her son **Afonso Henriques**. But in 1128 the latter forced his mother to relinquish her power (see GUIMARÃES); in 1139 he broke the bonds of vassalage imposed upon him by Alfonso VII of Castile and proclaimed himself King of Portugal under the name Afonso I; Castile finally agreed in 1143.

Afonso Henriques continued the reconquest and after the victory at Ourique (1139) took Santarém and then Lisbon (1147) with the aid of the Second Crusade's fleet.

The capture of Faro in 1249 marked the end of Moorish occupation.

BURGUNDIAN DYNASTY (1128–1383) – WARS WITH CASTILE

1279–1325 — King Dinis I founds the University of Coimbra and establishes Portuguese, a dialect of the Oporto region, as the official language.

1369–83 — Taking advantage of the trouble in Castile, Fernando I attempts to enlarge his kingdom; in failing he proposes the marriage of his only daughter, Beatriz, to the King of Castile, Juan I.

13 June 1373 — First Treaty of Alliance with England (signed in London).

AVIS DYNASTY (1385–1578) – THE GREAT DISCOVERIES

(☝see The Great Discoveries section)

1385 — Upon Fernando I's death in 1383, his son-in-law Juan of Castile claims the succession; but João, bastard brother of the late king and Grand Master of the Order of Avis is acclaimed to rule; the **Cortes** in Coimbra proclaims him King of Portugal under the name **João I**.

Seven days later, on 14 August, Juan of Castile confronts João of Avis at the **Battle of Aljubarrota** but fails.

To celebrate his victory, João builds the monastery at Batalha. He marries Philippa of Lancaster, thus sealing the alliance with England that is to last throughout Portugal's history.

1386 — Treaty of Windsor with England.

1415 — The **capture of Ceuta** in Morocco by João I and his sons, including **Prince Henry**, puts an end to attacks on the Portuguese coast by Barbary pirates and marks the beginning of Portuguese expansion.

1420–44 — Settlement of the Madeira archipelago begins in 1420 and that of the Azores in 1444.

1481–95 — **João II**, known as the Perfect Prince, promotes maritime exploration; however, he mistakenly rejects Christopher Columbus' project. During his reign Bartolomeu Dias rounds the Cape of Good Hope (1488) and the **Treaty of Tordesillas** is signed (1494), dividing the New World into two spheres of influence, the Portuguese and the Castilian.

1492 — Christopher Columbus discovers America.

1495–1521 — Reign of **Manuel I**. In order to marry Isabel, daughter of the Catholic Monarchs of Spain, he expels the Jews in 1497 and Portugal loses a great many traders, bankers and learned men. **Vasco da Gama** discovers the sea route to India in 1498 and **Pedro Álvares Cabral** lands in Brazil in 1500. **Magellan**'s expedition from 1519–22 is the first to circumnavigate the world.

August 1578 — **Sebastião I** is killed (☝*see box*) and succeeded

Detail of 15C miniature depicting Battle of Aljubarrota

©Scala, Florence/Hip/British Library

Sebastião I, the "Regretted"1554–1578

Dom Sebastião came to the throne in 1557 at the age of three. He was educated by a Jesuit priest who instilled in him the old-fashioned values of chivalry, whichhis romantic, proud nature was prone to exacerbate. He believed that a mission had been conferred upon him: namely, to conquer Africa from the Moorish infidels. In 1578, having made the decision to fulfil his destiny, he set sail for Morocco along with 17 000 men and the finest of Portuguese nobility. However, with his soldiers poorly prepared and encumbered by their stately armour under a ruthless sun, his dream was to end in brutal

Museu Nacional de Arte Antiga/akg-images

Portrait of Dom Sebastião (1571) by Cristóvão Morais

fashion in the muddy reaches of the Malhazin river at Alcácer Quibir, where half of his armada was to die and the other half to be taken prisoner. His body was never found. The Spanish domination that followed encouraged the development of **Sebastianism**, which transformed the young king into a long-awaited Messiah to save Portugal, thus enriching the Portuguese soul with yet another type of nostalgic longing *(saudade)*.

by his great uncle and former regent, **Henrique I**, a pious man, whose reign lasts two years and ends without heir.

1580 — Three of Henrique's cousins lay claim to the crown: **Dom António**, Prior of Crato, the **Duchess of Bragança** and the King of Spain, **Philip II**, son of the Infante, Isabel. The Prior of Crato seeks support in the Azores (*see The AZORES*). Philip II sends the Duke of Alba in November 1580 to claim Portugal by force. Lisbon soon falls and Philip is elected king.

SPANISH DOMINATION (1580–1640)

1580 — **Philip II** of Spain invades Portugal and is proclaimed king Felipe I. Spanish domination lasts 60 years.

1 Dec 1640 — Uprising against the Spanish; the war of restoration of Portuguese supremacy ensues. Duke João of Bra-

gança takes the title João IV of Portugal; the **Bragança family** remain as the ruling dynasty until 1910.

1668 — Spain recognises Portugal's independence.

THE 18C

1683–1706 — **Pedro II** on the throne.

1703 — Britain and Portugal sign the Methuen Treaty and a trade treaty facilitating the shipping of port to England.

1706–50 — The reign of **João V**, the Magnanimous, is one of untold magnificence – sustained by riches from Brazil – in keeping with the luxurious tastes of a king of the Baroque period. The finest testimony to the period is the monastery at Mafra (*see MAFRA*).

1 Nov 1755 — An earthquake destroys Lisbon.

1750–77 — **José I** reigns assisted by his minister, the **Marquis of Pombal**. Through the latter's policies, Portugal becomes a model of enlightened despotism. Pombal expels the Jesuits in 1759.

THE NAPOLEONIC WARS

Portugal joined the first continental coalition against Revolutionary France in 1793. In 1796 Spain left the Convention and allied itself to France. Spain invaded in 1801 when Portugal refused to renounce its alliance with England; the resulting conflict was known as the **War of the Oranges**. To ensure a strict application of the blockade on Britain, Napoleon invaded Portugal, but his commanders had little success in a country supported by English troops under the command of Wellesley. The future **Duke of Wellington** preferred guerrilla tactics and finally forced the French from the Peninsula.

Portugal suffered violence and depredations at the hands of both armies with a long-term effect on the politics of the country. **General William Carr** (1768–1854) was assigned to take command of the British forces in Portugal. With the king in Brazil (until 1821), Carr took full advantage of his power. Named Viscount of Beresford following a string of victories resulting in the **Sinatra Accord** (which allowed French soldiers to return home), Carr was appointed regent by the absent **João VI**. By 1821 Beresford's tyranny provoked a conspiracy by liberal forces. He fled the country and in 1822 the same liberals obliged João to accept a liberal constitution.

THE DOWNFALL OF THE MONARCHY

1828–34 — Civil War between liberals and absolutists. In 1822 Brazil is proclaimed independent and Pedro IV, older son of João VI, becomes Emperor Pedro I of Brazil. In 1826, on his death Pedro I retains the Brazilian throne and leaves the throne of Portugal to his daughter **Maria II**. Dom Pedro's brother Miguel, who has been appointed regent, champions the cause for an absolute monarchy and lays claim to the crown, which he eventually obtains in 1828. A bitter struggle ensues between the absolutists and the liberal supporters of Dom Pedro. Aided by the English, Dom Pedro returns to Portugal to reinstate his daughter on the throne in 1834; the Evoramonte Convention puts an end to the Civil War. In 1836 Maria II marries Prince Ferdinand of Saxe-Coburg-Gotha who becomes king-consort the following year.

1855–90 — In spite of political restlessness during the reigns of **Pedro V** (1855–61), **Luís I** (1861–89) and **Carlos I** (1889–1908), a third Portuguese empire is reconstituted in Angola and Mozambique. The British Ultimatum ends endeavours by the Governor, **Serpa Pinto**, to set up a territorial belt linking Angola and Mozambique.

1899 — Treaty of Windsor.

1 Feb 1908 — Assassination in Lisbon of King Carlos I and the Crown Prince. Queen Amélia manages to save her youngest son who succeeds to the throne as **Manuel II**.

5 Oct 1910 — Abdication of Manuel II and Proclamation of the Republic.

THE REPUBLIC

1910–33 — The Republic cannot restore order. Entering the war against Germany in 1916 and sending troops to France only aggravates the domestic situation. General Carmona calls upon Oliveira Salazar, professor of economics at Coimbra University. **Dr Salazar** is appointed Minister of Finance, then in 1932, Prime Minister: he restores economic and political stability but in 1933 promulgates

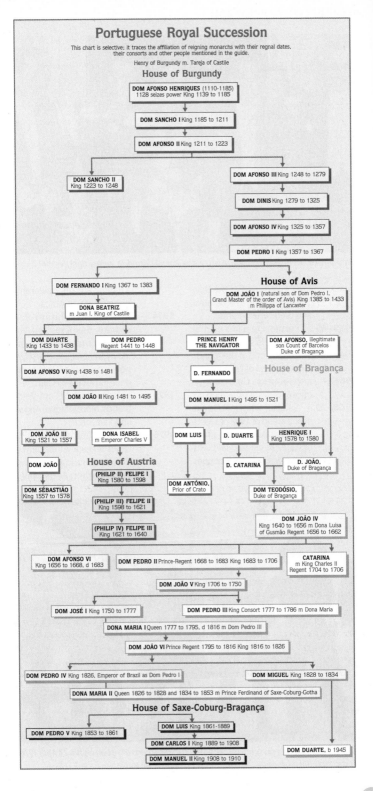

Portuguese Royal Succession

This chart is selective: it traces the affiliation of reigning monarchs with their regnal dates, their consorts and other people mentioned in the guide.

Henry of Burgundy m. Tareja of Castile

House of Burgundy

DOM AFONSO HENRIQUES (1110-1185)
1128 seizes power King 1139 to 1185

DOM SANCHO I King 1185 to 1211

DOM AFONSO II King 1211 to 1223

DOM SANCHO II King 1223 to 1248

DOM AFONSO III King 1248 to 1279

DOM DINIS King 1279 to 1325

DOM AFONSO IV King 1325 to 1357

DOM PEDRO I King 1357 to 1367

DOM FERNANDO I King 1367 to 1383

DONA BEATRIZ m Juan I, King of Castile

House of Avis

DOM JOÃO I (natural son of Dom Pedro I, Grand Master of the order of Avis) King 1385 to 1433 m Philippa of Lancaster

DOM DUARTE King 1433 to 1438

DOM PEDRO Regent 1441 to 1448

PRINCE HENRY THE NAVIGATOR

DOM AFONSO, illegitimate son Count of Barcelos Duke of Bragança

DOM AFONSO V King 1438 to 1481

D. FERNANDO

House of Bragança

DOM JOÃO II King 1481 to 1495

DOM MANUEL I King 1495 to 1521

DOM JOÃO III King 1521 to 1557

DONA ISABEL m Emperor Charles V

DOM LUIS

D. DUARTE

HENRIQUE I King 1578 to 1580

DOM JOÃO

House of Austria

(PHILIP II) FELIPE I King 1580 to 1598

DOM ANTÓNIO, Prior of Crato

D. CATARINA

D. JOÃO, Duke of Bragança

DOM SÉBASTIÃO King 1557 to 1578

(PHILIP III) FELIPE II King 1598 to 1621

DOM TEODÓSIO, Duke of Bragança

(PHILIP IV) FELIPE III King 1621 to 1640

DOM JOÃO IV King 1640 to 1656 m Dona Luisa of Gusmão Regent 1656 to 1662

DOM AFONSO VI King 1656 to 1668, d 1683

DOM PEDRO II Prince-Regent 1668 to 1683 King 1683 to 1706

CATARINA m King Charles II Regent 1704 to 1706

DOM JOÃO V King 1706 to 1750

DOM JOSÉ I King 1750 to 1777

DOM PEDRO III King Consort 1777 to 1786 m Dona Maria

DONA MARIA I Queen 1777 to 1795, d 1816 m Dom Pedro III

DOM JOÃO VI Prince Regent 1795 to 1816 King 1816 to 1826

DOM PEDRO IV King 1826, Emperor of Brazil as Dom Pedro I

DOM MIGUEL King 1828 to 1834

DONA MARIA II Queen 1826 to 1828 and 1834 to 1853 m Prince Ferdinand of Saxe-Coburg-Gotha

House of Saxe-Coburg-Bragança

DOM PEDRO V King 1853 to 1861

DOM LUIS King 1861-1889

DOM CARLOS I King 1889 to 1908

DOM DUARTE, b 1945

DOM MANUEL II King 1908 to 1910

António de Oliveira Salazar (centre left) with General Carmona (centre right) in 1941

the Constitution of the New State instituting a corporative and dictatorial regime.

1939–45 — Portugal remains neutral during World War II.

1949 — Portugal is one of the founding members of NATO.

1961 — India annexes Goa, a Portuguese territory since 1515.

1968–70 — Salazar, whose accident near the end of 1968 prevents him from taking part in affairs of state, dies in July 1970. His successor, Caetano, continues

a ruinous and unpopular anti-guerrilla war in Africa.

1974 — **Carnation Revolution** (Revolução dos Cravos): the Armed Forces Movement, led by General Spínola, seizes power on April 25. Independence of Guinea-Bissau.

1975 — Independence of Cape Verde Islands, Mozambique, Angola and São Tomé.

1976 — General António Ramalho Eanes is elected President of the Republic. Independence of East Timor. Autonomy is

Armed Forces Movement soldiers take position in the streets of Lisbon on the 28 April 1974, 3 days after the coup d'etat that overthrew the Salazar dictatorship.

granted to Macau, Madeira and the Azores.

1980 — The conservative party wins the general election. Sá Carneiro forms a government, but dies in a plane crash. General Eanes's presidential mandate is renewed.

1986 — Portugal becomes a member of the EEC on 1 January. Mário Soares is elected President on 16 February.

March 1986 — 600 years of friendship between Britain and Portugal celebrated with Queen Elizabeth and Prince Philip's state visit.

1991 — Mário Soares is re-elected president.

1994 — Lisbon chosen as European Capital of Culture.

1996 — Jorge Sampaio elected President of the Republic.

1998 — Lisbon hosts **Expo'98**.

1999 — Portugal converts its currency to the Euro.

2001 — Socialists win elections and Sampaio becomes Premier.

2002 — Another change as Social Democrats take over with José Barroso becoming the leader.

2004 — Barosso resigns to become President of the European Commission. Social Democrat Pedro de Santana Lopes becomes Premier. Portugal hosts the Euro '04 football championships.

2005 — Socialists win over 50per cent of the parliamentary seats and José Pinto de Sousa becomes Premier. Droughts and forest fires devastate large parts of the country.

2006 — Aníbal Cavaçao Silva elected President of the Republic.

2007 — Portugal takes over the Presidency of Europe and tries to restore relations with Africa. The Lisbon Treaty, binding the nations of Europe closer together, is signed in December.

The Great Discoveries

On 25 July 1415, some 200 ships under the command of Dom João I and his three sons, including Prince Henry, set sail from Lisbon. The **capture of Ceuta** in Morocco ended attacks by Barbary pirates, resulting in Portuguese control of the Straits of Gibraltar. The Potuguese also hoped that the expedition would reward them with gold and slaves from the Sudan.

At the end of the Middle Ages wealth lay in the hands of the Moors and Venetians, who monopolised the spice and perfume trade brought overland from the Orient to the Mediterranean. To bypass these intermediaries, a sea route had to be found, and Henry the Navigator was to devote his life to this dream.

THE SAGRES SCHOOL

Prince Henry the Navigator (1394–1460) retired to the Sagres promontory together with cosmographers, cartographers and navigators to try and work out a sea route from Europe to India. **Madeira** was discovered in 1419 by João Gonçalves Zarco and Tristão Vaz Teixeira, the **Azores** in 1427 (supposedly by Diogo de Silves), and in 1434 **Gil Eanes** rounded **Cape Bojador**, then the farthest point known to western man. Each time they discovered new land the mariners erected a **padrão**, a cairn surmounted by a cross and the arms of Portugal, to mark their presence. Prince Henry inspired new methods of colonisation by setting up **trading posts** *(feitoras)*, exchanges and banks. These offices, set up and run by private individuals, sometimes fostered the development of towns independent of the local powers, such as Goa. Companies were created to control trade in a particular commodity, for which the monopoly rights were often acquired. There were also **deeds of gift**, usually of land, to ships' captains with the proviso that the area be developed. Henry died in 1460, but the stage was set.

Classic - Image/World Illustrated/Photoshot

Prince Henry the Navigator (from a 15C polyptych of the Adoration of St Vincent)

NEW TERRITORIES

The major discoveries were made during the reigns of João II and Manuel I who were both grand nephews of Henry the Navigator. **Diogo Cão** reached the mouth of the Congo in 1482 and the whole coast of Angola then came under

Portuguese control. In 1488 **Bartolomeu Dias** rounded the Cape of Storms, which was immediately rechristened the Cape of Good Hope by Dom João II. A few years earlier **Christopher Columbus**, a Genoese navigator with a Portuguese wife, had the idea of sailing to India by a westerly route. His proposals, rebuffed in Lisbon, found favour with the Catholic Monarchs and in 1492 he discovered the New World. In 1494, under the **Treaty of Tordesillas** and with the Pope's approval, the Kings of Portugal and Castile divided the newly discovered and as yet undiscovered territories of the world between them: all lands west of a meridian 370 sea leagues west of the Cape Verde Islands were to belong to Castile, all east to Portugal. The position of the dividing meridian has led some historians to speculate as to whether Portugal knew of the existence of Brazil even before its official discovery by **Pedro Álvares Cabral** in 1500.

The exploration of the African coast by the Portuguese continued. On 8 July 1497 a fleet of four ships commanded by Admiral **Vasco da Gama** sailed from Lisbon with the commission to reach India by way of the sea route round the

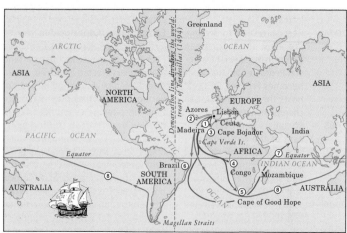

PRINCIPAL PORTUGUESE EXPEDITIONS (1419–1522)

1   Madeira (João Gonçalves Zarco and Tristão Vaz Teixaira, 1419)
2   The Azores (1427)
3   Cape Bojador (Gil Eanes, 1434)
4   Mouth of the Congo River (Diogo), Cão, 1482)
5   Cape of Good Hope (Bartolomeu Dias, 1488)
6   Brazil (Pedro Álvares Cabral, 1500)
7   Mozambique and India (Vasco da Gama, 1498)
8   Circumnavigation of the globe (Magellan's expedition, 1522)

Cape. By March 1498 Vasco da Gama had reached Mozambique and on 20 May he landed in Calicut (Kozhicode, southern India): the sea route to India had been discovered. This epic voyage was later sung in **The Lusiads** *(Os Lusíadas)* by the poet Camões.

In 1501 **Gaspar Corte Real** discovered Newfoundland, but King Manuel was interested primarily in Asia. Within a few years the Portuguese had explored the coastlines of Asia. By 1515 they were in control of the Indian Ocean, thanks to fortified outposts like Goa, which had been established by **Afonso de Albuquerque** in 1510.

It was, however, on behalf of the King of Spain that the Portuguese **Fernão de Magalhães** (Magellan) set out in 1519 and landed in India in 1521. Though he was assassinated by the natives of the Philippines, one of his vessels continued the journey to become the first to circumnavigate the world in 1522.

In 1517 King Manuel I sent an ambassador to **China** but this proved a failure and it was not until 1554 that the Portuguese were able to trade with Canton and make contact with Macau. In 1542 the Portuguese arrived in Japan where they caused political upheaval by introducing firearms. The Jesuits, whose Society of Jesus had been founded in 1540, became very active there and by 1581 there were almost 150 000 Christians. The Discoveries had a huge impact on western civilization. New products – the sweet potato, maize, tobacco, cocoa and indigo – were introduced to Europe; gold from Africa and America flooded in through the Tagus. Portugal and Spain became great powers.

A DIFFERENT WORLD

The sea faring age and Europe's discovery of new lands and civilizations disrupted every sphere of global society. For instance in Europe, the discovery of the existence of formerly unknown peoples posed religious problems: did the men of the New World have a soul and were they marked by original sin? These doubts presaged the Reformation and the development of the critical approach led to the advancement of modern science. Emerging trade empires began to thrive on cheap manual labour, bringing about history's most ignominious period of international slave trading, escalating existing slaving on a massive scale.

EVANESCENT RICHES

Portugal overspent its strength; many went overseas and the population halved from two to one million; riches encouraged idlers and adventurers; land was not tilled and wheat and rye had to be imported; crafts and skills were lost while the cost of living rose steeply. Gold was exchanged for goods from the Low Countries and France, until Portugal's riches were dissipated and little remained. The final blow came on 4 August 1578, when the young King Sebastião I was killed at El-Ksar El-Kebir in Morocco. Two years after his death Portugal came under Spanish control.

Monument of Discoveries in Belém, Lisbon

R. Mattes/MICHELIN

ART AND CULTURE

Architecture

RELIGIOUS ARCHITECTURE

Cross-section of a church

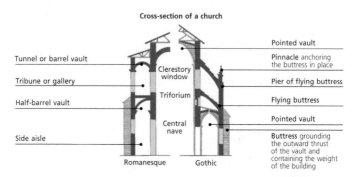

Tunnel or barrel vault

Tribune or gallery

Half-barrel vault

Side aisle

Clerestory window

Triforium

Central nave

Romanesque

Pointed vault

Pinnacle anchoring the buttress in place

Pier of flying buttress

Flying buttress

Pointed vault

Buttress grounding the outward thrust of the vault and containing the weight of the building

Gothic

LISBON – Ground plan of Igreja de Santa Maria (Mosteiro dos Jerónimos), Belém

This church is a **hall-church** (the nave is the same height as the aisles; when these have different heights a distinction is made between the central nave and the aisles).

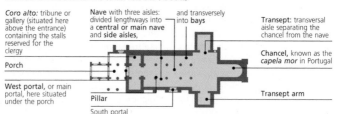

Coro alto: tribune or gallery (situated here above the entrance) containing the stalls reserved for the clergy

Porch

West portal, or main portal, here situated under the porch

Nave with three aisles: divided lengthwise into a **central or main nave** and **side aisles**, and transversely into **bays**

Pillar

South portal

Transept: transversal aisle separating the chancel from the nave

Chancel, known as the *capela mor* in Portugal

Transept arm

FREIXO DE ESPADA-À-CINTA – South porch of the church

The small parish church is attributed to Boytac and displays the main characteristics of the **Manueline style**: twisted columns interspersed with rings, vegetal decoration and spiral pinnacles. This decoration, an extension of the Mudéjar style, is not unlike the Plateresque style found in Spain. In this church, the style is only evident on the portals, but it later became more popular and could also be found inside buildings and on façades.

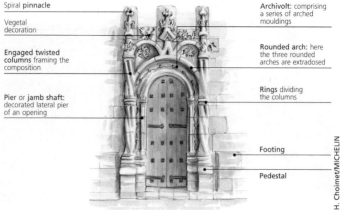

Spiral **pinnacle**

Vegetal decoration

Engaged twisted columns framing the composition

Pier or **jamb shaft**: decorated lateral pier of an opening

Archivolt: comprising a series of arched mouldings

Rounded arch: here the three rounded arches are extradosed

Rings dividing the columns

Footing

Pedestal

H. Choimet/MICHELIN

RATES – Chevet of Igreja de São Pedro (12C–13C)

This church is typical of the Portuguese Romanesque style and is part of the remains of a monastery founded by Henry of Burgundy for the monks of Cluny.

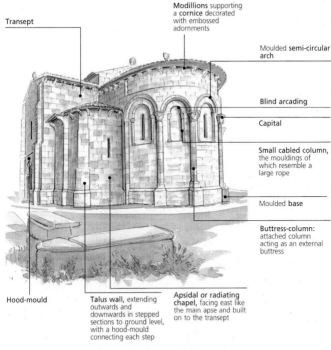

Transept

Modillions supporting a **cornice** decorated with embossed adornments

Moulded **semi-circular arch**

Blind arcading

Capital

Small cabled column, the mouldings of which resemble a large rope

Moulded **base**

Buttress-column: attached column acting as an external buttress

Hood-mould

Talus wall, extending outwards and downwards in stepped sections to ground level, with a hood-mould connecting each step

Apsidal or radiating chapel, facing east like the main apse and built on to the transept

BATALHA – Monastery: Capela do Fundador (15C)

The chapel housing the tombs of João I, his wife Philippa of Lancaster, and their sons, including Henry the Navigator, is a magnificent example of Flamboyant Gothic architecture. It is a square room crowned with an octagonal two-storey lantern and a ribbed vault shaped like an eight-pointed star.

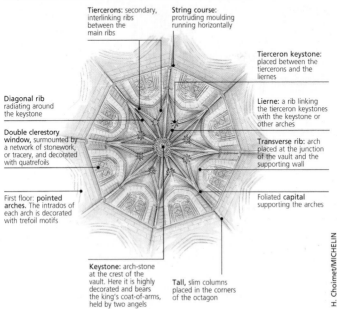

Tiercerons: secondary, interlinking ribs between the main ribs

String course: protruding moulding running horizontally

Tierceron keystone: placed between the tiercerons and the liernes

Diagonal rib radiating around the keystone

Lierne: a rib linking the tierceron keystones with the keystone or other arches

Double clerestory window, surmounted by a network of stonework, or tracery, and decorated with quatrefoils

Transverse rib: arch placed at the junction of the vault and the supporting wall

First floor: pointed arches. The intrados of each arch is decorated with trefoil motifs

Foliated **capital** supporting the arches

Keystone: arch-stone at the crest of the vault. Here it is highly decorated and bears the king's coat-of-arms, held by two angels

Tall, slim columns placed in the corners of the octagon

H. Choimet/MICHELIN

MAFRA – Basilica (18C)

This basilica is a masterpiece of 18C Portuguese architecture, which is heavily influenced by Italian neo-Classicism and German Baroque. It took its inspiration from Saint Peter's in the Vatican and the Gesù Church in Rome.

Twinned transverse arch which supports the barrel vault, decorated with caissons

Triangular pediment decorated with a group of sculptures (Christ crucified, the Glory and two angels in adoration)

Rounded arch decorated with flowerets

Pendentive: a concave triangle connecting the surface of the dome and the walls

Cornice with a hood-mould underlined by dentils between two moulded strips

Lunette: part of a barrel vault which does not extend as far as the keystone and which opens out the upper sections of a bay

Corner piece

Tuscan capital

Pink marble frieze

String course running horizontally along the capitals

Architrave with two **fasciae** (banding edged with fillets) crowned with a moulded strip

Pink marble columns framing the high altar

Organ

Overhanging organ loft

Retable or altarpiece

Communion table

Twinned pilasters adorned with fluting

Composite capital

Triforium

H. Choimet/MICHELIN

CIVIL AND MILITARY ARCHITECTURE

ÓBIDOS – Castle (13C-14C)

The fortress built by the Moors on the site of a Luso-Roman hillfort was considerably modified after the reconquest of Óbidos. However, Arab influence is still evident, particularly in the pyramidal shape of the merlons on the Dom Ferdinand Tower and in the absence of architectural features such as machicolations on the 42ft/13m-high walls.

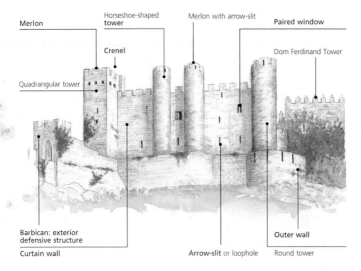

Merlon

Horseshoe-shaped tower

Merlon with arrow-slit

Paired window

Crenel

Dom Ferdinand Tower

Quadrangular tower

Barbican: exterior defensive structure

Curtain wall

Arrow-slit or loophole

Outer wall

Round tower

Mudéjar influence (13C-16C)

After the Christian Reconquest an artistic style developed in the Iberian peninsula which borrowed certain decorative features from Islamic art and which became known as Mudéjar, the name given to Muslims who had remained under Christian rule. In Portugal this influence is particularly noticeable in the **Évora** region, where King Manuel I had a palace built, of which only one pavilion remains.

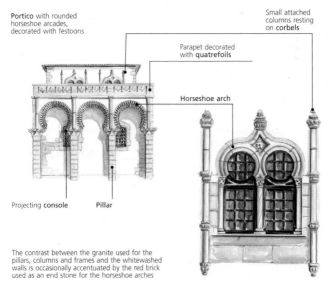

Portico with rounded horseshoe arcades, decorated with festoons

Small attached columns resting on **corbels**

Parapet decorated with **quatrefoils**

Horseshoe arch

Projecting **console**   Pillar

The contrast between the granite used for the pillars, columns and frames and the whitewashed walls is occasionally accentuated by the red brick used as an end stone for the horseshoe arches

Paired windows under rounded horseshoe arches with a curved moulded frame

H. Choimet/MICHELIN

GUIMARÃES – Paço dos Duques de Bragança (15C)

Built by the first Duke of Bragança, the palace has been restored to its original appearance and bears traces of both Norman and Burgundian influence. Its defensive character can be seen in the huge corner towers, crenels and covered machicolations. It prefigures the buildings dating from the Renaissance period with their sloping roofs, numerous chimney pots and large windows.

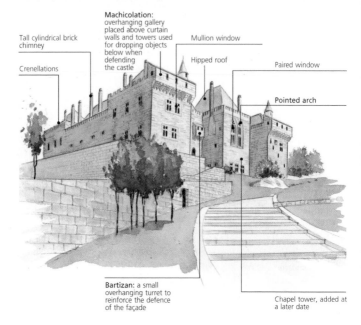

Tall cylindrical brick chimney

Crenellations

Machicolation: overhanging gallery placed above curtain walls and towers used for dropping objects below when defending the castle

Mullion window

Hipped roof

Paired window

Pointed arch

Bartizan: a small overhanging turret to reinforce the defence of the façade

Chapel tower, added at a later date

ÉVORA – Cloisters of the old university (16C)

The former Jesuit university (Antiga Universidade dos Jesuítas) was inspired by the Italian Renaissance. The central triple-bayed avant-corps, flanked by attached pilasters topped by statues, leads to the Sala das Actas (Hall of Acts). Above the central bay a crowned attic ornamented with an escutcheon bears a broken pediment decorated with a group of sculptures. Note the rounded arcades supported by slender columns and a pedestal in the upper gallery and by columns in the portico.

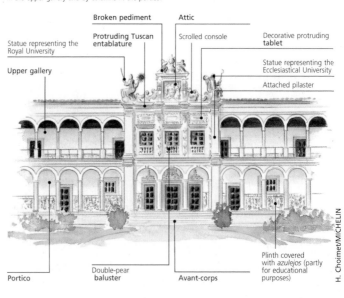

Broken pediment

Attic

Protruding Tuscan entablature

Scrolled console

Decorative protruding tablet

Statue representing the Royal University

Upper gallery

Statue representing the Ecclesiastical University

Attached pilaster

Portico

Double-pear baluster

Avant-corps

Plinth covered with *azulejos* (partly for educational purposes)

H. Choimet/MICHELIN

LISBON – Praça do Comércio (18C)

After the earthquake on 1 November 1755, the Marquis of Pombal decided to demolish and rebuild the Baixa district. Between Terreiro do Paço, renamed Praça do Comércio, and the Rossio, he created a district built on a grid plan, with streets intersecting at right angles where all the buildings had three floors and where just a few decorative features distinguished one street from the next. This new style, partly inspired by the city's architectural past, became known as the **Pombaline style**.

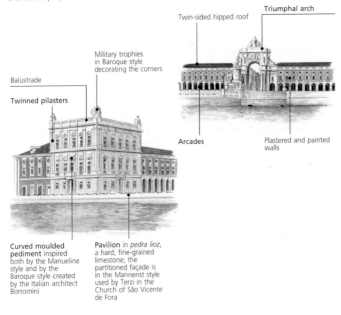

Twin-sided hipped roof

Triumphal arch

Military trophies in Baroque style decorating the corners

Balustrade

Twinned pilasters

Arcades

Plastered and painted walls

Curved moulded pediment inspired both by the Manueline style and by the Baroque style created by the Italian architect Borromini

Pavilion in *pedra lioz*, a hard, fine-grained limestone; the partitioned façade is in the Mannerist style used by Terzi in the Church of São Vicente de Fora

LISBON – Main railway station, Praça do Rossio (19C)

Built in 1886-87 by José Luis Monteiro, the façade of this building, a beautiful example of the neo-Manueline style, conceals an iron structure. The harmony of the three sections on the first floor is achieved through slender polygonal columns which rest on the sloping retaining walls of the ground floor. The crowning aedicule above houses a clock. The decorative elements used (cabling, rings and spiral pinnacles) are typical of the Manueline style.

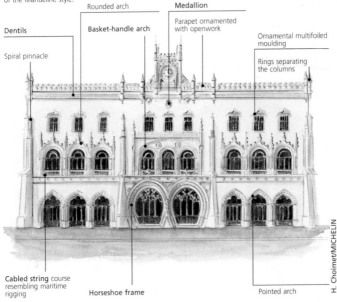

Rounded arch

Medallion

Dentils

Basket-handle arch

Parapet ornamented with openwork

Ornamental multifoiled moulding

Spiral pinnacle

Rings separating the columns

Cabled string course resembling maritime rigging

Horseshoe frame

Pointed arch

H. Choimet/MICHELIN

ARCHITECTURAL TERMS

(**Cadeiral:** *words in bold italics are in Portuguese or Spanish*)

Adufa: A protective lattice screen made of small strips of wood arranged on the outside of windows.

Ajimez: a paired window or opening.

Apse: the generally rounded end of a church behind the altar. The exterior is called the east end.

Altar Mor: the high altar.

Armillary sphere: a globe made up of hoops to show the motions of the heavenly bodies. As the emblem of King Manuel I, it is often portrayed in Manueline art.

Artesonado: a marquetry ceiling in which raised fillets outline honeycomb-like cells in the shape of stars. This particular decoration, which first appeared under the Almohads, was popular throughout the Iberian Peninsula in the 15C and 16C.

Atlas (or **telamon**): support in the form of a carved male figure.

Atrium: a forecourt or open central courtyard in a Roman house.

Azulejos: glazed, patterned, ceramic tiles *(see p 53)*.

Bastion: a projecting part of a fortification built at the angle of, or against the line of, a wall.

Cadeiral: the choir stalls in a church.

Campanile: a bell-tower, often detached from the church.

Chicane: a zig-zag passageway.

Chrisma: the monogram of Christ, formed by the Greek capital letters *khi* (X) and *rhô* (P), the first two letters of the word Christos.

Churrigueresque: in the style of the Churrigueras, an 18C family of Spanish architects. Richly ornate Baroque decoration.

Citânia: a term used to describe the ruins of former Roman or pre-Roman settlements on the Iberian Peninsula.

Coro: the part of a chancel containing the stalls and used by canons and other members of the clergy.

Cupola (or **dome**): curved roof, most often hemispherical, crowning the top of a building.

Empedrado: a typical surface covering for Portuguese pavements and streets made from stones of various types and colours to create attractive designs.

Entablature: beam member made up of the architrave, frieze and cornice.

Foliage (or **foliated scrolls**): sculptural or painted ornamentation depicting foliage, often in the form of a frieze.

Gable: the decorative, triangular upper portion of a wall which supports a pitched roof.

Glacis: an embankment sloping gently down from a fort.

Grotesque: (from *grotta* or *grotto* in Italian); a fantastic or incongruous ornament used in the Renaissance.

Windows with adufa screens in the Algarve

©Hani Alex Latif/iStockphoto.com

Detail of empedrado in Rossio, Lisbon

Hypocaust: a space under a floor in a Roman house where hot air or furnace gases were used for heating.

Impluvium: a square basin in the atrium of a Roman house for collecting rain water.

Jacente: a funerary statue.

Judiaria: an old Jewish quarter.

Lantern: the part of a dome which opens laterally.

Lavabo: a fountain basin in cloisters used by monks for their ablutions.

Levada: Irrigation channels used to provide water.

Lombard arches: a decorative device in Romanesque architecture consisting of small slightly projecting blind arcades linking vertical bands.

Modillion: a small console supporting a cornice.

Moucharaby: a wooden lattice-work screen placed in front of a window.

Mouraria: a former Moorish district.

Mozarabic: the work of Christians living under Moorish rule after 711. On being persecuted in the 9C, they sought refuge in Christian areas bringing with them Moorish artistic traditions.

Mudéjar: the work of Muslims who remained under Christian rule following the Reconquest. It is used to describe work reminiscent of Moorish characteristics which was undertaken between the 13C and 16C.

Padrão: a stone monument erected by the Portuguese to denote possession of lands they discovered.

Peristyle: a row of columns surrounding a court, garden or façade.

Plateresque: a style that originated in Spain in the 16C and is derived from the word *plata* (silver); it is used to describe finely carved decoration inspired by the work of silversmiths.

Predella: the lower part of a retable.

Púlpito: a pulpit.

Retable: an altarpiece; marble, stone or wood decoration for an altar.

Rinceau: used in painting and sculpture. An ornamental motif of scrolling foliage, usually vine. Often part of a frieze.

Rococo: a late-Baroque style of decoration with asymmetrical patterns involving scroll-work, shell motifs etc.

Sé: a cathedral or episcopal seat; from the Latin *sedes* meaning seat.

Stucco: a type of moulding mix consisting mainly of plaster, used for coating surfaces.

Tree of Jesse: a genealogical tree showing Christ's descent from Jesse through his son David.

Talha dourada: carved, gilded woodwork typical of Portuguese Baroque.

Tracery: intersecting stone ribwork in the upper part of a window, a bay or rose window.

Triptych: a painting or sculpture comprising three hinged panels which can be folded over.

Art

FROM PREHISTORY TO THE LATE MIDDLE AGES

Prehistoric sites such as the megaliths around Évora, the rock engravings in the Vale do Côa, as well as Iron Age ruins in Citânia de Briteiros, and the Roman remains at Conímbriga, Tróia and Évora will interest the lover of Antiquity. There are also small pre-Romanesque churches that recall the different architectural influences that swept across the Iberian Peninsula from the north and the east. These influences include Visigothic (Igreja de São Pedro de Balsemão near Lamego and Igreja de Santo Amaro in Beja), Mozarabic (Capela de São Pedro de Lourosa in Oliveira do Hospital) and Byzantine (Capela de São Frutuoso near Braga).

THE MIDDLE AGES (11C–15C)

Romanesque Art

The Romanesque influence arrived in Portugal in the 11C. Brought from France by Burgundian knights and monks, it retained many French traits. Nevertheless, the influence of Santiago de Compostela, particularly in northern Portugal, produced a style more Galician than French, which was further enhanced through the use of granite. Monuments have a massive and rough appearance with capitals that show the granite's resistance to the mason's chisel.

Cathedrals were rebuilt at the same time as local fortified castles and often resemble them. The cathedrals in Coimbra, Lisbon, Évora, Oporto and Braga are good examples. Country churches, built at a later date, sometimes have richly carved main doorways. The interior design, frequently including pointed arches and even groined vaulting, was often transformed by Manueline or Baroque additions.

Gothic Art

While the Romanesque style blossomed in chapels and cathedrals in the north, Gothic architecture developed most vigorously at the end of the 13C in Coimbra and Lisbon in the form of large monasteries. The churches, designed with a nave and two corresponding aisles with polygonal apses and apsidal chapels, retain the proportions and simplicity of the Romanesque style. The *Mosteiro de Alcobaça* served as a model for the 14C cloisters of the cathedrals in Coimbra, Lisbon and Évora. Flamboyant Gothic found its most perfect expression in the **Mosteiro da Batalha** even though this was only completed in the Manueline period.

Sculpture

Gothic sculpture developed in the 14C for the adornment of tombs, but barely featured as decoration on tympana and

Mosteiro da Batalha

P. Martins/MICHELIN

doorways. Capitals and cornices were ornamented only with geometric or plant motifs with the exception of a few stylised animals or occasional human forms (capitals in the Mosteiro de Celas in Coimbra). Funerary art flowered in three centres, Lisbon, Évora and Coimbra from where, under the influence of **Master Pero**, it spread into northern Portugal, principally to Oporto, Lamego, Oliveira do Hospital and São João de Tarouca. The most beautiful tombs, those of Inês de Castro and Dom Pedro in the Mosteiro de Alcobaça, were carved from limestone. Coimbra's influence continued into the 15C under **João Afonso** and **Diogo Pires the Elder**. A second centre developed at Batalha inspired by **Master Huguet** (tombs of Dom João I and Philippa of Lancaster).

Military Architecture

The Portuguese, in the wars first against the Moors and then the Spanish, built castles. The first examples mark the successive stages of the **Reconquest**, the second, dating from the 13C to the 17C, guard the major routes of communication. Most of these castles, built in the Middle Ages, are similar in style, double perimeter walls circling a keep or *Torre de Menagem*, crowned with pyramid capped merlons, a trace of the Moorish influence.

THE MANUELINE PERIOD (1490–1520)

The Manueline style marks the transition from Gothic to Renaissance in Portugal; its name recalls its appearance during the reign of Manuel I. Despite the brevity of the period in which it developed, the Manueline style's undeniable originality has given it major importance in all aspects of Portuguese art.

It reflects the passion, which inspired all of Portugal at the time, for the sea and of faraway territories which had just been discovered, and manifests the strength and riches accumulating on the banks of the Tagus.

Architecture

Churches remained Gothic in their general plan, in the height of their columns and network vaulting – but novelty and movement appeared in the way columns were twisted to form spirals; triumphal arches were adorned with mouldings in the form of nautical cables; ribs of plain pointed arched vaulting were given heavy liernes in round or square relief; these, in their turn, were transformed by further ornamentation into four-pointed stars or were supplemented by decorative cables occasionally intertwined into mariners' knots. The contour of the vaulting itself evolved, flattening out and resting on arches supported on consoles. The height of the aisles was increased, so giving rise to true hall-churches.

Sculpture

The Manueline style shows its character in the form of decoration. Windows, doorways, rose windows and balustrades are covered with sprigs of laurel leaves, poppy heads, roses, corn cobs, acorns, oak leaves, artichokes, cardoons, pearls, scales, ropes, anchors, terrestrial globes, armillary spheres and lastly the Cross of the Order of Christ, which forms a part of every decorative scheme.

Artists

Diogo de Boytac was responsible for the first Manueline buildings, the Igreja do Convento de Jesus at Setúbal, and the cathedral *(sé)* at Guarda. He also contributed to the construction of the Mosteiro dos Jerónimos in Belém, Lisbon, the Igreja do Mosteiro da Santa Cruz in Coimbra and the Mosteiro da Batalha. His artistry lay in magnificent complication: twisted columns, of which he was the master, were covered with overlapping laurel leaves, scales and rings; doorways, which were a major element in Manueline art, stood in a rectangular setting bordered by turned columns crowned with spiralled pinnacles; in the centre of the whole or above it stood the Manueline emblems of the shield, the Cross of the Order of Christ and the armillary sphere.

Mateus Fernandes, whose art was distinctly influenced by the elegance of Flamboyant Gothic, brought a Manueline touch to Batalha. Decoration, which he usually designed as an

Photolocation/Picture Colour Library

Manueline style window of the Convento do Cristo, Tomar

infinitely repeating plant, geometric or calligraphic motif, takes precedence over volume – the doorway to the Capelas Imperfeitas (Unfinished Chapels) at Batalha is outstanding for the exuberance of its decoration.

Diogo de Arruda was the most original Manueline artist. He designed the famous and marvellously inventive Tomar window. Nautical themes were a positive obsession with this artist.

Francisco de Arruda was the architect of Lisbon's Torre de Belém. He rejected the decorative excesses of his brother, preferring the simplicity of Gothic design embellished with Moorish motifs.

The Arruda brothers were recognised equally as the "master architects of the Alentejo", where they displayed their skill in combining the Manueline style with Moorish themes which gave rise to an entirely new style, the **Luso-Moorish**. This is characterised by the horseshoe arch adorned with delicate mouldings. Most of the seigneurial mansions and castles in the Alentejo, as well as the royal palaces in Sintra and Lisbon, bear the stamp of this style.

Simultaneously, as Manueline architecture was reaching its peak at the end of the 15C, Portuguese sculpture came under Flemish influence due to **Olivier de Gand** and **Jean d'Ypres** – their masterpiece is the carved wooden altarpiece in Coimbra's Sé Velha. **Diogo Pires the Younger** followed, adopting Manueline themes in his work, the best example of which is the font in the Mosteiro de Leça do Bailio (1515).

In the early 16C artists came from Galicia and Biscay to work in northern Portugal. There they helped build the churches at Caminha, Braga, Vila do Conde and Viana do Castelo. The obvious influences in their work are Flamboyant and Spanish Plateresque. From 1517 onwards, two Biscayan artists, **João** and **Diogo de Castilho** worked successively in Lisbon, Tomar and Coimbra. Their art, which had much of the Plateresque style in it, became integrated in the Manueline style (Mosteiro dos Jerónimos).

PAINTING FROM 1450 TO 1550

The Primitives (1450–1505)

The early painters were influenced by Flemish art, which was introduced into Portugal partly through the close commercial ties between Lisbon and the Low Countries.

Only **Nuno Gonçalves**, author of the famous **São Vicente polyptych** *(see Museu de Arte Antiga, Lisbon)* remained truly original, not least in the way the picture's composition evoked a tapestry more than a painting. Unfortunately none of his other works are known except for the cartouches for the Arzila and Tangier tapestries which hang in the Collegiate Church of Pastrana in Spain. A group of "masters", including the **Master of Sardoal**, left a good many works that may be seen throughout the country's museums in the sections on Portuguese Primitives. Among the Flemish painters who came to Portugal, **Francisco Henriques** and **Carlos Frei** stand out for their rich use of colour.

The Manueline Painters (1505–50)

The Manueline painters created a true Portuguese School of painting which was characterised by delicacy of design, beauty and accuracy of colour, realism in the composition of the backgrounds, life-size human figures and an expressive naturalism in the portrayal of people's faces tempered, however, with a certain idealism. The major artists in the school worked in either Viseu or Lisbon.

The **Viseu School** was headed by **Vasco Fernandes**, known as Grão Vasco (Great Vasco), whose early works, including the altarpiece at Lamego, reveal Flemish influence. His later work showed more originality, a richness of colour as well as a sense of the dramatic and of composition (as in his paintings from Viseu cathedral which may now be seen in the town's Museu Grão Vasco). **Gaspar Vaz**, whose works can be seen in the Igreja São João de Tarouca, began painting at the Lisbon School, but painted his best pictures while at Viseu.

The **Lisbon School** – established around **Jorge Afonso**, painter for King Manuel I – saw the development of several very talented artists:

- **Cristóvão de Figueiredo** evolved a technique that recalls the later impressionists and the use of black and grey in portraiture. His style was imitated by several artists including the Master of Santa Auta in his altarpiece for the original Igreja da Madre de Deus in Lisbon.

- **Garcia Fernandes**, archaic in style, showed a preciosity in his portraits.

- **Gregório Lopes**, whose line and modelling were harsher, painted Court life. He excelled in backgrounds which present contemporary Portuguese life in exact detail (altarpiece in the Igreja de São João Baptista in Tomar).

©Scala, Florence/Museu Nacional de Arte Antiga

Ecce homo (Behold the Man) (16C) by Cristóvão de Figueiredo

THE RENAISSANCE

The Renaissance style, which retained its essential Italian and French characteristics in Portugal, spread – particularly in sculpture – from Coimbra, where several French artists had settled.

Nicolas Chanterene, whose style remained entirely faithful to the principles of the Italian Renaissance, undertook the decoration of the north door of the Mosteiro dos Jerónimos in Belém before becoming the master sculptor of the Coimbra School. The pulpit in the Igreja da Santa Cruz in Coimbra is his masterpiece. **Jean de Rouen** excelled in altarpieces and low reliefs, as may be seen in the Mosteiro de Celas in Coimbra. **Houdart** succeeded Nicolas Chanterene in 1530 at Coimbra as grand master of statuary. His sculptures are easily recognisable for their realism.

The advance in architecture, which came later than in the other arts, was brought about by native Portuguese: **Miguel de Arruda** introduced a classical note to Batalha after 1533; **Diogo de Torralva** completed the Convento de Cristo in Tomar; **Afonso Álvares** began the transition to classical design by giving buildings a monumental simplicity.

CLASSICAL ART

The classical period saw the triumph of the Jesuit style with **Filippo Terzi**, an Italian architect who arrived in Portugal in 1576, and **Baltazar Álvares** (1550–1624); churches became rectangular in plan and were built without transepts, ambulatories or apses.

Painting came under Spanish influence and produced only two major artists: **Domingos Vieira** (1600–78), whose portraits are vividly alive, and Josefa de Ayala, known as **Josefa de Óbidos** (1634–84). A feeling for classical composition is apparent in the work of the gold and silversmiths of the period. The 17C was marked by the Indo-Portuguese style of furniture, typified by marquetry secretaries, rare woods and ivory.

BAROQUE ART (LATE 17C–18C)

The Baroque style, which owes its name to the Portuguese word *barroco* – a rough pearl – corresponds to the spirit of the Counter Reformation.

Architecture

Baroque architecture abandoned the symmetry of the classical style and sought movement, volume, a sense of depth through the use of curved lines and an impression of grandeur. The beginning of Baroque architecture coincided with the end of Spanish domination. In the 17C, architecture took on an austere and simple appearance under **João Nunes Tinoco** and **João Turiano**, but from the end of the century onwards façades became alive with angels, garlands and the interplay of curving lines, particularly at Braga. The architect **João Antunes** advocated an octagonal plan for religious buildings (Igreja da Santa Engrácia in Lisbon). In the 18C King João V invited foreign artists to Portugal. The German **Friedrich Ludwig** and the Hungarian **Mardel**, both trained in the Italian School, brought a monumental style, best be seen in the Mosteiro de Mafra. True Baroque architecture developed in the north and can be seen in both religious and civic buildings (Igreja de Bom Jesus near Braga and Solar de Mateus near Vila Real), where the whitewashed façades contrast with the pilasters and cornices which frame them. In Oporto, **Nicolau Nasoni**, of Italian origin, adorned façades with floral motifs, palm leaves and swags, while in Braga, architecture bordered on Rococo in style (Palácio do Raio in Braga, Igreja de Santa Maria Madalena in Falperra).

Decoration

Azulejos and *Talha Dourada* were popular forms of decoration, the latter being the Portuguese name for the heavily gilded wood used in the adornment of church interiors, including, from 1650 onwards, high altarpieces which were first carved before being gilded. In the 17C altarpieces resembled doorways; on either side of the altar, surrounded by a stepped throne, twisted columns rose up while the screen itself was covered in decorative motifs in high relief including vines, bunches of grapes, birds and cherubim. Altarpieces in the 18C were often out of proportion, invading the ceiling and the chancel walls. Entablatures with broken pediments crowned columns against which stood atlantes or other statues. Altarpieces were also surmounted by baldaquins.

Statuary

Many statues, generally in wood, were to be found on the altarpieces that decorated the churches. In the 18C statuary largely followed foreign schools: at Mafra, the Italian **Giusti** and his colleagues instructed many Portuguese sculptors, among them **Machado de Castro**; in Braga, Coimbra and Oporto, **Laprade** represented the French School; at Arouca, the Portuguese **Jacinto Vieira** gave his carvings a very personal, lively style. The idea of the Baroque cribs *(presépios)*, that can be seen in many churches, originate from southern Italy. In Portugal they are more naive but not without artistic merit. The figures in terracotta are often by **Machado de Castro**, **Manuel Teixeira** or **António Ferreira**. The talent of the Baroque sculptors is also evident in the many fountains found throughout Portugal especially in the Minho region.

The monumental staircase of Bom Jesus near Braga is made up of a series of fountains in the Rococo style.

Painting

Painting is represented by **Vieira Lusitano** (1699–1783) and **Domingos António de Sequeira** (1768–1837), the latter a remarkable portraitist.

LATE 18C–19C

Architecture

The second half of the 18C saw a return to the classical style, seen in the work of **Mateus Vicente** (1747–86 – Palácio Real in Queluz), **Carlos da Cruz Amarante** (Igreja de Bom Jesus), and the Lisbon architects, particularly **Eugénio dos Santos** who created the Pombal style. In the late 19C when the Romantic movement favoured a revival of former styles, Portugal developed the neo-Manueline,

an evocation of the period of the Great Discoveries exemplified by the Castelo da Pena in Sintra, the Palace-Hotel in Buçaco and the Estação do Rossio in Lisbon. At the time *azulejos* were being used to decorate entire house façades.

Sculpture

Soares dos Reis (1847–89) tried to portray the Portuguese *saudade* or nostalgia in sculpture; his pupil, **Teixeira Lopes** (1866–1918), revealed an elegant technique, particularly when portraying children's heads.

Painting

Portuguese painters discovered the naturalistic approach from the Barbizon school in France. Two painters, **Silva Porto** (1850–93) and **Marquês de Oliveira** (1853–1927) followed the Naturalist movement, while **Malhoa** (1855–1933), the painter of popular festivals, and **Henrique Pousão** (1859–84) were closer to Impressionism; **Sousa Pinto** (1856–1939) excelled as a pastel artist and **Columbano Bordalo Pinheiro** (1857–1929) achieved distinction with his portraits and still-life paintings.

20C

Architecture

The influence of Art Nouveau may be seen in buildings in Lisbon, Coimbra and Leira, while one of the finest examples of Art Deco in Portugal is the Casa de Serralves in Oporto. In the 1930s, the architect **Raúl Lino** built the Casa dos Patudos in Alpiarça, near Santarém. However, it was only in the 1950s that a noticeable development in housing came about which may be seen in council houses, garden cities and buildings like the Museu Gulbenkian in Lisbon. The Oporto School of architecture stands out for the modernism it advocates with internationally known architects such as **Fernando Távora** (b.1923) and **Álvaro Siza** (b.1933) who was commissioned to restore the Chiado quarter in Lisbon after it was partly destroyed by fire in 1988. The main architectural event in Lisbon in the 1980s was the construction of the post-modern Torres das Amoreiras designed by **Tomás Taveira**.

Casa de Serralves in Porto

©Gonçalo Carreira/Fotolia.com

Sculpture

Francisco Franco (1885–1955) held great sway over the official sculpture of the period, including the commemorative monuments so popular under Salazar. More recently, **João Cutileiro** has come to prominence with his original collection of statues (Dom Sebastião in Lagos, and Camões in Cascais), while **José Pedro Croft** (stonework), **Rui Sanches** (woodwork) and **Rui Chafes** (metal) are all contemporary artists who adhere to a more conceptual style of sculpture (installations).

Painting

In the early 20C Portuguese painting mainly stuck to Naturalism; only a few artists diverged to follow the general trend; **Amadeo de Souza Cardoso** (1887–1918), a friend of Modigliani, worked in Paris assimilating the lessons of Cézanne and found his true expression first in Cubism then in a highly coloured variant of Expressionism; his friend **Santa Rita** (1889–1918), who died unexpectedly, made a great contribution to the Portuguese Futurist movement but destroyed much of his work. **Almada Negreiros** (1889–1970) was influenced by Cubism while at the same time remaining a classical draughtsman. He was also a poet and playwright. He painted the large frescoes in Lisbon's harbour stations in 1945 and 1948. **Maria Helena Vieira da Silva** (1908–92), who moved to Paris in 1928, derived her art from the Paris School, although in her space paintings the *azulejo* influence may be seen.

Among the best known contemporary painters are **Paula Rego** (b.1935), who draws upon Op-Art, **Júlio Pomar**, Lourdes Castro, **José de Guimarães** and, more recently, Julião Sarmento, Pedro Cabrita Reis, Alberto Carneiro (installations), Pedro Calapez (abstraction and volumetric forms), Álvaro Lapa, Pedro Portugal, Pedro Casquiero (abstraction), Graça Morais and Pedro Proença (allegorical images).

Azulejos

Ever since the 15C the *azulejo* has been a component of the different styles of Portuguese architecture that have followed one another through the centuries. There is some controversy as to the etymological origin of the word *azulejo*; some say it comes from *azul* meaning blue, others that it in fact derives from the Arabic *az-zulay* or *al zuleich* which means a smooth piece of terracotta.

Origin

The first *azulejos* came from Andalucía in Spain where they were used as decoration in *alcázars* and palaces. They were introduced into Portugal by King Manuel I who, having been dazzled by the Alhambra in Granada, decided to have his Sintra palace decorated with these rich ceramic tiles. *Azulejos* at that time took the form of **alicatados**, pieces of monochrome glazed earthenware cut and assembled into geometric patterns. The process was superseded by that of the **corda seca** in which a fine oil and manganese strip were used to separate the different enamels, and when fired, blackened to form an outline for the various motifs. Another method for separating the motifs was known as **aresta** and consisted of drawing ridges in the clay itself. In the 16C the Italian Francesco Nicoloso introduced the Italian **majolica** technique, in which the terracotta was covered with a layer of white enamel which could then be coloured. *Azulejos* thus developed into another type of artistic medium with a wide range of decorative possibilities. The Portuguese created a standard square with 14cm/5.5in sides and opened their own workshops in Lisbon.

Renaissance and Mannerist styles

Towards the middle of the 16C Flemish influence took precedence over Spanish, and more complex *azulejo* panels were used to decorate churches; the transept in the Igreja São Roque in Lisbon is a good example. *Azulejos* were in great demand for decorating summer houses and gardens. The finest examples may be seen at Quinta da Bacalhoa and date from 1565. They consist of wonderful multicoloured panels with an Italian majolica-ware quality, which illustrate allegories of great rivers. The panel of Nossa Senhora da Vida, in the Museu do Azulejo in Lisbon, dates from the same period.

17C

Portugal entered a period of austerity under Spanish domination. In order to decorate church walls without incurring great expense, simple monochrome tiles were used and placed in geometric patterns. The Igreja de Marvila in Santarém is a fine example. A style known as *tapete*, a sort of tile-carpet or tapestry, was developed, repeated in blocks of four, 16 or 36 tiles, which resembled oriental hangings on account of their geometric or floral patterns.

The restoration of the monarchy was followed by a period of great creative development. There was a return to figurative motifs on panels with illustrations of mythological scenes or caricatures of contemporary society life. Traditional blues and yellows were enhanced by greens and purples; there are fine examples at the Palácio dos Marqueses da Fronteira in Lisbon. Little by little, multicoloured tiles gave way to cobalt blue motifs on a white enamel background as may be seen in the Victory Room of the Palácio dos Marqueses da Fronteira.

Panel from 1670, Museu Nacional do Azulejo, Lisbons

M. Gurfinkel/MICHELIN

18C

Tiles in the 18C were almost exclusively blue and white. This fashion developed from Chinese porcelain, popular at the time of the Great Discoveries. *Azulejos* were decorated by true artists and masters including **António Pereira**, **Manuel dos Santos** and especially **António de Oliveira Bernardes** and his son **Policarpo**. Their works include the Capela dos Remédios in Peniche, the Igreja de São Lourenço in Almansil and the Forte de São Filipe in Setúbal.

The reign of João V (1706–50) was characterised by magnificence, with gold from Brazil funding all manner of extravagance. The taste of the day was for dramatic effect which expressed itself particularly well in *azulejos*. Panels became veritable pictures, with surrounds of intermingling festoons, tassels, fluttering angels and pilasters – the **Baroque style** in full bloom. The main artists at the time were **Bartolomeu Antunes** and **Nicolau de Freitas**.

The second half of the 18C was marked by the **Rocaille style** (rock and shell motifs). There was also a return to polychromy with yellow, brown and purple being the dominant colours; painting became more delicate; smaller motifs were popular and frames were decorated with scrolls, plant motifs and shells as may be seen at the Palácio de Queluz, particularly along the Grand Canal. The opening of the Fábrica Real de Cerâmica in Rato in 1767 meant that *azulejos* could be manufactured in great quantity. The **neoclassical style** during the reign of Maria I is notable for the refreshing subject matter of its tiles which were framed by garlands, pilasters, urns and foliage.

Literature

While remaining open to outside influences which are quickly and successfully assimilated, Portuguese literature is nonetheless original and reflects the lyrical and nostalgic spirit – the famous *saudade* of the people, as in the *fado*. Poetry has always held a privileged position with, as a figurehead, the monumental work of Camões.

The Middle Ages

The earliest known Portuguese literature dates from the late 12C with the poetry of the troubadours, influenced by Provençal lyricism. There were **Cantigas de Amor** for male voices, the more popular **Cantigas de Amigo** and the satirical **Cantigas de Escárnio e Maldizer** which were collected in anthologies or *cancioneiros*. The most famous of these, the *Cancioneiro Geral,* compiled by the Spaniard Garcia de Resende in the 16C, covered all the poetry written in Portuguese and Castilian over more than a century. King Dinis I, a poet himself, imposed the official use of Portuguese in the 13C. Dom Pedro was the major literary figure of the 14C. However, **Fernão Lopes** (born c.1380–1390), the chronicler of Portuguese kings and queens *(Chronicles of Dom Pedro, Dom Fernando, Dom João I and Dom Dinis)*, is considered *the* great name in medieval literature.

The Renaissance

The 16C introduced humanism and a revival of poetry and dramatic art which can be seen at its best in works by **Francisco Sá de Miranda** (1485–1558), **Bernardim Ribeiro** (1500–52), author of the famous novel *Child and Damsel (Menina et Moça)*, **António Ferreira** (1528–69) in his *Lusitanian Poems (Poemas Lusitanos)* and *Castro*, and especially **Gil Vicente** (1470–1536), a great dramatist whose 44 plays painted a satirical picture of Portuguese society in the early 16C.

The greatest figure of the period, however, remains **Luís de Camões** or Camoens (1524–80) who, having demonstrated his virtuosity of verse in *The Lyric (A Lírica)*, shows himself to be the poet of the Great Discoveries in his vast portrait of *The Lusiads (Os Lusíadas,* 1572), which relates the epic voyage of Vasco da Gama in a similar way to the *Odyssey*. He led an adventurous life, which took him to Morocco (where he lost an eye) and to Goa.

Classicism

During the 60 years of Spanish domination, Portuguese literature was confined to the Academies in Lisbon and the provinces; Baroque affectation prevailed, but at the same time "Sebastianism" developed, a belief in the return of King Sebastião and the restoration of the country's independence. Much of the literary output consisted of chronicles and travel narratives including work by **Fernão Mendes Pinto** (1509–83) who wrote *Peregrination (Peregrinação)*. The Jesuit **António Vieira** (1608–97) revealed the growing personality of the immense colony of Brazil in his sermons and letters as a missionary.

18C

The Age of Enlightenment was represented in Portugal by scholars, historians and philosophers. Theatre and poetry came under French influence. **Manuel MB do Bocage** (1765–1805), of French descent, was the great lyric and satirical poet of this century.

19C

Romanticism took a firm hold thanks to **Almeida Garrett** (1799–1854), who was not only a poet (*Fallen Leaves – Fôlhas Caídas* and *Flores Sem Fructo*) and master of a whole generation of poets, but also a theatre reformer, playwright *(Frei Luís de Sousa)* and novelist *(Travels in My Homeland – Viagens na Minha Terra)*. The century's other outstanding poets included **António F de Castilho** *(Amor e Melancolia)* and **João de Deus**.
Alexandre Herculano (1810–77) introduced the historical novel and his *História de Portugal* was a great success. Among fellow historians, mention should be made of **Oliveira Martins**. The transition to realism came about with work by **Camilo Castelo Branco** (1825–90) whose best-known novel *Fatal Love (Amor de Perdição)* gives an account of society at the time. The end of Romanticism was signalled by the work of the Azorian **Antero de Quental** (1842–91), whose *Odes Modernas* were an instrument of social unrest. **Eça de Queirós** (1845–1900), a diplomat and a novelist, made a critique of the morals of his day through his works *(Cousin Bazilis, The Maias, Barbaric Prose, The Sin of Father Amaro (O Primo Basílio, Os Maias, Prosas Bárbaras, O Crime do Padre Amaro)*. **Guerra Junqueiro** (1850–1923) wrote satirical and controversial poems.

World Illustrated/Photoshot

So we ploughed our way through waters where none save Portuguese had ever sailed before. To our left were the hills and towns of Morocco, the abode once of the giant Antaeus; land to our right there was none for certain, though report spoke of it. And now our course took us into regions and past islands already discovered by the great Prince Henrique.

Luís de Camões
The Lusiads, Canto V

Contemporary authors

Fernando Pessoa (1888–1935), a complex and precursory genius, revived Portuguese poetry by using different names and personae, among them Ricardo Reis, Álvaro de Campos, Alberto Caeiro and Bernardo Soares, which enabled him to express himself in different styles. His *Book of Disquietude (Livro do Desassossego)* was published forty years after his death. Among his contemporaries and successors mention should be made of his friend **Mario de Sá Carneiro**, who committed suicide at the age of 26 leaving some very fine poems, **José Régio** *(Poems of God and the Devil – Poesias de Deus e do Diabo)*, **Natália Correia**, **António Ramos Rosa** and **Herberto Helder**. Among the main novelists are **Fernando Namora** *(The Wheat and the Chaff – O Trigo e O Joio)*, **Ferreira de Castro** (1898–1974), who drew upon his experiences during a long stay in Brazil *(The Jungle and The Mission – A Selva, A Missão)*, **Carlos de Oliveira** (1921–81), who wrote about life in small villages *(Uma Abelha na Chuva)*, **Manuel Texeira Gomes** *(Letters with No Moral – Cartas sem nenhuma moral)*, **Urbano**

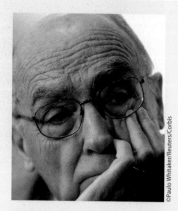

©Paulo Whitaker/Reuters/Corbis

José Saramago, Winner of the 1998 Nobel Prize for Literature

Born in 1922 in Azinhaga, near Santarém, José Saramago lived in Lisbon from the age of three. He worked in a number of jobs (mechanic, draughtsman, social security employee, editor, translator and journalist) before publishing his first novel *(Terra do Pecado)* in 1947. He then worked for a publishing house and was the literary critic for the *Seara Nova* magazine. His second book, *Os Poemas Possíveis*, was not published until 1966, although his great literary success came in the 1980s with *Memorial do Convento* (1982), which retraces the construction of the Mafra monastery, *The Year of the Death of Ricardo Reis* (1984), *The Stone Raft* (1986), *History of the Siege of Lisbon* (1989) and *The Gospel According to Jesus Christ* (1991).

T. Rodrigues (*Bastards of the Sun – Bastardos do Sol*), **Agustina Bessa Luís** (*The Sibyl – A Sibila* and *Fanny Owen*), as well as regionalist authors like **Aquilino Ribeiro** and **Miguel Torga**. **Vergílio Ferreira** first wrote neo-realistic novels before adopting a very personal style in which he tackles existential problems (*Aparição*).

Over the last few decades Portuguese literature has undergone a veritable revival with writers such as **José Cardoso Pires** (*Ballad of Dog's Beach – Balada da Praia dos Cães*), **Lídia Jorge** (*A Costa dos murmúrios, Notícia da Cidade Silvestre*), **Vitorino Nemésio** and his beautiful novel *Mau Tempo no Canal* which takes place in the Azores, **António Lobo Antunes** (*South of Nowhere* and *An Explanation of the Birds – O Cús de Judas, Explicação dos Pássaros*), **Sofia de Melo Breyner**, whose work is mainly poetical and in a similar vein to **Nuno Júdice** (*Theory of Sentiment, A Field in the Depths of Time*), and Nobel Prize-winner **José Saramago**, who mixes all the great legends and figures of Portuguese history, including João V and Fernando Pessoa in his novels (*Memorial do Convento, The Year of the Death of Ricardo Reis, The Gospel According to Jesus Christ*).

Mention should also be made of the philosopher **Eduardo Lourenço** (*O Labirinto da Saudade*), **Eugénio de Andrade**, a major, prolific post-war poet, **Almeida Faria** who writes about memory, exile and nostalgia, and **Maria Judite de Carvalho** who is continuing her demanding work (*Os Armários Vazios*).

The former Portuguese colonies, particularly Brazil, contribute greatly to Lusitanian literature with authors such as **Jorge Amado**, José Lins do Rego etc. Angola also has a tradition of great storytellers and poets such as Luandino Vieira (*Velhas Estórias, Nós os de Makuiusu*), Pepetela (*As Aventuras de Ngunga*) and José Eduardo Águalusa (*A Nação Crioula, A Estação da Chuva*), as has Mozambique, with Mia Couto (*A Varanda do Frangipani, Contos do Nascer da Terra*) and Luís Carlos Patraquim (*Litemburgo Blues*). In Cape Verde the philologist Baltazar Lopes (*Chiquinho*) and the storyteller Manuel Lopes (*Os Flagelados do Vento Leste*) bear witness to the literary wealth of these West African islands.

Cinema

During the 1930s and 1940s the development of Portuguese cinema was marked by popular-based themes, rural films and moralistic comedies with leading actors such as Beatriz Costa and António Silva. The ideology of the Salazar regime then began to dominate with the almost-official producer António Lopes Ribeiro. From the 1950s onwards, directors became a fundamental part of Portuguese cinema, which became known for its creativity and independence, while the 1960s were marked by the exodus of young Portuguese to France and Great Britain to study cinema. The best known directors of the time were **Paulo Rocha**, who was Jean Renoir's assistant, **Fernando Lopes** (Belarmino) and **António de Macedo** (Domingo à tarde). Paulo Rocha distinguished himself in 1963 with The Green Years (Verdes Anos) which made a break with films under the dictatorship and was the precursor for the "Cinema Novo" (New Cinema) movement, the equivalent of "New Wave" in France. He then went on to film in Japan (The Island of Loves – A Ilha dos Amores and The Mountains of the Moon – As Montanhas da Lua). Many directors returned to Portugal after the Carnation Revolution to make films with a militant, political bent, such as O Recado, which was produced during the dictatorship by **José Fonseca e Costa**. Other important directors of the period include **António Reis** (Jaime), **António Pedro de Vasconcelos** (O lugar do Morto) and **Lauro António** (A manhã Submersa).

The new generation of directors in the 1980s and 1990s imparted a certain artistic quality to Portuguese cinema. These directors set themselves apart by their great originality and include names such as **Joaquim Pinto**, **João Mário Grilo** (O Processo do Rei, Longe da Vista), **João Botelho** (A Portuguese Farewell – Um Adeus Portugûes, Three Palm Trees – Três Palmeiras and Tráfico), **João César Monteiro** (Recollections of the Yellow House – Recordações da Casa Amarela and God's Comedy – A Comédia de Deus), **Pedro Costa** (O Sangue, A Casa da Lava and Ossos) and **Teresa Vilaverde** (Os Mutantes).

Portuguese cinema is dominated abroad by the extraordinary personality of **Manoel de Oliveira**, born in 1908. His early films were dedicated to his home town, Oporto, where he filmed from 1931 onwards. Later he turned to

Still from Valley of Abraham

more imaginary themes and mainly drew upon Portuguese literature with works by Camilo Castelo Branco (Fatal Love – Amor de Perdição and The Day of Despair – O Dia do Desespero), and Agustina Bessa Luís (Francisca, adapted from Fanny Owen, which he co-wrote), as well as a number of Italian works such as Dante's Divine Comedy. French literature also provided him with inspiration, including Le Soulier de Satin by Paul Claudel, Valley of Abraham (Vale Abraão), inspired by Flaubert's Madame Bovary, and La Lettre, an adaptation of La Princesse de Clèves by Madame de Lafayette, and winner of the Prix du Jury at the 1999 Cannes Film Festival. Luís Miguel Cintra and Leonor Silva are actors who have frequently figured in his films, as have international stars such as Catherine Deneuve and John Malkovitch (The Convent), Michel Piccoli and Irène Papas (Party), and Chiara Mastroianni (La Lettre).

THE PORTUGUESE LANGUAGE

Portuguese is a Romantic language originating from Latin. Although the syntax and etymology are similar to Castilian, the pronunciation is totally different, being closer to French for letters such as j, c, z, ç and ch, but dissimilar with regard to its palato-alveolar fricatives (the pronunciation of s as sh), its nasals and its sibilants. With a very rich and expressive vocabulary, Portuguese lends itself very well to poetry and fado. More than 180 million people worldwide speak Portuguese; it is the seventh most widely spoken language.

THE COUNTRY TODAY

Portugal today has a thriving economy, as seen from the vast amount of construction work in progress. It has become a vital part of the European Union and continues to play its part in the world economy. Tourism is of great importance, and the infrastructure within the country, so crucial to tourism, continues to be developed and modernised.

Economy

At the time of the 1974 Carnation Revolution, Portugal had fallen behind many of its European neighbours. Lack of investment in the country's industry and infrastructure under the Salazar regime was the cause, even though Portugal had significant gold reserves originating mainly from its mining con-

cerns in its former colonies. Traditional activities, such as agriculture and fishing, still formed the basis of the country's economy until its membership of the European Economic Community in 1986, which marked a transitional point in Portugal's development, thanks in part to EEC aid. Today Portugal remains one of the world's largest producers of wine and is the leading producer of cork – while leading industries in the industrial and transformation fields include shoe, textile and paper production, car manufacturing, metallurgy and mechanical engineering. Tourism is still very important.

PROVINCES AND DISTRICTS

o Braga   District boundaries and capitals

MINHO   The old provinces

Government

The **Constitution**, promulgated on 2 April 1976, brought in a semi-presidential form of government. **Executive power** is held by the **President of the Republic** who is elected by universal suffrage for a five-year term (renewable once). The president appoints the **Prime Minister**, who represents the Parliamentary majority, and, on his suggestion, the rest of the government. The revised Constitution of 1982 has limited the president's powers although he retains the right to veto laws approved by straight majority vote in the Assembly. **Legislative power** is held by a single Chamber of between 240 and 250 members who are elected for four years. The

The Portuguese Flag

The green vertical stripe at the hoist and red stripe in the fly are divided by an armillary sphere bearing the Portuguese coat of arms. The sphere supports a white shield with five blue shields, each with five white disks symbolising Christ's wounds. The seven yellow castles represent the strongholds retaken from the Moors.

archipelagos of Madeira and the Azores are Autonomous Regions with their own Regional Government and Regional Assembly. The Assembly is elected by universal suffrage. The President of the Republic appoints a **Minister of the Republic** for each of the autonomous regions, who then appoints a **Regional Government President**.

ADMINISTRATIVE ORGANISATION

The old historical provinces of the Minho, Trás-os-Montes, Douro, Beiras (Alta, Baixa and Litoral), Ribatejo, Estremadura, Alentejo and Algarve no longer fulfil an administrative role but still denote the main regions of the country.

Portugal's present administrative organisation is as follows:

♦ **Distritos**: There are 18 districts in mainland Portugal, three in the Azores and one in Madeira. Health, education and finance are managed at district level.

♦ **Concelhos**: These councils represent municipal authority. There are 305 in all. A *concelho* is similar to a district borough or a canton. Each one has a town hall or *Paço do Concelho* and an executive committee or *Câmara Municipal* led by a president who acts as mayor. Both the president and the municipal assembly are elected by universal suffrage every four years.

♦ Lastly, each *concelho* consists of several **freguesias**, the smallest administrative unit, some of which represent a village, and others a district. There are approximately 4 200 *freguesias* in Portugal, responsible for keeping public records, civil status, the upkeep of natural heritage, and organising festivals and other local events.

Architectural Traditions

DOMESTIC ARCHITECTURE

Portugal has preserved different styles of traditional housing; these styles are most apparent in the Alentejo and the Algarve.

The North

The most popular building material is granite. Houses are massive with tiled roofs. As chimneys are very small or even non-existent, the smoke has to escape through gaps in the roof, the doorway or the windows. The outside stairway leads to a stone balcony or verandah large enough to be used as a living room.

On country estates in the Douro valley, simple cottages stand alongside elegant manor-houses *(solares)*, which are often whitewashed.

The Centre: Estremadura and Beira Litoral

The limestone used in the region's houses adds a pleasant touch to their appearance. The façades are often ornamented with cornices and stucco; outside staircases have disappeared.

Alentejo

The houses, built to shelter the inhabitants from the summer glare and heat, are low-lying single storey structures

Alentejo

Algarve

with whitewashed walls and small doors and windows. Nevertheless, the winters are so harsh that huge square or cylindrical chimneys are a local feature. Building materials vary according to the region: usually *taipa* (dried clay), or adobe (mud mixed with cut straw and dried in the sun), which was used in Moorish times. Bricks are used for decorative features, for chimneys, crenellations and verandahs, while around Estremoz marble is common.

The Algarve

The white houses squat low, several juxtaposed cubes making up each dwelling. The white flat-roofed houses in Olhão and Fuseta resemble the villages of North Africa. Very occasionally the terrace is replaced by a four-sided peaked roof, *telhado de tesoura*, which some attribute to a Chinese influence. Peaked roofs are mostly to be seen in Faro, Tavira and Santa Luzia. Chimneys are slender and elegant, gracefully

pierced, painted white or built of brick laid in decorative patterns, crowned with a ball, a finial, a vase, or an ornament of some kind.

Madeira and the Azores

In Madeira, traditional mountain dwellings have a thatched roof with two eaves that descend right down to the ground, thus covering the whole house. The main door on the front of the house is flanked by two small windows, with an occasional third one above it. All these openings are set into the wall with colourful surrounds. Houses in the Azores are similar to those in the Algarve, offering a reminder of the islands' first inhabitants. The Empires (*Impérios*) of the Holy Ghost are brightly-coloured original buildings, similar in style to chapels, which have large windows and are used to house objects for the worship of the Holy Ghost.

Minho

Madeira

Stone monuments (Padrões)

These public monuments, memorials bearing the cross and the arms of Portugal, were erected by Portuguese explorers when they reached new lands. They may be seen in former colonies and in Madeira and the Azores.

Handicrafts

Portugal's arts and crafts are remarkably varied and unpretentious. The weekly markets held in most towns give a good idea of the skill of Portuguese craftsmanship.

TRADITIONAL URBAN FEATURES

Pavements

Throughout the country and even in Madeira and the Azores, pavements and squares are paved with beautifully patterned compositions of alternating blocks of black basalt, golden sandstone, white limestone and grey granite. These are known as **empedrados**.

Windmills (Moinhos)

There were about 2 000 windmills in Portugal several years ago but most have now been abandoned and are in ruins. They may still be seen on hilltops around Nazaré, Óbidos and Viana do Castelo. Those most common today are the Mediterranean type in which a cylindrical tower built of stone or hard-packed clay supports a turning conical roof bearing a mast. The mast carries four triangular sails.

Ceramics and pottery

There are many village potters *(olarios)* producing domestic and decorative earthenware which varies in shape and colour according to the region. In Barcelos, pots are glazed, colours bright with ornamentation consisting of leaves, stems and flowers; handsome multicoloured cocks are also made locally. Around Coimbra, the colour used is green with brown and yellow overtones and the decoration is more geometric. The potters of Caldas da Rainha use bright green and produce items with surprising shapes. Continuing the tradition set up by Rafael Bordalo Pinheiro (&see LISBOA, Museu Rafael Bordalo Pinheiro), water jugs, salad bowls and plates are all heavily adorned with leaves, flowers and animals. In Alcobaça and Cruz da Légua the potters work with more classical designs, distinguishing their ware by the variety of blues they use in its decoration.

In the Upper Alentejo (in Redondo, Estremoz and Nisa) the clay is encrusted with shining quartz particles or marble chips; in the Algarve amphorae are still made based on Greek and Roman models, while in Tras-os-Montes the potters damp down their ovens at the end of the firing to give the ware a black colour.

Lace

Lace is made virtually only along the coast. The decorative motifs used are fir cones and flowers, trefoils at Viano do Castelo where the lace looks more

Windmill in Sesimbra, Setúbal

Best-Known Handicraft Markets and Fairs

Barcelos: Pottery fair on Thursday mornings.
São Pedro de Sintra: Antiques fair on the second and fourth Sunday of the month.
Estremoz: Pottery market on Saturdays.
Estoril: Handicraft fair (Feira do Artesonato) in July and August.
Santarém: Agricultural fair in October.
Golega: Horse fair in November.

like tulle, and seaweed, shells and fish at Vila do Conde.

Embroidery

Madeira's embroidery is particularly well-known, although mainland Portugal also produces wonderful shawls, tablecloths and bedspreads. The best-known bedspreads *(colchas)* are from Castelo Branco and are embroidered with silk on linen. The tradition is a long-standing one, the work painstaking.

Filigree work

The working by hand of gold or silver wire which reached its height in the reign of King João V (1706–50) is still held in high regard in Portugal. The chief centre is the small town of Gondomar not far from Oporto. Delicate, intricate jewellery in the shape of hearts, crosses, guitars and above all caravels is fashioned from this extremely pliable wire. In the Minho, filigree earrings and brooches are worn to set off the regional costume.

Weaving and carpet-making

Hand weaving still flourishes in some mountain villages. Lengths of heavy frieze are woven on old looms to make capes and tippets. Guimarães specialises in bedspreads and curtains in rough cloth bordered with classical motifs in bright colours. The hemp or linen-based carpets embroidered in wool at Arraiolos are the best known of their type and have simpler designs.

Woodwork

In the Alentejo many items made of wood, including trays, chairs and cupboards, are painted with brightly-coloured, naive motifs.

Painted whitewood is an important feature of traditional Portuguese handicraft and may be seen all over the country. Examples include ox yokes (the most famous being in the Barcelos region), painted carts (in the Alentejo and the Algarve) and carved and painted fishing boats (in the Ria de Aveiro and on many of the country's beaches).

Madeira enbroidery

DRT Madeira

Eggs play an important part in Portuguese food, being used in soups and often to accompany fish and meat dishes. Rice, for which the Portuguese developed a liking following their voyages to Asia, is the most favoured vegetable. Fried potatoes are also commonly served.

Soups

Soup is served at most meals. Among the many varieties are *canja de galinha*, chicken soup with rice, *sopa de peixe*, fish soup, *sopa de marisco*, seafood soup, *sopa de coelho*, rabbit soup, and *sopa de grão*, chickpea soup.

The most famous is the Minho **caldo verde** which is served north of the Mondego. This dish consists of a mashed potato base to which finely shredded green Galician cabbage is added; lastly olive oil and slices of black pudding, *tora*, are mixed in.

Bread soups or **açordas** are to be found in all regions, those of the Alentejo having many variations such as the *sopa de coentros* made with coriander leaves, olive oil, garlic and bread, with a poached egg on top.

In the south, **gaspacho**, a soup of tomatoes, onions, cucumbers and chillies seasoned with garlic and vinegar, is served cold with croutons.

Fish and seafood

Fish is a basic element of Portuguese cuisine. Cod, **bacalhau**, is the most common fish, particularly in the north, though there are issues involved with the dwindling stocks of cod in the Atlantic and surrounding areas. There are, it is said, 365 ways of preparing it (*see recipe for Bacalhau à Brás below*).

Many other fish, however, are to be found in some part or other of the country: the aroma of grilled sardines wafts the streets of every coastal town; many types of fish are put into the **caldeirada** or stew made by fishermen on the beach. You will get tunny fillets in the Algarve, river lampreys and salmon beside the Minho and shad beside the Tagus. Seafood (*mariscos*) including octopus is plentiful. Shellfish are delicious and varied especially in the Algarve where a special copper vessel, a *cataplana*, is used to cook clams and sausages spiced with herbs.

Crayfish (*lagosta*) prepared in the Peniche way, or steamed, are rightly famous.

Meat and game

Apart from pork and game, Portuguese meat is often very ordinary. Pork is cooked and served in a variety of ways. The **leitão assado**, or roast suckling-pig, of Mealhada (north of Coimbra) is

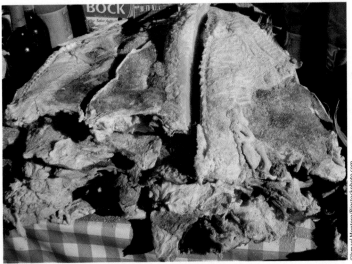

Bacalhau - 365 ways of preparing it

©Ismael Montero/Bigstockphoto.com

delicious. Meat from various parts of the pig can also be found in stews, in **linguiça** or smoked pigs' tongue sausages, in smoked pork fillets, *paio,* and in smoked ham, *presunto,* at Chaves and Lamego. Ham and sausages are added to the **cozido à Portuguesa**, a hotpot of beef, vegetables, potatoes and rice, also to the local tripe prepared in the Oporto way, *dobrada,* a dish of pig or beef tripe cooked with haricot beans.

Pork in the Alentejo way, or **carne de porco à Alentejana**, is pork marinated in wine, garnished with clams. Other meat is mostly minced and consumed as meat balls, although lamb and kid are sometimes roasted or served on skewers.

Queijo fresco with Portuguese bread

© Mauro Rodrigues/Fotolia.com

Cheeses

Cheeses are made all over Portugal with several special varieties being made in the Azores. It is possible to visit several cheese producers, many of which are small-scale cottage industries where you will get a personal tour as well as the opportunity to try (and hopefully buy) some of the often hand-made product. Ewes' milk cheese should be

A "faithful friend"

Cod *(bacalhau)* has played an important role in Portugal's maritime history, and is such a standby in family dining that it is commonly known as the "faithful friend". Fished in the cold, far-off waters of Newfoundland, it had to be salted to preserve it until the fishing fleet returned home. Emblematic of Portuguese cooking, a traditional dish for Christmas, a delicacy enjoyed by fishermen and peasants alike, cod is enjoyed throughout the country, particularly served as fish balls. **Bacalhau à Brás**, a cod recipe which originates from Lisbon, is now served the length and breadth of Portugal.

Ingredients for 4 people:

500g (about 1lb) of cod
500g of potatoes, fried
3 medium-sized onions
5 eggs, beaten
2 cloves of garlic
4 tablespoons of oil

Chopped parsley, black olives, salt and pepper

Soak the cod overnight, changing the water several times.

Shred the cod, taking care to remove the skin and any bones, and rinse through a cloth.

Peel the potatoes and cut into strips.

Slice the onions into thin rings.

Heat the oil in a frying pan with the garlic and remove when golden. Fry the onions until golden and add the cod. Leave on the heat for 5min, add the potatoes and garlic. Season with salt and pepper and add the beaten eggs and mix well. Sprinkle with parsley and decorate with the black olives.

tried between October and May, notably the *Queijo da Serra da Estrela,* the *Queijo de Castelo Branco* and the creamy *Queijo de Azeitão* as well as goats' milk cheeses such as the *cabreiro,* the *rabaçal* from the Pombal region and the small soft white cheeses or *quejinhos* from Tomar, often served as an hors d'œuvre as is the fresh goat's cheese, *Queijo fresco.*

Desserts

Portugal has an infinite variety of cakes and pastries. Nearly all recipes include eggs and come in most instances from old specialities prepared in convents such as the **Toucinho-do-Céu, Barriga-de-Freira** and **Queijadas de Sintra**, with almonds and fresh sheep's milk. The dessert most frequently seen on menus, however, is the **pudim flan**, a sort of crème caramel, while the **leite-creme** is a creamier pudding made with the same ingredients. Rice pudding, **arroz doce**, sprinkled with cinnamon is often served at festive meals.

In the Algarve, the local figs *(figos)* and almonds *(amêndoas)* are made into the most appetising sweetmeats and tidbits.

A particularly delicious pastry is the **pasteis de nata**, a small custard tart sprinkled with cinnamon.

Wine

Portugal is the seventh largest wine-producer in the world and has a rich variety of wines, including the world famous **Port** and, although not quite as popular as it once was but still important, **Madeira**. The reasonably-priced wines bought locally or enjoyed in a restaurant are of good quality, suitable for all occasions and deserve to be better known.

ORT

vines of the Upper Douro and its
 produce a generous wine
from the city that
only after it

Pasteis de nata

The English and Port

In the 14C some of the wines produced in the Lamego region were already being exported to England. In the 17C the Portuguese granted the English trading rights in exchange for their help against the Spanish. By the end of the 17C, once the port process had been developed, some Englishmen acquired country estates *(quintas)* in the Douro valley and began making wine. Through the **Methuen Treaty** (1703) the English crown obtained the monopoly of the Portuguese wine trade. However in 1756, to combat this English invasion, King Dom José I and the Marquis of Pombal founded the **Company of the Wines of the Upper Douro** *(Companhia Geral da Agricultura dos Vinhos do Alto Douro)* which fixed the price for all exported port. The following year the company defined the area in which port vines could be grown. Various English companies were set up, among them Cockburn, Campbell, Offley, Harris, Sandeman, Dow, Graham etc. The Portuguese followed suit in 1830 with their own companies with names like Ferreira and Ramos Pinto. In 1868 phylloxera raged throughout the region but the vineyards were rapidly rehabilitated – many of the vineyards were grafted from phylloxera-resistant American stocks – and "vintage" port was being produced by the end of the 19C.

The vineyards

The area defined by law in 1757 for the cultivation of vines covers 240 000ha/593 000 acres of which a tenth consists of vineyards that stretch for about sixty miles along the Douro to the Spanish border. The approximate centre is situated at Pinhão. There are 25 000 vineyard owners. Port's inestimable quality is due to the exceptional conditions under which the grapes are grown and ripened – hot summers, cold winters, and schist soil – and the processing of the fruit when harvested. The vines grow on steep terraces overlooking the Douro, a striking picture not only from an aesthetic point of view but also in terms of the extraordinary amount of work involved.

WINES AND REGIONAL SPECIALITIES

Wine-producing regions

Bucelas Major vineyards

The making of port

The grape harvest takes place in late September. Men carry the bunches of grapes in wickerwork baskets on their backs. The cut grapes go into the press where mechanical crushing has taken the place of human treading which, with its songs and rhythmic tunes, was so highly picturesque. The must is sealed off during fermentation which reduces the sugar content to the right amount, then brandy – from Douro grapes – is added to stop the fermentation and to stabilise the sugar. In the spring the wine is taken by lorry and train to Vila Nova de Gaia. Up until a few years ago it was transported 150km/90mi along the Douro to Oporto in picturesque sailing craft known as *barcelos rebelos*. Some of these boats may be seen at Pinhão and Vila Nova da Gaia.

The wine is stored with the 58 port wine companies that have set up in Vila Nova da Gaia and matures in huge casks or, more commonly, in vats containing up to 1 000hl/26 400 imperial gallons. It is then decanted into 535l/118 gallon barrels *(pipes)* in which the porous nature of the wood augments the ageing process. The Wine Institute (Instituto do Vinho do Porto) sets the rules and controls the quality.

Types of port

Port, which is red or white according to the colour of the grapes from which it is made, has many subtleties – it can be dry, medium or sweet. The variety of port also depends upon the way it is made. Port aged in casks matures through oxidation and turns a beautiful amber colour; port aged in the bottle matures by reduction and is a dark red colour. The alcohol content is about 20%.

Vintage ports are selected from the best wines of a particularly fine year and are bottled after two years in casks. They then mature in the bottle for

Harvesting grapes in the Douro Valley

at least ten years or more before being served. Since 1974 all Vintage Port must be bottled in Portugal.

White port or **Branco** is less well known than the reds. It is a fortified wine made from white grapes. Dry or extra dry, it makes a good apéritif.

Blended ports are red ports made from different vintages from different years. The blending and ageing differ according to the quality required. They include:

+ **Tinto**, the most common, which is young, vigorous, distinctly coloured and fruity.

+ **Tinto-Alourado** or **Ruby**, which is older, yet rich in colour, fruity and sweet and is the result of the blending of different vintages from different years.

+ **Alourado** or **Tawny** is blended with different vintages from different years and ages in wooden cakes. Its colour turns to a brownish gold as it ages. It should be drunk soon after it is bottled.

+ **Alourado-Claro** or **Light Tawny** is the culmination of the former.

CHOOSING AND SERVING PORT

White port, which should be drunk chilled and is best served as an aperitif, is the least expensive followed by the reds (**Ruby** and **Tawny**). Very good quality Tawny ports will provide an indi-

cation of their age on the label (10, 20, 30 or more years spent in the barrel). Next come the ports which bear their vintage date *(colheita)*; they have been made with wines from the same year. The best and most expensive are **Vintage ports** and **Late Bottled Vintage Ports (L.B.V.)**. The former are made with wine from an exceptionally good year and are bottled after two to three years; likewise, the latter are made with wine from the same vineyard and are bottled after four to six years. These can be kept for many years provided that they are laid down horizontally and are stored at a suitable temperature. Vintage port should be served in a carafe and drunk quickly, preferably on the day the bottle is opened. All ports, with the exception of the whites, are a perfect accompaniment to game, hams, foie gras, cheeses, dried fruit etc.

For additional information on port, contact the Instituto do Vinho in Oporto (website: http://www.ivp.pt) which, in association with other official organisations, particularly the Port Wine Route association in Peso da Régua and the region's tourist offices, has created a Port Wine Route within the official Douro region. The itinerary passes through 54 sites, including estates, **co-operatives** and wine information centres, providing visitors with an ideal opportunity to discover the beautiful landscapes of the region and to taste its most famous product.

Since 1963 the French have replaced the English as the largest importers of port.

MADEIRA

Madeira wine, which deserves to be more widely celebrated, has always been particularly popular with the English. *See MADEIRA.*

OTHER WINES

Several regions in Portugal produce perfectly respectable wines that can be enjoyed in restaurants. One can ask for the *vinho da casa*, usually the local wine.

Vinho Verde
Vinho Verde from the Minho and the Lower Douro valleys can be white (tendency to gold) or deep red. Its name, "green wine" comes from its early grape harvest and short fermentation period which gives the wine a low alcohol content (8% to 11%) and makes it light and sparkling with a distinct bouquet and what might be described as a very slightly bitter flavour. It is best enjoyed young and chilled. It is an ideal aperitif and is a perfect accompaniment to both fish and seafood. The most renowned *vinho verde* is produced from the Alvarinho grape, which enables the wine to be kept longer than wine produced from other grape varieties.

Dão
Vines growing on the granite slopes of the Dão valley produce a fresh white wine as well as a sweet red wine with a velvety texture and a heady bouquet which most closely resembles Bordeaux *crus*. *Quinta* wines are the equivalent of French *château* wines.

Bairrada
This very old vine-growing region produces a robust, fragrant red, as well as a natural sparkling wine which goes wonderfully well with roast suckling pig.

Colares
The vines grow in a sandy topsoil over a bed of clay in the Serra de Sintra. The robust, velvety, dark red wine has been famous since the 13C.

Bucelas
Bucelas is a dry, somewhat acidic straw-coloured white wine produced from vineyards on the banks of the Trancão, a tributary of the Tagus.

Other table wines
The Ribatejo vineyards produce good everyday wines; full bodied reds from the Cartaxo region and whites from Chamusca, Almeirim and Alpiarça on the far bank of the Tagus.

Also worth trying are the wines of Torres Vedras, Alcobaça, Lafões and Agueda, and the Pinhel and Mateus rosés.

In the Alentejo, full-bodied reds such as Reguengos, Borba and Redondo predominate. The one exception to this is the white Vidigueira wine.

In the Algarve, a small amount of wine is still produced in Lagoa, home to the country's oldest **co-operative**.

Dessert wines
Setúbal moscatel from the chalky clay slopes of the Serra da Arrábida is a generous fruity wine which acquires a particularly pleasant taste with age.

Fruity amber-coloured Carcavelos is drunk as an apéritif as well as a dessert wine.

Spirits
The wide variety of Portuguese brandies includes *ginginha*, cherry brandy from Alcobaça, *medronho*, arbutus berry brandy and *brandimel*, honey brandy from the Algarve. *Bagaço* or *bagaceira*, a grape marc, served chilled, is the most widely drunk.

Mineral water
Portugal produces fine mineral waters, such as the Água de Luso and the sparkling waters of Castelo, Carvalhelhos, Vidago and Pedras Salgadas. The most common beer served is light and similar to lager. The country's fruit juices, both still *(sem gás)* and sparkling *(com gás)*, are also excellent and refreshing.

For the best little places, follow the leader.

Looking for the latest news on today's best hotels and restaurants? Pick up the Michelin Guide and look for the Bib Gourmand and Bib Hotel symbols. With 45,000 addresses in Europe, in every category and price range, the perfect place to dine or stay is never far away.

MICHELIN
A better way forward

Praia da Boneca, Lagos, Algarve
Associação Turismo do Algarve

ABRANTES
SANTARÉM
POPULATION 42 436– MICHELIN MAP 733

Abrantes occupies an open site★ on a hillside overlooking the right bank of the Tagus. Its fortress had fallen into decay more than 200 years before the Peninsular War, when the town was entered first by French troops in 1807 and later by Wellesley, who briefly made it his headquarters in 1809. The town is known for its delicious confections, "Abrantes straw" or *palha de Abrantes*, so called because the eggs from which they are made leave yellow straw-like streaks.

▪ **Information:** Largo 1° de Maio. 2200-320. ☎241 36 25 55.
▸ **Orient Yourself:** North east of Santarém, 146km/90.7mi from Lisbon.
⊛ **Don't Miss:** The castle and the church.
⊙ **Organizing Your Time:** About a day to see everything worthwhile. Allow longer if you plan to visit Constância, the home to Portugal's great poet, Camões.

Sights

Castle
Praça da República.
⊙*Open Tue–Sun 10am–5pm.*
The keep has been converted into a **belvedere** from which there are excellent views of the middle valley of the Tagus, the Serra do Moradal and the foothills of the Serra da Estrela.

The **Igreja de Santa Maria** (⊙*church open 9am–6pm (5pm in winter); ☎241 37 17 24),* rebuilt in the 15C, includes a small **museum** with a 16C carving of the Trinity in polychrome stone and, on the high altar, a beautiful statue of the Virgin and Child dating from the 15C. The tombs of the Counts of Abrantes date from the 15C and 16C. Also worthy of note on one of the walls are the 16C Hispano-Moorish *corda seca azulejos*.

Igreja e Hospital da Misericórdia
⊙*To visit, contact Santa Casa da Misericórdia, up the street on the right. ☎241 36 00 20.*
The church (1584) contains six 16C oil paintings on wood. Attributed to Gregório Lopes, they evoke the life of Christ. Also see the 18C gilded wood altar and organ. The Sala do Definitório in the former hospital is decorated with attractive 18C *azulejo* panels beneath a coffered wood ceiling. The room also contains seven paintings representing the seven works of the Misericord.

The collection of furniture includes a 16C *burra* (literally a she-ass) and an iron chest used to transport precious objects.

Igreja de São João Baptista
Located left of Igreja da Misericórdia, this church was founded in 1300 by Queen Saint Isabel and rebuilt at the end of the 16C. The interior contains gilded wood Renaissance altars.

Excursions

Constância
15km/9.3mi west of Abrantes.
Regarded as Portugal's national poet, Luís de Camões (1534–80) lived in this village from 1547–1550, having sought refuge from the King who was angry at him for having written love sonnets to a lady for whom the King himself had a passion. His house is now a centre for the study of his many works and there is a memorial to him: Casa Memória de Camões. Attractive with flower-bedecked cobbled streets, the village holds a huge fair every Easter Monday.

Castelo de Belver in Gavião
37km/23mi east of Abrantes.
The Castelo de Belver is one of the prettiest castles in Portugal, looking out over the river far below. It dates from the 12C and was built to resist the Moors. The reliquary is of particular interest.

ALBUFEIRA★
FARO
POPULATION 35 281 – MICHELIN MAP 733
LOCAL MAP SEE ALGARVE

Albufeira is a former Moorish stronghold that has kept its Arab name, meaning "castle on the sea". Midway between Faro and Lagos it has, over the past few decades, become the most famous seaside resort in the Algarve with its international visitors and fashionable nightlife. Mass tourism has altered the charm of the old fishing village in the centre. The beaches, which are very good, are packed all summer and unless you are staying in one of the numerous hotels, which are fine for family holidays or for the younger crowd, it is not the sort of place to go if you are seeking peace and quiet.

- ℹ **Information:** Ruta de Outubro. ☎289 58 52 79.
- ▶ **Orient Yourself:** On the Algarve coast, midway between Faro and Lagos
- 👁 **Don't Miss:** The beaches.
- 🕐 **Organizing Your Time:** Set aside a week for this area. Try and get to all the local beaches – Praia da Galé, Praia da Oura, Praia da Falésia.
- 🧒 **Especially for Kids:** Krazy World theme park, and Zoo Marine.

B. Brillion/MICHELIN

Praia dos Barcos, Albufeira

Nightlife

Once the sun goes down, the lights come up in Albufeira and the places to be include Rua Cândido dos Reis, Rua São Gonçalo de Lagos, Rua Alves Correira or Largo Engenheiro Duarte Pacheco, where masses of mainly younger tourists intent on having a good time congregate. There seems to be a constant contest to see who can play the loudest music and mix the most intoxicating and outlandish cocktails – but everyone seems to have fun. Happy Hour seems to last most of the night, though many of the bars are not exactly for the budget-conscious. The bars are open until 3am, the clubs until 6am and many of them have a British or Irish theme, catering to their most prominent clients. There is live music in several of the bars and in the clubs top DJs from all over Europe are attracted here during the summer.

The most famous nightclub is **Kiss** (on the beach at Praia da Oura) which has a terrace overlooking the beach itself. Other notable and popular establishments include **Sir Harry's Bar**, **Steps**, **Blue Bell**, **Barracuda**, **Augusto's** and **Planet C**. There are other places where you can just get a quiet(ish) drink and a snack, but Albufeira at night is not the sort of place to go for a quiet night out.

ALCOBAÇA★★
LEIRIA
POPULATION 56 823 – MICHELIN MAP 733

One of the most beautiful Cistercian abbeys dating from the Middle Ages stands in the heart of this small town. Alcobaça is set in an agricultural region at the confluence of the Alcoa and Baça rivers which gave the town its name. Its main activities are fruit growing, wine-making and the production of a cherry liqueur called *ginginha*. Alcobaça is also an active commercial centre for local pottery, which is predominantly blue.

- **Information:** Praça 25 de Abril. 2460-018. ☎262 58 23 77.
- **Orient Yourself:** Inland from Nazaré, midway between Lisbon and Coimbra.
- **Don't Miss:** The Monastery of Santa Maria.
- **Organizing Your Time:** Spend at least a morning in the monastery and wander around in the afternoon.
- **Also See:** ÓBIDOS, TOMAR, FÁTIMA, BATALHA.

Mosteiro de Santa Maria★★ 45min

Open Apr–Sept, 9am–7pm; Oct–Mar, 9am–5pm. Closed 1 Jan, Good Fri, Easter Sun and 25 Dec. ☎262 50 51 20. €4.50; entry to the church is free.

The external appearance of the 18C Santa Maria Monastery belies the splendid Cistercian architecture within. Of the original façade, altered by successive 17C and 18C reconstructions in the Baroque style, only the main doorway and the rose window remain. It originally housed 999 monks who, by all accounts, enjoyed their life here to the full. Certainly they were very hospitable to visitors, according to some early 19C reports.

Church★★

The Abbey church (*igreja*), the largest in Portugal, has been restored to the nobility and clean lines of its original Cistercian architecture. The **Nave** is spacious; the quadripartite vaulting is supported on transverse arches which, in turn, rest on mighty pillars and engaged columns. By terminating the latter 3m/9.8ft above the ground, the architect increased the space available for the congregation considerably and gave the church a unique perspective. The aisles have striking vertical lines; they are almost as tall as the nave is long.

Dom Pedro's tomb

B. Barbier

Inês de Castro's tomb (Túmulo de Inês de Castro)★★

In the north transept (1).

Inês de Castro was the maid of Constance, the wife of Prince Pedro, son of King Afonso IV. Pedro and Inês fell in love and on the death of Constance, secretly married. Afonso, who had other ideas for his son, had her murdered. On his succession, Pedro had Inês' body exhumed, dressed in Queen's robes and crowned, insisting that everyone paid homage to her by kissing her decomposing hand. Her reclining figure now lies upon a tomb on which the four panels depict scenes from the Life of Christ. *The Last Judgement*, which adorns the panel at the statue's feet, is particularly realistic; at the bottom on the left, the dead are standing in judgement before God.

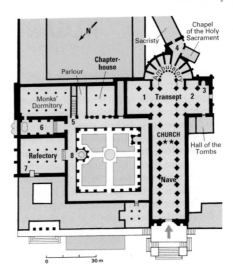

Dom Pedro's tomb (Túmulo de Dom Pedro)★★

In the south transept (2).

Beneath a severe reclining figure, Dom Pedro's tomb depicts, on its sides, the life of St Bartholomew, the King's patron saint. The panel at the foot depicts Dom Pedro's last moments. The **Transit of St Bernard** (3), a damaged terracotta depicting the death of the saint, stands in a chapel off the south transept. It was modelled by monks in the 17C. The **Chancel** is surrounded by a vast ambulatory off which open two beautiful **Manueline doors** (4) dating from the 16C, and nine chapels adorned with polychrome wooden statues from the 17C and 18C.

Abbey buildings★★

Claustro do Silêncio

The cloisters, built in the early 14C, have an attractive simplicity of line; between buttresses slender twin columns support with great elegance three rounded arches which are surmounted by a rose.

A staircase (5) leads to the **Monks' Dormitory**, a vast Gothic hall over 60m/197ft long. Two rows of columns with capitals divide the room into three sections. The **Kitchens** (6), which were enlarged in the 18C, are flanked to the east by the storeroom. The white tiled chamber is 18m/58ft high and with enormous open fireplaces; water is provided by a tributary of the Alcoa river.

The **Refectory** is a large hall with ribbed vaulting. A stairway, built into the thickness of the wall and surmounted by a fine colonnade, leads to the reader's pulpit (7). Opposite the door, a **lavabo** and 17C fountain (8) jut out into the close.

In the 18C **Sala dos Reis** (Kings' Hall) a frieze of *azulejos* illustrates the foundation of the monastery; the statues carved by monks represent the Portuguese kings up to Dom José I. Note also a beautiful Gothic Virgin and Child.

Additional Sight

Museu da Junta Nacional do Vinho

1km/0.6mi along the N 8 towards Leiria, on the right. ○*Open Mon–Fri 9am–12.30pm, 2pm–5.30pm, Sat–Sun 9am–12.30pm, 2pm–5.30pm.* ○*Closed public holidays.* ⊚€1.50. ☎262 58 22 22.

A wine **co-operative**'s warehouses are the setting for this wine museum with its collections of bottles (old Port and Madeira), wine vats, wine presses and stills.

ALGARVE★★

MICHELIN MAP 733

The Algarve is Portugal's playground. It stretches across the whole of southern Portugal. Its name derives from the Arabic *El-Gharb* meaning "west". The landscape and climate, which is mild all year round, resemble that of North Africa, with figs, carobs, bougainvillaeas, geraniums and oleanders. The beaches, which are extremely popular have attracted extensive tourist development which has unfortunately disfigured some parts of the coast. The beaches in the east are excellent: long stretches of golden sand, many of which are on *ilhas* – reef-like islands, some of which you can only reach by boat. In the south west there are more rocky little bays and coves. The west coast is wild and rugged, perfect for surfing. Of the towns, **Faro**, **Lagos**, **Albufeira** and **Portimão** are the main names you will come across, though you should also try to visit **Cabo de São Vicente** – the end of the world, or at least the most southwesterly point of mainland Europe.

Driving Tours on the East Coast and Offshore

1 From Vila Real de Santa António to Faro

65km/40.4mi – allow a day

From the Spanish frontier to Faro the coast is broken up by several *ilhas* – sandy reefs that form the beaches of the area and are well developed with restaurants and campsites. They are linked to the mainland by boats as well as footbridges over the lagoon. The entire coast from Manta Rota to Ançao near Quinta do Lago is a protected area, the **Parque Natural da Ria Formosa**, is 60km/37mi long, and covers 18 400ha/45 467 acres of dunes, channels and islands of great ornithological interest. There are many opportunities for deep-sea fishing expeditions and the fish restaurants are very good.

Vila Real de Santo António and Monte Gordo

See VILA REAL DE SANTO ANTÓNIO.

Cacela Velha★

This pleasant hamlet is built around the ruins of a medieval fortress and a small church with an attractive doorway. From its rocky bluff you have a fine **view** over the lagoon and fishing boats below. During the summer, the main lake, with its two small restaurants, is a popular place to savour local Algarve delicacies.

You next come into **Tavira**★ – *See TAVIRA*, before reaching **Pedras d'el Rei,** a holiday village of villas and attractive gardens with a rail link *(10min)* to the offshore sandbank and its beautiful beach, **Praia do Barril**.

The Renaissance church on the outskirts of **Luz de Tavira** has an attractive Manueline doorway and flame ornaments around the roof. Continue to **Olhão** – *See OLHÃO* and on towards **Faro**★ – *See FARO.*

The Interior

2 Circuit around Faro via the Serra do Caldeirão

107km/66.4mi – allow a day

This tour takes you into a relatively unknown area of the Algarve, between the limestone hills of the Serra do Caldeirão just a few kilometres (couple of miles) from the coast, yet far from its madding crowds. The flower-bedecked villages have managed to preserve their traditional appearance; handicrafts are still an important industry. In January and February the flowering almond trees carpet the mountains in a mass of white; spring heralds the appearance of the rock-rose with its white bloom, while in summer and winter oranges stand out against the green backdrop of the cottage gardens. The year-round scents of eucalyptus, pine, lavender and rock-rose alone are worth the visit.

▸ *Leave Faro on the N 2 heading north east. After 10km/6.2mi, turn right along the Estoi road (towards Tavira).*

Estoi
Estoi's main attractions are the Milreu Ruins and Estoi Palace.

Roman Ruins of Milreu
🕐 *Open Tue–Sun 9.30am–12.30pm, 2pm–6pm (5pm winter).* ⊙€2. ☎289 99 78 23.
A square-shaped apse and two marble columns are all that remain of a 1C Roman settlement which was built around a temple. The brick foundations of the houses and baths surround the living quarters and pools, some of which still retain their mosaic designs. Particularly worthy of note is the **mosaico dos peixes grandes**, a mosaic of large fish on the wall of one of the pools.

Gardens, Palácio de Estoi
From Estoi head 1km/0.6mi beyond Milreu.
The gardens are bordered with orange trees leading up to the Baroque façade of this small 18C palace. The enclosed verandas, decorated with pools, statues, marble and earthenware vases, blue and multi-coloured *azulejos* give an overall atmosphere of romantic charm.

▸ *Return to the N 2 and head north.*

São Brás de Alportel
This peaceful small town is built on elevated ground dotted with white houses. The town used to be the country's main centre for cork extraction and still retains a few cork-related industries.

Casa da Cultura António Bentes (Museu Etnográfico do Trajo Algarvio)
🕐*Open Mon–Fri 10am–1pm, 2pm–5pm, Sat, Sun and public holidays 10am–1pm.* ⊙€2.50. ☎289 84 26 18.

This ethnographic museum, housed in an attractive 19C bourgeois mansion, contains an interesting collection of old carts and carriages, dolls and typical local dress. The beautiful garden of the former residence of the bishops of the Algarve can be seen in front of the museum.

▸ *Continue along the N 2 for 14km/8.7mi. The road winds its way through groves of eucalyptus and pine before reaching Barranco Velho. Here, head towards Querença along the N 396.*

Querença
The village nestles on the slope of a hill at an altitude of 276m/905.5ft. The foundation of the **Igreja de Nossa Senhora da Assunção** on the summit is attributed to the Knights Templar. Although the church was completely remodelled in 1745, it has retained its Manueline door. The interior contains some fine gilded carvings. Arbutuses abound in the surrounding fields, producing strawberry-like berries used to make the well-known **aguardente de medronho**, a local brandy.

▸ *Retrace your route, then take the road to Aldeia da Tôr, close to where you will see a Roman bridge. Head towards Salir.*

Salir
There is a fine view of the mountains from the ruined Moorish castle. To the north east of the village, the Rocha da Pena sits atop a steep, rugged hill at an altitude of 479m/1571ft with its two walls dating from the Neolithic period.

▸ *Take the N124 toward Alte.*

Alte★
The white houses of this attractive village with its narrow, winding streets cling to the sides of a hill in the *serra*. In the lower part of the town, two rustic fountains, the Fonte Pequena and the Fonte Grande, provide a pleasant place in which to have a picnic.

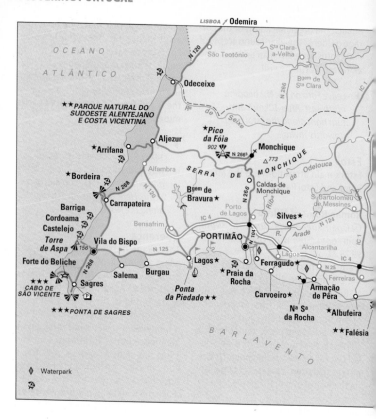

Street in Alte village

▶ *Rejoin the N 124. At Benafim Grande, turn right on to a small road leading to the N 270, which you join at the village of Gilvrazino. Then head towards Loulé.*

Loulé

The town, which was inhabited by the Romans, has preserved a few remnants from the walls of its Moorish castle. Loulé is also famous for its Carnaval, reputed to be the predecessor of the carnival in Rio de Janeiro. Held every February it attracts a large following with its fantastic costumes and dances. The Senhora da Piedade *romaria* held on the second Sunday after Easter originates from pre-Christian times.

▶ *Return to Faro on the N 125-4.*

The Rocky Coast

③ From Faro to Portimão

100km/62mi – allow a day

This is the Algarve's most famous stretch of coast. Ochre-coloured cliffs plunge down to the beach as far as Vilamoura,

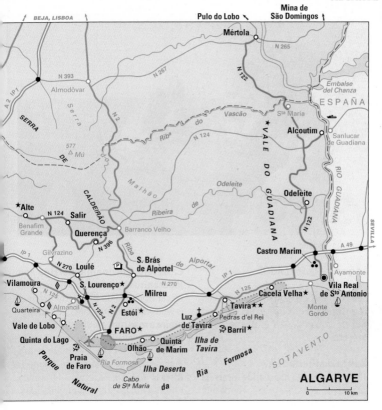

BEJA, LISBOA

Pulo do Lobo

Mina de
São Domingos

Mértola

N 265

N 393

Almodôvar

N 267

N 122

Embalse
del Chanza

ESPAÑA

SERRA

IP 1

A 2

Serra

N 2

Vascão

do

Sta Maria

Alcoutim

Sanlucar
de Guadiana

577
Mú

DE

Maihão

Riba

N 124

V A L E   D O   G U A D I A N A

RIO GUADIANA

Odeleite

Odeleite

★Alte

N 124

Salir

CALDEIRÃO

Ribeira

de

Benafim
Grande

Querença

Barranco Velho

N 396

Castro Marim

N 122

A 49

SEVILLA

IP 1

Gilvrazino

N 270

Loulé

Riba

S. Brás
de Alportel

Alportal

Ayamonte

Vilamoura

N 125

S. Lourenço★

N 270

IP 1

N 2

Milreu

N 125

Cacela Velha★

Vila Real
de Sto Antonio

Quarteira

Almancil

N 125-4

Estói★

Tavira★★

Monte
Gordo

Vale de Lobo

FARO★

Luz
de Tavira

Pedras d'el Rei

Barril★

Quinta do Lago

Olhão

Quinta
de Marim

Ilha de
Tavira

SOTAVENTO

Parque

Praia
de Faro

Ria Formosa

Ilha Deserta

Ria

Formosa

Natural

Cabo
de Sta Maria

da

ALGARVE

0   10 km

where the turquoise sea surges into coves and grottoes, some of which may be explored by boat. Unfortunately, the natural beauty has been marred in many places by intensive tourist development. Small harbours look lost among tall white apartment blocks, and in summer fishing boats are crowded out by beach umbrellas.

You arrive first in the hamlet of **São Lourenço★** (&See ALMANCIL) before getting on towards **Quinta do Lago and Vale do Lobo**, two holiday villages with golf courses, country clubs and smart hotels around which are dotted villas nestling among umbrella pines. There are footbridges across the lagoon to the beaches. You next pass **Quarteira and Vilamoura** (&See VILAMOURA) before reaching **Albufeira★** (&See ALBUFEIRA) **Carvoeiro★** (&See CARVOEIRO) and **Portimão** (&See PORTIMÃO). After Portimão is one of the best beaches on the Algarve, Praia da Rocha.

Lagos and the West Coast

⑤ From Portimão to Odeceixe

140km/87mi – about one day

The south coast after the busy town of Lagos attracts fewer tourists and its small fishing villages have managed to retain some of their character. The west coast heading north from Cabo de São Vicente is still very wild with tall, grey cliffs. The hinterland is undulating, with eucalyptus, pine trees and aloes, while the bright white villages have remained unspoiled. The region is ideal for anyone seeking a quiet spot and is particularly popular with campers. There are many golf courses along the south-west coast, normally less busy than those around Vilamoura, for example, and at Sagres there are surf schools.

Ponta da Piedade

Lagos★ – ⓒ*See LAGOS.*

Several roads lead southwards between Lagos and Vila do Bispo to beaches and fishing villages such as **Burgau** and **Salema**

Ponta da Piedade★★

The **setting**★★ of this seaside resort, its **sea caves** and clear green sea make it especially attractive.

Vila do Bispo

The bright white village is a junction for roads to the north, the Algarve and Sagres. The Baroque **church** (ⓒ*open Thu–Tue mornings)* has a chancel in gilded wood and its walls are decorated with *azulejos*. A door to the left of the chancel opens into a small museum which contains a beautiful crucifix. You then reach the very western end of the Algarve.

Ponta de Sagres and Cabo de São Vicente★★★

ⓒ*See Ponta de SAGRES and Cabo de SÃO VICENTE.*

▶ *Return to Vila do Bispa.*

The **Torre de Aspa** belvedere *(6km/3.7mi west. Take the Sagres road, then bear right and follow the signs)*, which stands at an altitude of 156m/512ft, has a beautiful **view**★ of Cabo de São Vicente and Ponta de Sagres.

Castelejo, **Cordoama**, **Barriga** and **Mouranitos beaches** may be reached by car from Vila do Bispo. The scenery is wild with tall, grey cliffs. At **Carrapateira** a road runs around the headland west of the village. There are fine views of the steep rock-face and Bordeira's long sandy beach, before you approach **Aljezur** which consists of white-walled houses with brightly painted borders. A road from here leads west *(9km/5.6mi)* to **Arrifana**★ with its beach and fishing harbour nestling at the foot of a tall cliff. The whole of this coast is perfect for surfing and many surf camps, official and unofficial, can be found, especially in Spring when the Atlantic surf is at its best. Finally you come into **Odeceixe** through eucalyptus trees. A road runs for 4km/2.5mi alongside the Seixe, small coastal river and estuary with **beach** at its mouth.

Monchique and its Spas

Inland a little from the west coast you come to the mountain village of Monchique, in itself nothing much to speak of, though its twice-weekly markets are famed throughout the Algarve, especially for its smoked meats and sausages. But near Monchique you'll find the natural spas at **Caldas de Monchique**, a village that has been totally renovated by a Spanish company and now has hotels and other attractions surrounding its natural spa centre.

AMARANTE★
PORTO
POPULATION 11 261 – MICHELIN MAP 733
LOCAL MAP SEE VALE DO DOURO

Amarante is a picturesque riverside town, with its 16C, 17C and 18C houses, complete with wooden balconies and wrought iron grilles, on a hillside overlooking the Tâmega. The town, well known for its pastries (lérias, foguetes, papos de anjo) and its *vinho verde* wine, has recently become very popular with weekenders from Porto.

- 🚹 **Information:** Rua Cândido dos Reis ~~~~~~ ☎255 43 22 59 or 255 43 29 80.
- ▶ **Orient Yourself:** Inland from Porto, halfway to Vila ~~~~
- ⊗ **Don't Miss:** All the churches in this village.
- 🕐 **Organizing Your Time:** Spend the morning here and then have lunch; it should be enough.

Sights

Igreja e Convento de São Gonçalo

The church, erected in 1540, and modified in the 18C, has some lovely gilded wooden Baroque furnishings: an altarpiece in the chancel, two pulpits and the superb **organ case**★ (early 17C) supported by three Tritons.

Igreja de São Pedro

This 18C church has a Baroque façade decorated with statues of St Peter and St Paul. The nave is decorated with 17C bands of blue and yellow *azulejos*; the chancel has a gilded wooden altar. There is a coffered chestnut wood **ceiling**★, with elegant carving in the sacristy.

AROUCA
AVEIRO
POPULATION 4 374 – MICHELIN MAP 733

Arouca Monastery and a few houses on its perimeter lie deep in the hollow of a small green valley surrounded by wooded hills. Founded in 716 but rebuilt in the 18C after a fire, the monastery forms a baroque but unadorned group.

- 🚹 **Information:** Praça Brandão Vasconcelos – 4540-110. ☎256 94 35 75.
- ▶ **Orient Yourself:** An hour south east of Porto on the N 224.
- 🕐 **Organizing Your Time:** A pleasant way to spend a long afternoon, after having had lunch here.
- ⓺ **Also See:** VISEU.

Sights

Igreja do Mosteiro

🕐 *Open Tue–Sun; church open 9am–7pm.* 👥 *Guided tours 9.30am–12 noon, 2pm–5.50pm.* 💰*€2.50.*

The church and monastery dominate this small town, their walls towering above everything. The single nave of the abbey church contains numerous gilded Baroque altars and several statues in Ançã stone carved by Jacinto Vieira. The 18C tomb worked in silver, ebony and quartz in the second chapel on the south side of the church contains the mummy of Queen Mafada (1203–52), daughter of King Sancho I; she retired here in 1217 after her marriage to Dom Henriques I of

Castile was annulled. In 1792, 400 years after her death, the Monastery was threatened by a huge fire and she is believed to have been seen dousing the flames. Her remains were exhumed and beatified shortly after.

The richly carved choir stalls are worth examining and if you have a chance to hear the organ played (sadly rare) you'll be very impressed. It has 1 352 notes.

Holy Week celebrations are impressive in this town, culminating on Easter Saturday with a huge candlelit procession.

Lower Chancel

The lower chancel (coro baixo) is ornamented with an 18C gilded organ loft, stalls with richly-carved backs and

graceful statues of religious figures by Jacinto Vieira.

Museu de Arte Sacra de Arouca

🕐 Open Wed–Sun 10am–noon, 2pm–5.30pm, Tue 10am–noon 🕐 Closed 1 Jan, Good Fri, Easter Sun, 1 May and 25 Dec. ⊛€2.50.

The extensive museum on the first floor of the cloisters contains many of the treasures of Queen Mafada, including an exquisite silver diptych dating from the 13C, several Portuguese Primitive **paintings**★ dating from the late 15C to early 16C from the Viseu School, and works, including an Ascension, by the 17C artist Diogo Teixeira. There is also a statue of St Peter dating from the 15C.

SERRA DA **ARRÁBIDA**★
SETÚBAL
MICHELIN MAP 733

The Serra da Arrábida rises and falls over the southern part of the Setúbal peninsula, covering 35km/21.7mi between Cabo Espichel and Palmela. The line of hills is made up of the ends of Secondary Era limestone deposits, pushed back, broken and buried beneath more recent deposits, and which reappear on the north side of the Tagus abutting the Sintra Massif. The Parque Natural da Arrábida, which covers 10 800ha/26 688 acres between Sesimbra and Setúbal, was created to protect the local scenery and architecture.

- 🛈 **Information:** Praça do Quebedo, Setúbal. ☎265 534 402.
- ▶ **Orient Yourself:** Cross the Vasca da Gama bridge from Lisbon and just keep going towards Setúbal.
- 🕐 **Organizing Your Time:** You'll need an entire day to do the full tour.
- Kids **Especially for Kids:** The Oceanographic Museum in Portinho da Arrábida.
- ♿ **Also See:** LISBON, SETÚBAL.

Driving Tour

Round trip from Sesimbra

77km/47.8mi – about 4hr

The itinerary described below takes in the two very different sides of this small range of mountains, which is a mere 6km/3.7mi wide. The **southern side** slopes down to the ocean, ending in cliffs 500m/1 640ft high. The indented coastline, with its wonderful array of colours, is more reminiscent of the Mediter-

ranean than the Atlantic. The **northern side**, with a more rounded relief, has a landscape of vineyards, orchards and olive groves and, on poorer ground, its original brush and pine woods.

Sesimbra – ♿ See SESIMBRA.

After Santana, the N 379 to the right winds between hills enlivened by orange trees and windmills.

- ▶ 2.5km/1.5mi before Vila Nogueira de Azeitão, turn right on N 379-1 towards Arrábida.

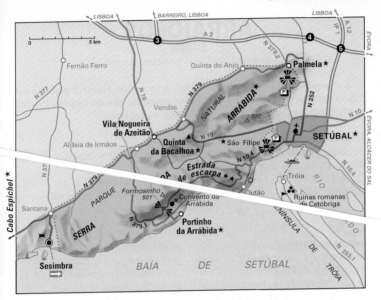

After a brief run through olive groves and vineyards, the road begins a winding climb through dense vegetation. The sea is visible far below.

▸ *Follow the signs to Portinho.*

Portinho da Arrábida★

The bay of Portinho da Arrábida, at the foot of the *serra*, forms an even curve, edged by a semicircular beach of fine white sand that is very popular at weekends. At the entrance to the village, the **Forte de Nossa Senhora da Arrábida**, built in the 17C as a protection against pirates, now houses a small 🄺🄸🄳🅂 **Museu Oceanográfico** (🕘open Tue–Fri 10am–4pm, Sat 3pm–6pm; 🕘closed public holidays; ⊗€1.50. ☎212 18 97 91) with fine displays of sponges and various marine species. Steps lead from the left of the fort entrance down to a cave.

▸ *Continue along the N 379-1, leaving the lower corniche road on the right.*

Corniche road★★

The Corniche road *(estrada de escarpa)* follows a section of the mountain crestline with views of both the northern and southern slopes. On the left there is a view of Monte Formosinho (499m/1 637ft) the *serra's* highest peak,

and on the right of Portinho and the Sado estuary. Below, in the foreground, abutting on a cliff overlooking the sea stands the **Convento da Arrábida**, founded by Franciscans in 1542.

Setúbal★ – 🕭 *See SETÚBAL.*

▸ *Leave Setúbal heading north on the N 252 and, before the motorway, take the N 379 to the left. You then reach* **Palmela★** *(🕭 See PALMELA). The N 379 runs near Bacalhoa (on the N 10 opposite the Rodoviária Nacional bus station), which can be reached from Vendas on the left, before you reach* **Quinta da Bacalhôa★.** *The N 10 passes through vineyards and orchards to Vila Nogueira de Azeitão.*

Vila Nogueira de Azeitão

Set amidst beautiful *quintas,* this town is famous for its moscatel wine. The main street is bordered with lovely Baroque fountains and the graceful buildings and gardens of the **Casa Vitícola José Maria de Fonseca**, a firm which has been making moscatel wine since 1834.

▸ *Return to Sesimbra on the N 379 via Santana.*

ARRAIOLOS
ÉVORA

POPULATION 7 567 – MICHELIN MAP 733

This charming village, perched on a hill in the great Alentejo plain about 22km/14mi north of Évora, has long been famous for its wool carpets. The 14C castle dominates the narrow streets of white-walled houses.

- **Information:** In the tiny main square ☎266 490 254
- **Orient Yourself:** 20km/12mi north of Évora in the Alentejo region.
- **Don't Miss:** Window-shopping for carpets!
- **Organizing Your Time:** A couple of hours will show you all you need to see.
- **Also See:** The *Pousada Nossa Senhora da Assunção* – even if you're not staying the night.

Arraiolos carpets

In the second half of the 17C, a small industry was established in the Arraiolos region, manufacturing hemp and linen carpets which were then embroidered with wool and used as chest and wall coverings. The carpets first followed Indian and Persian designs with animal figures and plant motifs but later the Oriental patterns and colourings were abandoned in favour of more popular, regional themes. They can be found on sale in the village in several shops ranging in price from €75 to over €2 500.

Castle

The castle *(partially restored)* has a fine view of the village and olive groves beyond. The **Convento dos Lóios** has been converted into a *pousada*.

AVEIRO ★
AVEIRO

POPULATION 73 521 – MICHELIN MAP 733
PLAN OF THE BUILT-UP AREA IN THE RED GUIDE PORTUGAL

Canals, small bridges, colourful barges that evoke the gondolas of Venice, and a fine museum give Aveiro the feel of a city of culture. The centre has many fine buildings, some in an Art Nouveau style, but the surrounding areas are impressive as well, canals and marches to the north, dunes and the beaches to the west.

- **Information:** Rua João Mendonça 8 – 3800-200. ☎234 42 36 80.
- **Orient Yourself:** 77.5km/48mi south of Porto, 63km/39mi north of Coimbra.
- **Parking:** Difficult in town with 2hr metered maximum. There is a covered car park or you can use the road by the train station, 10min walk from the centre.
- **Don't Miss:** The museum, but walk the old town to really see all the sights.
- **Organizing Your Time:** To get to know Aveiro stay a couple of days.
- **Especially for Kids:** Take them for an adventure cruise on the lagoon.
- **Also See:** COIMBRA, VISEU.

A Bit of History

Aveiro was once a busy fishing port, with boats returning from cod fishing off Newfoundland. However, in 1575 disaster struck: a violent storm closed the lagoon; the harbour silted up and the city, deprived of its livelihood, fell into decline, over 70 per cent of its population left for work elsewhere.

An effort by the Marquis of Pombal to rehabilitate it in the 18C came to noth-

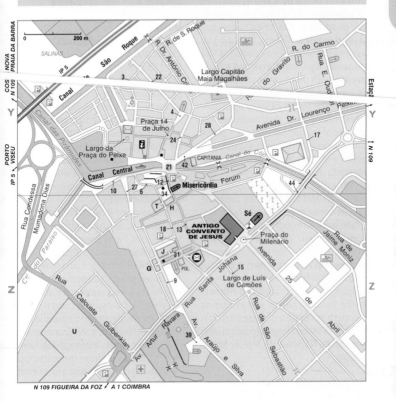

ing, as did several plans to reconnect the town to the sea. Finally in 1808, with the aid of breakwaters built from stones taken from the old town walls, a passage was opened once more from the lagoon to the sea.

Ceramic and chinaware industries developed locally (Ílhavo and Vista Alegre), bringing prosperity, and with it came expansion and artistic renown: Aveiro became a centre of Baroque art with a famous school of sculpture.

Aveiro today – Saltpans, grazing, rice paddies and land made fertile with seaweed gathered from the sea floor are important, but Aveiro remains primarily a fishing town: lamprey and sea perch

are caught in the lagoon, sardines and skate offshore. Aveiro is Portugal's third-largest industrial centre after Lisbon and Porto, yet has a quiet charm. The best way to see it is either to walk or use the free bike service, *BUGA* (www.moveaveiro.pt). Gourmets visiting the town should try the *ovos moles*, a type of egg dessert, usually served in miniature, painted wooden barrels. In July or August, during the Ria Festival, a competition takes place on the central canal to find the best painted prow from the fleet of wide-bottomed *moliceiros*.

A distinctive feature – Canals crisscross the town spanned by several small humpbacked bridges which give an almost Dutch feel to it, especially with the bicycles; at the same time the graceful *moliceiros* (flat-bottomed boats used for inshore fishing and for gathering seaweed) as well as their mooring posts inevitably bring to mind Venetian gondolas and their *palli*. The immediate proximity of the river and its labyrinth of waterways gives Aveiro its originality. In addition, the town centre has several lovely buildings, including its azulejo-covered railway station, a fine museum, a pleasant park and a main avenue with plenty of shade (*Avenida Dr Lourenço Peixinho*).

Some of the town's canal bridges have been nicely decorated with bronze statues of traditional workers – prime among them is the *salineira* (the salt seller) with her tray of salt for sale. The Mercado do Peixe (fish market) is also worth a visit.

For locals and tourists alike the huge Forum Aveiro shopping mall is a major draw, and although you might not consider it "art" its design does blend in with the rest of the town. However, the jewel in Aveiro's crown is without doubt its magnificent museum, highlighting the exuberance and richness of the Baroque period and exhibiting a superb collection of sacred art. It is Portugal's second largest museum after the Museu Nacional de Arte Antiga in Lisbon.

Address Book

For coin ranges, see cover flap.

WHERE TO EAT

Restaurant-Bar Salpoente – *Canal São Roque, 83.* ☎*234 38 26 74.* This soberly decorated restaurant is situated alongside the canal in a former salt warehouse, as is shown by several features which remind visitors of its original purpose. The cuisine is both well prepared and tasty, with the accent on fish specialities, such as eel *caldeirada* (a type of chowder) and a variety of cod dishes. From 11pm onwards the restaurant becomes a bar, hosting regular concerts.

Sights

Antigo Convento de Jesus★★

🕐 *Open Tue–Sun 10am–5.30pm.* 🕐*Closed Jan, Good Fri, Easter Sun, 1 May and 25 Dec.* €*2 (no charge on Sun and mornings of holidays).* ☎*234 42 32 97 or 234 38 31 88. – Rua Santa Joana.*

Museum★★

The Convent of Jesus was built between the 15C and 17C. Princess Joana, daughter of King Afonso V, wanted to become a nun but she was barred from doing so by here father, who wanted her married off for political reasons. To escape this planned union she "retired" here in 1472 and remained for the last 18 years of her life. She was later beatified for her determination to escape the material world. Her tomb and the chapel in which it rests are striking, the tomb a masterpiece of 17C marble mosaic.

The museum exhibits various collections including sculptures of the Coimbra School (16C) and Portuguese Primitive paintings on wood. One is a lovely **portrait**★ of Princess Joana (late 15C), attributed to Nuno Gonçalves, remarkable for the severe sculptural features of the young girl dressed in court finery.

In the rooms devoted to Baroque art, there are statues in polychrome wood of the Aveiro angels, a strange Holy Family in earthenware from the workshop of Machado de Castro, and a lacquered wooden writing desk. The room where Saint Joana died in 1490 is now an oratory decorated with altarpieces and gilded wood.

Church★★

The church dates from the 15C, but the interior decoration was completed in the early 18C. The interior has some sumptuously carved and gilded wood, particularly in the **chancel**★★, a masterpiece of Baroque exuberance with its columns; scenes from the life of Saint Joana can be seen on *azulejos* panels. The **lower chancel**★*(coro baixo)*, with its painted wood ceiling, holds **St Joana's tomb**★★ (early 18C). This masterpiece by the architect João Antunes, a mosaic in polychrome marble, is supported by sitting angels, also in marble.

The Renaissance-style **cloisters** are surrounded by chapels, one of which contains the beautiful 15C **tomb of João de Albuquerque**. The refectory is totally covered with 17C *azulejos* decorated with floral motifs.

A tour of the Museum includes a visit to the church gallery or **coro alto** which is decorated with paintings and a 14C Crucifixion in which Christ's expression changes according to the angle.

Cathedral

This cathedral *(sé)* is the only remaining vestige of the former Convento de São Domingos, founded in 1423, but it has been greatly modified since it was first built. It has a Baroque façade and, inside, a strange mixture of styles, including 17C and 18C polychrome *azulejos* on the walls of the nave and a 17C organ in the north arm of the transept. To the left of the entrance, there is an early Renaissance *Entombment*.

Cruzeiro de São Domingos

This Gothic-Manueline -tyle Calvary in front of the cathedral is an exact reproduction of the original, which is now housed inside the church.

Igreja da Misericórdia

The Church of the Misericord has an imposing finely-worked 17C doorway. Inside, the height of the nave and the 17C *azulejos* should be noted, as well as the churchwardens' pew opposite the pulpit.

Canal Quarter★ 2hr

Some canals of the Ria de Aveiro continue right into the town; they are shored up by embankments which the water laps over at high tide.

Canal Central

Part of the canal is bordered by beautiful old buildings, their classical façades reflected in the water. The canal features a continuous spectacle of small boats, *moliceiros*, flat bottomed boats traditionally used for gathering seaweed in the lagoon, their prows brightly painted. The best viewpoint is from the wide bridge-tunnel with balusters which divides it at the halfway point; this bridge is the main crossroads in the town *(Praça Humberto Delgado)*.

Canal de São Roque

This canal borders the built-up area to the north, and is spanned (in front of Rua Dr. António Cristo) by an elegant stone humpback footbridge. It divides the salt marshes from the salt warehouses which line the embankment among the low-roofed houses of the fishing quarter.

Ria de Aveiro★

The Ria de Aveiro empties into a vast lagoon marked by tides, dotted with islands and crisscrossed with channels. It is bordered by salt marshes and pine forests, behind an offshore bar some 45km/28mi long and not more than 2.5km/1.5mi wide, with a narrow bottleneck *(Estreito da Barra)* linking it to the ocean. The lagoon takes the shape of a triangle, and at high tide covers about 6 000ha/23sq mi, with an average depth of 2m/6.5ft. Rich in fish and fertile in the parts above high tide mark, the *ria* is particularly famous for its seaweed, which is used as a fertiliser. The seaweed is traditionally collected in **moliceiros**, flat-bottomed boats with prows curved like swans' necks and painted with in vivid colours. The boats either have a sail or are propelled with a pole, similar to the gondolas of Venice. The rakes' prongs *(ancinhos)* for scraping or gathering up seaweed are hung around the tip of the prow. Unfortunately, the number of these boats is decreasing (some can be seen in front of the tourist office), although there is still an annual competition in July and August for the best-decorated vessel.

Boat trips

Allow a whole day for the complete tour. Departures daily from Aveiro's Central Canal from mid-Jun–mid-Sept at 10am (return at about 5pm). For information and reservations: Tourist Information Centre in Aveiro (Região de Turismo de Rota da Luz, Rua João Mendonça 8, 3800-200 Aveiro). Prices vary but are about €12 (€8

R. Mattes/MICHELIN

Moliceiros

for children). You can also find, at certain times of the year, one-hour trips round the lagoon for about €8. ☏234 42 36 80 or 234 42 07 60.

Around Aveiro

Although Aveiro itself has no beaches there are plenty around, all very popular in summer. In fact the entire coast is almost one continuous run of glorious sand. The beaches closest to the town are **Barra**, about 9km/5mi west of Aveiro and then **Costa Nova**, 3km/2mi south of Barra. Both are reachable by bus from Aveiro. Both are good venues for surfing and there is also a diving centre for scuba-diving. There are plenty of restaurants and beach bars along the edge of the beach.

Bico

To the north of Aveiro one of the better beaches is at Bico, a small fishing port with plenty of restaurants, which is reached after crossing Murtosa. You can normally see many *moliceiros* that are tied up here most days.

Torreira

This is a small port on the *ria* where beautiful *moliceiros* may still be seen. The Pousada da Ria, located between the two ports, is on the water's edge.

The Reserva Natural das Dunas de São Jacinto is situated 2km/1.2mi before São Jacinto.

Reserva Natural das Dunas de São Jacinto

This nature reserve, which covers 666ha/1 645 acres of some of the best preserved dunes in Europe, is particularly interesting for its scenery, flora and fauna. Over 100 different types of birdlife can be seen here, including goshawk and there are many hides along the trails. To ensure the preservation of this area visitors are only allowed to enter between 9am and 9.30 am, or between 2pm and 2.30pm and it is necessary to book at least one day in advance as numbers are limited. You can only stay for 2hrs 30min.

The **visitor centre** contains exhibits and details of the reserve including a 7km/4mi walking trail with map, though you can also find someone who will be happy to give you a guided tour. ☚ *Guided tours (2hr 30min) Fri, Sat, Mon–Wed 9am and 1.30pm.* ◷ *Closed public holidays.* ☏234 33 12 82.

São Jacinto

The small resort in the pine woods at the end of the northern offshore bar on the Estreito da Barra is also a busy little port with plenty of restaurants.

Vista Alegre

Vista Alegre, 5km/3mi west of Aveiro, has been a manufacturing centre of fine chinaware and glass since 1824. It acquired royal patronage shortly after opening and has since been regarded as the most important centre of porcelain in Portugal. A small **museum** (⊙*open Tue–Fri 9am–12.30pm and 2pm–4.30pm (5pm Sat–Sun and public holidays;* ⊙*closed 1 Jan, Good Fri, Easter Sun, 1 May and 25 Dec;* ⊚*€1.50;* ☎*234 32 50 40/46)* on the factory premises recounts the developments in production since its earliest days through displays of machines, tools and examples of most of the pieces produced since its foundation. You can take an inclusive bus tour to include admission from Aveiro on Weds and Fri |P12.

Southern arm of the Ria

Ílhavo

This small former fishing port has become developed with some attractive early 20C villas such as the "Villa Africana", covered with *azulejos* in varying shades of yellow. Its fascinating **museum**★, devoted to fishing and the sea, has a comprehensive section on cod fishing, while a documentary dating from the 1970s shows the harsh reality of the fishing expeditions, some of which would last six months in the fishing grounds off Newfoundland.

AVIS
PORTALEGRE
POPULATION 4 893 – MICHELIN MAP 733

The first glimpse of Avis comes as a welcome sight as you cross the Alentejo plateau, covered mostly with cork oaks and olive trees. The town, about midway between Évora and Portalegre, has kept traces of its early fortifications and overlooks the confluence of the Seda and Avis rivers, now submerged below the waters of the reservoir serving the Maranhão power station, 15km/9.3mi downstream.

▸ **Orient Yourself:** 40km/28mi north of Évora
⊛ **Don't Miss:** The Convent and town ramparts.
⊙ **Organizing Your Time:** You will probably only stop here en route, for a coffee perhaps and maybe an hour or so of rest and calm.
⚲ **Also See:** CRATO.

Visit

The N 243 from the south offers the best **view**★ of the town. Ramparts, a few medieval towers and the church of the Convento de São Bento, rebuilt in the 17C, stand witness today of the city's brilliant past. It was here, at the beginning of the 13C, that the military order founded in 1147 by Afonso Henriques to fight the Moors became geographically established. The oldest order of chivalry in Europe bore several names and followed the rules of several other orders before finally becoming the Order of St Benedict of Avis. It prospered in the Tagus region until 1789.

Avis was also the cradle of the dynasty which was to reign over Portugal from 1385 to 1580. On 7 August 1385 João (bastard son of Pedro I), Grand Master of the Order of Avis, was proclaimed king under the name **João I**. In February 1387 he married Philippa of Lancaster.

QUINTA DA **BACALHÔA**★
SETÚBAL
MICHELIN MAP 733

This seigneurial residence, built at the end of the 15C and remodelled in the early 16C by the son of Afonso de Albuquerque, Viceroy of India, has both Renaissance and Moorish styles and rich **azulejo**★ decoration.

▶ **Orient Yourself:** The Quinta da Bacalhôa is on the N 10 as you leave Vila Fresca de Azitão heading towards Setúbal, opposite the bus station.
🅿 **Parking:** Parking spaces should be readily available here.
🕐 **Organizing Your Time:** An hour should be just right. Take an extra hour or two to visit nearby Cabo Espichel and its fantastic views over the vast Atlantic.

Visit

In the manor house a graceful loggia giving onto the gardens is adorned In the manor house a graceful loggia giving onto the gardens is adorned with polychrome *azulejo* panels depicting allegories of great rivers, including the Douro, Nile, Danube and Euphrates. The **Gardens** (🚶guided visits Mon–Sat 1pm–5pm; 🕐 closed public holidays; ☜€5; ☎212 18 00 11; www.bacalhoa. com; advance reservations essential)

were inspired by the style current in 16C France. An ornamental kitchen garden, where mandarins and walnut trees, bamboo and cinerarias grow, ends at an attractive pavilion and ornamental pool. The walls inside the pavilion are decorated with Spanish *azulejos* with geometrical patterns but the most impressive panel is the Florentine-style depiction of **Susannah and the Elders**★, the oldest figurative panel in Portugal (1565).

BARCELOS
BRAGA
POPULATION 125 000 – MICHELIN MAP 733

Barcelos is an attractive town on the north bank of the Cávado. It was the capital of the first county of Portugal and residence of the first Duke of Bragança, who was also the Count of Barcelos (🌀see BRAGANÇA). It is now a busy agricultural centre and is well known for the production of pottery, ornamental crib figures, carved wood yokes and decorated cocks.

🛈 **Information:** Largo da Porta Nova. ☎253 81 18 82 or 253 81 21 35.
▶ **Orient Yourself:** 65km/40.3mi north east of Porto.
👁 **Don't Miss:** The market on Thursdays.
🕐 **Organizing Your Time:** Spend the whole of Thursday morning here for the market.
🌀 **Also See:** BRAGA, VIANA DO COSTELO, PONTE DE LIMA.

The market

The lively **market**, held on Thursday mornings, is one of Portugal's oldest and largest with agricultural products on one side and arts and crafts from

the region and further afield (pottery, baskets, hand-embroidered household linen, leather goods, harnesses) on the other. They come mainly from the region which is more based on cottage industries and smallholdings than anything more industrialised. Like most markets across Portugal there's a fair selecytion of "branded" goods that are not quite the real thing.

Old Quarter

The main sights are centred on the **medieval bridge** over the Cávado in the southern part of the town.

Parish church

This 13C church, which was modified in the 16C and 18C, has a plain façade, flanked on the right by a square belfry, and a Romanesque doorway. The **interior**★ is glittering with gold and bordered with Baroque chapels. The walls are decorated with 18C **azulejos**. Some of the capitals are historiated.

Solar dos Pinheiros

This beautiful 15C Gothic manor house built of granite is adorned with three-storey corner towers.

Ruínas do Paço dos Duques de Bragança ou Condes de Barcelos

These 15C palace ruins are the setting for a small open air **Museu Arqueológico** (⊙open 9.30am–6pm; ⊙closed 1 Jan, Good Fri, Easter Sun, 1 May and 25 Dec; ☎253 82 12 51).
Of particular interest are the steles and coats-of-arms of the House of Bragança, as well as the 14C monument set up in honour of the Barcelos cock.

Museu da Olaria

⊙Open Tue–Fri 10am–5.30pm, Sat–Sun and holidays, 10am–12.30pm, 2pm–5.30pm. ⊙Closed 1 Jan, Good Fri, Easter Sun, 15 Aug, 1 Nov and 24–25 Dec.≈€1.45; free Sun. ☎253 82 47 41.
The ceramics museum in the basement of the palace contains one of the largest collections of its kind in Portugal, with pride of place given to the town's colourful emblem. An entire section is also devoted to the black tableware from the village of Prado, with illustrations of this age-old technique which is no longer used today. The museum is an ideal place in which to purchase the work of

Barcelos cocks

P. Martins/MICHELIN

modern-day ceramists at reasonable prices. The best known include Mistério, who is continuing his family's traditions, and Júlia Ramalho, the grand-daughter of the already famous Rosa Ramalho.

Additional Sights

Campo da República

This vast esplanade in the centre of the town is the scene of the famous **market** held on Thursday mornings.

Igreja de Nossa Senhora do Terço★

On the northern side of Campo da República.
The Church of Our Lady of Terço was formerly part of a Benedictine monastery from 1707. The walls of the nave are covered with beautiful 18C **azulejos**★ depicting events in the life of St Benedict. The coffered ceiling is painted with 40 scenes of monastic life. The pulpit of gilded wood is richly ornamented.

Torre de Menagem

This tower, part of the remains of the 15C ramparts, now houses the Tourist Information Centre, where visitors can also purchase a range of arts and crafts.

Igreja do Bom Jesus da Cruz

The Church of Jesus, which is built in the Northern Baroque style, has an interesting plan in the shape of a Greek cross. According to legend, on 20 December 1504 a cross appeared on this very spot, following which a church was built to commemorate this miracle.

MOSTEIRO DA **BATALHA**★★★
LEIRIA
MICHELIN MAP 733

The Monastery of Batalha (Battle) is a mass of gables, pinnacles, buttresses, turrets and small columns standing majestically in a green valley. Although its setting is somewhat marred by the proximity of the N 1 road, vibrations from which are visibly damaging the building, the rose gold effusion of its architecture remains one of the masterpieces of Portuguese Gothic and Manueline art.

- **Information:** Praça Mouzinho de Albuquerque – 2440-109. ☎244 76 51 80.
- **Orient Yourself:** On the N 1 road, 11.8km/7.3mi south of Leiria.
- **Parking:** Plenty of parking at the Abbey, plus an overspill nearby.
- **Don't Miss:** The Tomb of the Unknown Warriors.
- **Organizing Your Time:** To explore it fully allow best part of a day.
- **Also See:** ALCOBAÇA, LEIRIA, CASTELO DE ALMOUROL.

A Bit of History

On 14 August 1385 on the plateau of Aljubarrota, 15km/9.3mi south of Batalha, two pretenders to the throne of Portugal faced each other, prepared to do battle: Juan I of Castile, nephew of the late king, and João I, Grand Master of the Order of Avis, who had been crowned king only seven days previously.

The opposing forces were of very different strengths: against the organised forces and 16 cannon of the Castilians, the Constable **Nuno Álvares Pereira** could only muster a squad of knights and foot soldiers. João I of Avis, knowing that defeat would mean Portugal passing under Spanish domination, made a vow to build a superb church in honour of the Virgin if she were to grant him victory. The Portuguese troops resisted and were victorious. Three years later the Mosteiro de Santa Maria da Vitória, subsequently known as the Mosteiro da Batalha, (Battle Abbey) began taking shape.

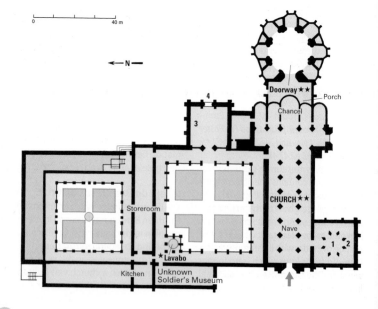

Claustro Real, Mosteiro da Batalha

Visit *2hr*

🕐 *Open 9am–6pm (5pm Oct–Mar).*
🕐 *Closed 1 Jan, Good Fri, Easter Sun, 1 May and 25 Dec.* ✆*The entrance to the Church and the Capelas Imperfeitas is free; Cloisters €4.50, no charge Sun and public holidays before 2pm).* ☎*244 76 54 97.*

The **exterior** of the monastery, which in accordance with the Dominican rule has no belfry, possesses innumerable pinnacles, buttresses and openwork balustrades above Gothic and Flamboyant windows. The building is in fine-textured limestone, which has taken on a lovely

ochre colour with time. The complicated structure at the east end of the church demonstrates the architectural problems arising from joining onto an earlier apse an octagonal rotunda which, by means of pillars, was to bear a vaulted ceiling.

The **Capela do Fundador**★ (Founder's Chapel), off the south aisle, is surmounted by an octagonal lantern supported by flying buttresses. The main façade is divided into three: the central part, decorated with a network of lancet-shaped blind arcades, is pierced by a beautiful Flamboyant window; the main doorway is richly carved, bearing statues of Christ in Majesty, surrounded by the Evangelists, the twelve Apostles on the sides, and angels, prophets, kings and saints on the covings. The doorway's proportions appeared to better advantage when the church stood, as it did originally, below the level of the terrace outside.

Church★★

The church's vast **interior** is very plain with strong English Perpendicular influences, the outstanding element being the upward sweep of the vaulting. In fact English architects were used in the design of the Abbey following the marriage of King João I and his queen Philippa of Lancaster, the daughter of John of Gaunt. The chancel is lit by **stained-glass windows**★ which date from the 16C and depict scenes from the Life of the Virgin and Jesus Christ.

Capela do Fundador★

This square chamber, known as the Founder's Chapel, lit by Flamboyant windows, on the right as you enter, is covered with an octagonal lantern topped by a star-shaped cupola.

In the centre are the tombs (1) of King João I and his queen Philippa of Lancaster, the two figures reclining beneath delicately carved canopies. They are depicted holding hands in an expression of the cordial relations between England and Portugal. The Avis and Lancaster coats of arms appear on the tomb. Bays on the south and west sides contain the tombs of the founder's four younger sons (Duarte, the eldest was buried in the sanctuary), Fernando, João, Pedro and Prince Henry the Navigator, whose tomb (2) is covered with a canopy.

Claustro Real★★★

The Gothic and Manueline styles mix most successfully in the Royal Cloisters, the simplicity of the original Gothic design not being obscured by Manueline detail. The fleur-de-lis balustrade and the flowered pinnacles provide a motif which harmonises well with the Manueline tracery backing the carved marble arcades.

Chapter-House★★

The chapter-house (sala do capitulo) contains the tomb (3) of the Unknown Soldiers where the bodies of two Portuguese soldiers lie. Both died during World War I, one in France, the other in Africa. The **vaulting**★★★ is an outstandingly bold feat; after two unsuccessful attempts the master architect Huguet managed to launch a square vault of some 20m/60ft without intermediary supports. The chamber is lit by a window containing early 16C **stained glass**★ (4) representing scenes of the Passion.

Lavabo★

The lavabo in the northwest corner of the cloisters consists of a basin with a festooned curbstone surmounted by two smaller basins. The light, filtering through the stone tracery between the arches, gives a golden glow to the stone and the water. The old refectory, which has a fine Gothic ceiling, houses the Museum of the Unknown Soldiers.

Claustro de D Afonso V★

The coats of arms on the keystones to the vaulting in these fine Gothic cloisters are those of King Duarte I and King Afonso V.

▶ *Go round the outside of the chapter-house and through the porch to the Unfinished Chapels.*

Capelas Imperfeitas★★

Dom Duarte commissioned a vast mausoleum for himself and his descendents but he and his queen alone lie buried in the unfinished building open to the sky. A vast transitional Gothic Renaissance porch connecting the east end of the church with the doorway of the octagonal chamber was added later by Dom Manuel. This **doorway**★★, initially Gothic in style, was ornamented in the 16C with Manueline decoration; it opens towards the church with a curved arch beneath a powerful multilobed arch. The cut-away ornament of the festoons as well as the detailed decoration on the covings and the columns are particularly worthy of note.

BEJA★
BEJA
POPULATION 26 659 – MICHELIN MAP 733

Having been a brilliant Roman colony *(Pax Julia)*, the town became the seat of a Visigothic bishopric and then fell under Muslim control for four centuries. Today the capital of the Baixo Alentejo, it is a town of white houses and straight streets that is a flourishing agricultural market town.

- **Information:** Rua Capitão Francisco de Sousa 25 – 7800-451. ☎284 31 19 91.
- ▶ **Orient Yourself:** Beja is 79.7km/49.5mi south of Évora. On the main railway line south from Lisbon or along the E 802 by car.
- ☺ **Don't Miss:** The cloisters in the old convent.
- ⏱ **Organizing Your Time:** You should see all you need within one day.

Sights

Antigo Convento da Conceição★
⊙*Open Tue–Fri and Sun 9.30am–12.30pm, 2pm–5.15pm.* ⊙*Closed public holidays.*
The Poor Clares Convent was founded by Dom Fernando, father of King Manuel, in 1459. The graceful Gothic balustrade crowning the church and the cloisters recalls that of the Mosteiro da Batalha. During the occupation of the town by French forces in the early 17C a young nun, Sister Mariana Alcoforada, from this Convent fell in love with a young French officer, Count Chamilly. Her letters to him, published in 1669, caused a scandal.

Today the convent houses the regional museum, also known as the **Museu da Rainha Dona Leonor**. ⊙*Open 9.30am– Tue–Fri and Sun 12.30pm, 2pm–5.15pm.* ⊙*Closed public holidays.* ⊛*€2 (no charge Sun morning); ticket also gives you free entry to the Museu Visigótico nearby.* ☎284 32 33 51.

The Baroque **church** is richly decorated with gilded and carved woodwork from the 17C and 18C. The walls of the cloisters on the right are covered with *azulejos*. The chapter-house is richly decorated with beautiful 16C Hispano-Moorish *azulejos* from Seville and the vaulting is adorned with 18C floral motifs. A collection of Crucifixes is also on display. The rooms beyond contain paintings including a *St Jerome* by Ribera (17C) and a 15C *Ecce Homo*.

The first floor contains the Fernando Nunes Ribeiro archaeological collection of engraved flagstones from the Bronze Age and Iron Age epigraphic stelae.
A second convent, that of São Franciso, has been turned into a *pousada*.

Castle
⊙*Open summer, Tue–Sun 10am–1pm, 2pm–6pm; winter, Tue–Sun 9am–noon, 1pm–4pm.* ⊙*Closed 1 Jan, 25 Dec and local holidays.* ⊛*€1.35 (no charge on Sun and public holidays).* ☎284 31 19 12.
The town is dominated by the 13C castle's crenellated perimeter wall (housing a military museum), flanked by square towers, is overlooked at one corner by a high **keep**★ reached by 197 steps, topped by pyramid-shaped merlons. The views from the top over the surrounding countryside are magnificent. The first floor, reached by a spiral staircase, has fine star vaulting resting on Moorish-style veined corner squinches.

Igreja de Santo Amaro★
This small Visigothic church, parts of which date back to the 5C, now houses the Visigothic art section ⊙*Same opening times as the Museu da Rainha Dona Leonor in the Convent (◖left).*

Sé (Cathedral)
Beja's Cathedral looks rather dull and dour from the outside but the interior is richly decorated.

BELMONTE ★
CASTELO BRANCO
POPULATION 7 662 – MICHELIN MAP 733

This delightful, isolated town perched high on a line of hills near the Serra da Estrela, has many churches that help create a vision of architectural harmony. The great navigator **Pedro Álvares Cabral**, who discovered Brazil in 1500, was born here. His statue stands on the main street which is named after him.

- **Information:** Praça da República, 18 – 6250-034. ☎275 91 14 88.
- **Orient Yourself:** 29km/18mi south of Guarda.
- **Don't Miss:** The castle and as many churches as you wish to visit.
- **Organizing Your Time:** A full morning spent here will be well rewarded.
- **Also See:** GUARDA, SERRA DA ESTRELA.

Sights

Castle
🕐*Open 10am–1.30pm, 3pm–6pm.*
The castle was built in the 13C–14C by King Dom Dinis I; only the keep, the corner tower on the right with 17C balconies, and the section of the wall adjoining it on the left remain. A walk round the perimeter wall offers a fine **view**★ of the countryside below.

Igreja de São Tiago
🕐*Open Tue–Sun 9.30am–12.30pm, 2pm–6pm.* ◎€1.
Next to the castle and of an earlier period but modified in the 16C, the church still has some interesting elements inside dating from the Romanesque and Renaissance periods; a baptismal font, 16C frescoes in the chancel and 12C examples on the wall to the right. The Nossa Senhora da Piedade chapel, built in the 14C, contains a strange pulpit with a sounding-board and a polychrome Pietà carved from a single block of stone, as well as capitals which refer to the exploits of Fernão Cabral I, the father of Pedro Álvares Cabral, the man who "discoverd" Brazil and had been born in the castle in 1467. The family mausoleum containing the tombs of his parents can be seen in the adjoining **Panteão dos Cabrais** though his own tomb is in Santarém rather than here.

Belmonte also has a restored Jewish Quarter just below the walls of the castle. This was one of the largest Jewish communities in Portugal and details of a synagogue dating back to 1297. At the time of the Inquisition many Jews fled though have since returned. Many pretended to convert to Catholicism but practised their own religion in secret, right up to 1974. There is a new **synagogue** (🕐*open Tue–Sun 9.30am–12.30pm, 2pm–6pm;* ◎€2) and a **Museu Judaico** (🕐*open Tue–Sun 9.30am–12.30pm, 2pm–6pm;* ◎€2.50; ticket gives access to all the town's museums, same opening hours).

Parish church
🕐*Open 9am–9pm.*
The church, built in 1940, contains the picture of Our Lady of Hope, which, according to tradition, accompanied Pedro Álvares Cabral on his voyage of discovery to Brazil, as well as a replica of the cross used in the first mass celebrated there. The original can be seen in Braga Cathedral.

Torre Romana de Centum Cellas ★
4km/2.5mi to the north. Take the N 18 towards Guarda then, on the right, the road to Comeal (sign marked Monumento) where there is a road leading to the foot of the tower.
This impressive ruin is thought to be part of a 1C Roman villa which was connected to the tin trade along the road linking Mérida and Braga. Its square mass, made of pink granite blocks laid with dry joints, still stands with rectangular openings on three levels.

ILHA DA **BERLENGA**★★
LEIRIA
MICHELIN MAP 733

The Ilha de Berlenga, a reddish-coloured mass, which protrudes 12km/7.4mi out to sea from Cabo Carvoeiro (Peniche, close to Óbidos), is the main island in an archipelago consisting of a number of rocky islets, the Estelas, the Forcadas and the Farilhões. Berlenga, 1 500m/4 921ft long and 800m/2 625ft at its widest point, reaches a height of 85m/279ft. The major attractions of this block of bare granite lie in its numerous indentations and headlands and in its marine caves.

- **Information:** In Peniche, Rua Alexandre Herculano. ☎262 789 571.
- ▶ **Orient Yourself:** An almost uninhabited island 12km/7.4mi off Peniche.
- P **Parking:** You'll need to leave your car by the harbour in Peniche.
  Make sure you park legally or you could get a steep fine.
- **Don't Miss:** The grottoes as you approach the island by boat.
- ⊙ **Organizing Your Time:** This is normally no more than a half-day trip.
- **Kids Especially for Kids:** The bird colonies on the island will fascinate them.

Visit

Access
⊙ *There is a regular boat service to the island from Peniche between 15 May and 20 Sept. In July and August they leave Peniche harbour at 9.30am and 11.30am, other months 10am. They return from the island at 4.30pm, 6.30pm in July and Aug, 4pm other months. Return (round trip) ticket: ☞€18 per person; crossing time: 45min. For bookings, contact Viamar☎262 785 646, or contact the Tourist Office in Peniche. ☎262 789 571.*

Boat trip★★★
⊙ *For bookings, contact Viamar: ☎262 785 646. Ticket office opens at 8.30am and a maximum of 300 tickets are sold daily. July and August are very busy. Other companies operate from the harbour in Peniche with "island trips" that include a brief stop on the island. Tickets should cost no more than ☞€20.*

On a calm day the trip is glorious but if the sea is a bit on the rough side you could be a little uncomfortable. Among the most striking sights of the trip are, south of the inn, the Furado Grande, a marine tunnel 70m/229.6ft long which ends in a small creek (Cova do Sonho) walled by towering cliffs of red granite; beneath the fortress itself is a cave known locally as the "Gruta Azul" or "Blue Grotto", where light refracts on the sea within, producing an unusual and most attractive emerald green pool.

Walk★★
2hr.

The island is almost uninhabited though there is an inn where you can stay the night, though it is fairly basic. There is also a campsite, but you need permission from the tourism office in Peniche first. The island is a **bird colony** and thousands of gulls screech and swoop. If you take a picnic, guard it carefully. There is no shade on the island so if it's a hot day make sure you have a hat at least, and some sun-cream. The walk can be rough so take good boots – it is not recommended for those who find walking difficult.

The island and two other islands close by make a wonderful location for diving – there are diving operators in Peniche.

Take the stairway from the inn to the lighthouse. Halfway up turn to look at the fortress (Forte de São João Baptista) in its **setting**★; on reaching the plateau take a path on the left which goes to the west coast or Wild Coast. There is a good **view**★ from the top, of the rocks. Return to the lighthouse and descend a path leading to a small bay bordered by a beach and a few fishermen's cottages. Halfway down, to the left, the view of a creek where the sea roars and pounds in bad weather is particularly impressive.

BRAGA ★
BRAGA
POPULATION 170 858 – MICHELIN MAP 733

Braga is regarded as the religious capital of Portugal, equivalent, in Portuguese eyes, to Rome. There are dozens of churches to go alongside its Cathedral, and a little outside you will find the impressive sanctuary of Bom Jesus. Yet it is also an important and lively town, so the sacred and secular live comfortably together. Holy Week here is a time of major celebration.

- **Information:** Av. da Liberdade 1 – 4710-305. ☎253 26 25 50.
- ▶ **Orient Yourself:** About 54km/33.5mi north east of Porto.
- 🅿 **Parking:** Difficult – use the underground parking in the town centre.
- 👐 **Don't Miss:** Holy Week when the entire town is richly decorated with flowers and processions.
- 🕐 **Organizing Your Time:** Allow a complete day.
- 👁 **Also See:** ALTO VALE DO CÁVADO, PORTO, GUIMARÃES.

A Bit of History

A very religious city

Bracara Augusta, an important Roman town, was made into their capital by the Suevi when they advanced upon the area in the 5C. The town was subsequently captured by the Visigoths (who built the Igreja de São Frutuoso) and then by the Moors and only regained prosperity after the Reconquest when it became the seat of an archbishopric. From this time onwards the influence of the Church became paramount, a fea-ture now particularly apparent in the richness of the architecture; in the 16C the archbishop and patron Dom Diogo de Sousa presented the town with a palace, churches and calvaries in the Renaissance style; in the 18C the two prelates, Dom Rodrigo of Moura Teles and Dom Gaspar of Bragança, made Braga the centre of Portuguese Baroque art. Braga, once the seat of the Primate of All Spain, is still strongly ecclesiastical in character. Holy Week is observed with devotion and is the occasion for spectacular processions. The Feast of St John the Baptist on 23 and 24 June attracts crowds of local people and even many from as far as Galicia; they attend the processions, folk dancing and firework displays in the highly decorated town.

Cathedral ★

🕐 Open 8.30am–6.30pm. ☎253 26 33 17.

Only the south doorway and the arching over the main doorway remain from the original Romanesque cathedral. The portico with festooned Gothic arches is by Biscayan artists brought to Braga in the 16C by Diogo de Sousa. The moulded window frames

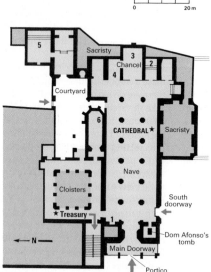

0   20 m

5

Sacristy

3
Chancel   2
4

Courtyard

6

CATHEDRAL ★   Sacristy

Nave

Cloisters

South
doorway

★ Treasury   1

Dom Afonso's
tomb

◄ — N —

Main Doorway

Portico

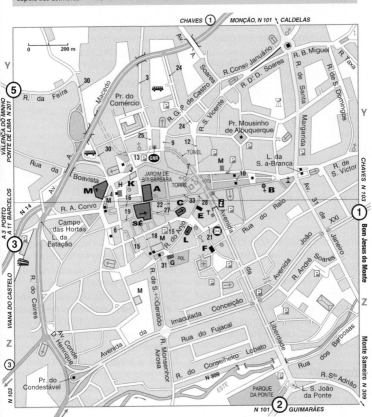

date from the 17C. This same archbishop is responsible for the cathedral's east end bristling with pinnacles and balusters. The graceful **statue**★ of the Nursing Madonna (Nossa Senhora do Leite) beneath a Flamboyant canopy which adorns the east end exterior is said to be by Nicolas Chanterene.

Interior★

The interior, which was transformed during the 18C, is striking in its contrast between the richness of the Baroque woodwork and the simplicity of the nave. The font (1) is Manueline: to the right, in a chapel closed by a 16C grille, lies the bronze tomb (*túmulo*, 15C) of the Infante Dom Afonso. The Chapel of the Holy Sacrament (Capela do Sacramento) contains a fine 17C polychrome wooden altar (2) representing the Church Triumphant after a picture by Rubens.

The chancel, covered with intricate ribbed **vaulting**★, contains a Flamboyant **altar**★ (3) of Ança stone carved on the front with scenes of the Ascension

Address Book

For coin ranges, see cover flap.

WHERE TO STAY

Albergaria Bracara Augusta – *Avenida Central, 134.* ☎*253 20 62 60. www.bracaraaugusta.com. 19 rooms.* A new-ish hotel (2005) in a beautiful building. The rooms are very comfortable and well decorated in a contemporary style. A small garden at the rear is ideal for breakfast in good weather.

Hotel Residencial Dona Sofia – *Largo São João do Souto, 131,* ☎*253 26 31 60. 34 rooms* ☄. This comfortable hotel close to the cathedral is housed in an old mansion with comfortable rooms.

WHERE TO EAT

Anjou Verde – *Largo da Praça Velha.* ☎*21 253 26 40 10. Closed Sun.* Lovely décor, lively and fresh; a very good vegetarian restaurant where the portions and flavours will leave you delighted. A warm welcome.

Inácio – *Campo das Hortas, 4.* ☎*253 61 32 35. Closed Christmas, Easter, 2 weeks in Mar and Sept.* A restaurant where typical menus are served with exquisite care. The restaurant enjoys a high reputation and it is well deserved.

INTERNET

Biblioteca Pública da Universidade do Minho - *Antigo Paço Episcopal, Largo do Paço (2 places). Free.*

Café-Bar James Dean - *Rua Santo André, 85. 253 61 76 02. Daily 8am-10pm, Sun 1pm-7pm.* ☄*30min €1; 60min €1.75.*

TRANSPORT

Railway station – *Largo da Estação* ☎*253 27 82 52.* Trains for Porto (journey 1hr) every 30min during the day.

Buses – *Praça da Estação Rodoviária* ☎*253 20 94 00.* There are extensive services with connections to many towns, particularly in the region. A comfortable and inexpensive way to travel.

---

and of the Apostles. Above the altar is a 14C statue of St Mary of Braga. To the left of the chancel is a chapel (4) decorated with 18C *azulejos* by António de Oliveira Bernardes depicting the life of St Pedro de Rates, first bishop of Braga. A harmonious Baroque group is formed by the two 18C **cases**★ on either side of the balustraded organ loft.

Treasury★

Open 9am–noon, 2pm–6pm. ☄*€2.* The cathedral treasury *(tesouro)* is the most magnificent in Portugal and has a fine collection of 16C–18C vestments as well as a Manueline chalice, a 14C cross in rock crystal, a 17C silver-gilt reliquary cross, a 10C Mozarabic chest made of ivory, a 16C chalice, a 17C monstrance, Dom Gaspar of Bragança's 18C silver-gilt monstrance adorned with diamonds, and several statues including a 13C Christ and St Crispin and St Crispinian. You also come across a room dedicated to the treasures of Dom Rodrigo de Maura-Teles who commissioned 22 monuments (including Bom Jesus) during his years in office. He was a par-

ticularly popular Archbishop though is remembered mostly for his height – he was less than four feet tall and had shoes built up so he would look taller.

A tour of the treasury includes the **Capela de São Geraldo** and the **Capela da Glória**★, the walls of the former decorated with 18C *azulejos* illustrating the life of St Gerald who was the first archbishop of Braga. The Gothic Chapel of Glory is decorated with 14C mural paintings in the Mudéjar style. The sides of the Gothic **tomb**★ (5) of the founder, Dom Gonçalo Pereira, in the centre of the chapel, bear reliefs of the Crucifixion and the figures of the Apostles, the Virgin and Child and clerics at prayer.

Capela dos Reis

The Kings' Chapel, with Gothic vaulting resting on beautiful brackets sculpted with human heads, contains the 16C tombs (6) of Henry of Burgundy and his wife Teresa, parents of Afonso Henriques, the first king of Portugal, and the mummy of Dom Lourenço Vicente (14C), archbishop of Braga, who fought at Aljubarrota.

Medival city of Bragança

A. Cassaigne/MICHELIN

an elegant façade with a door which is framed by two twisted columns decorated with vine plants; inside a fine ceiling painted in *trompe-l'œil* depicts the Assumption.

Additional Sights

These may be seen in the lower town that was built in the 17C and 18C.

Largo da Sé (Cathedral Square)

The square is adorned with a large Baroque cross which was originally a pillory. This church is no longer the cathedral as that honour is now conferred on the **Igreja de Nossa Senhora Rainha**, a little to the west. The cross is in front of the city's modest cathedral, which is adorned with *azulejos* and features Baroque carved and gilded altars inside.

Igreja de São Vicente

St Vincent's church is Romanesque in origin, but was totally reconstructed in the 18C. The interior contains a profusion of *talha dourada* work from the 17C, and the chancel is topped by a gilded vault. According to tradition, it was in this church that the secret wedding between Dom Pedro and Dona Inês de Castro took place (*see ALCOBAÇA*).

Igreja de São Bento

This single-nave 16C church has a Renaissance-style painted wooden ceiling. The chancel, with its attractive **Mudéjar ceiling**, contains a valuable 18C gilded wooden altar screen.

Museu do Abade de Baçal★

Open Tue–Fri 10am–noon, 2pm–5pm (10am–6pm Sat–Sun and public holidays). Closed 1 Jan, Good Fri, Easter Sun, 1 May and 25 Dec. €2 (no charge on Sun and public holidays until 2pm). 273 33 15 95.

The museum is housed in the former Episcopal Palace. The collections include archaeological displays, paintings, items of local ethnological interest, coins and religious art. At the entrance, a video provides an insight into Trás-os-Montes costumes, and an interactive computer provides information on the museum, the region and its monuments. The ground floor contains a fine collection of funerary steles and milestones. On the second floor, the chapel of the former palace, with its painted ceiling, displays a set of 16C and 17C ecclesiastical vestments and polychrome pictures of saints. In Room 7, a 15C Virgin with Child in gilded and polychrome wood is worthy of particular note.

BRAVÃES★
VIANA DO CASTELO
POPULATION 582 – MICHELIN MAP 733

Bravães is a tiny village in a secluded spot along the road between Ponte da Barca and Ponte de Lima. Its church is one of the finest Romanesque buildings in Portugal and is worth a visit.

- **Information:** In nearby Ponte de Lima. *See PONTE DE LIMA.*
- **Orient Yourself:** In the very north of Portugal, close to Ponte de Lima.
- **Don't Miss:** The church – the only thing of note in the village.
- **Organizing Your Time:** Bravães is the sort of place you would visit if you were passing through, though it is worth a diversion from Ponte de Lima or Braga. If you stop here, continue to nearby Ponte de Lima for its Roman bridge.

Sight

Igreja de São Salvador★
Open 8am–7pm. ☎258 45 21 97. If the door is locked, ask at the cottage behind the church.

The façade of this small Romanesque church (12C) has a remarkable **doorway**★ whose arching is covered in an intricate decoration representing doves, monkeys, human figures and geometrical motifs; richly historiated capitals crown naively carved statue columns. The tympanum, resting on the stylised heads of a pair of bulls, is ornamented with two angels in adoration of Christ in Majesty. A low relief of the Holy Lamb is carved into the tympanum of the south doorway. There are two magnificent medieval murals of St Sebastian and the Virgin Mary. Inside, the triumphal arch is embellished by a frieze influenced by Arabic design.

MATA NACIONAL DO BUÇACO★★
BUÇACO FOREST – AVEIRO
MICHELIN MAP 733

The forest of Buçaco lies to the north of Coimbra near the Luso spa, crowning the northernmost peak of the Serra do Buçaco. It is enclosed by a stone wall pierced by several gates. The forest can be explored on foot and by car.

- **Information:** Rua Emidio Navarro –3050-201. ☎231 93 91 33.
- **Orient Yourself:** Due north of Coimbra, about 20km/12.4mi.
- **Don't Miss:** Explore the hidden forest. *See the itineraries below.*
- **Organizing Your Time:** You should spend a day here, including a picnic.
- **Especially for Kids:** An adventure and picnic in the heart of the forest.
- **Also See:** AVEIRO, COIMBRA, VISEU.

The Forest

In the 6C Benedictine monks built a hermitage in the forest at Buçaco. In 1628 the Carmelite monks built a community and surrounded the entire domain by a wall, which still stands to this day, totally enclosing the forest. They continued to preserve and develop the forest by planting new varieties of trees and other plants and obtained a papal bull from Urban VIII threatening anyone damaging the trees with excommunication. There are, today, over 700 species with the most impressive being some of the earliest, particularly the Mexican cedars.

P. Martins/MICHELIN

Palace-Hotel

Women were banned from the forest to guard the monks from any temptation. In 1834 all religious orders in Portugal were abolished and the Carmelite friars had to leave Buçaco. The forest was taken into royal care and then came under the Water and Forest Department of the government.

Visit

€2.50 per car, May–Oct; Nov–Apr free. The 105ha/250 acres of forest in Buçaco harbour 400 native varieties of tree and about 300 exotic species, including ginkgos, monkey-puzzles, cedars, Himalayan pines, thuyas, Oriental spruces, palms, arbutus, sequoias and Japanese camphor trees as well as tree ferns, hydrangeas, mimosas, camellias, magnolias, philarias and even lilies of the valley.

Palace-Hotel★

The hotel, on the site of the monastery, was built as a hunting lodge for King Carlos by the Italian architect Luigi Manini between 1888 and 1907. It is flanked by a small tower surmounted by an armillary sphere. The decoration inside is exuberant, its walls covered with huge *azulejo* panels depicting episodes from Camões' **The Lusiads**, and battle scenes

from the history of Portugal. Although it is a 5-star hotel they do tolerate visitors who just want to peer inside and it is worthwhile. You might even stop for a drink in the sumptuous bar.

Convento dos Carmelitas Descalços

Below the hotel . ⊙*Open Tue–Sat 10am–12.30pm, 2pm–5.30pm.* ⊙*Closed public holidays.* €0.60.
The remains of the Carmelite Convent completed in 1630, comprise a chapel, cloisters and a few monks' cells which were lined with cork to keep out the cold.

Walking Tours

1 Fonte Fria and Vale dos Fetos★★

1hr 15min round trip on foot.

Ermida da Nossa Senhora de Assunção

The Hermitage of Our Lady of the Assumption is one of ten hermitages in the forest to which the monks used to retire. After seeing this you can move on

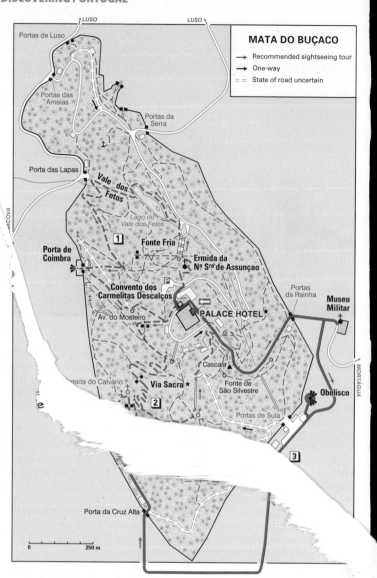

MATA DO BUÇACO

→ Recommended sightseeing tour
→ One-way
== State of road uncertain

Portas de Luso

LUSO   LUSO

Portas das Ameias

Portas da Serra

Porta das Lapas

Vale dos Fetos

Lago do Vale dos Fetos

1   Fonte Fria

Porta de Coimbra

Ermida da Nª Srª de Assunçao

Convento dos Carmelitas Descalços

Portas da Rainha

Museu Militar

Av. do Mosteiro

PALACE HOTEL

Cascata

Ermida do Calvário

Via Sacra ★

Fonte de São Silvestre

2

Obelisco

Portas de Sula

3

Porta da Cruz Alta

0   250 m

to the **Fonte Fria.** The water of the Cold Fountain rises in a cave and spills out to form a cascade down a flight of 144 stone steps; at the bottom, hydrangeas and magnolias surround the pool into which the water flows and which also mirrors some majestic conifers nearby. There is a gate from the forest, the **Porta de Coimbra** (Coimbra Gate), which was built at the same time as the 17C wall and has Rococo decoration.

▶ Return by way of Avenida do Mosteiro, an avenue of superb cedars.

2 **Via Sacra and Cruz Alta**★★

1hr round trip on foot.

▶ Take Avenida do Mosteiro below the convent, then turn left for the Via Sacra.

The **Via Sacra**★ (Way of the Cross) was built in the Baroque style in the late 17C. The chapels along the way contain life-size terracotta figures enacting the road to Calvary. You then reach the **Cruz Alta**★★ at an altitude of 545m/1 788ft.

▸ *Return by the woodland paths which lead past various hermitages.*

Driving Tour

The Cruz Alta *6km/3.7mi*

A few hundred yards from the hotel is the waterfall *(cascata)*, fed by the **Fonte de São Silvestro** nestling among ferns and hydrangeas.

Museu Militar

🕐*Open Tue–Sun 10am–5pm.* 🕐*Closed 1 Jan, Good Fri, Easter Sun and 25 Dec.* ✆*€1.* ☎*231 93 93 10.*

The military museum features the Battle of Buçaco and the campaigns of 1810, in which the Duke of Wellington faced the French.

Excursion

Luso

A little outside the forest to the north you come across **Luso**, a charming little spa town that has, for the past century or so, been pulling in crowds of mainly Portuguese visitors eager to "take the waters" which are renowned for curing rheumatism and other complaints. Luso water, bottled, is sold all over the country and you can fill up a small container free of charge. Or you can stop for an afternoon and immerse yourself in the hot, curing waters that bubble up from deep within the earth's core. Apart from this, Luso is worth a visit if for nothing else than some welcome refreshment.

CAMINHA
VIANA DO CASTELO
POPULATION 1 878 – MICHELIN MAP 733

The fortified town of Caminha was part of Portugal's northern frontier defences against Galician aspirations. It occupied a key position at the confluence of the Coura and the Minho and also controlled the Minho estuary, overlooked on the Spanish side by Monte Santa Tecla. Caminha is now a fishing village and craft centre for coppersmiths.

- 🛈 **Information:** Rua Ricardo Joaquim de Sousa – 4910-155. ☎258 92 19 52.
- ▸ **Orient Yourself:** On the northern border, on the main road towards Vigo (Spain).
- 🚫 **Don't Miss:** The Igreja Matriz.
- 🕐 **Organizing Your Time:** A few hours will allow you time to see everything.
- 👁 **Also See:** VALENÇA DO MINHO, VIANA DO CASTELO.

Sights

Praça do Conselheiro Silva Torres

The square, locally referred to as *Largo Terreiro*, is still largely medieval in character with ancient buildings grouped round a 16C granite fountain. You can clearly see that the town was once very prosperous and although a little sleepy now it still has its charm and its pride. The 15C **Casa dos Pitas** is Gothic and its emblazoned façade is elegant with curved windows.

The battlemented town hall (**Paços do Concelho**) has a lovely coffered ceiling in the council chamber. The clock tower

(Torre do Relógio) was once part of the 14C fortifications.

▶ *Go through this gate to Rua Ricardo Joaquim de Sousa, which leads to the church.*

Parish church – Igreja Matriz

Built towards the end of the 15C – when Caminho rivalled Porto and was the main shipping point for the export of port wine – the church has recently undergone extensive renovation, and stands tight in against part of the old city walls.

Inside is a magnificent *artesonado* inlaid **ceiling**★ of maplewood. Each octagonal panel, framed in stylised cabling, bears a rose at its centre. On the right, stands a statue of St Christopher, patron saint of boatmen.

The Chapel of the Holy Sacrament, to the right of the chancel, contains a 17C gilded wood tabernacle illustrated with scenes from The Passion by Francisco Fernandes. There is a magnificent granite carved pulpit. There are some wonderful figures carved on the Renaissance doorways.

There is a small **museum** in the nearby library (○ *open 9.30am–12.30pm, 2pm–5pm*) with a motley collection of items found in nearby archaeological sites.

Ferry trip to La Guardia

From Caminha you can take a ferry across the river Coura to La Guardia in Spain (◎ with a one-hour time change!). *Ferries operate daily from 8am–7pm (from 10am Sun and until 8pm May–Jul); €2.50 per car; €0.70 on foot.*

CARAMULO
VISEU
POPULATION 1 546 – MICHELIN MAP 733

Caramulo, a little to the south west of Viseu, is a spa at an altitude of 800m/2 625ft on a wooded hillside in the Serra de Caramulo. Parks and gardens enhance this town on the schist and granite massif which is wooded with pines, oaks and chestnuts and also has crops such as maize, vines and olives. The western slope, which descends gently towards the Aveiro coastal plain, is completely different from the eastern slope where the sharper relief is cut away by tributaries of the Mondego.

- **Information:** Estrada Principal do Caramulo. 3475-031. ☎232 86 14 37.
- **Orient Yourself:** Inland from Porto, close to Viseu.
- **Don't Miss:** The Museu do Caramulo.
- **Organizing Your Time:** An all-day excursion to see its best parts.
- **Also See:** VISEU.

Sight

Museu do Caramulo★

○ *Open 10am–1pm, 2pm–5pm (6pm Mar–Sept).* ○ *Closed 1 Jan, Good Fri, Easter Sun, 25 Dec.* €6. ☎232 86 12 70. The museum, named after its founder Abel Lacerda, comprises two sections. An **Ancient and Modern Art Exhibition** contains statues from the 15C Portuguese School including a Virgin and Child, a series of tapestries from

Tournai representing the arrival of the Portugueuse in India and a large number of paintings: Picasso (still-life), Fernand Léger, Dufy, Dalí and Braque. The other part contains an interesting **Automobile Exhibition**★ with some 50 vehicles, all beautifully maintained in working order, on display. Among the oldest are an 1899 Peugeot and a 1902 Darraco; the most prestigious include Hispano-Suizas, Lamborghinis and Ferraris. There are also some bicycles and motorbikes.

Driving Tour

Pinoucas★ *3km/1.8mi.*

▶ *Leave Caramulo heading north on the N 230; after 2km/1.2mi bear left on a dirt track which ends at the watchtower 1km/0.6mi further on.*

From the top (alt 1 062m/3 481ft) there is an impressive **panorama** over the Serra de Caramulo.

Serra de Caramulo *7.5km/4.6mi.*

▶ *Leave Caramulo heading west on Avenida Abel Lacerda which becomes the N 230-3; 3km/1.8mi further on you pass on your left the road leading to Cabeço da Neve.*

Caramulinho★★

30min round trip on foot, by a rocky path which has 130 steps cut into its face.

The tip of the Serra do Caramulo (alt 1 075m/3 527ft) makes an excellent **viewpoint** over the Serra da Lapa in the north east, the Serra da Estrela in the south east, the Serra da Lousã and Serra do Buçaco to the south, over the coastal plain to the west, and over the Serra da Gralheira to the north.

▶ *Return to the intersection with the Cabeço da Neve road, which you then take to the viewpoint.*

Cabeço da Neve
Alt 995m/3 264ft.

This summit has plunging **views** to the south and towards the east across wooded hillsides dotted with tiny villages, the Mondego basin and the Serra da Estrela.

CARVOEIRO★
FARO
MICHELIN MAP 1 576 – LOCAL MAP SEE ALGARVE

Built into a narrow indentation in the cliff, this fishing village has become a pleasant seaside resort that has not yet been spoilt by modern buildings.

- **Information:** Praia do Carvoeiro – 8400-517 Lagoa. ☎282 35 77 28.
- ▶ **Orient Yourself:** On the Algarve coast between Faro and Albufeira.
- **Parking:** Difficult, especially in summer. There are car parks by the beaches.
- **Don't Miss:** The beaches.
- **Organizing Your Time:** It's the sort of place to stay, but not in July or August.
- **Especially for Kids:** Slide & Splash – near Lagos.
- **Also See:** SAGRES, LUZ.

Sight

Algar Seco★★
500m/546.8yd beyond the Miradouro de Nossa Senhora da Encarnação, plus 30min round trip on foot.
Leave the car in the car park.
Below Cabo Carvoeiro, the **marine site** of Algar Seco with its dramatic rock formations, is reached through a maze (including 134 steps) of reddish rocks sculpted by the sea in the shape of peaks and arches. On the right *(sign "A Boneca")*, a short tunnel leads under a conically formed ceiling into a cavern (converted into a refreshment room in summer) which has two natural "windows" from which there is a view encompassing the western cliffs. On the left, a path leads to a headland from which one can see the entrance to a deep underwater cave. There are several blow-holes that are dramatic when the sea is rough.

The **sea caves** of Cabo Carvoeiro can be visited by boat during the season. *To visit the sea caves, ask the fishermen in Algar Seco or on Praia do Carvoeiro.*

Address Book

For coin ranges, see cover flap.

WHERE TO STAY

⊖⊖ **Vila Horizonte** Estrada do Farol 1260, ☎*282 356 047*. Ten minutes from the beach this is a pleasant little place with a nice garden and pool.

⊖ **O Castelo** Rua do Casino, ☎*282 357 416* The other side of the bay a lovely castle-like guest house.

⊖ **Brigitte Lemieux** Rampa de Nossa Senhora da Encarnação, ☎*282 356 318*. Run by a Canadian lady this little place has a few rooms with kitchenettes .

WHERE TO EAT

⊖⊖ **Restaurante Boneca Bar**, Algar Seco, ☎*282 358 391*. By the rock formations at Algar Seco this is a lively restaurant that serves very good fish. On a warm evening sit outside by the sea.

⊖⊖ **Rafaiol Restaurante,** Rua do Barranco, ☎*282 357 164*. Set in a lovely old mansion surrounded by a terrace this is an ideal place for meat and fish, and some impressive desserts that are definitely not low-calorie!

Activities

The entire Algarve coast is wonderful for golf and Carvoeiro is no exception with an 18-hole championship course, a 9-hole course and a David Leadbetter Golf Academy.

You will also find a very good family-run diving school here, offering both rental of equipment and, for those less experienced, lessons, which cost about €60 for a three-hour introductory lesson; €120 for a full day and open-water scuba diving for €225/410 for two or four days.

CASCAIS ★
LISBOA

POPULATION 35 000 – MICHELIN MAP 733

Cascais is both a traditional fishing port of age-old tradition and a bustling holiday resort. It is progressively expanding into a smart suburb of Lisbon with its developed centre and pleasant pedestrian streets lined with shops and restaurants. It is a pleasant place to visit, popular with foreign visitors and Portuguese alike.

- **Information:** Rua Visconde da Luz – 2750-415. ☎214 86 82 04 or 214 86 70 44.
- **Orient Yourself:** About 30km/18.6mi west along the coast from Lisbon.
- **Parking:** Not too difficult, apart from Friday and Saturday evenings.
- **Don't Miss:** The old town hall square which is lively; Boca do Inferno.
- **Organizing Your Time:** It's the place to stay at least for a weekend. Make sure you visit the beaches here and get over to nearby Estoril with its huge casino!
- **Also See:** ESTORIL, SINTRA.

A Bit of History

In medieval times, Cascais relied on its fishing and agriculture industries, providing Lisbon with produce by the 13C. Tourism came to Cascais in 1870 when the court moved here for the summer to escape the heat of Lisbon. With the court came a tradition of elegance and a group of architects. The **royal palace**, or former citadel, sits on the promontory which protects the bay on the south west. It is now an official residence of the Head of State.

Sight

Museu-Biblioteca dos Condes de Castro Guimarães

Museum: ✏ *guided tours (30min), Tue–Sun 10am–5pm.* ◷ *Closed public holidays.* ✆€1.75 (no charge on Sun). ☎214 82 54 07. *Library:* ◷ *open Mon–Fri 9am–5pm (1pm Sat).* ◷ *Closed public holidays and Sat in Jul, Aug and Sept.* ☎214 82 54 07.

On the coast road, this 19C nobleman's residence, (originally owned by an Irishman which is why you will see cloverleaves everywhere – sadly he went bankrupt and had to sell the place) with a central patio, has a large collection of 17C Portuguese and Indo-Portuguese furniture and *azulejos*, 18C and 19C Portuguese gold and silversmith work and pottery, 18C bronzes, carpets and Chinese vases and many valuable books, the most valuable of which is an illustrated 16C *Chronicles of D. Afonso Henriques* and has a drawing of pre-earthquake Lisbon.

Excursions

From Cascais to Praia do Guincho★

8km/5mi heading west on the coast road – about 30min.

On leaving Cascais, pass the former royal palace on the left.

Boca do Inferno★

A restaurant with a few pines standing on the left marks the site of this **abyss**★ formed by marine erosion. The sea, entering under a rock arch, booms and crashes particularly in stormy weather. The power of the ocean is spectacular to watch.

The road continues as a *corniche* above the sea, offering some fine views of the wild coast. Beyond Cabo Raso (small fort), where the road turns off towards the Serra de Sintra, stretches of sand pounded by rough seas can be seen between the rocky points before you come to Praia do Guincho.

Praia do Guincho★

This immense beach is backed by windswept dunes and a small fort; the imposing headland, Cabo da Roca, can be seen. This is a popular spot for surfing and windsurfing (the World Windsurfing Championships have been held here) with the Atlantic waves crashing onto the crescent-shaped beach but there are strong undercurrents and it can be dangerous for inexperienced surfers. From this beach you can see the imposing cliffs of Cabo da Roca quite clearly.

Golf in Cascais

Golfers have two very good courses to choose from on the outskirts of Cascais. In the grounds of the Quinta da Marinha hotel is an excellent 18-hole course with some very challenging holes. A short walking distance away you will come across one of the newest courses in Portugal, **Oitavos**: a links course laid out in traditional fashion – nine out, nine back. It runs straight out towards Cabo da Roca, the most westerly point of mainland Europe. There are several other courses close by, all within 30 minutes' drive.

Address Book

✆ *For coin ranges, see cover flap.*

WHERE TO STAY

▭▭ **Solar Dom Carlos** – *Rua Latina.* ☎214 828 115. A lovely 16C mansion is the setting for this mid-price hotel.

▭▭ **Hotel Baia** – *Ave Com da Grande Guerra.* ☎214 831 095. *www.hotelbaia.com.* A modern seafront hotel with a rooftop pool, good restaurant and some balcony rooms.

WHERE TO EAT

▭▭ **O Pescador** – *R das Flores* ☎214 832 054. The name tells you this is the finest fish restaurant in town.

▭▭ **Jardim dos Frangos** – *Ave Com da Grande Guerra.* And this is the place for chicken, indoors or outside.

▭ **Dom Manolo's** *Ave Com da Grande Guerra.* ☎214 831 126. Good value for money.

CASTELO BRANCO
CASTELO BRANCO
POPULATION 56 001 – MICHELIN MAP 733

The town was well fortified as it lay strategically close to the Spanish border, but nevertheless it suffered a number of invasions and occupations – events which have left few historic monuments. The maraudings of the Napoleonic troops in 1807 were among the most devastating. The scant ruins of a Templars' stronghold dominate the town. Today the capital of Beira Baixa is a peaceful, flower-decked city living on its trade in cork, cheese, honey and olive oil. It is particularly known for the fine bedspreads (colchas) embroidered in different colours in a tradition going back to the 17C.

- **Information:** Alameda da Liberdade – 6000-074. ☎272 33 03 39.
- **Orient Yourself:** The southern edge of the Serra da Estrela, a little north of the Tagus as it spills into Portugal from Spain.
- **Don't Miss:** The new Cargaleiro museum and the village of Monsanto.
- **Organizing Your Time:** Give yourself up to a full day here.
- **Also See:** SERRA DA ESTRELA.

Sights

Museu Francisco Tavares Proença Júnior

Open Tue–Sun 10am–12.30pm, 2pm–5.30pm. Closed 1 Jan, Good Fri, Easter Sun, 1 May and 25 Dec. €2 (no charge Sun and public holidays 10am–12.30pm). ☎272 34 42 77.

This museum is housed in the old episcopal palace and contains an interesting collection of coins, earthenware, ancient weapons and Roman pottery on the ground floor, and 16C Flemish tapestries (Story of Lot) on the staircase. Perhaps of more interest to many visitors is the large collection of colchas (silk embroidered bedspreads) for which the town is famous. Exhibits upstairs include more tapestries, paintings of the 16C Portuguese School (a **Santo António** attributed to Francisco Henriques) and antique Portuguese furniture.

Gardens, Antigo Paço Episcopal★★

Open 9am–5pm (7pm in summer). Closed 1 Jan and 25 Dec. €2.

The 17C gardens belonged to the Episcopal Palace and now form an unusual ensemble of topiary, banks of flowers, azulejo-covered ornamental pools, fountains (one of which is activated by a clap – apparently one particular 18C bishop used to like 'surprising' visiting ladies by clapping his hands as they passed the fountain, giving them a soaking) and Baroque statues.

An alley, which runs beside the Crown Lake and ends in two flights of steps, is lined by balustrades peopled with statues: the Apostles and the Evangelists on the right, Kings of Portugal on the left.

Convento da Graça e Museu de Arte Sacra da Misericórdia

Guided tours (20min) Mon–Fri 9am–noonm 2pm–5pm. Closed public holidays. €0.50. ☎272 34 44 54, ext 57.

Opposite the palace is the Convento da Graça, which has retained a Manueline door from its primitive early-16C construction. Inside the Santa Casa da Misericórdia, a small sacred art museum contains the statues of Queen Saint Isabel and St John of God with a pauper, a Virgin and Child, a 16C St Matthew and two marble statues of Christ on the cross.

Medieval town

The medieval town, with its traditional stone-paved narrow streets, clothes and birdcages hanging from the windows, has preserved a few interesting buildings such as the former Paços do Conselho (Town Hall) on the Praça Velha, dating from the 1600s but significantly

Gardens, Antigo Paço Episcopal

H. Champollion/MICHELIN

remodelled since, the 17C Arco do Bispo on the attractive Praça Camões, as well as several other delightful palaces.

Museu Cargaleiro★

🕐 *Open Tue–Sun 10am–1pm, 2pm–6pm.* 💶 *€2.* ☎ *272 33 73 94.*

This is a museum of contemporary works by the Portuguese artist Manual Cargaleiro (who was responsible for the decoration of the Champs-Élysées-Clémenceau metro station in Paris). Works by his friends are also here, including a Picasso. Engravings, ceramics and paintings fill this interesting gallery.

Driving Tour

Tour via Monsanto

150km/94mi.

▸ *Leave Castelo Branco by ② on map and follow the N 233 north east to Penamacor.*

Penamacor

Situated at an altitude of 600m/1 968ft, the village, which dates from Roman times, is crowned by a castle, the construction of which was ordered by Dom Sancho I in 1209; parts of the wall and the keep can still be seen today. The panoramic view over the plains and surrounding hills is impressive, and the walk through the old part of Penamacor is particularly pleasant.

The **Igreja da Misericórdia** (🕐 *open Mon–Sat 9am–5pm;* 🕐 *closed public holidays;* ☎ *272 39 41 33)* has a fine Manueline door and a high gilded wood altar.

The **Convento de Santo António** (🕐 *same opening times as Igreja da Misericórdia)* founded in the 16C, contains a chapel with a roof and pulpit in lavish **talha dourada** style.

▸ *Take the N 332 south as far as Medelim, and then the N 239 east.*

Monsanto★★ – 👁 *See MONSANTO.*

▸ *Return to Medelim and take the N 332 south.*

Idanha-a-Velha★

This tiny village, once a prosperous Roman settlement, seems more like an open-air museum with excavations everywhere. By following the signposted path you will pass the 13C Torre dos Templários, a Templars' tower built on top of a Roman temple; the cathedral (**sé**), rebuilt five times on a site with paleo-Christian origins; a Roman bridge rebuilt during the Middle Ages; and many other historical remains.

▸ *Rejoin the N 332 south to Alcafozes, then follow the N 354 towards Ladoeiro. From here, return to Castelo Branco on the N 240.*

CASTELO DE VIDE★
PORTALEGRE
POPULATION 2 558 – MICHELIN MAP 733
LOCAL MAP SEE SERRA DE SÃO MAMEDE

Castelo de Vide lies at the foot of its castle, which stands perched on an elongated foothill of the Serra de São Mamede just to the north of Portalegre, very close to the Spanish border. It owes its attraction to old whitewashed houses stepped high up the hillside along winding alleys brilliant with flowers. The town is also a spa; its waters are allegedly beneficial for various ailments.

- **Information:** Rua Bartolomeu Álvares da Santa, 81-83 – 7320-117. ☎245 90 13 61 or 245 90 13 50.
- **Orient Yourself:** 20km/12.4mi north of Portalegre, on the Spanish border.
- **Don't Miss:** The Jewish Quarter and Synagogue.
- **Organizing Your Time:** About a half day is plenty to see all you need.
- **Also See:** MARVÃO.

Sights

Castle
🕐*The castle is always open. The keep is open from 9am–12.30pm, 2pm–5.30pm (10am–7pm in summer).*
From the top of the **keep** in the old castle there is a very good **view**★ of the town. Also visit the **Praça de Dom Pedro V** where you will see the Igreja de Santa Maria opposite two 17C buildings, the Baroque Palácio da Torre and the Santo Amaro Hospital. The 13C Sinagoga is the oldest building in town, set in the old alleyways of the Judairia, the Jewish Quarter.

CASTRO MARIM
FARO
POPULATION 4 549 – MICHELIN MAP 733
LOCAL MAP SEE ALGARVE

Castro Marim abuts a high point overlooking the marshy Lower Guadiana plain near its outflow into the Gulf of Cádiz. Facing the town across the estuary – and the border – is the Spanish town of Ayamonte. Castro Marim, which was in existence in Roman times, became the seat of the Knights of Christ on the dissolution of the Order of Templars in Portugal in 1321, until it was transferred to Tomar in 1334.

- **Information:** Praça 1º de Maio, 2–4 – 8950-150. ☎281 53 12 32.
- **Orient Yourself:** Eastern end of the Algarve, a little inland from the coast.
- **Don't Miss:** The nearby salt marshes – with their flamingoes.
- **Organizing Your Time:** Half a day would be ideal.
- **Also See:** VILA REAL DE SANTO ANTÓNIO, TAVIRA.

Visit

The ruins of Castro Marim's fortified **castle**, (🕐*open daily 9am–7pm (6pm Oct–Apr),* are to the north of the village, and the view from the parapet gives a wonderful view not only over the extensive salt marshes around the town but also the remains of the 17C Forte de São Sebastião. Within the partly restored walls are the foundations of yet another castle dating back to the 12C.

ALTO VALE DO RIO **CÁVADO**★
UPPER CÁVADO VALLEY – BRAGA AND VILA REAL
MICHELIN MAP 733

The course of the Cávado river above Braga is steeply enclosed between the Serra do Gerês and the Serras de Cabreira and do Barroso. In this rocky upper valley, as in its tributary, the Rabagão, a series of dams control reservoir lakes of a deep blue colour which are surrounded by wooded mountain slopes crested by bare peaks – altogether a highly picturesque landscape.

- **Information:** In Montalegre – Turismo in town centre. ☎276 511 010; in Chaves – Terreiro de Cavalaria. ☎2476 340 660.
- **Orient Yourself:** In the very north of Portugal just below the Parque Nacional da Peneda-Gerês – the lakes form part of the frontier with Spain.
- **Don't Miss:** Montalegre, Braga or Chaves.
- **Organizing Your Time:** You could spend a couple of days here.
- **Also See:** PARQUE NACIONAL DA PENEDA-GERÊS.

A Bit of History

The Cávado, which is 118km/73mi long, rises to 1 500m/4 859ft in the Serra do Larouco not far from the Spanish frontier; after crossing the Montalegre plateau, the river drops sharply as it follows a series of rock faults running north east–south west. The hydro-electric development of this upper valley began in 1946. There are dams at Alto Cávado, Paradela, Salamonde and Caniçada on the Cávado, at Alto Rabagão and Venda Nova on the Rabagão and at Vilarinho des Funas on the Homen.

Driving Tour

From Braga to Chaves
235km/146mi

Allow about half a day (not including visit to Braga). ♿*For local map, see PARQUE NACIONAL DA PENEDA-GERÊS.*

Braga★ ♿*See BRAGA.*

- *Leave Braga by ① in the direction of Chaves.*

On leaving Braga, the Cávado valley becomes deep and wild; the road climbs along the south slopes which are covered with pine and eucalyptus. 11km/6.8mi further, the castle of Póvoa

de Lanhoso can be seen. After this village, the Cávado valley is hidden, while on the right the parallel valley of the Rio Ave appears. Then the road climbs up through a bare and rocky landscape. A little before Cerdeirinhas, the N 103 turns and descends following the Cávado river, running along the edge of the Parque Nacional da Peneda-Gerês. The road then twists and turns, giving stunning **views**★ of two reservoirs: the 15km/9.3mi-long **Represa de Caniçada**★ and the Salamonde. Both lie below pine scattered slopes, dominated by the bare summits of the Serra do Gerês.

- *Bear left off the N 103 on the Paradela road over the crest of the Vanda Nova dam; at the next crossroads bear right.*

As the road rises rapidly, the **views**★★ of the Serra do Gerês become even more beautiful. A little before Paradela, on the left, there is a village built on a rocky projection at the foot of a shale hillock, which has been hollowed out at the back by a gigantic quarry.

- *The road crosses Paradela and arrives at the dam of the same name.*

At Paradela you enter the eastern part of the **Parque Nacional da Peneda-Gerês**, known as the Barroso region,

Upper Cávado Valley

where life seems to have stood still, before reaching **Represa da Paradela**★. This reservoir lake, sitting at an altitude of 112m/367ft above the Cávado river, has a lovely mountain **setting**★.

Pitões das Júnias, a village 15km/9.3mi north of Paradela, has some Romanesque ruins belonging to a Benedictine monastery which dates back to the Visigothic period. Several arches indicate where the cloisters once stood.

▶ *Return to the N 103. The road runs alongside the* **Venda Nova reservoir**.

Vila da Ponte

This village perches upon a rock spur.

▶ *After Pisões, a path to the right leads to the Alto Rabagão dam.*

Barragem do Alto Rabagão★

The dam stands as a massive concrete wall. Go to the crest, where there is a good **view** over the reservoir-lake.

▶ *Return to the N 103. The road skirts the north edge of the lake before turning left to Montalegre.*

Montalegre

Montalegre was built at an altitude of 966m/3 170ft. Old red-roofed houses encircle the walls of the ruined 14C castle, the keep of which looks out over the wild and mountainous plateau.

The pine and heather-lined N 308 on the plateau returns to the N 103. Then the road crosses arid rock-strewn moors covered with heather. The plateau suddenly disappears as the **view**★★ extends dramatically to take in a vast green and cultivated basin at the far end of which can be seen the low-lying old villages of **Sapiãos** and **Boticas**.

Serra do Barroso★

Continuing along the N 311, pass through **Carvalhelhos**, famous for its spa waters. On the next summit, with access via a dirt road, you find the **Castro de Carvalhelhos**, a settlement dating from the Iron Age, with its foundations, doors and walls still clearly visible. A road leads from Carvalhelhos to **Alturas do Barroso**, a traditional village in these harsh, isolated mountains. From there, head to **Vilarinho Seco**★, the most traditional mountain village in this area. It has no modern buildings, and the rural two-storey dwellings of loose, dark stone with wooden veranda and staircase and thatch roof appear not to have changed in centuries. Hens and goats run loose, with the most frequent traffic on the street the pairs of the impressive breed of Barroso oxen.

▶ *Rejoin the N 311 at Viveiro towards Sapiãos, then follow the N 103 to Chaves.*

CHAVES
VILA REAL
POPULATION 14 300 – MICHELIN MAP 733

Chaves is one of the most attractive little towns in Trás-os-Montes. Built on the banks of the Tâmega, the small town of Aquae Flaviae was known to the Romans for its thermal springs, and became an important stopping point on the Astorga-Braga road when Trajan built a bridge over the Tâmega. In 1160, after being recaptured from the Moors, Chaves was fortified to ensure its command of the valley facing the Spanish fortress of Verín. Today the old castle and dozens of picturesque white houses with wooden verandas give the quiet spa town considerable style.

- **Information:** Terreiro de Cavalaria – 5400-193. ☎276 34 06 61.
- ▶ **Orient Yourself:** 72km/44mi north east of Vila Real, near the Spanish border.
- **Parking:** Difficult in the town centre but plenty of space around the Forte de São Francisco.
- **Don't Miss:** Try the natural spas whilst you're here.
- **Organizing Your Time:** Half a day should be just enough but if you are 'taking the waters' you'll need a few days.
- **Also See:** BRAGANÇA, VILA REAL.

Sights

Ponte Romana
With the passing of the years this Roman bridge has lost its stone parapets and even some arches, but adds a considerable charm to the town.

Igreja da Misericórdia★
The façade of this small 17C Baroque church is embellished with verandas and twisted columns. The inside walls are covered with *azulejos* showing scenes from the Life of Christ attributed to Oliveira Bernardes. There is a large gilded wooden altarpiece; the ceiling is decorated with 18C paintings, one of which, in the centre, is a Visitation.

Museu da Região Flaviense
○*Open Mon–Fri 9am–12.30pm, 2pm–5.30pm, Sat–Sun 2pm–5.30pm.* ○*Closed public holidays.* ✆*€1 (includes visit to Museu Militar).* ☎*276 34 05 00*
This museum, housed in a fine 17C building, contains collections which trace the history of the town including prehistoric stone relics – the main piece in the display is a megalithic **figure in human form** (about 2000 BC) – and

Roman remains including sculptures and military columns. Exhibits also include ancient coins, a banknote plate, a magic lantern and radio receivers dating from the early wireless days (pre-1930).

Torre de Menagem
This massive square tower with battlements at the corners is all that remains of the castle. Built by King Dinis in the 14C, the castle was the residence of the first Duke of Bragança, illegitimate son of Dom João I.

The Spas (Termas)
In **Chaves** itself is one spa with waters rich in minerals, recommended for digestive disorders and rheumatism.
The Termas de Vidago *(11km/6.8mi from Chaves)* are set in a top-class hotel situated in a beautiful park. The water from the spa is used for treating digestive disorder and is also bottled and sold throughout Portugal.
The **Caldas Santas de Carvalhelhos** *(30km/18.6mi from Chaves)* are surrounded by mountains – the sparkling water is also good for digestive problems and is bottled for sale as well being sold throughout Portugal.

COIMBRA★★
COIMBRA
POPULATION 148 1443– MICHELIN MAP 733

Overlooked by the tall tower of its old university, Coimbra stands on a hillside at the foot of which flows the Mondego. Many poets, inspired by the romantic setting★, have immortalised the charm of the city, an old capital of Portugal, and have helped to make it a centre of fine arts and letters. Although the town has spread substantially over recent decades, and has been surrounded by modern districts, the centre is still distinctly divided into the upper town *(A Cidade Alta)*, which is traditionally the university and episcopal quarter, and the lower town *(A Cidade Baixa)* or shopping area.

- **Information:** Largo Dom Dinis. ☎239 83 25 91. Praça da República. ☎239 83 32 02.
- ▶ **Orient Yourself:** Midway between Porto and Lisbon, inland a little.
- **P Parking:** There is a large parking area *(free)* on the south side of the Santa Clara bridge, along the banks of the Mondego river. In town, parking is hard to find.
- **Don't Miss:** The University library in particular.
- ◷ **Organizing Your Time:** At least a full day to fully explore.
- **Especially for Kids:** Portugal dos Pequeninos.
- **Also See:** CONÍMBRIGA, FIGUEIRA DA FOZ.

Background

The University
The University, the oldest in Portugal, was originally established in Lisbon by King Dinis in 1290 and only transferred to Coimbra in 1308 though it was not until 1537 that Coimbra became its permanent home. Teachers from Oxford (England), Paris, Salamanca and Italy were drawn to the new university, making the town one of the most important humanist centres of the period.

The Coimbra School of Sculpture
In 1530 several French sculptors formed a group of artists under the protection of their patron, Cardinal Georges d'Amboise. They were joined by a few prominent Portuguese artists of the day and created a school of sculpture in the town. Their art was inspired by Italian decorative forms: doorways, pulpits, altarpieces and the low reliefs surrounding altars in local churches were delicately carved out of Ança stone.

View of the city from the Mondego

A. Cassaigne/MICHELIN

Address Book

♿ *For coin ranges, see the Legend on the cover flap.*

WHERE TO STAY

🛏🛏🛏 **Astória** – *Av. Emídio Navarro 21.* ☎*239 85 30 20. www.almeidahotels. com. 64 rooms* ⬜. The Astória is magnificently situated overlooking the Mondego river in an elegant, Parisian-style early 20C building. The hotel, which in the past was popular with artists and writers, retains a certain charm, particularly in its dining and reading rooms.

🛏 **Pensão Santa Cruz** – *Praça 8 de Maio, 21 (reception on 2nd floor).* ☎*239 82 61 97. www.pensaosantacruz.com. 14 rooms.* The main charm of this little *pensão* is its location, close to the University and right in the heart of things. The staff are welcoming, but remember that this is the heart of the night-life area so it's not exactly quiet at night.

🛏 **Residencial Vitória** – *R. da Sota, 11-19.* ☎*239 82 40 49 or 239 84 28 96. 20 rooms* ⬜. The rooms at this small hotel are comfortable, if somewhat basic. Good location and some rooms are air conditioned.

🛏 **Residencial Domus** – *R. Adelion Veiga, 62 (reception on 1st floor).* ☎*239 83 85 84. 20 rooms* ⬜. A good welcome at this quiet and comfortable family-run hotel set back from the road. Rooms are furnished in rustic style and most have an en-suite bathroom.

🛏 **Residencial Coimbra** – *R. das Azeiteiraas, 55–61.* ☎*239 83 79 96/7. 15 rooms* ⬜. In a small side street in the city centre this quiet hotel has very comfortable rooms. The class and comfort at budget rates come as a nice surprise.

WHERE TO EAT

🍴 **Shmoo Café** – *R. Corpo de Deus, 68.* ☎*965 21 45 75 (mobile). www. shmoocafe.blogspot.com. Closed Sun.* Near the Santa Clara church, this tiny café, painted bright red, serves beautiful salads, exotic fruit and vegetables, and meat and cheese dishes served on wooden platters.

🍴 **Snack-Bar Daniel Sun** – *R. da Lousa, 50-52.* ☎*934 83 09 76 (mobile). Closed Sun.* This little bar close to Praça 8 de Maio is very traditional and well-frequented by the locals, who will sit at the bar and order octopus salad, mussels, grilled cod and other tasty dishes of meat as well as fish. If you want to feel like a local, this is the place.

🍴 **Adega Paço do Conde** – *R. Paço do Conde, 1.* ☎*239 82 56 05. Closed Sun.* A traditional Portuguese restaurant offering quality fish and meat dishes. You can eat in one of two small salons or in a larger dining room, the latter obviously not quite as intimate and quiet as the others. Very good service.

🍴🍴 **Feb** – *R. do Corvo, 8–16.* ☎*239 82 81 48. Closed Sun.* In a road off Praça 8 de Maio, this restaurant is highly prized by the locals for the quality of its cuisine. Ignore the ground-floor bar as the restaurant is on the first floor.

🍴 **Zé Neto** – *R. das Azeiteiras, 8;* ☎*239 826 786.* An excellent family-run restaurant serving inexpensive local food with cabrito (kid) often on the menu. Very busy but with excellent, rapid service, you will find this to be one of the best choices in town.

NIGHTLIFE

The town, very quiet in the summer, bursts into life once the academic year starts in early autumn. The students start the evening by meeting at the outdoor cafés in the Praça da República for an apéritif, though these places are full of coffee-drinkers during the day.

Café Teatro is well known and features live performances some evenings (ticket holders only). **Café Santa Cruz** (close to the church) is one of the best places to watch the world go by and has the most attractive interior. **Piano Negro** (*R. Borges Carneiro*) is a smoky yet lively place with good music. Then as the evening wears on the venues change to the clubs, many of which do not open much before 10pm but stay open late (2am–4am) such as **Vinyl** or **RMX**), which have live music, or to places such as **Via Latina** (with its outdoor terrace), **Scotch Club** (which stays open latest) or **OK Bar**. Also currently in fashion are the bars and clubs on the other side of the river. The

Galeria Bar Santa Clara with its pleasant garden (in front of one of the side gates of Portugal dos Pequenitos) and the **Bar de São Francisco**, a little further along, are also very popular, as are **le Calhabar** (*R. do Brasil*) and **Noites Longas** (*R. Almeida Garret*). Back in the old town Shmoo Café is a popular haunt for the chic crowd, unlike Café Tropical which caters for the students. **Quebra Costas** (*Escadas do Quebra Costas 45-49; ☎239 82 16 61; www.quebra costas.com*) is another hotspot at night, but not in the Praça da República area – this one is near the old Cathedral and has a terrace to escape the heat inside.

Open until 4am. Finally, **À Capela** (*Capela de Nossa Senhora da Vitória; 239 83 39 85*) has nightly fado shows at 9.30pm, 10.30pm and 11.30pm. Very good value and nice surroundings. You'll find the Coimbra brand of *fado* on the streets at certain times of the year, mainly on Thursday and Saturday evenings. Unlike the Lisbon variety, here it is sung by men accompanied by a guitar and tells primarily of student loves.

Student life

The city, peaceful throughout the summer, reawakens with a start at the beginning of the academic year and the return of the 20 000 students, many of whom live in groups known as "republics" in an ancient tradition (*⌖ see below*). They wear different coloured ribbons to denote their faculty.

Old Town and University★

The old town lies on the Alcáçova hill, reached by a tangle of narrow alleys cut by steps with expressive names such as Escadas de Quebra-Costas (Broken Ribs Steps).

Queima das Fitas (Burning of the Ribbons)

The ribbons worn on the students' black capes indicate the academic subject studied: blue for arts, yellow for medicine, red for law. At the beginning of May, the old cathedral square is the setting for a festival marking the end of the university year, during which the ribbons are burned. This ceremony has today become one vast, week-long party fuelled by free beer handed out by breweries. It can get pretty wild.

Porta de Almedina

This gateway with an Arab name (*medina* means city in Arabic) is one of the last remaining sections of the medieval wall. It is topped by a tower and adorned with a statue of the Virgin and Child, which stands between two coats of arms.

Sé Velha★★

⌚Open Mon–Thu and Sat 10am–6pm, Fri 10am–1pm. ⌚Closed public holidays.
The **old cathedral**, Portugal's earliest, was built between 1140 and 1175 by two French master craftsmen in a fortress-like style (the Moors were still a threat at the time). In the **Interior** a wide gallery above the aisles opens onto the nave by means of a graceful triforium with Byzantine capitals, which, like the lantern over the transept crossing, show Oriental influence. The Flamboyant Gothic **altarpiece★** in gilded wood at the high altar is by the Flemish masters Olivier de Gand (Ghent) and Jean d'Ypres. At the base, the four Evangelists support the Nativity and the Resurrection; above, surrounded by four saints, an attractive group celebrates the Assumption of the Virgin.

In the **Capela do Sacramento★** there is a good Renaissance composition by Tomé Velho, one of Jean de Rouen's disciples. Below a figure of Christ in Benediction surrounded by ten Apostles, the four Evangelists face the Virgin and Child and St Joseph across the tabernacle.

The Republics

Republics were created at the end of the 18C by students who wanted to introduce the French revolutionary ideas of the time into their communities. Although they were residences in which debate and protest flourished, as time passed they were also to become a cheap and practical form of accommodation. They generally number between 12 and 20 students, usually from the same region, who live together, renting vast apartments and managing the group budget in turn. Traditionally, they employ the services of a maid *(tricana)* to prepare meals, which are eaten communally. As you wander around the city you will probably come across some of these republics, which are recognisable by flags or paintings on the façades of their buildings. The **República dos Kágados** *(Rua do Correio, 98)*, which was founded in 1933, is currently the oldest republic in the city, while the **Real República Corsário das Ilhas** *(Couraça dos Apóstolos, 112)* is distinguishable by the pirates on its flag. Most of the republics have humorous names, often based on puns.

The late 13C **cloisters** *(€1)* are an example of transitional Gothic architecture; they were restored in the 18C. Blind arcades are surmounted by round bays filled with a variety of tracery. In the chapter-house, on the south side, are several tombs, including that of Dom Sesnando, the first Christian governor of Coimbra, who died in 1091.

Sé Nova

Open Tue–Sat 9am–12.30pm, 2pm–6.30pm; Sun for services only. Closed public holidays.

The **'new' cathedral**, the construction of which started in 1598, was part of the Jesuits' college of the "Eleven Thousand Virgins" until the order was disbanded in 1759. The façade comprises two superimposed sections; the four niches in the lower part house statues of saints from the Society of Jesus. The vast, single-nave interior is covered by a barrel vault topped by a high lantern. The Baroque style predominates in the side chapels and the high altar, where an imposing gilded wood altarpiece and a magnificent silver throne are of particular note. The baptismal font to the left of the entrance is Manueline in style and was originally part of the old cathedral.

Universidade Velha★★

Open Apr–Oct, 9am–7.30pm; Nov–Mar, 9.30am–5.30pm. Closed 1 Jan, 25 Dec. €6 (library only, €3.50; Ceremonial Hall only, €3.50). ☎239 85 98 00.

Courtyard, Universidade Velha

A. Cassaigne/MICHELIN

COIMBRA

8 de Maio Pr.	Y 56	Brasil R. do	X	J. de Almeida R.	V	
Adelino Veiga R.	YZ	Carmo R. do	Z	Dr Dias da Silva Av.	VX	
Afrânio Peixoto R.	V	Colégio Novo R. do	Y 12	Dr João Jacinto R.	Y 18	
Ameias Largo	Z 2	Combatentes de Gde		Dr Júlio		
Antero de Quental R.	V 3	Guerra R. dos	X 13	Henriques Alameda	X 21	
António Augusto		Comércio Pr. do	Z	Elísio de Moura R.	VX	
Gonçalves R.	X 4	Cónego Urbano		Emídio Navarro Av.	Z	
Augusta R.	V 5	Duarte Av.	X	Erva Terreiro da	Z	
Augusto Rocha R.	V 6	Couraça dos		Fernandes Tomás R.	Z 25	
Aveiro R. de	V 8	Apóstolos R.	YZ	Fernando Namora Av.	X	
Bernardo de		Coutinhos R.	Y 15	Fernão de Magalhães Av.	Y	
Albuquerque R.	V 9	Direita R.	Z	Ferreira Borges R.	Z 27	
Borges Carneiro R.	Z 10	Dom Afonso		Figueira da Foz R. da	V 28	
		Henriques Av.	V 17	Guerra Junqueiro R.	Z 30	
		Dom Dinis Largo	ZDr A.	Guilherme Moreira R.	Z 31	

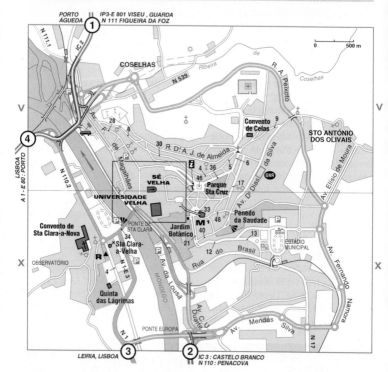

The old university is housed in buildings that once belonged to the royal palace and were restored and modified to become the Paço dos Estudos in 1540. The **courtyard** (pátio) is dominated by an 18C tower. To the left, the courtyard extends to a terrace that provides a fine view of the Mondego. Opposite are the library and chapel and, on the right, the graceful Paços da Universidade. This Manueline building was endowed with a colonnaded gallery called the Via Latina in the late 18C. The central body of the building is surmounted by a triangular pediment (tickets should be purchased at the entrance to this building). A staircase leads to the first floor and the loggia, formerly for women only, which gives on to the **Sala dos Capelos** (Ceremonial Hall) where formal events such as the inauguration of rectors, the defence of theses and the conferring of degrees take place. The name derives from the cap (capelo) given to students on graduating. The vast hall, once the palace assembly-room, has an exquisite 17C painted ceiling and is adorned with a series of portraits of the kings of Portugal. Beside it is the private examination room which was remodelled in 1701. It

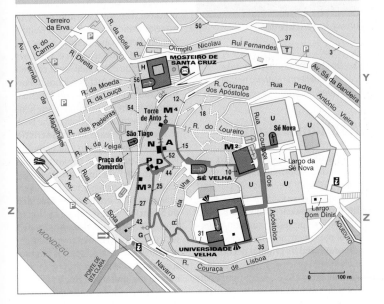

has a painted ceiling and is hung with portraits of former rectors.

An exterior balcony provides a beautiful **view**★ of the city, the old cathedral and the more recent districts near the Mondego.

Chapel★

This Manueline chapel (capela), with an elegant door, is by Marcos Pires. It is decorated with 17C azulejos and a painted ceiling and also possesses a fine 18C **organ loft**★★. A small **Museum of Sacred Art** adjoins the chapel.

Library★★

The library was built during the reign of João V in 1724 and consists of three large rooms, where precious wood furnishings are highlighted by Baroque decorations of gilded wood. Gilded Chinese-style patterns have been painted on green, red or gold lacquer work. The ceilings painted in false perspective are by Lisbon artists influenced by Italian art. Ladders have been fitted into the shelving itself for easy access. The 30 000 books and 5 000 manuscripts are classified according to subject matter.

P. Bourget/MICHELIN

Library, Universidade Velha

▶ *On leaving the university, take Rua Guilherme Moreira to the Almedina gate.*

Additional Sights

Casa Museu Bissaya-Barreto

Guided visit (45min) Tue–Sun, 3pm–5pm. ○ *Closed weekends in Oct and public holidays.* €2.50. 239 85 38 00. The former residence of Bissaya-Barreto (1886–1974), professor, surgeon, member of parliament and friend of Salazar, has preserved its original decoration. Built in 1925 in neo-Baroque style, it is surrounded by a small, delightful garden decorated with statues and *azulejos*. The interior reveals the aesthetic tastes of its former owner: a 19C French lounge, *azulejos* from different periods, ceilings painted with frescoes, porcelain from the Indies company and from Saxony, silverware, Italian marble, an interesting library with books dating from the 16C and 17C, a collection of paintings based on the theme of the mother and child (including a *Virgin and Child* by Josefa de Óbidos), and several canvases by José Malhoa, Sousa Pinto and António Vitorino.

Jardim da Sereia or Parque de Santa Cruz

The entrance to this delightful 18C garden is through two towers adorned with arches. A staircase leads to a grotto-like fountain decorated with statues. Picnic tables, a lake surrounded by sculpted boxwood creating a maze effect and exotic trees provide welcome cool and a haven of peace and quiet.

Mosteiro de Santa Cruz★

○ *Church open Mon–Sat, 7.30am–noon, 2pm–6pm; Sacristy and cloisters Mon–Sat 9am–noon, 2pm–5pm; Sun 4pm–5pm* €2.50.

The Manueline ceiling of the **Church★** is supported by twisted columns and brackets. The walls are adorned with *azulejos* depicting the life of St Augustine. The Renaissance **pulpit★** by Nicolas Chanterene is a masterpiece. Two bays on either side of the high altar contain the tombs of the first two kings of Portugal Afonso Henriques and Sancho I, surrounded by a late Gothic–early Renaissance decoration. A door at the back of the chancel leads to the **Sacristia** (sacristy) in which hang four early 16C Portuguese paintings. The visit continues with the **Sala do Capitulo** (chapter-house) which has a fine Manueline ceiling and 17C *azulejos*. The **Claustro do Silêncio★** were designed by Marcos Pires in 1524. The galleries are decorated with *azulejos* of parables from the Gospel. Three low-relief sculptures illustrate scenes of the Passion after Dürer engravings. In the **gallery** (coro alto – access through the sacristy) at the entrance to the church are beautiful 16C wooden **stalls★** carved and gilded by Flemish artists and the Frenchman, François Lorete.

Botanical Gardens

○ *Open 9am–5.30pm (8pm Apr to Sept).* 239 82 28 97. *Free, though entry to the greenhouses is* €2.

The terraced botanical gardens (*jardim botânico*), which were laid out in the 18C in accordance with reforms introduced by Pombal, have a wide variety of rare trees including many tropical species.

Holy Queen Festival

At the beginning of July in even-numbered years, the city pays homage to its patron saint. On the Thursday evening, the statue of the saint is removed from the Convento de Santa-Clara-a-Nova and carried in procession across the bridge and through the city's streets to the Igreja da Graça, where it remains until the following Sunday, when it is returned to the convent. The streets are crowded with people, some of whom make the journey barefoot or on their knees, and the statue often takes several hours to travel just a few metres. The youngest members of the procession dress up as cherubs, King Dinis or Queen Isabel in memory of the miracle of the roses. When the queen, who was hiding bread in her lap to give to the poor, was asked by the king what she was carrying, she was said to have replied: "these are roses, my lord..."; when she went to remove the bread from the folds of her dress, a quantity of rose petals miraculously fell out. This is why Coimbra's inhabitants throw rose petals onto the statue from their windows, which are draped with brightly coloured bedspreads and large flags for the occasion. At midnight, a huge firework display illuminates the Mondego.

They were once one of the best-known of the world's botanical gardens though less renowned these days, but still an interesting and relaxing place to visit. The **Museu Botânico** (entry included in the greenhouse ticket) is also well worth a visit.

South Bank of the Mondego

Convento de Santa Clara-a-Nova

◷*Open Tue, 8.30am–6.30pm; Thur, Fri, Sat 8.30am–6pm; Weds 8.30am–noon; 2pm–6pm; Sun 8.30am–noon; 3pm–6pm. Free for the church but Cloisters* ⊚€1.50 ☎239 44 16 74.

The chancel in this vast convent contains the 17C silver tomb of Queen St Isabel by Teixeira Lopes. At the end of the lower chancel (*coro baixo*), behind the wrought-iron screen, is the queen's original **tomb**★ (14C) of painted Ança stone made during her lifetime.

Portugal dos Pequeninos Kids

◷*Open Mar-1 May 10am–7pm; Jun–15 Sept, 9am–8pm; 16 Sept-Feb 10am–5pm.* ⊚€7 *(€3.50 under 14yrs and over 65s; reduced prices for gardens only and only in low season.)* ☎239 80 11 70.

An attraction for children where scale models of Portuguese monuments including those of former overseas colonies may be seen. One of the houses

contains a children's museum, the **Museu da Criança**.

Quinta das Lágrimas

◷*Open 9am–5pm.* ⊚€0.75. ☎239 80 23 80.

The name of this wooded park, the Villa of Tears, recalls the legend described in verse by Camões of Inês de Castro's murder here on 7 January 1355 by King Afonso's Chief Justice and two of his henchmen.

Miradouro do Vale do Inferno

4km/2mi. Leave by ③ and take a narrow road on the right towards the Vale do Inferno (steep climb); at a fork bear right.

The belvedere provides a good **view**★ of Coimbra.

Portugal dos Pequeninos

B. Brillon/MICHELIN

CONÍMBRIGA★
COIMBRA
MICHELIN MAP 733

The Roman ruins of Conímbriga are among the finest in the Iberian Peninsula. A Celtic city stood on this spot as long ago as the Iron Age. The present ruins, however, are those of a Roman town situated on either side of an important road that connected Lisbon and Braga. In the 3C, threatened by Barbarian invasion, the inhabitants were compelled to build ramparts, leaving some of the houses outside the wall. Material from these houses was used in the construction of the fortifications. In spite of these measures, Conímbriga fell to the Suevi in 468 and the town declined.

- **Information:** Rua Emídio Navarro 136. ☎231 939 133.
- ▶ **Orient Yourself:** Just 14km/9mi south of Coimbra. You can get to Conimbriga either by car or by bus from Coimbra. The bus is €1.80 one way, takes 30 minutes and leaves Coimbra at 9.35am and returns at 5pm, with additional buses at 9am out and 1pm return on weekdays. There is also a half-hourly service from Coimbra to Condeixa but the walk from there to Conimbriga is about 2km/1.2mi and poorly signposted.
- **Don't Miss:** Particularly the mosaics in the House of Fountains.
- **Organizing Your Time:** About three hours.
- **Especially for Kids:** A great place for them to begin to understand how people (including children) lived in an age now largely forgotten.
- **Also See:** COIMBRA, FIGUERA DA FOZ.

Visit

Open Jun–Sept, 9am–8pm; Oct–Apr, 10am–6pm. Closed public holidays; museum closed Mon. €3, no charge Sun (includes the ruins and museum). ☎239 94 11 77. www.conimbriga,pt. Leave the car

Mosaics in the Casa da Cruz Suástica

in front of the museum and take the path towards the ruins, following the route marked on the plan.

Visit the Museum and its café first to see the information on display – this gives you a very good overview of the site and will help you understand everything much better.

The first thing you notice on entering the site itself is the amazing wall that was put up literally overnight in 465 in a frantic, but futile attempt to repel a threatened Suevi invasion. The wall even cuts through the middle of several houses and was constructed of absolutely anything that came to hand. The inhabitants, fearing their own destruction, eventually fled the city and hid in the surrounding countryside, leaving the invaders to take control of the city without further destruction.

Cross the **Casa da Cruz Suástica** (House of the Swastika) and the **Casa dos Esqueletos** (House of the Skeletons), paved with fine mosaics, before reaching the baths and the interesting *laconicum* (a type of sauna) (1). You then come to the **Casa de Cantaber**★, which is one

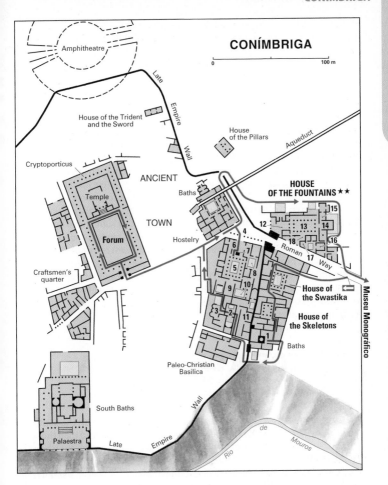

CONÍMBRIGA

Amphitheatre

Late

House of the Trident
and the Sword

Empire

Wall

House
of the Pillars

Aqueduct

Cryptoporticus

ANCIENT

Baths

**HOUSE
OF THE FOUNTAINS** ★ ★

Temple

TOWN

15

Forum

Hostelry

12

13

14

4

18

16

Roman

17

Way

Museu Monográfico

6

7

Craftsmen's
quarter

5

8

House of
the Swastika

9

10

11

**House of
the Skeletons**

3

2

1

Baths

Paleo-Christian
Basilica

Wall

South Baths

Late

Empire

de

Mouros

Palaestra

Rio

of the largest in the western Roman world and is said to have belonged to Cantaber, whose wife and children were captured by the Suevi during the attack on the town in 465. The tour begins with the private baths: the *frigidarium* (2) with its cold baths, the *tepidarium* (warm baths) and the *caldarium* (hot baths) (3) over the *hypocaust* (heated space connected with the furnace). The hypocaust's layout gives an idea of the plan for the fireplaces and the underground system of warm air circulation; a few lead pipes remain.

You then arrive at the northern entrance to the house: a colonnade (4) preceded the *atrium* (entrance vestibule) (5). As you pass from the *atrium* to the central peristyle (6), you will note an unusual stone (7) in the pavement, cut away to

a rose tracery through which the drain can be seen. The *impluvium* (a basin for collecting rain water) (8) is to the left of the peristyle. Leading off from the *impluvium* were the bedrooms.

From the *triclinium* (sitting and dining room) (9) you can see three pools. The most interesting of these pools (10) is encircled by columns of which one has retained its original stucco painted in red. A suite of three rooms (11) adjoining the wall has a lovely pool and flower beds in the shape of a cross.

Excavations north west of the Casa de Cantaber have uncovered the centre of the **ancient town** *(cidade antiga)*, in particular the **forum**, a hostelry and baths. To the south west, the craftsmen's quarter and the monumental baths have also been discovered.

You can also see the remains of the **aqueduct** (*aqueduto*), which was some 3.5km/2mi long, brought water from Alcabideque to the supply tower by the reconstructed arch abutting on the wall.

Casa dos Repuxos (House of the Fountains)★★

Access by footbridge to the north.
The villa, which belonged to a Roman named Rufus, dates from the early 2C although it was built on the site of a 1C building. The layout of the rooms is easy to follow on account of the column bases and the paving which consists largely of wonderful mosaics. Inside are the *atrium* (12), the peristyle (13) and the *triclinium* (14), which was bordered by a pool. Around these rooms were the living quarters and communal rooms. The **mosaics**★★ covering the floors show extraordinary variety.

In a room to the left of the *triclinium*, a fine polychrome composition (15) shows hunting scenes, the Four Seasons and a quadriga.

Another room (16) giving onto the *impluvium* presents some elegant figures at a deer hunt. A *cubiculum* (bedroom) (17) has ornamental tiling with geometrical designs and plant motifs surrounding Silenus astride an ass being pulled forward by its halter. Next door, a sitting room (18), opening on to the peristyle, is decorated with an outstanding mosaic: in the centre of an ornament representing wading birds, dolphins and sting rays, a marine centaur surrounded by dolphins brandishes a standard and a fish. Lastly, in the southwest corner of the peristyle, Perseus stands, holding in his right hand Medusa's head which he appears to be offering to a monster from the deep.

COSTA DA CAPARICA
SETÚBAL
MICHELIN MAP 733 LOCAL MAP P9

The Costa da Caparica is the nearest seaside resort to Lisbon on the southern shore of the Tagus. With its vast beaches, which are less polluted than those on the northern shore, it is one of the most popular weekend spots with Lisbonites (*Lisboetas*). The resort is constantly being developed parallel to the ocean and the ridge of sand dunes which protects it from the wind. In season, a **small train** runs along the coast for 11km/6.8mi, giving access to the immensely long beach. Fishing boats, their prows adorned with a painted star or eye, may still be seen bringing in their nets helped by holidaymakers.

- **Information:** Avda da Liberdade 18. ☎212 900 071.
- ▶ **Orient Yourself:** On the opposite side of the Tagus from Lisbon.
- **Parking:** No major problems along the roads leading to the beaches.
- **Don't Miss:** The statue of Christ – Cristo Rei.
- **Organizing Your Time:** A day out from the hustle and bustle of Lisbon.
- **Especially for Kids:** There's a beach! In fact, several; they'll have fun.

Sights

The vast Rio-like statue of Cristo Rei dominates the Tagus and can be seen from Lisbon as well. You can visit (*Open 9.30am–6pm; €3*) and take the lift to the top, 80m/262.5ft above ground from where you have a magnificent view as far as Sintra. The other reason to go to Caparica is to laze on the beach, though surfers and windsurfers find this a great place. There is a little road-train that is well worth a ride and stops at dozens of places along the coast, each of them different in character, from family-orientated to nudist sunbathing to a gay community. Choose the right stop carefully!

CRATO
PORTALEGRE
MICHELIN MAP 733

As early as 1350, Crato (about 20km/12.4mi due west of Portalegre) became the seat of a priory for the Order of the Knights Hospitallers of St John of Jerusalem, which later became the Order of the Knights of Malta. The title of Grand Prior of Crato was bestowed up until the late 16C. In 1356 the command of the knights' residence was transferred to the monastery-fortress in the neighbouring village of Flor da Rosa; Crato, however, retained its role as a priory. While Crato's castle was burnt in 1662 by Don Juan of Austria, several old houses may still be seen.

- **Information:** Largo do Município. ☎245 9 71 61.
- ▶ **Orient Yourself:** 21km/13mi west of Portalegre, in the Alentejo region.
- **Don't Miss:** The Varanda do Grão Prior; the church and the monastery.
- **Organizing Your Time:** A couple of hours will suffice.

Sight

Mosteiro de Flor da Rosa★
Entrance is free – ask for key at pousada Reception.
The monastery-fortress of the Order of the Knights of Malta was built in 1356. It forms a compact group of fortified buildings within a crenellated perimeter wall. The **church**★ on the right has been extremely well restored; the simplicity of its lines and the height of its nave are outstanding. The small flower-decked cloisters in the centre are robust in design but are given an overall elegance by their graceful Late Gothic network vaulting.

VALE DO DOURO★★
MICHELIN MAP 733

The Douro, which rises in Spain, flows in an erratic course before reaching the Atlantic near Oporto. Its valley is fertile, with vineyards, orchards and olives growing in abundance as they have done for centuries. The valley itself is quite steep and can be very hot in mid summer, though cooler at high temperatures and further downstream. The landscape has been enhanced by beautifully built quintas. Port is the main wine produced here but the valley is also the centre for the famous *vinho verde*.

- ▶ **Orient Yourself:** The valley runs across the northern part of Portugal from the Spanish border to the Atlantic, emptying into the sea at Porto.
- **Don't Miss:** The wine route!
- **Organizing Your Time:** Two or three days of peace and quiet are ideal.
- **Also See:** PORTO.

Visit

The Douro was the first officially designated wine-growing region on the planet, predating even the great regions of France. The valley of the river Douro is beautiful and one of the most interesting (though not cheap) ways of seeing it is on an all-inclusive river cruise. These normally start in Porto on a Sunday, returning the following Saturday. The hills climbing from the valley floor are lined with vineyards from which both red and white wines are made, and not just port, though obviously this is very important. The higher altitudes as well as the vineyards further downstream are best for white wines while the intense summer heat of the upper part of the valley is perfect for full-bodied reds.

Driving Tour around the Vinho Verde Region★

①From the Barragem do Carrapatelo to Lamego

62km/38.5mi – about 2hr 30min –
⏱*See map.*

The lower valley of the river, near Oporto, is not the domain of the great wine of that name but that of the well-known **vinho verde** (green wine), so-called because the local climate is such that the grapes cannot fully ripen here. The description of the wine reflects its

youth rather than its colour. Port is made much further east, between Régua and the Spanish border. The Douro, widened by successive dams, runs hemmed in by steep hills and winds round in great twists and turns. The shale and granite slopes, more wooded on the north bank and more cultivated on the south bank, where little white villages seem to hang between the vines, terraced olive groves and corn fields, with the river below, have created a delightful landscape, despite the reminders of industrial civilization evidenced by the railway line, the Carrapatelo dam *(barragem)*, a few factories, and the installations for transporting coal from the Pejão mines on the south bank.

Barragem do Carrapatelo

This dam is 170m/558ft long. A hydro-electric station and a fish ladder occupy its south bank. On the north bank, a lock with the greatest displacement in Europe drops 43m/141ft.

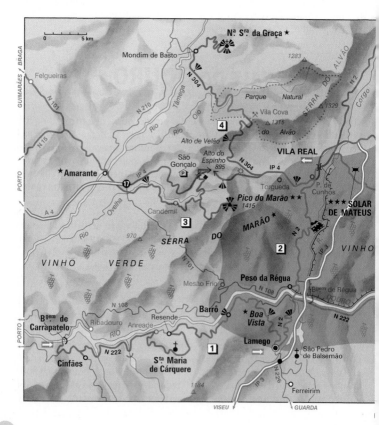

Cinfães
Cinfães is the commercial centre for *vinho verde* but apart from that there is nothing much of interest to see.

▶ *Continue along N 222 to Anreade; turn right on the road towards Ovadas, heading south; 5.5km/3.4mi on, bear left.*

Priorado de Santa Maria de Cárquere
Only the church and the funeral chapel of the Lords of Resende remain, linked by a monumental arch. The church, restored in the 13C, 14C, 16C and 17C (the square crenellated tower and chancel are Gothic, the façade and nave Manueline) still has a Romanesque doorway decorated with small columns and capitals with interlacing. The chancel, under diagonal ribbed vaulting, has a door on the left with a high pediment and a double string course of billets. The chapel, which has a remarkable Roman-

esque window with capitals of sculpted pelicans, contains four stone sarcophagi carved with animals and inscriptions.

▶ *Return to N 222 and turn right.*

Resende is an important wine production centre. From the village of Barrô, there is a good view of the valley's wooded slopes; the 12C Romanesque church has a richly carved tympanum and a beautiful rose window.

▶ *After 6km/3.7mi turn right on N 226.*

Miradouro da Boa Vista★
There is a magnificent view from this belvedere of the Douro valley. High up, cut out against the sky, are the whitish summits of the Serra do Marão.

▶ *Continue until you arrive at* **Lamego** *(⟨ See LAMEGO).*

The Port Region★★

②Round trip from Lamego

112km/69.5mi – about 3hr – ⟨ See map.

As the local saying goes: *"God created the Earth and man the Douro"*. One has to see the way the steep banks of the Douro have been shaped meticulously into terraces, each one comprising several rows of vines, to understand the enormous amount of work man has put into these hillsides for more than 20 centuries. The sight is particularly fascinating between mid-September and mid-October when the terraces are invaded by thousands of grape-pickers. The vineyards cover an area of 42 500ha/105 000 acres and it is their grapes, which ripen in the shelter of the valley, where the temperature in summer can easily reach 40°C/106°F, that pro-

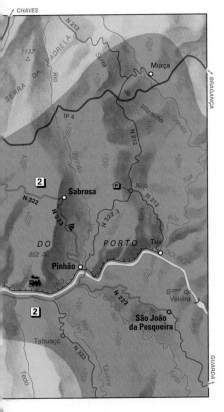

View of vineyards in the Douro Valley

H. Champollion/MICHELIN

duce port wine. There are many opportunities to taste port (and other wines) at some of the quintas along the way, though take care if driving. In **Peso da Régua** you will find the beautiful **Instituto do Vinho do Porto** (R. dos Camilos) or the **Solar do Vinho do Porto** (R. da Ferreirinha) where you can not only taste various wines but also pick up some brochures with full details.

Leave Lamego and take the picturesque N 2 above the Corgo valley to **Vila Real**. *See VILA REAL.*

▶ *Leave Vila Real on N 322 and continue east towards* **Sabrosa** *(the town is Magellan's birthplace), passing, on the way* **Solar de Mateus** ★★. *See VILA REAL.*

Road from Sabrosa to Pinhão★★

After Sabrosa, the N 323 descends towards the Douro and overlooks the deep valley of the Pinhão. 7km/4.3mi before Pinhão there is a fine **view**★ of a bend in the Douro and its confluence with the Pinhão river.

Pinhão

Pinhão, which stands at the junction of the Douro and Pinhão rivers, is an important port production centre and is said to produce the very best port. The **railway station** is decorated with *azulejos* illustrating the sites and the traditional costumes of the valley. Nowadays, all the wine is transported by road rather than on the flat-bottomed boats that look like Venetian gondolas – some of which can still be seen on the river in Porto.

By making an excursion eastwards to **São João da Pesqueira** *(18km/11mi of hairpin bends on N 222)* you will see the terraced hillsides of vineyards in the Torto valley. São João da Pesqueira is a large village on the plateau with an arcaded main square around which stand beautiful white balconied houses. After Pinhão, N 222 follows the valley westwards between shale slopes which have been terraced and contained by small drystone walls. The land is exclusively given over to vines.

An important diversion is to take the train from Paso de Régua to Vila Real on the Corgo Line, renowned as one of the most picturesque train rides in the world. Take the camera.

Serra do Marão★

③ From Vila Real to Amarante

See Serra do MARÃO

④ From Vila Real to Mondim de Basto

See Serra do MARÃO

ELVAS ★
PORTALEGRE
POPULATION 25 843 – MICHELIN MAP 733

Elvas is an impressive fortification still surrounded by its ramparts, only 19km/11.8mi from the Spanish citadel of Badajoz. The town was not liberated by the Christians from the Moorish occupation until 1229, almost a hundred years later than Lisbon. Elvas subsequently resisted many assaults by the Spanish until 1580 when it was attacked by Philip II's troops. Today Elvas is a charming little frontier town with cafés and restaurants in its main square making a perfect interlude to an otherwise busy schedule. It is famous for its markets.

- **Information:** Praça da República; ☎268 622 236
- ▶ **Orient Yourself:** On the Spanish border 208km/129mi east of Lisbon.
- P **Parking:** Plenty outside the city walls – not very much inside.
- **Don't Miss:** The fortifications, most of which you can walk round.
- **Organizing Your Time:** You'll find it easy to spend a full day here.
- Kids **Especially for Kids:** They will love the fortifications.
- **Also See:** ESTREMOZ.

Sights

City walls (Muralhas)★★
The Elvas fortifications are the most accomplished example of 17C military architecture in Portugal. Fortified gates, moats, curtain walls, bastions and glacis form a remarkable defensive group completed to the south and north by the 17C Santa Luzia and the 18C Graça forts, each perched on a hill.

Aqueduto da Amoreira★
The aqueduct was constructed between 1498 and 1622. It begins 7.5km/4.6mi south west of the town and still brings water.

Cathedral
The cathedral *(sé)*, originally Gothic, was rebuilt in the 16C by Francisco de Arruda in the Manueline style. The interior, whose pillars were decorated in the Manueline period, contains an 18C chancel entirely faced with marble.

Igreja Nossa Senhora da Consolação★
The Renaissance style Church of Our Lady of Consolation on Largo de Santa Clara was built in the 16C. Its interior, covered by a cupola resting on eight painted columns, is entirely decorated with 17C multi-coloured **azulejos**★. The pulpit, supported by a marble column, has a 16C wrought-iron balustrade.

Castle
Open 9am–5pm. Closed 1 Jan, Easter Sunday, 1 May and 25 Dec. €1.50, free on Sundays and holidays.
The castle was constructed by the Moors and reinforced in the 14C and 16C. From the top of the ramparts there is a view of the town, its fortifications and the surrounding countryside scattered with olive trees and isolated farmsteads.

Pillory on the Largo Santa Clara

C. Champagnon/MICHELIN

ERICEIRA★
LISBOA
POPULATION 8 780 – MICHELIN MAP 733

Ericeira is a lively seaside resort perched on a cliff facing the Atlantic, and has preserved its old quarter around the church, its maze of alleyways and its picturesque fishing harbour. It was from here in 1910 that King Manuel II sailed into exile while the Republic was being proclaimed in Lisbon. It has a picturesque harbour and the area around the Parish Church is also worth a visit. Its nearby beaches are renowned worldwide for their surfing.

- **Information:** Rua Dr Eduardo Burnay, 46. ☎261 863 122. www.ericeira.net.
- **Orient Yourself:** On the west coast about 53km/33mi north west of Lisbon.
- **Parking:** Can be difficult in the old town; it's free near the market.
- **Don't Miss:** The beaches north and south of the town.
- **Organizing Your Time:** You could easily spend several days based here.
- **Especially for Kids:** Fantastic beaches to play on.

Visit

Ericeira was, until the 19C, a major port, though since then it has declined and its sea trade these days consists of little more than fishing boats. However, the quality of its seafood and the restaurants that dot the old town centre and the promenades lining its beaches, are renowned far and wide. The centre of the town, based round the **Praça da República**, is mainly pedestrianised and has dozens of bars, restaurants and shops around it. The main street, **Rua Dr Eduardo Burnay**, leads from the square to the main beach near the fishing harbour.

It was from this harbour that the last Portuguese King, Dom Manuel II, set sail on 5 October 1910. Alerted by his staff that a mob was on its way from Lisbon after the proclamation of a Republic, he hurriedly left his palace at Mafra and sailed south to Gibraltar and the safety of the Royal Navy. He was taken to England, where he lived out his exile.

The best **beaches** are to the north and south and have, in the past decade, become extremely popular with surfers. So much so, in fact, that the World Surfing Championships have been held here, on the **Praia da Ribeira d'Ilhas**, the beach about 3km/1.8mi north of the town. Several surf camps and schools have been set up and are at their busiest in Spring and autumn when the sea is rougher. You can hire boards and wetsuits for about €25 for 24 hours.

In the summer it's calm, hot and lovely and although many Lisboetas spend their holidays or weekends here (and many apartments have sprung up along the sea road) there is still plenty of room on the wide and glorious beaches. Praia do Norte and Praia do São Sebastião, the latter just round the headland, are also worth a visit and are slightly less busy. A further option is to go 2km/1.2mi south to Foz de Lizandro, where river bathing is safe and calm.

Ericeira has plenty of hotels and *pensões* and rates can be competitive, apart from the height of summer (July, August) when, unless you have a reservation you might struggle to find a room. Restaurants are plentiful and renowned for their quality and there are plenty of bars and cafés. Most of the nightlife is out of town though a few bars are clustered along the Praça dos Navegantes close to the Praia do Sul.

Ericeira is very handy for nearby Mafra with its wonderful palace (*See MAFRA*) and also for the UNESCO World Heritage Site town of Sintra (*See SINTRA*).

CABO ESPICHEL★
SETÚBAL
MICHELIN MAP 733

Cabo Espichel (Cape Espichel), at the southern tip of the Serra da Arrábida, is a true World's End, beaten continuously by violent winds. The cliff drops a sheer 100m/328ft to the sea. It was off this cape that Dom Fuas Roupinho vanquished the enemy in 1180 in a brilliant victory at sea, when Portuguese sailors succeeded in capturing several enemy ships. The remains of the Santuário de Nossa Senhora do Cabo have been a popular pilgrimage centre ever since the 13C, though these buildings were erected during the 18C by pilgrims.

▶ **Orient Yourself:** Cape Espichel lies at the tip of the Seúbal Peninsula.
🅿 **Parking:** No problems parking here.
🚫 **Don't Miss:** The views from the cliff.
🕐 **Organizing Your Time:** No more than an hour is needed here.

Cape

Cabo Espichel is remote, wild and desolate, with very little left of what was once an arcaded pilgrimage and lodgings. Today they are totally run-down and look more like a former prison. The reason for coming here is to see the wonderful views out over the Atlantic from the edge of the imposing cliffs. You can easily see why the place has been used as a location for several films. Dinosaurs' footprints have been found close by.

Santuário de
Nossa Senhora do Cabo
🕐 *Open 9.30am–6pm.* ☎*212 68 10 31.* This large though now crumbling church, built in the classical style at the end of the 17C, has a Baroque interior.

ESTORIL★
LISBOA
POPULATION 25 769 – MICHELIN MAP 733
PLAN IN THE MICHELIN GUIDE SPAIN AND PORTUGAL

Estoril has developed into a refined and attractive beach and winter resort, favoured by a mild climate and a temperature that averages 12°C/54°F in winter. It lies on the sea road linking Lisbon and Cascais, a point on the Costa de Estoril that is famous for its luminous skies. Formerly a small village known to a few for the healing properties of its waters, Estoril now attracts an elegant international circle who come for the resort's entertainments (golf, casino and sea fishing), its sporting events (horse-racing and regattas), its pleasant location facing Cascais bay, its park of tropical and exotic plants and trees, palm-lined avenues, beaches of fine sand and its highly successful festivals (Festival of the Sea in July).

ℹ **Information:** Opposite the station. ☎214 663 813. www.estorilcoast.com.
▶ **Orient Yourself:** On the coast road about 35km/21.7mi west of Lisbon.
🅿 **Parking:** Can be very difficult though the Casino has a huge car park.
🚫 **Don't Miss:** The Casino with its shows each night; fireworks on Saturdays.
🕐 **Organizing Your Time:** A day trip is fine though it's good to be based here.
Kids Especially for Kids: They'll love the beach.
👣 **Also See:** Nearby Cascais and, of course, Lisbon – go by train along the coast.

Resort

Estoril was once a sedate and refined resort reserved for the well-heeled and it tries to maintain this image, largely succeeding despite the influx of tourism, attracted by its wonderful beach and, at night, its **Casino**, with spectacular cabaret shows. It was in this Casino that Ian Fleming, in the last days of the War, prowled around tracking Dusko Popov, a Yugoslav double-agent.

From this experience came the novel-turned-film *Casino Royale*. Graham Greene, another intelligence officer-turned-novelist, was also a frequent visitor in those days when the area around Lisbon teemed with exiles, spies and sundry ne'er-do-wells.

The Casino stands in a large palm-lined square whose gardens are maintained to a very high standard. As well as the cabaret shows there are obviously gam-ing rooms and several shops, though an unusual attraction is a very good art gallery, in which, each October, the International Naïve Painting Salon holds its show, the largest in Iberia.

During the summer there is a nightly crafts market outside the Casino, from 6pm to midnight. On Saturday nights in the summer there is a large fireworks display on the beach between Estoril and Cascais. Both towns claim to hold it but it is spectacular and worth staying up for.

Estoril is also known for the quality of its nearby **golf courses**, which include Oitavos, a relatively new course (www.quintadamarinha-oitavosgolfe.pt) that is expensive but spectacular, running out to Cabo da Roca, the westernmost part of mainland Portugal, Quinta da Marinha, based in the eponymous hotel, Penha Longa, designed by Robert Trent Jones Jnr, and the oldest course in Portugal, Estoril GC.

SERRA DA ESTRELA★
GUARDA AND CASTELO BRANCO
MICHELIN MAP 733
MICHELIN ATLAS SPAIN & PORTUGAL PP 35 (K 6,7) AND 48 (L 6,7)

The Serra da Estrela *(Mountain range of the Star)*, **a great mountain barrier 60km/37mi long by 30km/18.6mi wide, is the highest massif in Portugal. Above the cultivated and wooded slopes appear the arid and boulder strewn summits, the tallest of which is Torre with an altitude of c. 1 993m/6 539ft. Tourism is developing in this formerly isolated area: Penhas da Saúde has become a winter sports resort; Covilhã, Seia, Gouveia and Manteigas, small towns within reach of the plain, have become starting points for mountain excursions.**

- 🛈 **Information:** Av. Frei Heitor Pinto. ☎275 319 560. www.rt-serradaestrela.pt.
- ▶ **Orient Yourself:** In the triangle formed by Coimbra, Viseu and Guarda.
- ⊚ **Don't Miss:** The Zêzere glacial valley and the view from the summit of Torre.
- ◑ **Organizing Your Time:** A couple of days midweek to look around the region.
- ⓒ **Also See:** MOURA.

Driving Tours

Monte da Torre Road★★

1 From Covilhã to Seia
49km/30.4mi – about 2hr. This itinerary includes the highest road in Portugal.

On leaving **Covilhã**, the road rises rapidly before you arrive at **Penhas da Saúde**, a popular winter and summer spot though it is not exactly a town and has limited supplies of food and drink.

▶ *Leave the Manteigas road on the right.*

After a bend bringing the road parallel with the upper valley of the Zêzere, the **landscape**★ becomes desolate. There is

Zézere glacial valley

an interesting **view**★ from a belvedere on the left, a short distance from the summit, of the glacial upper valley of the Zêzere. The river's source is hidden by a 300m/984ft-high granite cone.

▶ *Bear left to Torre.*

Torre★★

In 1817 King João VI decreed that an obelisk 7m/23ft high should be placed atop the Torre, bringing the official "height" of Portugal to exactly 2000m/5 651.6ft. The best thing about Torre, though, is the road leading up and back. Although from the summit the **panorama** includes the Mondego valley, the Serra da Lousã and the Zêzere valley, the top itself is ruined by radar domes and a tacky souvenir shop. The "long lake", Lagoa Comprida is the largest single expanse of water in the *serra*. The descent into the Mondego valley is swift and the **views**★★ are magnificent. After **Sabugueiro**, a village of granite-walled houses, the road drops steeply into **Seia**, a small town pleasantly situated at the foot of the *serra*.

Zêzere Upper Valley★★

②Gouveia to Covilhã via Manteigas

77km/47.8mi – about 2hr 30min.
This route crosses the massif by way of the upper valley of the Zêzere.

Gouveia is a small, attractive town built halfway up the side of the Mondego valley. The upper plateaux are soon reached; some of the granite boulders have been worn into astonishing forms, such as the Old Man's Head, **Cabeça do Velho**, which rises from a mass of rocks on the left of the road. The source of the Mondego (Nascente do Mondego – *signposted*), the longest river flowing solely in Portugal, rises to an altitude of 1 360m/4 462ft just before Penhas Douradas. The road runs past the Pousada de São Lourenço with a fine view of Manteigas and the Zêzere valley opposite. The descent becomes brutal as hairpin bends twist down to the Zêzere valley; a belvedere, not far from the *pousada*, affords an upstream **view**★ of the valley which is commanded by **Manteigas** with its 17C houses with wooden balconies.

▶ *At Manteigas leave the N 232 and turn right.*

A short distance beyond the small spa of **Caldas de Manteigas**, with its still-functioning hot springs (well worth a few hours to visit and sample), the mountain solitude takes over. However, cultivated terraces can be seen on the lower slopes. After the bridge over the Zêzere, the road (in poor condition) continues upstream until it reaches the rock

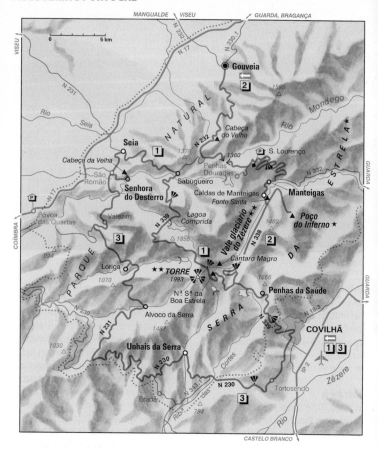

face of the glacial valley (ℓ*see opposite*); it then climbs to the top.

▶ *Turn left into a narrow unsurfaced road to Poço do Inferno (6km/3.7mi).*

Poço do Inferno★

The Well of Hell is a wild, wooded defile with a beautiful **waterfall**★. It is well worth a few hours to walk this area.

Vale Glaciário do Zêzere★★

This valley is a perfect example of glacial relief with U-shaped contours with steep slopes, hanging tributary valleys and connecting gorges, a cirque at the highest point, cascades, enormous erratic boulders strewn on the bottom, and scraggy vegetation on the slopes. The road bears westward and passes near the source of the Zêzere – signposted

"Cântaros" (the source is not visible from the road, but it can be reached on foot through huge boulders). A little further, at a fountain, there is a lovely extensive **view**★ across the glacial valley.

▶ *At the final pass, take the N 339 on the left towards Covilhã.*

Covilhã

Covilhã, spread over the wooded foothills of the Serra da Estrela, is both a health resort and an excursion centre, as well as the dormitory town for the Penhas da Saúde winter sports resort.

Western Serra★

3 From Covilhã to Seia via Unhais da Serra

81km/50.3mi – about 2hr

This route goes round the *serra* by the west along a road that runs almost constantly at an altitude of between 600m–700m/1 968.5ft–2 296.6ft.

▶ *Leave Covilhã by the N 230 going south. The Serra da Estrela's high peaks come into sight beyond Tortosendo.*

Unhais da Serra

This small spa and health resort enjoys a lovely **setting**★ at the mouth of a torrent-filled valley. Villages such as **Alvoco da Serra**, situated half way up the hillside, and **Loriga**, perched upon a spur in the valley, now come into view.

▶ *At São Romão turn right in the direction of Senhora do Desterro.*

Senhora do Desterro

The road climbs the Alva valley to Senhora do Desterro. Leave the car and take the path on the left which will bring you *(15min round trip on foot)* to the Cabeça da Velha (Old Woman's Head), a granite rock worn by erosion.

▶ *Return to the road, which leads to* **Seia** *(a useful base for weekends with good hotels and an interesting Bread Museum) and to the itinerary described.*

ESTREMOZ★
ÉVORA
POPULATION 16 657 – MICHELIN MAP 733

Approached from the south, the old town appears perched on a hill overlooking the bright whitewashed houses of the modern town below. Estremoz, standing in a region of marble quarries, is a pleasant city, still possessing its 17C ramparts and dominated by its medieval castle. It is well known for Alentejo pottery, which can be seen at the Saturday market in the Rossio (main square).

- **Information:** Rossio do Marquês de Pombal. ☎268 33 35 41.
- ▶ **Orient Yourself:** Halfway between Elvas and Évora.
- **Parking:** Not too difficult except on Saturdays when there is a huge market.
- **Don't Miss:** The Saturday morning market; the Capela de Santa Isabel.
- **Organizing Your Time:** A full morning allows you to see all you need.
- **Also See:** VILA VIÇOSA, ELVAS, ÉVORA.

Sights

Torre de Menagem

The keep has now been converted into one of the most famous *pousadas* in Portugal. It was built in the 13C and is crowned with small pyramid-shaped merlons and flanked in its upper part by galleries supported on consoles.

Capela da Rainha Santa Isabel

⏱*Open Tue–Sun 9.30am–11.30pm, 2pm–5pm.* ⏱*Closed public holidays. For the key, ask at the Museu Municipal.*
The chapel walls are covered with beautiful *azulejos* depicting scenes from the

life of **Queen Saint Isabel of Aragon**, wife of King Dinis. The Miracle of the Roses scene is the most delightful: in it, the queen, surprised by the king as she is carrying bread to distribute to the poor, opens the pleats of her skirt to banish her husband's suspicions: only rose petals fell out.

Sala de Audiência de Dom Dinis

A beautiful **Gothic colonnade**★ is the outstanding feature of King Dinis' Audience Chamber whose stellar vaulting dates from the Manueline period. Queen Saint Isabel and King Pedro I both died in this room.

Museu Municipal

🕐*Open Tue–Sun 9am–12.15pm, 2pm–5.15pm.* 🕐*Closed public holidays.* 👝*€1.50.* ☎*268 33 92 00 (ext 246).*

The museum is housed in a beautiful old almshouse. Among its collections are some fine examples of Estremoz pottery which was particularly important in gypsy weddings. As the bride and groom met in the town square the bride would suddenly make a dash for "freedom" hotly pursued by the groom. As he caught her and kissed her several bowls would be thrown into the air. As they broke on hitting the ground the couple were pronounced man and wife.

Museu de Arte Sacra

🕐*Open 9.30am–noon, 2.30pm–5.30pm* 👝*€1.*

Located in a 16C convent this small museum has some very ornate examples of sacred art. You also get to see the marble church and some wonderful views form the rooftop terrace.

Igreja de Nossa Senhora dos Mártires

2km/1.2mi south on the road to Bencatel. The church dates from 1744 and has a monumental Gothic east end. The nave, which is preceded by a triumphal Manueline arch, contains beautiful *azulejos (Flight into Egypt, The Last Supper, The Annunciation)* as does the chancel *(Nativity, Presentation in the Temple).*

ÉVORA★★★
ÉVORA

POPULATION 55 619 – MICHELIN MAP 733

Évora, a walled town since Roman times, is attractively Moorish in character with alleys cut by arches, brilliant white houses, flower-decked terraces, openwork balconies and tiled patios. From its rich past Évora retains several medieval and Renaissance palaces and mansions which in themselves provide a panoply of Portuguese architecture. They are at their most impressive at night (floodlit during the summer from 9pm to midnight) standing out against a starry sky. Today it is an important agricultural market and the base for several dependent crafts and industries (cork, woollen carpets, leather and painted furniture).

- 🛈 **Information:** Praça do Giraldo. ☎266 702 671.
- ▶ **Orient Yourself:** Along the A 6 about 132km/82mi east of Lisbon.
- 🅿 **Parking:** Park outside the town where it is free and unrestricted.
- 👁 **Don't Miss:** The university, the Roman temple and the cathedral.
- 🕐 **Organizing Your Time:** The tourist buses from Lisbon arrive about 11am. You might like to get there earlier – spend a day. It's quiet in the evenings too.
- 🧒 **Especially for Kids:** The Vasco da Gama palace with its history of the Great Discoveries.
- 👣 **Also See:** ELVAS, MONSARAZ.

Old Town
(Cidade Velha)

Praça do Giraldo

The bustling town centre is a vast square partly bordered by arcades. An 18C marble fountain by Afonso Álvares stands on the site of a former triumphal Roman arch. Several little streets and alleys lead off the square, including the famed **Rua**

5 de Outubro, a narrow street lined with houses with wrought-iron balconies, as well as arts and crafts shops; no 28 has a niche decorated with *azulejos*.

Cathedral★★

🕐 *Open 9am–12.30pm, 2pm–5pm.* 🕐*Museum closed Mon.* 👝*€1 (church only) €1.50 (church and cloisters) €3 (church, cloisters, museum).*

©Eneko Salaberria/iStockphoto.com

Cathedral

The cathedral was built in the late 12C in the Transitional Gothic style on the site of a former mosque. While it has Romanesque characteristics, the cathedral was completed under Gothic influence.

The plain granite façade of the **exterior** is flanked by two massive towers crowned by conical spires added in the 16C. The tower on the right consists of several turrets similar to those on the Romanesque lantern-tower over the transept.

The main doorway is decorated with figures of the Apostles supported by consoles. The sculptures were probably carved in the late 13C by French artists.

In the **interior**★ the large nave, with broken barrel vaulting, has an elegant triforium. To the left, on a Baroque altar, is a 15C multicoloured stone statue of the Virgin with Child; opposite is a 16C statue, in gilded wood, of the Angel Gabriel attributed to Olivier of Ghent. A very fine octagonal **dome**★ on squinches, from which hangs a chandelier, stands above the transept crossing. The arms of the transept are lit by two Gothic rose windows: the north one shows the Morning Star and the south the Mystic Rose.

In the north transept the Renaissance archway to a chapel is decorated with a marble sculpture by Nicolas Chanterene. The south transept contains the tomb of the 16C humanist André de Resende.

The chancel was remodelled in the 18C by Friederich Ludwig, architect of the monastery at Mafra. The **Cadeiras do coro**★ **(choir stalls)**, made of oak, were carved in the Renaissance period by Flemish artists. They are decorated with sacred and secular motifs; note in particular the scenes on the lower panels showing peasants at their daily tasks (grape-picking, pig-sticking and sheep-shearing). The large Renaissance organ is thought to be the oldest in Europe.

Museu de Arte Sacra★

This museum contains vestments, a collection of ecclesiastical plate, including an ivory 13C French figure-triptych of the **Virgin**★★, and a 17C reliquary cross of St Lenho in silver gilt and multicoloured enamel decorated with 1426 precious stones.

The **Gothic cloisters**★, which were built between 1322 and 1340, have a massive appearance which is further accentuated by their granite composition, despite the elegance of rounded bays with radiating tracery. Statues of the Evangelists stand in each of the four corners. The southwest corner provides a good view of the Romanesque belfry. An adjoining chapel contains the 14C tomb of the founder-bishop and 14C statues of the Angel Gabriel and a polychrome Virgin, whose posture shows French influence.

ÉVORA

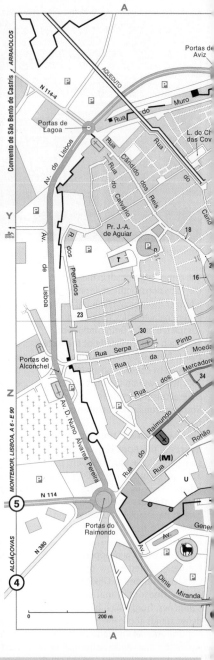

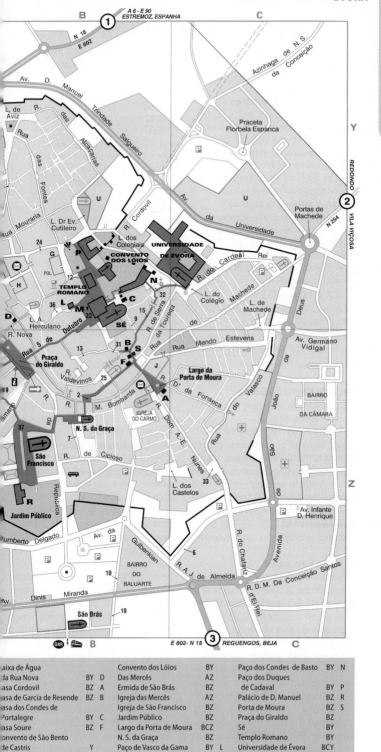

Address Book

&For coin ranges, see the Legend on the cover flap.

WHERE TO STAY

◎◎ **Residencial Policarpo –** R. da Freiria de Baixo, 16. ☎266 702 424. www.pensaopolicarpo.com. 20 rooms ⊟🅿. An old house beautifully restored is now a small hotel. The rooms are not all large but are comfortable and breakfast on the terrace is a nice change. Good quality for this price range.

◎◎🅢 **Albergaria Solar de Monfalim**. Largo da Misericórdia, 1. ☎266 750 000. www.monfalimtur.pt. 26 rooms ⊟🅿. All the rooms in this peaceful hotel, set in a 16C mansion, are different, though the comfort level remains the same.

◎◎🅢 **Casa de São Tiago –** Largo Alexandre Herculano, 2. ☎266 702 686. www.casa-stiago.com. 7 rooms. A delightful 16C house with its own inner garden and small orchard in the historical centre of the town. All the rooms are decorated with antique furniture.

◎🅢🅢🅢 **Hotel da Cartuxa –** Tv. da Palmeira, 4. ☎266 739 300. www. hoteldacartuxa.com.91 rooms ⚖&. A modern hotel close to the city walls west of the old town. Very well furnished, the rooms are ideal and at the rear, have balconies. Lovely pool and gardens that look out over the city walls.

◎◎🅢🅢 **Pousada dos Lóios –** Largo Conde de Vila Flor, ☎266 704 051 - www.pousadas.pt. 36 rooms ⚖. This elegant, luxurious pousada is situated in the buildings of the 16C Lóios convent. White-covered tables in the restaurant surround a patio on which orange trees grow. The chef has chosen to produce traditional cuisine which is delicious. There is a pool and solarium.

Paço de Vasco da Gama

🕐Open Mon–Sat 9am–5pm. Ring the bell for entry. ☎266 70 33 27.
This 15C mansion was built by the famous navigator and contains many items relating to the Great Discoveries, among them many paintings (which detail some of the fantastic animals encountered around the world) and frescoes. The building itself is impressive with cloisters, arcades and a chapel. Part of it is still used as lodging for Jesuit priests.

Templo Romano★

This Corinthian-style Roman temple erected in the 2C is often thought of as having been dedicated to Diana, though that is now considered unlikely. The capitals and bases of the columns are of Estremoz marble, the 14 Corinthian column shafts of granite. The temple is probably the best preserved in the Iberian peninsula and owes its present condition to its conversion into a fortress in the Middle Ages when it was walled up, after which it was used as a prison and later as an abattoir, only having been restored about a century ago.

Convento dos Lóios★

The Dos Lóios or St Eligius monastery, dedicated to St John the Evangelist, was founded in the 15C. It is now home to the city's pousada, as well as a **church★** (🕐open Tue–Sun 10am–12.30pm, 2pm–6pm (5pm winter); ◎€3 (€5 combined with the halls in the Palace of the Dukes of Cadaval); ☎266 70 47 14).
The church façade was remodelled after the earthquake of 1755 with the exception of the porch, which protects a Flamboyant Gothic doorway.
The nave, with lierne and tierceron vaulting, is lined with beautiful azulejos (1711) by António de Oliveira Bernardes, depicting the life of St Laurence Justinian, patriarch of Venice, whose writings influenced the Lóios monks. Two grilles in the pavement enable the castle's cistern, on the left, and an ossuary, on the right, to be seen.

Conventual buildings

The conventual buildings have been converted into a pousada. The chapter-house **door★** has outstanding architectural elegance and is a good

©Manuel Fernandes/iStockphoto.com

Templo Romano

example of the composite Luso-Moorish style; the crowning piece over the doorway and the piers topped by pinnacles which serve as a framework to the door are Gothic inspired; the columns are twisted and Manueline in style and the twin bays with horseshoe arches are, like the capitals, reminiscent of Moorish design.

Paço dos Duques de Cadaval

🕒*Open Tue–Sun 10am–12.30pm, 2pm–6pm (winter 5pm).* 🕒*Closed public holidays.* 💶*€2.50 (combined ticket with the church of the Couvent dos Loios).* ☎*266 70 47 14.*

The **Palace of the Dukes of Cadaval** (presently occupied by the Direcção de Estradas de Évora – Évora Road Network Department) is protected by two crenellated towers and has a façade that was remodelled in the 17C. It was given by King João I to his councillor, Martim Afonso de Melo, *alcalde* of Évora, in 1390. Kings João III and João V also lived within its walls at different periods.

The Dukes of Cadaval's **art gallery** contains a collection of historic documents on the Cadaval family and two fine Flemish commemorative plaques in bronze, dating from the late 15C.

▶ *Retrace your steps to the street between the Convento dos Lóios*

and the Museu Regional. Turn left into the street running perpendicular to the east end of the cathedral.

Paço dos Condes de Basto

The Palace of the Counts of Basto was built over the remains of the Roman wall including the Sertório Tower. The Gothic palace's main front has several paired Mudéjar windows.

▶ *Return to the east end of the cathedral and continue round.*

Casa dos Condes de Portalegre is a delightful Gothic and 16C Manueline-style mansion with a patio surrounded by a hanging garden and an openwork balcony. The **Casa de Garcia de Resende** is a 16C house in which the humanist Garcia de Resende (1470–1536) is said to have lived. Manueline decoration adorns the three sets of paired windows on the first floor.

The **Porta de Moura** gateway with its two towers formed part of the medieval town fortifications. A niche at the foot of the left tower contains a crucifix.

The picturesque **Largo da Porta de Moura** square is divided into two parts. On the larger of the two, in the centre, stands a beautiful Renaissance **fountain**★ which consists of a column surmounted by a white marble sphere.

Several lovely houses border the square: the 16C **Casa Cordovil** on the south side has an elegant loggia with twin arcades, festooned horseshoe arches and Moorish capitals, and a crenellated roof surmounted by a conical spire. On the west side, steps descend to the church of the former Carmelite Convent which has a Baroque **doorway**. On the east side are the Law Courts, housed in a modern building.

The 15C **Casa Soure** was formerly a part of the palace of the Infante Dom Luís. The Manueline façade has a gallery of rounded arches crowned by a conical spire.

▶ *Head toward Largo da Graça by way of Travessa da Caraça.*

Igreja de São Francisco

This early 16C church, which is preceded by a portico pierced by rounded, pointed and horseshoe arches, is crowned with battlements and conical pinnacles. The Manueline doorway is surmounted by a pelican and an armillary sphere, the respective emblems of João II and King Manuel.

The **interior★**, with ribbed vaulting, is surprisingly wide. The chancel contains two galleries, on the right, Renaissance, on the left, Baroque. The former chapterhouse is furnished with a balustrade of fluted marble and turned ebony columns and, as a covering to the walls, *azulejos* depicting scenes from the Passion.

▶ *Take the door to the left of the balustrade in the former chapter-house.*

Capela dos Ossos★

◷*Open 9am–12.30pm, 2.30pm–5.45pm (5.15pm in winter).* ✺€1. ☎266 70 45 21. This macabre ossuary chapel was built in the 16C by a Franciscan to induce meditation in his fellow men. The bones and skulls of 5 000 people have been used to face the walls and pillars.

Public Gardens (Jardim Público)

The public gardens are just to the south of the Igreja de São Francisco. Part of the 16C **Palácio de Dom Manuel** and the ruins of another 16C palace still stand in the gardens. Note the paired windows with horseshoe arches in the Luso-Moorish style.

Additional Sights

Fortifications★

Traces of the 1C Roman wall, reinforced by the Visigoths in the 7C, can be seen between the Paços dos Duques de Cadaval and dos Condes de Basto (Largo dos Colegiais). The 14C medieval wall marks the towAn limits to the north and west. The 17C fortifications now form the boundary of the public gardens to the south.

Universidade de Évora (Antiga Universidade dos Jesuitas)

◷*Open Mon–Fri 8am–6pm (8pm in Aug), Sat–Sun and public holidays, 8am–1pm, 3pm–6pm.* ◷*Closed public holidays.* The university occupies the former Jesuit University; the building's inner courtyard is of particular interest.

Buildings in the 16C Italian Renaissance style surround what is known as the main **Students' Cloisters★** *(Claustro Geral dos Estudos)* with its arched gallery. Facing the entrance, the pediment over the portico to the Sala das Actas (Hall of Acts) is decorated with statues personalising the royal and the ecclesiastical universities.

The classrooms opening onto the gallery are adorned with 18C *azulejos* representing the subjects taught here – physics, history, philosophy, mathematics.

Aqueduto da Água de Prata

The "Aqueduct of Silver Water" was completed in 1530 to bring clean water into the town. Below its huge arches, particularly at is end on Rua do Como, shops and restaurants have established themselves, giving a self-contained village feel to the area.

ÉVORAMONTE★
ÉVORA
POPULATION 700 – MICHELIN MAP 733

The small fortified town of Évoramonte, along the A 6 about 25km/15.5mi east of Évora, has a remarkable **setting**★ at the top of a high hill in the Alentejo. It was at Évoramonte on 26 May 1834 that the **Convention** was signed, which ended the civil war and under which the son of João VI, Pedro IV, Emperor of Brazil, compelled his brother Miguel I, an extremist whom he had vanquished at the Battle of Asseiceira, to abdicate in favour of his niece, Maria, and to go into exile.

- **Information:** There is a tiny information office just behind the castle.
- **Parking:** No problems parking here.
- **Don't Miss:** The castle and the house where the Convention was signed.
- **Organizing Your Time:** The place you would stop at for a coffee and a brief walk round on the way to somewhere else.
- **Also See:** ESTREMOZ, ÉVORA.

A Bit of History

Born at Queluz in 1798 Pedro was the son of the man who later became King John VI of Portugal. The family escaped Napoléon's advance and went to Brazil where Pedro was crowned King Pedro II and later Emperor. In 1831 he abdicated in favour of his son and returned to Portugal, planning to regain the crown that was rightly his, but which he had ceded to his daughter Maria. As she was still an infant Pedro's brother, Miguel, had become Regent and de facto monarch. Arguments and, later, battles ensued but in May 1834 an agreement was reached restoring Pedro as King Pedro IV and banning Miguel. That agreement was signed in Évoramonte. Pedro only had a few months to enjoy his throne, dying in October of the same year.

Access

1.5km/1mi from the modern village. Follow the signs to "Castelo de Évoramonte". After skirting the base of the 14C–17C ramparts, go through the entrance gate. If you are coming by bus, you will find it a struggle to get from the bus stop to the old town on foot.

Castle, Évoramonte

B.Brillion/MICHELIN

Sights

Castle★

🕐Open Jun–Sept, 10am–1pm, 2.30pm–6.30pm; Oct–Apr 10am–1pm, 2pm–5pm. 🕐Closed 1 Jan, Easter Sun, 1 May and 25 Dec. ⊕€1.50 (free Sun and public holidays 10am–1pm). ☎268 95 00 25.

The castle, which was first Roman, then Moorish, then radically remodelled in the 14C, emerges as a Gothic-style military monument in spite of further reconstruction in the 16C to repair damage caused by the 1531 earthquake. The medieval keep is girdled by rope motifs that knot in the middle of each façade. Inside, the central part of the castle consists of three superimposed storeys; each storey is covered with nine Gothic arches

resting on sturdy central pillars, those on the ground floor being massive and twisted. Three vaulted chambers have intricately carved granite capitals.

From the top, there is a **panorama★** of the surrounding countryside speckled with olive trees and small white villages, and to the north east, Estremoz.

Casa da Convenção

The house where the Convention was signed bears a commemorative plaque. It is said that the signing ceremony took so long that by the end of it there was only stale bread left to eat, though it was fashioned into what has since become a famed Portuguese dish, açorda – a soup of bread with water, coriander, garlic and olive oil.

FARO★

FARO

POPULATION 58 305– MICHELIN MAP 733
LOCAL MAP SEE ALGARVE

The capital of the Algarve is sited on Portugal's most southerly headland. Faro is these days one of the most important tourist towns on the Algarve though it still manages to retain its original charm, unlike some other resorts. Fishing (tunny and sardine), cork factories and marble works, food processing (beans) and canning, are still important. Faro's vast sandy beach, on an island, also attracts a great many tourists.

- 🛈 **Information:** Rua da Misericórdia 8–12. ☎289 803 604.
- ▶ **Orient Yourself:** On the Algarve coast, midway between east and west.
- 🅿 **Parking:** Very difficult – stay outside the town at the Largo de São Francisco.
- 👁 **Don't Miss:** The old town, the promenade and the beaches.
- 🕐 **Organizing Your Time:** An ideal place to be based for a week on the Algarve.
- 👶 **Also See:** PORTIMÃO, SILVES, TAVIRA.

Old Town★

The old town lies south of the Jardim Manuel Bivar, a peaceful quarter resting in the shadow of the circle of houses which stand like ramparts around it. It has dozens of restaurants, bars, cafés and hotels though still has charm.

Arco da Vila

The Arco da Vila is the finest of the gateways in the old Alfonso wall. It has Italian-style pilasters and, in a niche, a white marble statue of St Thomas Aqui-

nas. The top of the bell-tower above the arch has long been a nesting spot for a family of storks.

Cathedral

🕐 Open Mon–Sat 10am–6pm (Sat 10am–1pm). 🕐Closed public holidays. ⊕€2.50.

Only the entrance's imposing tower-portico remains from the original church built on the site of an old mosque following the Reconquist in 1251. Today, it combines a mix of styles, including a panelled ceiling covered with 17C azule-

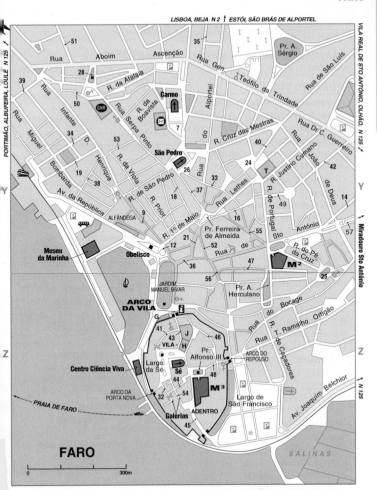

FARO

		Ferreira de Almeida Pr.	Y	16	Pé da Cruz Largo do	YZ	25
		Filipe Alistão R.	Y	18	Rasquinho R.	Z	46
1° de Maio R.	Y		Francisco Barreto R.	Y	19	Rebelo da Silva R.	Y	47
1° de Dezembro R.	YZ	56	Gil Fanes R.	Y	38	Repouso R. do	Z	48
5 de Outubro Av.	Y	57	Gomes Freire R.	Y	39	Sacadura Cabral R.	Y	49
Arco R. do	Z	32	Horta Machado R.	Y	40	Santo António R. de	Y	
Baptista Lopes R.	Y	33	Ivens R.	Y	21	São Pedro Largo de	Y	26
Carmo Largo de	Y	7	José Estevão R.	Y	37	São Sebastião Largo de	Y	28
Conselheiro Bivar R.	Y	9	Monsenhor Boto R.	Z	41	São Sebastião R.	Y	50
Conselheiro Tomas			Mouras Velhas Largo das	Y	24	Senhora da Saúde		
Ribeiro R.	Y	34	Mouzinho de			Estrada da	Y	51
Cunha Matos R.	Y	35	Albuquerque R.	Y	42	T. Valadim R.	Y	52
D. F. Gomes Pr.	Y	12	Município R. do	Z	43	Teófilo Braga R.	Y	53
D. F. Gomes R.	Y	36	Norberto Silva R.	Z	44	Trem R. do	Z	54
Dr Teixeira Guedes R.	Y	14	Nova do Castelo R.	Z	45	Vasco de Gama R.	Y	55

Museu de Etnografia Regional	Y	M³	Museu Municipal	Z	M²

Address Book

For coin ranges, see the Legend on the cover flap.

WHERE TO STAY

Pensão Residencial Central – *Largo Terreiro do Bispo, 12.* 289 807 291. *8 rooms*. A small, pleasing hotel with light and comfortable rooms overlooking the main square. One of the best addresses in town at this price.

Pensão Residencial Oceano - *Trv. Ivens, 21-1°.* 289 805 591. *22 rooms.* Ideal location in the pedestrianised area close to the marina. The rooms are clean and light. The staircase leading to reception is a little narrow so don't take really big bags! Good value.

Pensão Residencial Adelaide – *R. Cruz das Mestras, 9.* 289 802 383. *19 rooms*. A small hotel with big rooms (some with terraces) and pleasant furnishings. The only drawback is that many of the rooms overlook the street, which can be busy, particularly at weekends.

Faro – *R. D Francisco Gomes, 2* 289 830 830 - www.hotelfaro.pt; *90 rooms*. Simplicity and light are the two words that come to mind in describing the rooms at this newly opened hotel near the port. Breakfast is served on the top floor terrace, shaped like a boat and with a magnificent view over the marina and old town.

Residencial Dandy – *R. Filipe Alistão 62.* 289 824 791. *19 rooms*. A good value place that looks very smart inside and out though the best rooms are at the front: those in the back are not so well maintained.

Pensão São Filipe – *R. Infante Dom Henrique 55.* 289 824 182. *19 rooms.* A very good value hotel with en-suite rooms, cable TV and high fans in place of a/c, though the noise from the main road outside can be a bit testing at times, especially on summer weekends.

Hotel Dom Bernardo – *R General Teófilo da Trinidade 20.* 289 889 800. www.hoteldombernardo.com. A good modern hotel with striking interior design: try to get a room with a sea view for a few extra euro – it's worth it as other rooms overlook a busy street.

WHERE TO EAT

Chalavar – *R. Infante D Enrique, 120.* 289 82 24 45. *Closed Sun*. A lively and friendly restaurant owned by a fisherman - so you'll not be surprised that the menu has lots of fish!. Big portions and very tasty.

Pontinha – *R. Pé da Cruz, 5* 289 82 06 49. *Closed Sun*. At the back of the pedestrian zone on the praça da Liberdade, a simple restaurant which has a large choice, among them many local specialities, so if you want to eat like a local, this could be the place.

Mesa dos Mouros – *Largo da Sé, 10.* 289 878 873. *Closed Mon.* If you are passing the cathedral on your evening stroll do not hesitate to stop here for a refined and elegant dinner, often accompanied by a concert from the local family of storks. Very reasonably priced for this quality of food.

O Aldeão - *Largo de S. Pedro, 54–57.* 289 823 339. On the square where S Pedro's church is located, this restaurant has charm and style. Once inside you will delight in discovering the regional dishes from the Algarve and the Alentejo regions. Most enjoyable.

Camané – *Praia de Faro 9km/5.6mi to the west of Faro. Av. Nascente.* 289 81 75 39. *Closed Mon and 2 weeks in May*. This restaurant has a pleasant outdoor terrace overlooking the Formosa river. Seafood specialities.

Ve Re Pé – *Trav. Castilho 6.* 966 904 193. *Closed Sun eve.* A family-run restaurant for the budget-conscious though still good value. One main meat and one main fish menu each day though you can get toher things too.

Sol e Jardim – *Praça Ferreira de Almeida 22–23.* 289 820 030. *Closed Sun.* A good quality restaurant with a large dining room, good Portuguese food and live folk music Fridays.

Fim do Mundo – *R. Vasco da Gama 53.* 289 826 299. *Closed Mon and Tue.* A good value restaurant highly favoured by the locals, serving good grilled meat and fish.

Grutas de São Mamede

Guided tours (25min) Jul–Sept, 9am–7pm; Apr–Jun, 9am–6pm; Oct–Mar, 9am–5pm. 244 70 38 38. www.grutasmoeda.com. €5 .

Bandits were said to have hurled down the body of a traveller along with his purse, in their excessive haste, leading these spectacular caves to be called the Money Caves, **Grutas da Moeda**. There are nine "chambers", and the variety of colours, a waterfall, strange multi-coloured calcareous deposits in the Shepherd's Chamber, are worth seeing.

Grutas de Alvados

Guided tours (35min) Jun–Aug, 10am–8pm; Sept–May, 10am–5pm. €4.60 (€3 for children). www.grutasalvadas.com.

These caves were discovered in 1964 on the north west flank of the Pedra de Altar hill. They extend for 450m/1 476ft across about ten chambers linked by long tunnels, each having its own small limpid lake and colourful rock deposits. They have an additional attraction due to the golden colour of the walls, the number of stalactites and stalagmites joined together forming pillars, and the zigzag cracks in the ground.

Grutas de Santo António

Same as Alvados. €4.80 (children €3). The three chambers (the main one with an area of 4 000sq m/4 784sq yd is 43m/141ft high) and a short gallery all have delicate rose-coloured concretions. In one of the secondary chambers there is a small lake.

FIGUEIRA DA FOZ★
COIMBRA
POPULATION 62 601 – MICHELIN MAP 733
PLAN IN THE RED MICHELIN GUIDE SPAIN AND PORTUGAL

Figueira da Foz, on the mouth of the Mondego river, due west of Coimbra, is overlooked by the Serra da Boa Viagem. Tourists are attracted by the vast beach of fine sand which lines the wide curve of Figueira bay. This bay, previously known as Mondego bay, is overlooked by a fort of golden stone that was captured from the French by students of Coimbra University. Shortly before this momentous event Wellington landed the first British troops here in August 1808. From Figueira began the advance south that was to bring the first battles of the Peninsular War not far from Óbidos at Roliça and Vimeiro. Figueira, which was built in the last century, lives primarily from tourism, its fishing industry (sardines and cod) and its shipyards.

- **Information:** Av. 25 Abril. ☎233 422 610. www.figueiraturismo.com.
- **Orient Yourself:** On the coast close to Coimbra midway between Lisbon and Porto.
- **Parking:** Difficult in mid summer but not too bad at other times.
- **Don't Miss:** A quick excursion 4km/2.5mi north to Serra de Boa Viagem.
- **Organizing Your Time:** You could happily spend a few days here.
- **Also See:** COIMBRA, CONIMBRIGA, VISEU.

Sights

Figueira is a beach resort and as such the beaches close by are of major interest. They are all good and there is plenty of room, even in mid summer. Apart from that the headland of Serra de Boa Viagem, a heavily wooded headland, is a beautiful spot. In the town itself the **Museu do Mar** (*Tue–Fri 9.30am–12.30pm, 2pm–5pm*) and the **Mercado Municipal Dr Santos Rocha** (*9.30am–5.15pm; €1.40*) are worth a visit, the latter with its impressive archaeological selection.

GUARDA
GUARDA
POPULATION 26 400 – MICHELIN MAP 733

Guarda, a pleasant health resort and the highest town in Portugal, stands at an altitude of 1 000m/3 281ft in the eastern foothills of the Serra da Estrela. Its name "protector" recalls that at one time it was the main stronghold of the province of Beira Alta near Spain. Medieval castles and fortresses are dotted throughout the region guarding the border. Over the last few years the town has sprouted modern quarters around its medieval centre which is enclosed within the remains of ancient fortifications.

- **Information:** Praça Luis de Camões. ☎271 205 530.
- ▶ **Orient Yourself:** East of Viseu, not too far from the border with Spain.
- **Don't Miss:** The Eastern fortified towns which surround Guarda.
- **Organizing Your Time:** A couple of days would allow you to make several excursions.
- **Also See:** BELMONTE, VISEU.

Sights

Fortifications
Most of the once-impressive city walls have now fallen into decay, with the only preserved remains being the Torre dos Ferreiros (Blacksmiths' Tower), the 12C and 13C keep (Torre de Menagem) and the Porta d'El Rei and Porta da Estrela (King's and Star Gates). Public access is very limited and quite difficult, sadly.

Cathedral★
🕓Open 9am–noon, 2pm–5pm. ☎271 32 03 12. 🕓Closed Mon, 1 Jan, Easter Sun, 1 May and 25 Dec.
The cathedral (sé) was begun in 1390 in the Gothic style, but as it was only completed in 1540, Renaissance and Manueline elements are clearly visible in its decoration. The granite edifice is crowned with pinnacles and trefoils which give it a certain resemblance to the monastery at Batalha. The northern façade is embellished with an ornate Gothic doorway surmounted by a Manueline window. In the main façade, a Manueline doorway is framed by two octagonal towers emblazoned at their bases with the coat of arms of Bishop Dom Pedro Vaz Gavião, who played a part in getting the cathedral completed.

©Jorge Casais/Fotolia.com

Cathedral

Interior★
The lierne and tierceron vaulting over the transept crossing has a key-stone in the form of a cross of the Order of Christ. In the chancel is a Renaissance altarpiece made of Ançã stone in the 16C and gilded in the 18C. Attributed to Jean de Rouen, the high relief – which includes over 100 figures – depicts scenes from the Lives of the Virgin and Christ on four levels. A 16C altarpiece in the south apsidal chapel, also attributed to Jean de Rouen, represents the Last Supper.

Museu da Guarda

🕐 Open Tue–Sun 10am–12.30pm, 2pm–5.30pm. 🕐 Closed 1 Jan, Good Fri, Easter Mon, 1 May and 25 Dec. ✆€2 (no charge Sun or public holiday mornings). ☎271 21 34 60.

The regional museum, which is housed at the foot of the ramparts in the former bishop's palace, dates from the early 17C and has preserved its Renaissance cloisters. The collections include displays of regional archaeology as well as painting and sculpture.

The Eastern Fortified Towns

Distances indicated are from Guarda.

Medieval strongholds, built in the 17C–18C to protect the border, and numerous fortified small towns or villages still seem to mount guard at the top of a hillock or a steep headland, in the heart of the Beira Alta.

Almeida★

45km/28mi to the north east.
Less than 10km/6.2mi from the border, the peaceful little town of Almeida, perhaps the most impressive of all the fortified towns of the region, crowns a hill 729m/2 491ft high with its ramparts. Taken by the Spanish in 1762, then by the French under Massena in 1810, it has, nevertheless, kept intact its double **fortifications**★, in the form of a twelve-pointed star in pure Vauban style, which were completed in the 18C. Three arched gateways with monumental porches preceded by bridges, give access to the interior, the most important being the **Portas de São Francisco**. A medieval fortress dating from the time of King Dinis, this village clustered round a hill has only one ruined

tower remaining, next to a Gothic gate. The **Casamatas** (a stronghold that accommodated 5 000 men), is also well worth a visit.

Castelo Melhor★

77km/ 47.8mi to the north east.
Visible from the N 222, the village clings to the flanks of a rocky peak dotted with olive trees. A medieval **wall**★ reinforced with round towers encircles the grassy and bare summit.

Castelo Mendo

35km/ 21.7mi to the east.
Cobbled alleys crisscross on a rocky hillock among the remains of a Gothic wall, where the main gate is wedged between two towers. The village still has the marks of a flourishing past with a few Renaissance buildings, including a 17C church.

Celorico da Beira

28km/17.4mi to the north west.
This busy small town is on the extreme north of a wooded ridge at the end of the Serra da Estrela. The square keep of the ancient castle rises up at the top, surrounded by a small wall.

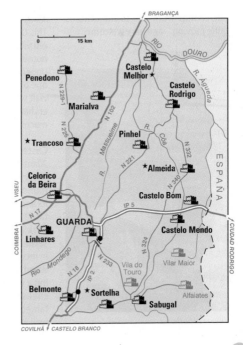

Linhares

*49km/30.4mi to the west (the last
6km/3.7mi after Carrapichana follow
a winding road).*

The beautiful outer wall of the castle,
built at the time of Dinis I, with its two
square crenellated towers, runs round
the top of a granite spur dominating
the upper valley of the Mondego. The
village has a 16C pillory with an armillary sphere.

Marialva

69km/42.8mi to the north.

Marialva is dominated by its ancient castle. Within its walls, built in 1200, there
is a complete, but deserted, village. A
town hall, houses, prison, watch-tow-
ers, all standing desolate, are now over-
grown by olives and other plants. For
some reason it was depopulated and
the only buildings now standing that are
visitable are the church (Igreja Matriz),
the keep, the bell-tower and the pillory. Visits are organised daily between
10am and 5pm, though you are better
off just going to the Turismo and asking
for access.

Outside the walls a newer, populated
village has taken hold and it makes a
pleasing change with chapels, fountains, squares, cafés and restaurants.
The change from one to the other is
quite moving – and very welcome.

Village of Soltelha

H. Champollion/MICHELIN

Penedono

74km/46mi to the north.

The town of Penedono is perched on
a rocky crest 947m/3 106ft high in
the Beira Alta. It is overlooked on its
northern side by a graceful and triangular fortified castle, the **Castelo
Roqueiro** (🕐open Mon–Fri 9am–5pm,
Sat 10am–12.30pm, 2.30pm–5pm; Sun
2.30pm–5pm; 🕐closed Good Fri and
Easter Sun; if closed, ask at the building
next to the castle; ☎254 50 41 50 or 254 60
57 70), crowned with pyramidal merlons.
A 16C **pillory** stands before the steps
leading up to the castle. Pass through
the ramparts and turn left towards the
simple entrance gate which is flanked by
two battlemented turrets. 🚶The climb
up to the castle is difficult.

Sabugal

33km/20.5mi to the south east.

The small city of Sabugal, on a hillock
round its fortified castle, dominates the
Côa valley. Founded by Alfonso X of León
at the beginning of the 13C, it became
Portuguese in 1282 on the marriage of
Isabel of Aragon and King Dom Dinis of
Portugal. The present appearance of the
castle dates from the late 13C.

Sortelha★

45km/28mi to the south.

This 12C **stronghold**★, hemming in the
old village with its picturesque granite
houses, stands on a spur dominating the
upper Zêzere valley. You enter it through
one of the Gothic gates of the fortified
wall, where the two existing square towers have their own surrounding wall with
machicolated gateways.

Castelo Rodrigo

20km/12mi north of Almeida.

The village of Castelo Rodrigo is surrounded by a new road and the entry to
its ancient heart is via three monumental 13C gates – though make sure you
park outside and walk in. Men have
settled here since at least 500 BC and
in recent years many of the once dilapi-
dated buildings have been restored, giving a very good feel to the place. Local
cheese, wine and smoked meats are
famed throughout the region and it's
well worth stopping to try them.

GUIMARÃES★★
BRAGA
POPULATION 161 870 – MICHELIN MAP 733

In the 10C, soon after it was founded by the Countess Mumadona, Guimarães consisted of a monastery with a defensive tower and a few neighbouring houses. In the Middle Ages new quarters were added. Nowadays Guimarães is a prosperous commercial city with cutlery, tanning and kitchenware industries and crafts such as gold and silversmith work, pottery, embroidery, linen damask and the carving of wooden yokes.

- **Information:** Praca de São Tiago. ☎253 518790.
- ▶ **Orient Yourself:** North-east of Porto about 22km/13.6mi south east of Braga.
- **Parking:** To visit the old town, leave your car in the underground car-park in the República do Brasil, south east of the town. There is also a large parking area at the rear of the castle except on Fridays (market day).
- **Don't Miss:** Make sure you stop for a glass of wine at one of the terrace cafés on the Largo da Oliveira or the praça da São Tiago.
- **Organizing Your Time:** A full day at least.
- **Also See:** BRAGA, PORTO.

A Bit of History

The cradle of Portugal
In 1095 Alfonso VI, King of León and Castile, bestowed the County of Portucale on his son-in-law, Henry of Burgundy. Henry had the tower at Guimarães converted into a castle and installed his wife, the Princess Teresa (Tareja), there. In about 1110 Teresa bore Henry a son, **Afonso Henriques**, who succeeded his father in 1112. The young prince revolted

against his mother, and on 24 June 1128 seized power following the Battle of São Mamede. He vanquished the Moors at Ourique on 25 July 1139 and was proclaimed King of Portugal by his troops.

Gil Vicente (1470–1536)
The poet and goldsmith, Gil Vicente, born in Guimarães in 1470, lived at the courts of King João II and King Manuel I. He wrote plays to entertain the king and the court, and mysteries *(autos)* to be

Address Book

For coin ranges, see cover flap.

WHERE TO STAY
Residencial das Trinas – *R. das Trinas, 29.* ☎253 517 358 11. *rooms.* A small, welcoming *pensão* in the old town. The rooms are furnished in a traditional style with TV and air-conditioning, and look aout over the street, though the view from the rear is better. The quality is very good for this price range.

Residencial Mestre d'Avis – *R. D João I, 40.* ☎253 422 770. *16 rooms.* Near the historic centre of town, this imposing building hides behind it very well appointed rooms, though some are a little on the small side. The proprietor

is very knowledgeable about the town and is a very good guide.

Paço de São Cipriano – Tabuadelo *(6km/3.7mi south of Guimarães).* ☎253 565 337. www.pacoscipriano. com. *7 rooms.* Set within a huge estate, this beautiful hotel will appeal to lovers of antiquity. The gardens are stunning, the aromas from flowers scintillating. All in all, a beautiful place to stay.

Pousada de Nossa Senhora da Oliveira – *Rua de Santa Maria.* ☎253 514 157. www.pousada.pt. *16 rooms.* This beautifully furnished and welcoming inn at the heart of the city's historical centre has a good restaurant serving regional specialities.

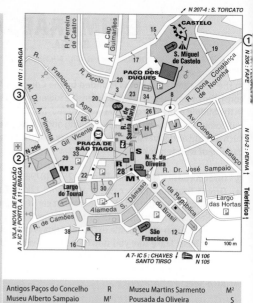

performed in the churches. His 44 plays provide a precise, if satirical, panorama of Portuguese society at the beginning of the 16C, while the variety of his inspiration allied to the lightness of his touch and finesse of his style make him the virtual creator of the Portuguese theatre.

Castle Hill

Castle★

🕐 Open Tue–Sun 9.30am–12.30pm, 2pm–5.30pm. 🕐 Closed 1 Jan, Good Fri, Easter Mon, 1 May and 25 Dec. ⬡€1.50 (keep). ☏253 41 22 73.

In the 10C Countess Mumadona had the 28m/91.8ft keep built to protect the monastery and small town in its midst. The castle was later built under Henry of Burgundy and reinforced in the 15C. Seven square towers surround the keep and although you can walk to the top you should take care as the stonework is not as secure as it might be. Afonso was born in the keep of this castle.

Igreja de São Miguel do Castelo

🕐 Open Tue–Sun 9.30am–12.30pm, 2pm–5.30pm. 🕐 Closed 1 Jan, Easter Sun, 1 May, 25 Dec. ☏253 41 22 73.

This small 12C Romanesque church contains a font in which Afonso Henriques was baptised, in addition to a great many funerary slabs.

Paço dos Duques de Bragança★

☚ Guided tours (30min) 9.30am–12.30pm, 2pm–6.30pm (5.30pm Sept–Jun) ⬡€3 (no charge on Sun and public holiday mornings). ☏253 412 273.

The palace was built in the early 15C by the first Duke of Bragança, Afonso I, illegitimate son of King Dom João I. The architecture shows a strong Burgundian influence, particularly in the roof and the unusual 39 brick chimneys. The palace was one of the most sumptuous dwellings in the Iberian Peninsula until the 16C when the court moved to Vila Viçosa (☚ see VILA VIÇOSA). The vast rooms were heated by huge fireplaces. On the first floor the **ceilings★** of oak and chestnut in the Dining and Banqueting Halls and the 16C and 18C **tapestries★** are special. The Tournai tapestries depicting the capture of Arzila and Tangiers are copies of the series woven after cartoons by Nuno Gonçalves.

Other decoration includes Persian carpets, 17C Portuguese furniture, Chinese porcelain, weapons and armour, as well as Dutch and Italian paintings.

Historic Centre★★

Wide avenues mark the limits of the harmonious, well-preserved historic quarter, which makes a pleasant stroll with its maze of streets, squares and old houses.

Convento de Nossa Senhora da Oliveira

The monastery dedicated to Our Lady of the Olive Tree was founded by Countess Mumadona in the 10C. Only the Gothic collegiate church with its Romanesque cloisters and chapter-house (now the museum) remains.

Colegiada de Nossa Senhora da Oliveira

The main doorway of this collegiate church is surmounted by a 14C Gothic pediment. Inside, note the silver altar in the Chapel of the Holy Sacrament (Capela do Santíssimo Sacramento). A Gothic **shrine** in front of the church contains a *padrão* commemorating the victory over the Moors at the Battle of the Salado in 1340. Legend has it that during the completion of the porch in 1342 the trunk of the olive tree, which stood in front of the church, suddenly sprouted leaves: thus, the church's name.

Museu Alberto Sampaio★

🕒*Open Tue–Sun 10am–6pm.* 🕒*Closed 1 Jan, Good Fri, Easter Sun, 1 May and 25 Dec.* ✎€2 (no charge Sun morning).

Façade of the buildings on Alameda São Damaso

H. Champollion/MICHELIN

The museum is housed in the conventual buildings. In a Gothic chapel to the right on entering is the fine **recumbent figure**★ in granite of Dona Constança de Noronha, wife of Dom Afonso, first Duke of Bragança. On the first floor are several statues including the 15C alabaster statue of Our Lady of Pity and a large wooden altarpiece from the 16C. The galleries that follow contain **church plate**★. Much of the collegiate church treasure was donated by Dom João I. In addition to the tunic worn by João I at the Battle of Aljubarrota, the room of the same name also contains the silver-gilt **triptych**★, which shows the Nativity, Annunciation, Purification and Presenta-

Recumbent figure of Dona Constança de Noronha

B. Brillion/MICHELIN

tion at the Temple on the left and, on the right, the Shepherds and the Magi. Among other pieces of the treasure, note a silver-gilt Gothic chalice with enamel embossing, a Manueline monstrance attributed to Gil Vicente and a finely engraved 16C Manueline **cross**★ depicting scenes from the Passion.

Additional Sights

Museu Martins Sarmento

Guided tours (30min) Tue–Sun 9.30am–noon, 2pm–5pm. ○ Closed public holidays and 24 Jun (local holiday). €1.50.
The museum, housed partly in the Gothic cloisters of the Church of São Domingos, includes a large collection of archaeological exhibits from the pre-Roman cities of Sabroso and Briteiros.

Igreja de São Francisco

This 15 church was remodelled in the 17C. The capitals in the main doorway represent the legend of St Francis. The chancel, with a Baroque altar carved in wood and gilded, is decorated with 18C **azulejos**★ depicting the life of St Anthony. In the **sacristy**★ (○ *open Tue–Sat 9.30am–noon, 3pm–5pm; Sun 9.30am–1pm*) is a fine coffered ceiling ornamented with grotesques and an Arrábida marble table standing against an elegant Carrara marble column. The chapter-house, which gives onto 16C Renaissance cloisters, is closed by a fine Gothic grille.

LAGOS★
FARO

POPULATION 27 041 – MICHELIN MAP 733
LOCAL MAP SEE ALGARVE

Lagos was the capital of the Algarve from 1576 to 1756. Today, in spite of great popularity with tourists, it has managed to preserve both character and charm with its fort, walls and old quarter. The most attractive approaches to Lagos are from Aljezur in the north along the N 120 or from Vila do Bispo in the west along the N 125. From both of these roads there are **views**★ of the town and the large marina that now lines the bay. Apart from being a seaside resort and a fishing port well sheltered by the Ponta da Piedade promontory, Lagos is also an important yachting centre organising international regattas.

- **Information:** R Vasco da Gama (São João). ☎282 763 031. www.cm-lagos.pt.
- ▶ **Orient Yourself:** On the Algarve coast, 23km/14mi west of Portimão.
- P **Parking:** A large parking area in the Avda. dos Desocobrimentos.
- **Don't Miss:** The church of S. Antonio.
- **Organizing Your Time:** Visit the sights in the morning and the beach in the afternoon.
- **Also See:** FARO, SAGRES, PORTIMÃO.

Some History

The harbour in the past

Lagos was an important harbour at the time of the Great Discoveries and it was from here that most of the African expeditions put to sea. It served as Prince Henry the Navigator's principal maritime base and as the port of registry to Gil Eanes who, in 1434, rounded for the first time in history Cape Bojador, a point on the west coast of the Sahara, which until then had been the last outpost of the habitable world. On Prince Henry's orders, one expedition followed another down the coast of Africa, each time adding to the knowledge of ocean currents and improving navigational techniques.

Forte da Ponta da Bandeira

© Inacio Pires/Dreamstime.com

Sights

Praça da República

A **statue of Prince Henry the Navigator**, erected in 1960 to commemorate the 500th anniversary of his death, stands in the middle of the square. Its presence explains why the square is better known as the Praça Infante Dom Henrique. The house with arcades on the right side of the square is the former slave market, **Mercado de Escravos**. The present building was reconstructed after the earthquake in 1755.

▶ *Take Rua Henrique Correia da Silva leading straight off the square.*

Igreja de Santo António★

🕑*Open Tue–Sun 9.30am–12.30pm; 2pm–5pm.* 🕑*Closed public holidays.* 🎫*€2.20*

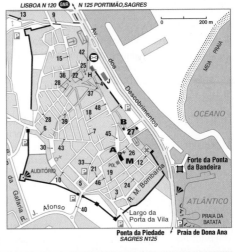

(combined ticket with Museu Municipal below). ☎282 762 301.

The plain façade gives no inkling of the exuberance and virtuosity of the **Baroque decoration**★ which reigns inside. Outstanding are the ceiling painted in false relief, the Eucharistic symbols and statues of gilded wood in the chancel, the walls and the gallery ceiling.

Museu Municipal

🕐*Open Tue–Sat 10am–1pm, 2pm–6pm, Sun 10am–1pm.* 🕐*Closed public holidays.* ⊙€2.20 (see church). ☎282 76 14 10.

The regional museum adjoining the Igreja de Santo António contains an interesting archaeological collection

(coins and fragments of mosaics) and an ethnographical section devoted to the Algarve (note the cork work).

Forte da Ponta da Bandeira

🕐*Open Tue–Sun 9.30am–12.30pm, 2pm–5pm.* 🕐*Closed public holidays.* ⊙€2. ☎282 76 14 10.

The 17C fort juts out into the sea guarding a small harbour. There are boat trips from the harbour to Ponta da Piedade. Cross the drawbridge to enter the inner courtyard. The halls contain displays on the Great Discoveries. The chapel is decorated with 17C **azulejos**. There is a **view** from the terrace of the town and the coast.

LAMEGO
VISEU

POPULATION 9 100 – MICHELIN MAP 733
LOCAL MAP SEE VALE DO DOURO

Lamego is an attractive small episcopal and commercial town known for its sparkling wine and its smoked ham. It lies near the Douro Valley in a landscape of green hills covered with vines and maize. The town, which is rich in 16C and 18C bourgeois houses, is overlooked by two hills on which stand respectively the ruins of a 12C fortified castle and the Baroque Santuário de Nossa Senhora dos Remédios, famous for the annual pilgrimages held in late August and early September. It hosted Portugal's first Parliament in 1143.

- **Information:** Av. Visconde Guedes Teixeira. ☎254 612 005.
- **Orient Yourself:** Just south of the River Douro, inland from Porto.
- **Don't Miss:** Santuário Nossa Senhora dos Remédios.
- **Organizing Your Time:** Allow two hours.
- **Also See:** VALE DO DOURO, VILA REAL.

Sights

Museu de Lamego★

🕐*Open Tue–Sun 10am–12.30pm, 2pm–5pm.* 🕐*Closed 1 Jan, Good Fri, Easter Sun, 1 May, 8 Sept and 25 Dec.*⊙€2 (no charge Sun morning). The museum is housed in the former episcopal palace, a majestic 18C building.

The right-hand section of the ground floor contains mainly religious sculpture from the Middle Ages to the Baroque period and a fine collection of coats of arms which adorned the façades of man-

sions belonging to the nobility. On the first floor two series of works – paintings and tapestries – are particularly noteworthy. The **five paintings on wood**★ (early 16C) by Vasco Fernandes were part of the altarpiece in Lamego's cathedral (👆 see VISEU: Viseu School of Painting). From left to right they show the Creation, Annunciation, Visitation (the most outstanding in the series), the Presentation at the Temple and Circumcision. The six **16C Brussels tapestries**★ are of mythological scenes (note the myth of Oedipus and the rich composition of the Temple of Latone). On the first floor are two Baroque chapels of carved and gilded wood, one of which, São João Evangelista from the Convento das Chagas, has statues and niches. There is also a Chinese room, gold and silver plate and ceramics.

The second ground-floor section contains another Baroque chapel and some fine 16C and 18C *azulejos*, in particular polychromed ones from the Palácio Valmor in Lisbon.

Capela do Desterro

🕐*Apply to Senhora Aurora Rodrigues, Rua Cardoso Avelino: ☎254 613 788.*

This chapel, built in 1640, is decorated inside with 18C carved and gilded wood-work and 17C *azulejos*; the coffered **ceiling**★ is outstanding with painted scenes from the Life of Our Lord.

Santuário de Nossa Senhora dos Remédios

The 18C façade, on which stucco serves to highlight the elegant granite curves, overlooks the crossed ramps of the **staircase** ornamented with *azulejos* and bristling with a multitude of pinnacles which recalls that of Bom Jesus near Braga.

The view from the church parvis *(access by car possible: 4km/2.5mi)* extends over Lamego to the heights on the horizon which border the Douro.

LEÇA DO BAILIO
PORTO
POPULATION 15 673 – MICHELIN MAP 733

It is said that after the First Crusade, the domain of Leça do Bailio was given to brothers of the Order of the Hospital of St John of Jerusalem who had come from Palestine, probably in the company of Count Henry of Burgundy, father of the first King of Portugal. Leça was the mother house of this Order (now the Order of Malta) until 1312 when this was transferred to Flor da Rosa.

▸ **Orient Yourself:** Just 8km/5mi north of Porto.
🕐 **Organizing Your Time:** A day trip up from Porto will suffice.
👍 **Don't Miss:** Lamego and the Mateus Palace near Vila Real.

Sight

Igreja do Mosteiro★

This fortress church, built in granite in the Gothic period, is characterised outside by pyramid-shaped merlons emphasising the entablature by the tall battlemented tower surrounded with balconies and watchtowers and by the plain façade adorned only with a door with carved capitals below and a rose window above. The historiated capitals portray scenes from Genesis and the Gospels – of particular note are Adam and Eve with the serpent and the angel. In 1372, the church hosted the royal wedding of King Fernando and Leonor Teles.

Several of the Hospitallers are buried here. The chancel, which has stellar vaulting, contains the 16C tomb of the bailiff Frei Cristóvão de Cernache, which is surmounted by a painted statue (16C) while the north apsidal chapel houses the tomb of the prior Frei João Coelho, with a reclining figure by Diogo Pires the Younger (1515). The Manueline-style **font**★ in the lateral apse is carved in Ança stone *(👍see COIMBRA: The Coimbra School of Sculpture)* by the same artist.

LEIRIA
LEIRIA
POPULATION 12 470 – MICHELIN MAP 733

Leiria is pleasantly set at the confluence of two rivers, the Liz and the Lena, and at the foot of a hill crowned by a medieval castle. Its role as a crossroads near well-known beaches – notably Nazaré – the sanctuary of Fátima and the magnificent architecture of Batalha and Alcobaça, makes it a favoured stopping place.

- **Information:** Jardim Luís de Camões. ☎244 823 773.
- **Orient Yourself:** Midway between Lisbon and Coimbra on the N 8 coast road.
- **Don't Miss:** The castle and the Igreja de Nossa Senhora da Penha.
- **Organizing Your Time:** A full day is fine, with time to relax.
- **Also See:** ALCOBAÇA, BATALHA, FÁTIMA.

Castle★

Open Apr–Sept, Tue–Sun 10am–6pm; Oct–Mar, Tue–Sun 9am–5pm. Closed 1 Jan and 25 Dec. €2.25.
In an exceptional **site★**, inhabited even before the arrival of the Romans, Afonso Henriques, first King of Portugal, had a fortified castle built in 1135. This castle formed part of the defence of the southern border of the kingdom of Portugal at the time, Santarém and Lisbon still being under Moorish domination. After the fall of these two cities in 1147, the castle lost its significance and fell into ruin. In the 14C, King Dinis, who undertook first the preservation and then the extension of the pine forest at Leiria, rebuilt the castle in order that he might live in it with his queen, Saint Isabel.

The present buildings, modified in the 16C, have been restored. After entering the perimeter of the castle walls through a door flanked by two square crenellated towers, you reach a pleasantly shaded garden courtyard. A stairway to the left leads to the centre of the castle. The royal palace is then on the left, the keep is straight ahead, and on the right the remains of the 15C chapel of Nossa Senhora da Pena with a graceful lanceolate Gothic chancel and an arcade decorated with Manueline motifs.

Paço Real (Royal Palace)
A staircase leads to a vast rectangular hall with a gallery adorned with depressed, three-centred arches resting on slender twin columns. The gallery, once the royal balcony, affords a good **view** of Leiria lying below.
The narrow streets of the town beneath the castle are pleasant for a stroll.

Pinhal de Leiria

This vast pine forest, planted over 700 years ago by Dom Dinis, extends to the west of town and leads onto one of the most beautiful stretches of coastline in Portugal. Come here to walk and relax.

Craftsmanship and Folklore

The Leiria region has kept alive its tradition of art and folklore. The glazed and multicoloured pottery of Cruz da Légua and Milagres, the decorated glassware of Marinha Grande, the willow baskets and ornaments and the woven coverlets of Mira de Aire are among the best known crafts of the district.
The traditional festivals and customs have lost none of their spontaneity. The folklore of the Leiria region is closely associated with that of its neighbour, the Ribatejo. The women's costumes consist of a small black felt hat with feathers, a coloured blouse edged with lace, a short skirt and shoes with wide low heels. It differs from that of the Ribatejo only by the addition of a gold necklace and earrings. Folk dancing displays are held every year (*see Calendar of Events*).

LINDOSO★
VIANA DO CASTELO
MICHELIN MAP 733
LOCAL MAP SEE PARQUE NACIONAL DA PENEDA-GERÊS

Built like an amphitheatre against the southern flanks of one of the last mountains in the Serra do Soajo, Lindoso, in the far north of Portugal on the border with Spain, sets out its austere granite houses in tiered rows up to a height of 462m/1 516ft, perfectly integrated into the rocky landscape – despite the presence of a few recent constructions – and surrounded by cultivated terraces (maize, vines). The castle stands on a hillock where there is also an unusual group of *espigueiros* (see below).

▶ **Orient Yourself:** Lindoso is a small village in the Serra Amarela mountains, part of the Parque Nacional da Peneda-Gerês.

Don't Miss: The granaries, which look like huge tombs.

Organizing Your Time: The type of place you will pass through, stopping for an hour or so.

Sights

Granaries★

Covering a rocky platform at the foot of the castle, the 60 or more *espigueiros* are grouped together, resembling a cemetery. They are small granite buildings, perched on piles, most with one or two crosses on the roof. Their construction dates back to the 18C and 19C. They are still used today for drying maize.

Castle

Open Apr–Sept, Tue–Sun 10am–12.30pm, 2.30pm–5pm. €1.

Facing the border, the castle was attacked several times by the Spanish during the War of Independence in the 17C. Restored, it appears again as a crenellated feudal keep in the middle of a small 17C square with a surrounding wall with bastions and watch turrets. From the watchpath there are views over the Lima valley and the surrounding Portuguese and Galician mountains.

B. Brillion/MICHELIN

Granaries

LISBOA★★★

LISBON – LISBOA
POPULATION GREATER LISBON 3.8 MILLION
MICHELIN MAP 733

The capital of Portugal stands midway between north and south. At the time of the Great Discoveries, Lisbon, according to the Portuguese poet Camões, was the "princess of the world… before whom even the ocean bows".

The old town was built on the northern shore of the "Straw Sea", as the bulge in the Tagus River (Tejo) was called on account of the golden reflections of the sun at this spot. Lisbon has a jumbled skyline, its buildings dotted over seven hills offering wonderfully varied views. The attraction of the city lies in its light, its pastel ochres, pinks, blues and greens, and the mosaic paving on its streets and squares – the small black and white paving-stones made of limestone and basalt known as *empedrados*. With its maze of narrow streets, alleys and steps in the old quarters, its magnificent vistas along wide avenues and its lively harbour and exotic gardens, Lisbon is a delightful city to explore.

Like any modern city, Lisbon is an eclectic mix of old and new and there are always construction and reconstruction works going on. Having said that Lisbon is doing its best to build and extend a modern urban mass transit system (the metro is excellent) whilst maintaining its original character. The choice of Lisbon as the site for Expo'98 resulted in a large-scale rebuilding programme along the Tagus, particularly at the Olivais docks, near the exhibition site, now a major tourist attraction and shopping centre, and the Santo Amaro, Santos and Alcântara docks, with their leisure facilities which include bars, restaurants and discos. Museums and other attractions abound, its restaurants provide wonderful traditional meals though with many modern chefs using novel new methods, and it still retains its "teashops" – almost a relic from another age. Above all, it must be said, Lisbon is probably one of the friendliest capitals in Europe.

- **Information:** The main tourist office is on Praça do Comércio (which is close to the Cais de Sodré station at the lower end of the Baixa and the arrival point for the bus from the airport (☎210 312 810/5; www.visitlisboa.com). There are also several "Ask Me" kiosks dotted around the city in summer and a tourist office at Lisbon airport.
- **Orient Yourself:** A little more than halfway down the coast from north to south, on the Atlantic at the mouth of the Tagus.
- **Parking:** Forget a car in the city and use public transport. If you do have a car, you will find parking almost impossible.
- **Don't Miss:** The most important thing you can do is buy the "Lisbon Card". Most museums are free on Sunday until 2pm.
- **Organizing Your Time:** Four days might be about right to soak up the atmosphere without cultural overload. Spend a day out along the coast (take the railway that runs right along the sea-wall) to Cascais (see CASCAIS). Or go the other way, across the Vasco da Gama bridge to Setúbal. And don't forget to go to Sintra with its wonderful palace and cosy town centre. Close by also is the wonderful Palace of Queluz. All these places are easily reachable by public transport from Lisbon.
- **Especially for Kids:** The Oceanarium with its wonderful marine life, the Calouste Gulbenkian Planetarium, the Museum of the Marionettes (puppets) and the Zoo.
- **Also See:** CASCAIS, SINTRA, ESTORIL, PARQUE DE PENA.

F. Fouché/MICHELIN

View of Castelo de São Jorge from Miradouro de São Pedro de Alcântara in Bairro Alto

A Bit of History

The Beginning

Lisbon, so legend has it, was founded by Ulysses but exactly where that comes from nobody really knows. It was, though, the Phoenicians who, in 1200 BC, landed here on their seaborne travels and named it "serene harbour" – a haven of peace and calm water after the rough water of the Atlantic after they had passed through what is now the Straits of Gibraltar.

It soon became a regular stopping point on the route to northern Europe for traders from the Mediterranean: Greeks, Carthaginians and eventually Romans, who conquered the city in AD 138. Subsequently, it was under Barbarian rule and then Moorish from 714 when it was given the name Lissabona. Not until 1147 did King Dom Alfonso retake the city for the Portuguese after a four-month siege aided by mainly British mercenaries on their way to and from the Crusades, though it did not become the capital of Portugal – that honour was given to Coimbra – until 1255 when Dom Afonso III chose Lisbon as the seat of his government.

The Age of the Great Discoveries

Lisbon benefited from the riches that accumulated after the voyages of Vasco da Gama to the Indies in 1497–1499 and the discovery of Brazil (and its gold) by Pedro Álvares Cabral in 1500. New trade routes developed; merchants flocked to Lisbon which was packed with small traders buying and selling gold, silver, spices, ivory, silks, precious stones and rare woods. Monuments, including the Mosteiro dos Jerónimos and Torre de Belém, were built and no expense was spared in decorating them. The decoration of these buildings, which was always inspired by the sea, became known as the Manueline style after King Manuel.

The earthquake

On 1 November 1755 at about 9.30am, just as much of the population was at Mass, the town was shaken by an exceptionally violent earth tremor: churches, palaces and houses collapsed; fire spread; survivors rushed to take refuge in the Tagus, but a huge wave came upstream, breaking over and destroying the lower town. Lisbon's riches were engulfed. At least two huge aftershocks did more damage and estimates suggest that as many as 90 000 people died of a total population then of about 270 000. The devastation was not just confined to the city either as many towns even as far away as the Algarve were destroyed.

The King, Dom João I, escaped as did his minister, Sebastião de Carvalho e Melo, the future **Marquis of Pombal**. The minister immediately began the rebuilding of Lisbon to plans in a style utterly revolutionary for the period. The

G. Bludzin/Michelin

Depiction of the earthquake in Lisbon in 1755

straight wide avenues and the plain and stylised houses to be seen in the Baixa today are Pombal's legacy.

In November 1807 Napoléon's troops took the city, remaining for four years. In 1908 the King, Dom Carlos and his son were assassinated in the Praça do Comércio and an era of republican revolution took hold. Another high-profile assasination, that of the President, Sidónio Pais, shook the city in 1918.

Lisbon remained neutral during World War II, though the place was teeming with spies and exiles.

The Carnation Revolution

At 4.30am on 25 April 1974, Portuguese radio broadcast a message from the command of the Movement of the Armed Forces (Movimento das Forças Armadas) calling upon the population to keep calm and remain indoors. This was the beginning of the *coup d'état* led by General António de Spínola against the regime of Salazar and his successor Caetano. Spínola's take-over was virtually bloodless and his soldiers, with a red carnation stuck in the barrel of their rifles, were acclaimed by the citizens of Lisbon, who surged onto the Praça do Comércio.

Lisbon Today

Lisbon is a delightful city with numerous focal points which can all be admired from the Tagus. Modern though the city is, its 18C layout and many buildings add to its charm. The Praça do Comércio encompasses a maze-like network of streets in the Baixa district, which is the lower part of town extending towards Rossio: the Praça dos Restauradores and the Avenida da Liberdade, the city's main boulevard, are lined with trees. On the hill to the right stands the imposing Castelo São Jorge surrounded by the ancient districts of Alfama and Mouraria, while the hill to the left houses the city's commercial area of Chiado, with the working-class residential areas of Bairro Alto and Madragoa beyond. Then you reach the slightly more refined areas of Lapa, Alcântara and Belém. The areas along the Tagus have been taken over by nightclubs, restaurants and bars, turning this old industrial area into a thriving, lively community.

Beyond the city many new housing developments continue to appear on the landscape, as you see when you fly into Lisbon airport. Yet despite the rush and bustle, Lisbon remains perhaps the friendliest capital city in Europe.

To get to know this lovely city better, follow our suggested itineraries further on.

The Baixa★★

Walking, this itinerary should take you 2–3 hours, but don't rush. Enjoy it!

Address Book

♿ *For coin ranges, see the Legend on the cover flap.*

USEFUL INFORMATION

TOURISM OFFICES

Main Tourist Board Office – *Palácio da Foz, Praça dos Restauradores (Rossio)* ☎ *213 463 314. Open 9am–8pm.*

Lisbon Welcome Centre – *Praça do Comércio (entrance Rua do Arsenal).* ☎ *210 312 810. www.visitlisboa.com.* Open 9am–8pm. Tourist information office, a fashion boutique, an auditorium, art-gallery, café and a food shop. Internet access.

Ask Me – In the summer there are several of these little kiosks dotted about the city centre at main tourist sites; they are handy for maps and little local tips.

LISBON CARD – CARTÃO LISBOA

A great idea to help visitors enjoy their stay so much more, the card gives free, unlimited travel on public transport (bus, tram, metro and funicular) together with free or reduced entry to many of the museums and cultural sites in Lisbon (including the Monastery at Belém and the Palace at Sintra – as well as travel to Sintra by rail).

Prices adult/child: €15/€8 (24hr); €26/€13 (48hr); €32/€16 (72hr). You can also buy this card at the airport, tourism offices and elsewhere.

Cartão do Parque (Parque das Nações) – €15.50; 4–12-year-olds and over 65 €8.50. This card gives visitors reduced prices on many attractions, including the Oceanário, the Pavilhaô do Conhecimento, rail journeys and the téléphérique, amongst others. It is valid for one month from the first time you use it.

Also available are Taxi Cards, Shopping Cards, Restaurant Cards and Taxi Vouchers. See *www.askmelisboa.com*.

EMERGENCY PHONE NUMBERS

✚ **Emergency Services** – 112
✚ **Emergency Pharmacy** – 118
✚ **Tourist Police** 213 421 634

OTHER USEFUL PHONE NUMBERS

Special telephone for assistance for international visitors – 800 296 296
Telephone enquiries – 118
Railways – ☎ *808 208 208 (www.cp.pt)*
Lisbon Airport – ☎ *218 413 700 (www.ana-aeroporto.pt)*

USEFUL WEBSITES

www.golisbon.com
www.visitlisboa.com

DANGERS & ANNOYANCES

Tourists are fair game for pickpockets and other petty criminals in Lisbon as in all big cities. The good thing is that violence is hardly ever used. These thieves, normally working in twos or threes, are opportunistic. Never carry money in a rear or top pocket, never have your handbag open and never leave a handbag, purse or wallet out on a desk, table-top or even on the floor beneath your legs in a restaurant. If you get credit cards out to pay in a store, hold on to everything at all times. Be aware of pickpockets on buses and metro – they tend to "crowd" you. It only takes a second for a petty thief to disrupt your holiday and leave you feeling helpless and distressed.

GETTING INTO AND AROUND LISBON

FROM THE AIRPORT

The airport is about 6km/3.7mi from the city centre. A bus (Aerobus no 91; €3) runs from the airport to the city (close to Praça do Comércio) with service from 7.45am–8.45pm, departures every 30min. Taxis from the airport to downtown cost around €15 with a surcharge for luggage of €1.50. There is a surcharge after midnight as well. Allow 30–40min for the trip by bus, more at peak periods. Only use licensed taxis. The tourist office inside the airport will sell you prepaid "taxi vouchers" to your hotel, though watch out for surcharges. Ask beforehand – the fare should not be more than about €15 to a downtown hotel.

A new airport is being planned, but it will be many years yet before it is built.

Estação do Oriente

There is, as yet, no metro or railway line serving the airport.

RAIL STATIONS

Cais do Sodré – services about every 15min to Estoril and Cascais. Journey takes about 40min to Cascais.

Santa Apolónia – services to the north of Portugal and international (Paris).

Rossio – suburban trains to the north-west and Sintra. Trains for Sintra leave every 10min or so. Journey takes about 35min. Last train 11pm.

Sul e Suesta – for services to Alentejo and the Algarve via the ferry that gives acces to the station at Barreiro.

Oriente – superb intermodal station (metro, bus, train) with services to the north, connecting with trains for Santa Apolónia and Sintra.

BOAT

The *cacilheiros*, which serve the towns on the opposite banks of the Tagus, give you a wonderful chance to cruise on the river. Throughout the day departures are about every 15min. Tickets are on sale from machines at the stations and cost €0.75 for Cacilhas.

- **Estação Fluvial do Terreiro do Paço** – for Montio, Seixal, Barreiro and trains to Alentejo and the Algarve. Also the departure point for Tagus river cruises.
- **Estação do Cais do Sodré** – serves Cacilhas and Almada.
- **Estação de Belém** – services to Brandão and Trafaria.
- **Estação Fluvial do Parque das Nações** – services to Barreiro.

CAR RENTAL

With Lisbon being a busy and compact city it is normally better to use public transport. Having a car in Lisbon is more of a hindrance than a help. By day the traffic is very heavy, particularly in the older quarters in the centre where the streets are narrow and very congested. Parking spaces are scarce though you will find some large underground car parks, though they are not cheap. Public transport is the easiest option.

If you do need to rent a car (maybe for a trip outside the city) there are several car rental agencies at the airport and also scattered around the city. If you have any problems ask your hotel concierge. Only the larger hotels will have parking spaces overnight and if you park on the street you may have to move the car fairly early. Never leave valuables in your car.

TAXIS

A good way of getting round Lisbon, taxis are plentiful and less expensive than you might imagine – certainly less than in any comparable city in Europe. Most of them are beige and the price is shown on meters, at least within Lisbon. Outside the city centre fares

P. Martins/MICHELIN

are calculated on a per kilometre rate, though if you go further afield you can negotiate a price.

ON FOOT

The best way to discover Lisbon and its various neighbourhoods – Baixa, Avenida da Liberdade, Chiado/Bairro Alta and Alfama – is on foot, or on the tram, using the lifts where possible. As parts of the city are quite hilly it helps to be in reasonably good physical shape.

METRO/BUS/TRAM

♿ *See the metro map on the inside back cover.*

In a city as hilly as Lisbon there are some interesting and novel means of transport, including funiculars, elevators and tramways – the old yellow trams are now only found on the no 28 route – others are newer models.

Times of Transport – Bus and trams operate to a regular timetable between 6am and 1am with a frequency of between 11–15min until around 9.30pm. There is a small network of night buses operating until 5am. Most of these leave from the Cais do Sodré station. The funiculars stop at 11pm.

Cost of Transport – You can buy individual tickets on the bus or tram (◉€1.20), but if you are staying a few days in Lisbon, it makes sense to buy a **Cartão Lisboa** *(see earlier)* or travel passes that can be used on bus, tram, metro and *elevadores*, and can be used on buses, trains, metro and funiculars. For longer stays you might like to buy a "7 Colinas" card – from ticket machines.

Funiculars/Elevadores – Elevador da Bica: R. de S. Paulo/Largo do Calhariz; Elevador da Glória : Restauradores/São Pedro de Alcântara; Elevador do Lavra: Largo da Anunciação/R. da Câmara Pestana; Elevador de S. Justa: . de Santa Justa (to viewpoint). They each cost ◉€1.20–€1.50.

Bus – Principal routes: no 45 (Prior Velho/Cais do Sodré); no 83 (Portela/Cais de Sodré); no 46 (Est. Sta. Apolónia/Damaia); no 15 (Cais do Sodré/Sete Rios); no 43 (Praça Figuira/Buraca).

Metro – Metro stations are shown on the plan on the inside back cover. The network comprises four lines:

- ◆ Blue (Baixa-Chiado/Amadora Este)
- ◆ Red (Odivelas/Rato)
- ◆ Green (Cais do Sodré/Telheiras)
- ◇ Yellow (Oriente/Alameda)

The metro operates from 6.30am until 1am. A few metro stations are user-friendly for those with disabilities: www.metrolisboa.pt.

Several stations are decorated with azulejos by well-known Portuguese artists. Worth a special mention are Cidade Universitária (Vieira da Silva), Alto dos Moinhos (Júlio Pomar), Campo Grande (Eduardo Nery) Marqués de Pombal (Menez) and Baixa-Chiado (Álvaro Sizo Vieira). Metro tickets cost ◉€1.10 per journey or you can buy a *caderneta* (ten tickets) for ◉€6.50. Or use your Lisbon Card, which is valid on the metro.

Tramways (Eléctricos) – The old tramways are one of the charms of Lisbon as well as being one of the best ways to see the city and avoid climbing its hills! The old yellow bone-shaker trams are being replaced by newer models that are more user-friendly and comfortable, which is a boon for travellers but maybe not enthusiasts! Two lines in particular serve a number of monuments and museums: **no 15**: Praça da Figuiera/Algés—Praça do Comércio—Mosteiro dos Jerónimos—Museu Nacional de Arqueológia—Museu da Marinha—Discoveries Monument—Tower of Belém; **no 28**: São Vicente de

Tram (eléctrico) no. 28

Turismo de Lisboa

Tile decoration on the building with a street lamp with a boat motif

Turismo de Lisboa

Fora church—Museum of Decorative Arts—São Jorge castle—Cathedral—Baixa—Chiado museum—Largo do Chiado—São Bento—Basilica d'Estrela.

Accessibility – Buses and trams in Lisbon are not user-friendly for disabled travellers, but there is a door-to-door minibus service (available for the same price as regular public transport) for those with special needs. It is, however, essential to make a reservation not less than two days in advance. ☎217 585 676 *(lines open 7am–midnight)*.

PARQUE DAS NAÇÕES

In the Parque das Nações there is a téléphérique (overhead cable car), which runs through the Park just above the banks of the Tagus, with a fine view over the Vasco da Gama bridge and, in the evening, of the sunset over the river. *Operates Jun–Sept 11am–8pm; weekend and holidays 10am–9pm; Oct–Apr 1am–7pm; weekend and holidays 10am–8pm. Parque das Nações* €5.50 *(return),* €3.50 *one-way.*

Electric train – An electric train makes a circuit of the Parque das Nações every 30min from 10am–6pm with a stop at the Centro Vasca da Gama. €1.50.

Cycle Rental – A good way to get round the Park is by bike and there are a couple of rental points: in front of the Centro Vasca da Gama; the Oceanário; near the Parque Adrenalina; midday–8pm from about €2 for 30min. You can pick them up and drop them off at different points within the park.

CITY TOURS

A very good way to see any city that is new for you is by an organised tour, either hop-on-hop-off or a regular tour. Lisbon has both: ☎213 582 334 *(Carris Tours)*. There is a very interesting 90min tram tour either around the Baixa and Alfama, or to Belém.

Cityrama *(Praça de Pombal;* ☎213 191 090; http://circuitos.cityrama.pt*)* offers a number of different tours around Lisbon, including a 5hr city trip, evening trips (with drinks) or full-day trips to Sintra and elsewhere.

Lisbon Cityline Bus offers hop-on-hop-off tours that start at Marquês de Pombal.

Tagus cruises – *Estação Fluvial do Terreira do Paço (Estação do Sul e Sueste;* ☎218 820 348; www.transtejo.pt; check times beforehand)*.* These are two-hour cruises that operate Apr–Oct and cruise past the Parque das Nações and along to Belém.

Tours for You *(R. do Possolo, 76, Escritório A; 213 904 208; www.tours foryou.pt)* runs half-day city tours and longer tours further afield.

Other tours go along the Tagus to Belém, another to the north east of the city to include the Parque das Nações. Ask at the tourist office for more information.

WHERE TO STAY

Choosing the right hotel is important. Naturally you want comfort and cleanliness along with a realistic price, but also you need to choose the area carefully, to be near enough to the main tourist sites but also to ensure that your nights won't be disturbed by a nearby disco. Briefly the Baixa area is fairly quiet at night though you will need to go a little way for restaurants, Rossio can be livelier though the side streets are calmer but café life goes on until about 1am; Bairro Alto and Chiado are the nightlife districts and can be noisy until 4am; Alfama is fairly residential and thus a good choice if you want quiet nights. It is obviously wise to pre-book, especially in the summer months from June to September.

BAIXA, ROSSIO & CHIADO

⊝ **Pensão Estrela do Mondego** – Calçada do Carmo, 25 2°. ☎213 240 840. 11 rooms. The rooms of this small pensão, next to the Rossio station, are comfortable and clean, and have air-conditioning. Tiny bathrooms with just a shower cubicle. Some rooms overlook the station so the area at night is not exactly quiet. Budget-friendly!

⊝ **Pensão Imperial** – Praça dos Restauradores, 78–4°. ☎213 420 166. 17 rooms. A small and friendly pensão close to the Restauradores metro station so very central. The rooms (not all en-suite) are well furnished. Try to get a room overlooking the square, which is not too noisy. The rooms occupy the top two floors of a five-storey building and there is no lift!

⊝ **Pensão Pérola da Baixa** – R. da Glória, 10–2°. ☎213 462 875. 11 rooms. A small, central pensão, neat and tidy. There are also some pious statuettes. A nice place.

⊝ **Residêncial Florescente** – R das Portas de Santo Antão. ☎213 425 062. www.residencialflorescente.com. 34 rooms. A nice little hotel with friendly staff, wifi connection, a lift and clean rooms. Good value. Well situated near Avda da Liberdade and plenty of restaurants close by.

⊝ **Residencial Iris** – Rua da Glória, 2-A, 1°. ☎213 42 31 57. 9 rooms. Set back from the Avda da Liberdade, this lodging is an ideal location for those on a budget. Most of the rooms

are reasonably sized and have showers that are not fully enclosed.

⊝⊝ **Hotel Portugal** – R. João das Regras, 4. ☎218 877 581. www.hotel portugal.com. 59 rooms. Centrally located, this hotel has spacious and comfortable rooms decorated with antique furniture. Internet access for guests. Without doubt a hotel of quality offering good service.

⊝⊝ **Residêncial Roma** – Trav da Glória. ☎213 460 557. www.residencial roma-lisbon.com. 40 rooms. The well-sized and clean rooms are ideal for a short break though there is no lift in this four-storey building. For longer stays they have apartments with kitchenette. Near Avda da Liberdade.

⊝⊝⊝ **Lisboa Tejo** – Rua dos Condes de Monsanto, 2. ☎218 866 182. www.evidenciahotels.com. 58 rooms. Next to the Praça da Figueira this hotel has comfortable and beautifully decorated rooms. Despite the double-glazing, some of the rooms overlooking the main road can be a little noisy. Very good breakfast.

⊝⊝⊝⊝ **Lisboa Regency Chiado** –R. Nova do Almada, 114. ☎213 25 61 00. 40 rooms ⎘P. Located above the Armazéns do Chiado retail gallery, this hotel designed by the celebrated architect Álvaro Siza is decorated with great taste in a Portuguese-Asian style; the rooms have every modern comfort and magnificent views over the Tagus, the castle and the city.

⊝⊝⊝⊝ **Metropole** – Praça do Rossio, 30. ☎213 219 030. www.metropole almeidahotles.com. 36 rooms. Very well located in the busy Rossio square (though noisy until 1am or so), the Metropole has classic and comfortable rooms in an early 20C building. Some rooms have a magnificent view over the castle.

BAIRRO ALTO

⊝⊝ **Residencial Alegria** – Praça da Alegria, 12. ☎213 220 670. 35 rooms. A lovely hotel with its façade painted bright yellow and its balconies filled with flowers, overlooking the beautiful, almost Parisian, Praça da Alegria. Ask for the rooms on the upper floors as they are quieter. There are reports of a disco close by becoming quite noisy at weekends.

⊝⊜–⊝⊜⊟ **Pensão Londres**
– *Rua Dom Pedro V. 53, 1.* ☎*213 462 203. www.pensaolondres.com. 40 rooms* ⊊. This *pensão* occupies four floors of a handsome building on the edge of the Bairro Alto, Lisbon's pulsating night-life district so don't go to bed too early. Certain rooms have original ceilings and good views of the Castelo São Jorge. A clean and well-maintained establishment offering reasonable rates in a good location.

⊝⊜⊟ **Casa de S. Mamede** –
R. da Escola Politécnica, 159. ☎*213 963 166. 28 rooms* ⊊. This charming hotel sits in an 18C mansion and still has a family feel to it, with *azulejos* and early 20C furniture. It really is in an ideal location, among the antique shops, close to the Principe Real and the botanical gardens and one of the top choices for discerning visitors.

⊝⊜⊟⊟ **Bairro Alto Hotel** – *Praça Luís de Camões, 8.* ☎*213 408 288. www.bairroaltohotel.com. 55 rooms* ⊊⊠. Located in the Luís de Camões square, this luxury hotel occupies the former Grand Hotel of Europe, one of whose regular guests was Sarah Bernhardt. Completely renovated in 2005, the rooms have every conceivable luxury and are decorated with refined taste. On the sixth floor is a terrace with great views over the city. There is a fitness centre for guests.

ALFAMA & GRAÇA

⊝ **Pensão Ninho das Aguias** –
Costa do Castelo, 74. ☎*218 85 40 70. 16 rooms* ⊠. Near the castle, this pretty villa has rooms with or without a bathroom, but all the balconies overlook the cathedral. On the top floor is a terrace with a good view over the city. This ideal location gives immediate access to the castle or to Alfama.

⊝⊜ **Comfort Principe** – *Avda Duque de Ávila, 201.* ☎*213 592 050 - www.hotelprincipelisboa.com. 59 rooms* ♿⊠⊊. Near the Gulbenkian Museum this is a very nice hotel, fairly quiet (though there might be some noise in the day from nearby construction); smallish rooms but very clean.

⊝⊜⊟ **Sé Guest House** – *R de São João de Praça.* ☎*218 864 400. 30 rooms* ⊊. In the same building as the previous hotel this is the more expensive version. Some of the rooms are described as romantic and are furnished with a motley collection of items. Very clean.

⊝⊜⊟ **Albergaria Senhora do Monte** – *Calçada do Monte 39.* ☎*218 866 002. 28 rooms* ⊊⊠. The principal attraction of this modern hotel located off the main tourist track (though near the Miradouro da Senhora do Monte) in the residential Graça district is the outstanding view of Lisbon from all but five of the rooms. Request one of the three rooms with terrace (higher rate). Hard climb to reach on foot, so plan on using taxis or the no 28 tram.

⊝⊜⊟ **Olissippo Castelo** – *R Costa do Castelo 112.* ☎*218 820 190. www.olissipohotels.com. 24 rooms* ⊊⊠. Near the São Jorge castle this clean, quiet and well-run hotel is ideal if you want a quiet neighbourhood. The downside is that the area is very steep, you will have to go out into town for dinner and coming back will probably need a taxi (but only about €5–7) rather than struggle up the hill. But it's lovely.

⊝⊜⊟ **Palácio Belmonte** –
Páteo D. Fradique, 14. ☎*218 816 600. www.palaciobelmonte.com. 11 suites* ⊊⊿. A hotel built in a 17C palace, perched on the highest point of the hill by the castle and renovated in a Franco-Portuguese style, this is one of the best. Private terraces with all suites and a black-marble pool await you if you have time to make use of them. If you really need to celebrate try the Himalaya Suite with a 360° bird's-eye view over the city.

⊝⊜⊟ **Pensão São João de Praça** – *R. de São João de Praça.* ☎*218 862 591. 20 rooms* ⊊. Immediately next to the cathedral (busy by day, quiet by night) this is a nice hotel at budget prices, though not all rooms are en-suite. In a lovely building with character. There is another, more expensive hotel next door – don't confuse them.

BELÉM

⊝ **Pensão Residencial Setubalense** – *R. de Belém, 28.* ☎*213 636 639. www.pensaosetubalense.pt. 30 rooms* ⊊. For those who prefer to stay in a quiet,

Breakfast served in the courtyard, York House

calm and elegant part of the city, away from the bustle of the centre, this little pensão is ideal, close to the Mosteiro dos Jerónimos. A beautiful pink-coloured façade and with rooms that are simple and comfortable. Ask for a room with a view.

NORTH OF THE CITY

NH Liberdade – Av de Liberdade, 180B. ☎213 514 060. www.nh-hoteles.com. 83 rooms. Lovers of refinement cannot afford to miss this elegant, ultra-modern hotel just off Lisbon's main street, in the small Tivoli Forum. On the roof is a pool and a terrace with wonderful panoramic views over the city and the Tagus. The rooms are decorated in minimalist style. Very chic!

As Janelas Verdes – R. das Janelas Verdes, 47, Lapa. ☎213 968 143. www.heritage.pt. 29 rooms. Located just a few steps from the Museu de Arte Antiga, this beautiful 18C mansion has been transformed into a welcoming and comfortable hotel, decorated with the personal touch. The rooms are not large and do look out over the busy street, so are not always quiet. At the back of the hotel is a lovely terrace/patio is the ideal place for breakfast in the open in the summer months. Internet access.

Britânnia – R. Rodrigues Sampaio, 17, Estrela. ☎213 155 016. www.heritage.pt. 32 rooms. Restored to its elegant 1940s appearance, this landmark hotel designed by Cassiano Branco (architect of the Éden Teatro on the nearby Praça dos Restauradores) is both charming and comfortable. Spacious, well-appointed and quiet rooms, a good location and an understated "retro" ambience make the Britânnia a good find.

York House – R. das Janelas Verdes, 32, Lapa. ☎213 962 544; www.yorkhouselisboa.com. 34 rooms. Lisbon's best known historic inn has every modern comfort, yet with an atmosphere of relaxed calm as befits the 17C convent in which it is housed. The rooms overlooking the street are best avoided, as this is the heart of the nightlife district. The handsome dining room looks onto a cobblestone courtyard. The inn's location near the Museu de Arte Antiga is not ideal for visiting Lisbon on foot.

WHERE TO EAT

Food is very important to Lisbon's population and their restaurants reflect this fact. Throughout the city the quality of cuisine is high, from the top-end restaurants with extensive wine lists to the smaller, back-street family-run variety catering almost exclusively to locals. In fact, stumble across one of these and you'll almost certainly have a very good and very inexpensive meal, washed down with a jug of wine of no particular provenance – but excellent. We have selected a few restaurants to guide you on your way. You'll discover more. Many are closed on Sundays or Mon.

CHIADO

Doce Real – *R. Dom Pedro V, 119-121 ☎213 465 923. Closed Sun.* A tiny, friendly café situated on the border of Bairro Alto between Príncipe Real and R. da Rosa. There's just enough space to enjoy a snack of shrimp or cod fritters. Whether at a table or standing at the counter, you'll find the food delicious.

Heróis Café Lounge – *Calçada do Sacramento, 18. ☎213 420 077. Closed Mon.* Frequented by lovers and designers of fashion, this café lounge is close the Carmelite church. A wonderful buffet at lunchtime will satisfy any appetite whilst in the evening the culinary inspiration is Mediterranean.

Bota Alta – *Trav. da Queimada 35. ☎213 427 959. Closed Sun.* Pleasant local restaurant with a lively atmosphere; the tables are crammed in and you'll get talking to your very-near neighbours. Good cuisine with fish featuring heavily on the menu. Gets very busy most nights by 8pm.

La Brasserie d'Entrecôte – *R do Alecrim, 117. ☎213 428 343. Closed Sat–Sun lunch.* The place in Lisbon for a steak, accompanied by some fine wine. Or you can choose from the extensive and not inexpensive à-la-carte menu.

Pap' Açorda – *Rua da Atalaia 57. ☎213 464 811. Reservations recommended. Closed Sun, and Mon lunch.* One of the highlights of the Bairro Alto. Excellent cuisine in an old bakery – a hit with the arty crowd, especially theatrical.

Tavares – *R. do Misericórdia, 37. ☎213 421 112. Closed Sat, and Sun lunch.* Classic international cuisine served with flair in a rich early 20C set-

ting. A salon-de-thé is at the side if you are in the area in the afternoon.

ALFAMA

Pateo 13 – *Calçadinha de Sto Estêvão, 13. ☎218 882 325.* In the warren of tiny streets in Alfama you will come across this lively and very typically Portuguese restaurant where grilled fish and meat form the basis of the menu. Good value.

Café Taborda – *R. Costa do Castelo, 75. ☎218 879 484. Closed Mon. Reservations recommended.* With an arty atmosphere this is a restaurant with an exceptional view over the city. A pleasant garden is the perfect place for an *apéritif.* Primarily vegetarian and fish – don't expect a steak!

Divina Comida – *Largo de S. Martinho, 6–7. ☎218 875 599. Closed Sun.* A nice name for the name of this elegant restaurant (*comida* means food). For a small place close to the Santa Luzia mirador it has a nice raised terrace under the trees, beautiful rooms filled with soft light and a carefully prepared internationally inspired menu with a good choice – prawns in ginger, fettucine with curry.

Malmequer-Bemmequer – *Rua de São Miguel 23. ☎218 876 535. Closed Mon, and Tue lunch.* This is well worth a visit for its excellent chargrilled fish and meat served on lovely flowery, light tables. Very good feeling.

Mesa de Frades – *R. dos Remédios, 139A. ☎218 884 599. Closed Mon.* An old chapel is the setting for this restaurant with a typically Brazilian and Portuguese cuisine. The terrace is the ideal place to sit on a warm day and watch the world go by.

Restô – *R. Costa do Castelo, 7. ☎218 867 334. Daily. Reservations recommended.* Unique for its view over Lisbon and the Tagus, and with a lively atmosphere, being part of an arts co-operative, this is really two restaurants: one in the open air with a good but simple tapas-style cuisine; the other inside with more elaborate menu and higher prices. Try to get there to watch the sunset over the Tagus.

Santo António de Alfama – *Beco São Miguel, 7. ☎218 881 328.*

P. de Franqueville/MICHELIN

Menu of a restaurant in Alfama

Evenings only; closed Mon, Tue. Reservation recommended⌨. Founded by two friends, one a pianist the other an actor, this restaurant is a meeting place for artists of all kinds. Three rooms on three floors give it an elegant bistrot feel.

◔◔◔ **Viagens de Sabores** – *R. S. João da Praça, 103.* ☎*218 870 189. Evenings only.* In the heart of Alfama a warm welcome awaits you in this elegant restaurant made up of several arched rooms overseen by its French chef. Everything matches the name – a voyage of flavours – tuna steak Thailandaise, veal *marocaine*, and something different, grapefruit with crab.

GRAÇA

◔◔◔ **Via Graça** – *Rua Damesceno Monteiro 9b.* ☎*218 87 08 30. www. viagracaclix.pt. Closed Sat–Sun lunch.* Situated below the Miradouro de Nossa Senhora do Monte, this sophisticated restaurant decorated in contemporary style offers superb views of Castelo São Jorge and the centre of the city. An ideal location for a romantic dinner for two.

BY THE TAGUS

◔◔◔ **Alcântara Café** – *Rua Maria Luisa Holstein 15.* ☎*213 637 176.* This brasserie-style café-restaurant is situated in an old factory, and adjoins the Alcântara-Mar night-club. A young, elegant and fashionable ambience in amazing industrial-baroque décor. The entrance is slightly hidden down a dark side-street in the port area but it's worth searching for. Attracts the trendy crowd and is open for dinner and drinks until 3am.

◔◔◔ **Café Malaca** – *Cais dos Gas (back of the Cais do Sodré station).* ☎*967 104 142.* On the first floor of the Naval Club of Lisbon, a small restaurant whose cuisine is inspired by the voyages of the Portuguese adventurers, with a particular Asian influence. Especially good are the Vietnamese dishes and you are guaranteed a very warm welcome.

BELÉM

◔◔◔ **Caseiro** – *Rua Belém 35.* ☎*213 638 803. Closed Sun and Aug.* An eclectic décor in which onions, garlic

and banknotes from around the world hang from the walls. Typical Portuguese cuisine.

◔◔◔ **O Funil** – *Av. Elias Garcia 82A.* ☎*217 966 007. Closed Mon and Sun evenings. Bacalhau à Funil* (cod) is one of the main specialities of this restaurant. Excellent wine list.

WEST OF THE CITY

◔◔ **Os Tibetanos** – *Rua do Salitre, 117.* ☎*213 142 038. Reservations recommended. Closed Sat, Sun, public holidays.* This small restaurant, slightly tucked away, is near the botanical garden and has tasty vegetarian cuisine with Tibetan inspiration at very reasonable prices. Pleasant ambience.

◔◔ **Pão de Canela** – *Praça das Flores, 27/28.* ☎*213 972 220.* Breakfast or lunch on the terrace, dinner inside where the décor is of light wood, and a menu based around fruit, light pastry or quiches: ideally located in the shadow of the Praça das Flores on the edge of Bairro Alto.

◔◔◔ **Comida de Santo** – *Calçada Engenheiro Miguel Pais, 39.* ☎*213 963 339.* On the side of the Principe Real this restaurant has a wonderful menu direct from Northeastern Brazil. You certainly won't go hungry here among the elegant and relaxed clientele.

◔◔◔ **Picanha** – *R. das Janelas Verdes, 96, Lapa.* ☎*213 975 540. Closed Sat–Sun lunch.* Very close to the Museu de Arte Antiga this is the place for meat-eaters with an appetite! Brazilian cuisine is again the theme and includes *pincanha (roast meat cut from large skewers carried by the waiters)*, served with rice and black beans.

◔◔◔ **Porco Preto** – *R. Marcos Portugal, 5.* ☎*213 964 895. Closed Sun.* On the beautiful Praça das Flores this beautifully designed restaurant has a concept unique to Lisbon: a menu exclusively devoted to the black pork of Alentejo (similar to *pata negra* in Spain). Exceptional value for food this good and a very intimate atmosphere.

◔◔◔◔ **Casa da Comida** – *Tv. das Amoreiras 1.* ☎*213 885 376. Closed Sat lunch, and Sun.* This immaculate, elegant restaurant in a verdant courtyard with an *azulejo*-covered fountain serves

B. Brillion/MICHELIN

Café Nicola, Rossio

TAKING A BREAK

Lisbon is known for its wonderful pastry shops and cafés and you can either take a break mid-morning or mid-afternoon to enjoy life the Lisbon way. One tradition in Lisbon is the *pastéis de nata* (egg custard tarts) that are eaten either with a coffee or with a small, cold glass of beer. With all the walking you'll do you'll soon work off the calories! You will find cafés everywhere, but here is just a brief selection of some of the more famous.

Café Nicola – *Praça Dom Pedro IV, 25. Daily.* A Lisbon landmark steeped in history. It was here that the first Portuguese women dared to put an end to the exclusively male character of the city's cafés by coming out for coffee.

Confeitaria Nacional – *Praça Figueira 18B. Closed Sun Oct–Apr.* This old pastry shop (1829) is one of the best in Lisbon and should be on your list. A huge choice of pastries and traditional sweets.

Pastelaria Suiça – *Praça. D. Pedro IV, 100, Rossio. Daily.* One of the busiest places in the Baixa and a good meeting place. Outdoor terraces in the Rossio and Praça da Figueira, with views of the Castelo de São Jorge. Snacks, excellent cakes and fruit juices.

Panificação Reunida de S. Roque – *Rua Dom Pedro V, 57B.* Ceramic tiles

NIGHTLIFE

Nightlife in Lisbon tends to mean "night" though the clubs come in two categories – the trendy, noisy disco variety for the young, and the more refined bar-clubs, some with live music, where you can at least hear yourself think whilst still enjoying the late-night ambience. We have tried to lean towards the latter. Many clubs and late bars do not open before about 10 or 11pm and no serious clubber would be seen out before midnight. As a result they tend to finish late, with 4am being the witching hour. The Baixa is fairly quiet with no main clubs though a couple of late bars, the most famous of which is **Ginginha do Rossio** (*Largo de São Domingos, 8; daily*) famous for its *ginginha* (cherry brandy) either at the bar or sitting at the pavement tables outside. A unique café with a unique atmosphere!

A Brasileira – *Rua Garrett 120. Daily.* A well-known café with a literary tradition. Artists, fashion designers, tourists and residents all meet in this legendary establishment.

Café No Chiado (*Largo do Picadeiro; daily*) is next to the San Carlos theatre and is where, it is claimed, you can taste the best mango mousse in the world. Well, at least in Lisbon! Lovely shaded terrace in the summer months.

In the **Bairro Alto** area, the real heart of the nightclub area, you will find **Frágil** (*Rua Atalaia 126–8; closed Sun*). One of the classics of Lisbon night-life. The décor in this bar-discotheque is always original and changes every three months or so. A trendy and eclectic clientele of night-time regulars. Then there's **Hot Clube** (*Praça da Alegria, 39; closed Sun; shows at 11pm and 12.30am*). The oldest jazz club in Lisbon. Many internationally renowned acts perform here on Fridays and Saturdays.

Pavilhão Chinês (*Rua D. Pedro V 89; daily*) was originally a grocer's shop that was transformed into a bar in 1986. The walls are covered with glass cases containing a varied collection of objects, including lead soldiers, contemporary engravings, humorous ceramics and models of war planes. Billiard table at the back of the bar.

Alfama has the **Bar das Imagens/Costa Do Castelo** (*Calçada Marqués de Tancos, 1-1B; closed Jan and Feb*). Halfway up the hill towards the castle this bar has a wonderful view out over the city and the 25 de Abril bridge. It combines two bars in one. Without having to go outside you can pass from a traditional bar to a terrace bar with DJ.

Kapital (*Av. 24 de Julho 68; closed Mon and Wed*). is one of the most popular Lisbon clubs. Elegant, airy decor on three floors, each with a bar. Terrace on the top floor.

Lux (*Av. Infante D. Henrique, Armazém A, Cais da Pedra in Santa Apolónia; closed Sun*). Created by the former owner of the legendary Frágil, Lux is currently one of the hottest venues in the city, housed in an old warehouse opposite Santa Apolònia railway station. The first floor is open for afternoon tea at 4pm, while the club takes on a "cocktail lounge" feel in the evening with its décor of 1960s chairs and tables. The disco above the lounge is open from Thursday to Saturday from midnight onwards. Another attractive feature is the terrace overlooking the Tagus.

ENTERTAINMENT

You cannot visit Lisbon without seeing **fado**, the traditional music that tells of love and often disaster. Fado is traditionally sung by women (though there are some fine male singers) and the *fadistas* are the pop stars of Portugal. The best places to see fado are in the working-class districts such as Alfama, normally fairly late on a Thursday to Saturday evening. There are, though, many fado clubs catering to tourists, many of which include a meal (though not always the very best dining in this city of great restaurants) with the show. They rarely begin before 9pm. Most are closed on Sundays. A selection of these clubs, together with details of other entertainment venues, is listed below. For details of all entertainment in Lisbon, look at the street posters or in one of the free magazines/papers on

A Brasileira

© World Pictures/Photoshot

offer. *L'Agenda Cultural* is a monthly publication with a schedule of all cultural events in Lisbon. It's available free from main tourist offices, hotels and on kiosks throughout the capital. Another publication, in English and Portuguese, is called "*Follow Me Lisboa*" with lists of shows and events: also available free from most tourist attractions.

ABEP– *Praça dos Restauradores*. A kiosk that sells tickets for different events theatres, sports and concerts.

Quiosque Cultural de S. Mamede – *R. de São Mamede, 30 – Principe Real*. This kiosk, set up by the city of Lisbon, has information on all the cultural activities in Lisbon.

BAIXA

Coliseu dos Recreios – *R. das Portas de Sto. Antão, 96*. ☎*213 240 580. www. coliseulisboa.com*. A huge auditorium, restored in 1994, which holds operas, concerts and shows of all kinds.

Teatro Nacional D. Maria II – *Praça D. Pedro IV 213 250 835. www.teatrodmaria. pt*. A varied classical programme.

CHIADO

Teatro Nacional de S. Carlos – *Largo de S. Carlos 213 253 045. www.saocarlos. pt*. Opera, ballet and classical concerts.

BAIRRO ALTO

Adega do Machado – *Rua do Norte 91*. ☎*213 224 660. Closed Mon*. An excellent folklore show early in the evening, followed by traditional *fado*.

Adega do Ribatejo – *Rua Diário Notícias 23*. ☎*213 468 343. Daily*. One of the venues with the most authentic *fado* and a lively, friendly atmosphere.

O Faia – *Rua Barroca 54/56*. ☎*213 426 742. Closed Sun*. Authentic Lisbon *fado* in a district where *fado* is the traditional form of expression.

Café Luso – *Tv. Queimada 10*. ☎*213 422 281. www.cafeluso.pt. Closed Sun*. Very popular with tourists. Evening entertainment begins with a folklore show, followed by *fado*.

ALFAMA

O Cabacinha – *Lg. Limoeiro 9/10*. ☎*218 872 040. Fado Fri–Sat 8.30pm*. A venue for true *fado* lovers.

Parreirinha de Alfama – *Beco Espírito Santo 1*. ☎*218 868 209. Closed Sun*. Traditional *fado* house popular with tourists.

Taverna del Rei – *Largo do Chafariz de Dentro 15 (corner of Rua São Pedro)*. ☎*218 876 754. www.tavernadelrey.com. Closed Sun*. Portuguese cuisine on offer to diners while they listen to authentic *fado*.

BELÉM

Centro Cultural de Belém – *Praça do Império*. ☎*213 612 400. www.fdesccb. pt*. The cultural centre organises a large number of events, including concerts and temporary exhibitions.

OTHER DISTRICTS

Culturgest – Caixa Geral de Depósitos – *Rua Arco do Cego*. ☎*217 905 155. www.cultgest.pt. Booking office open daily*. This enormous building in Neoclassical style is the headquarters of the Caixa Geral de Depósitos savings bank. It houses a cultural centre with two auditoriums and two exhibition galleries. The programme of musical events is of extremely high quality, while art exhibitions on show here often include works by contemporary international artists.

Grande Auditório Gulbenkian – *Av da Berna, 45A (next to the Museum)*. ☎*217 823 041. www.musica-gulbenkian.pt*. Various concerts from time to time.

Teatro da Comuna – *Praça de Espanha*. ☎*217 221 770*. A traditional programme of theatre, plus a bistro-style café-theatre for contemporary music concerts (rock, jazz, music from around the world) every Sun at 10pm.

Timpanas – *Rua Gilberto Rola 24 Alcântara*. ☎*213 906 655. www.timpanas.pt. Closed Tue*. A good place to hear some excellent *fado*.

Senhor Vinho – *Rua Meio Lapa 18, Lapa*. ☎*213 972 681 - www.restsrvinho. com. Closed Sun. Fado at 9.30pm*. Elegant, traditional *fado* venue with performances by some famous artists. Traditional Portuguese cuisine and a remarkable wine list.

The Lisbon Players – *R da Estrela 10, Estrela*. ☎*213 96 19 46. www.lisbonplayers.com.pt*. A group of amateur playwrights organising plays and operas in English with audience participation.

Escola Portuguesa de Arte Eques-tre – *Palácio Nacional de QUELUZ (see QUELUZ). ☎214 35 89 15. www.cavalonet. com. Shows Wed at 11am May–Oct (except Aug).* The school, which keeps alive the tradition of Portuguese equestrian art, particularly with Lusitanian thoroughbreds, was founded by King João V at the end of the 18C.

SHOPPING

Lisbon is probably Western Europe's least expensive capital and you'll find some great bargains as well as the normal international brand names – *Luis Vuitton, Armani, Trussardi, Burberry, Hugo Boss, Longchamp* and *Escada* – whose prices are pretty standard worldwide. Many of these international brand names are on the famous Avenida da Liberdade but if you want lesser-known but interesting Portuguese designers, at prices that might be more acceptable, go to the Bairro Alto and Chiado districts. Bairro Alto is popular with the alternative fashion set, with club and streetwear shops. Most of those only open after a late lunch and continue well into the night so if you go there in the morning you'll find them closed.

Rua Augusta is situated, in the Baixa, one of the busiest quarters of Lisbon. Closed to traffic, this pedestrian-only street offers a great variety of shopping options with European chain-stores like Zara, Mango or H&M, but you'll also find peddlers selling all sorts of things from neck-scarves to jewellery, from shoes to hand-made bags.

Some of the best bargains are leather with purses, handbags and shoes being good value. Look for antique hand-painted tiles, distinctive regional ceramics and textiles such as table-cloths and embroidery, and don't forget that all gold sold in Portugal is at least 19.2 karat and is one of the best buys in the country. In the Baixa in particular you will still find streets with names that indicate the work of their original inhabitants, Prata (Silver), Ouro (Gold) and Ferreiros (Blacksmiths).

There are plenty of shopping centres throughout the city. The biggest ones are at Colombo, Galerias Monumental, Saldanha, Vasco da Gama, Amoreiras and El Corte Inglés. Most of them have cinemas, gyms, restaurants as well and are open from about 10am to 11pm. There is also the Freeport Outlet Shopping, the biggest outlet in Europe, where you can find everything you may need. Many international brands offer discounts up to 50 per cent throughout the year.

M. Chaput/MICHELIN

Feira da Ladra

There are a couple of huge street markets, the biggest being the **Feira da Ladra** (translates as Thieves' Market!) all day Sat and Tuemorning, on Campo de Santa Clara, Alfama, where you'll find all sorts of things you never realised you needed. Arrive early if you want to avoid the crowds, and watch out for pickpockets.

Mercado da Ribeira Nova – *Av. 24 de Julho. Closed Sun.* Wonderful food market where colours, smells and the sales pitch of its vendors all blend together.

Feira de Carcavelos – *In the centre of Carcavelos 21km/13mi west of Lisbon on the Estoril road. Every Thursday morning.* Inexpensive clothes market selling seconds with minor – and often barely discernable – defects. A number of well-known French and British brand names are often on sale here, particularly cotton goods.

Also consider – **Feira de Sintra** – *Largo de São Pedro à Sintra – The second and fourth Sunday of the month, all day.* This large market in one of Sintra's delightful squares sells the same goods as most other markets, plus plants and animals. Around the square you will also find small craft and antique stalls.

ART GALLERIES

To buy original art visit one of the art galleries that are dotted around the city. Art galleries are usually closed on Sundays.

Associação José Afonso – *Rua Voz Operário 62 – Graça.* This traditional shop also contains an art gallery which makes a point of exhibiting the work of young artists.

Galeria 111 – *Campo Grande 114 – Campo Grande.*

Galeria 1991 – *Rua Marcos Portugal 28/30 – Príncipe Real.*

Galeria Arte Periférica – *Centro Cultural de Belém (Shops 5 and 6).*

Galeria Graça Fonseca – *Rua da Emenda 26C/V – Chiado.* A gallery which often hosts photographic exhibitions.

Galeria Luís Serpa – *Rua Ten. Raul Cascais 1B – Príncipe Real.* Exhibitions of paintings and sculpture by contemporary artists.

Galeria Módulo – *Cç. Mestres 34 A/B – Campolide.* Contemporary artists.

Galeria Palmira Suso – *Rua das Flores 109 – Bairro Alto.* Contemporary Portuguese artists.

Galeria de S. Francisco – *Rua Ivens 40 – Chiado.* Modern painting.

Novo Século – *Rua Século 23 A/B – Bairro Alto.* Contemporary art.

INDEX OF STREETS IN LISBON

INDEX OF SIGHTS IN LISBON

LISBOA

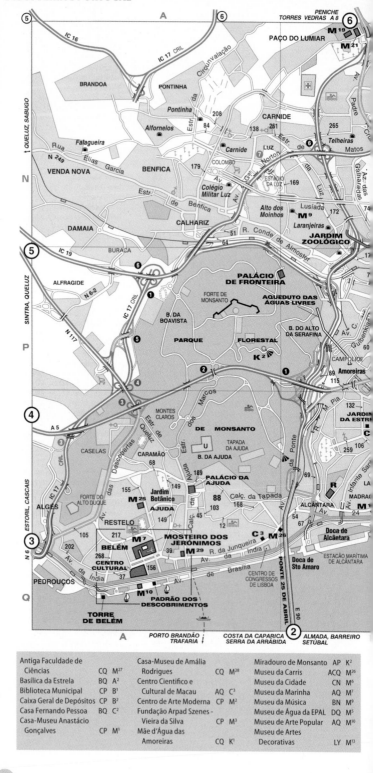

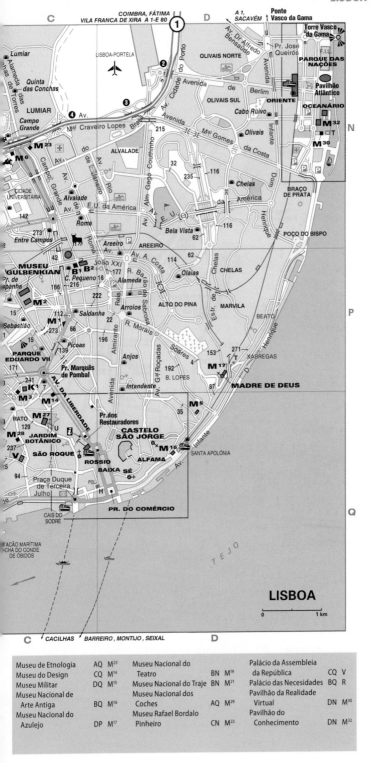

LISBOA

0   1 km

Museu de Etnologia	AQ	M²⁵	Museu Nacional do			Palácio da Assembleia		
Museu do Design	CQ	M¹⁴	Teatro	BN	M¹⁹	da República	CQ	V
Museu Militar	DQ	M¹⁵	Museu Nacional do Traje	BN	M²¹	Palácio das Necesidades	BQ	R
Museu Nacional de			Museu Nacional dos			Pavilhão da Realidade		
Arte Antiga	BQ	M¹⁶	Coches	AQ	M²⁹	Virtual	DN	M³⁰
Museu Nacional do			Museu Rafael Bordalo			Pavilhão do		
Azulejo	DP	M¹⁷	Pinheiro	CN	M²³	Conhecimento	DN	M³²

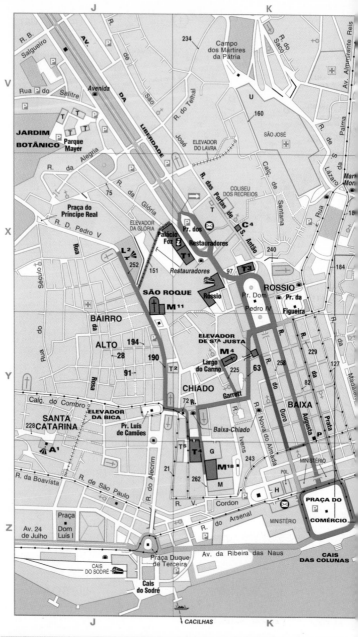

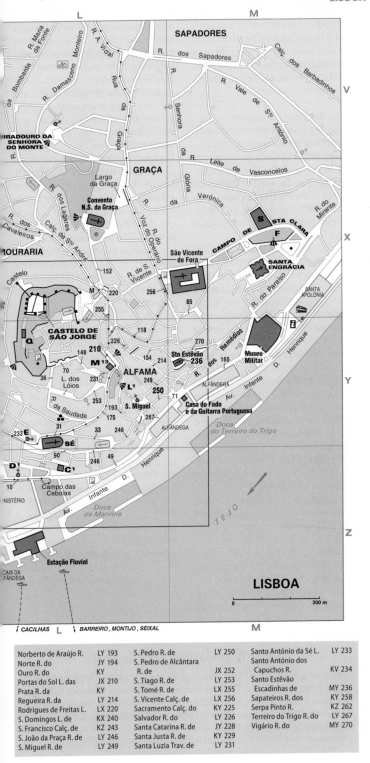

SAPADORES

GRAÇA

Largo da Graça

Convento N.S. da Graça

São Vicente de Fora

MOURÁRIA

SANTA CLARA

CAMPO DE

SANTA ENGRÁCIA

SANTA APOLÓNIA

Castelo

CASTELO DE SÃO JORGE

Sto Estêvão

Museu Militar

ALFAMA

L. dos Lóios

S. Miguel

Casa do Fado e da Guitarra Portuguesa

SÉ

Doca do Terreiro do Trigo

Campo das Cebolas

Doca da Marinha

T E J O

Estação Fluvial

CAIS DA FÁNDEGA

LISBOA

0   300 m

MIRADOURO DA SENHORA DO MONTE

This part of the city, which was completely devastated by the earthquake and tidal wave in 1755, was rebuilt to plans laid down by the Marquis of Pombal. Start at Praça dos Restauradores, just to the north of Rossio.

Praça dos Restauradores

The square owes its name to the men who in 1640 led the revolt against the Spanish and proclaimed the independence of Portugal. The fine red roughcast façade on the west of the square belongs to the **Palácio Foz** built by an Italian architect in the early 19C. Today it houses Lisbon's Tourist Information Centre *(Posto de Turismo)*.

Next door is the **Éden Teatro**, designed by Cassiano Branco in 1937. Part of its Art Deco façade and its monumental staircase remain from the original building which is now occupied by the Virgin Megastore. Avenida da Liberdade runs north east off the square to the Parque Eduardo VII. Parallel to the avenue is **Rua Portas de Santo Antão**, a pedestrian street with cinemas, cafés and shops. The **Casa do Alentejo** at no 58 has an unusual Moorish courtyard and a restaurant with abundant *azulejo* decoration.

Estação do Rossio, the station, has a 19C neo-Manueline, almost Italianate **façade★** with wide horseshoe-shaped openings, and serves the town of Sintra, among others. Although railway stations might not be on your list of must-see places, it is well worth a look, inside and out. It has some magnificent *azulejo* decoration.

Rossio★

Praça Dom Pedro IV, the lively main square of the Baixa, dates from the 13C. Its present appearance is due to Pombal: 18C and 19C buildings line it on three sides, the ground floors being given over to cafés such as the famous **Nicola** with its Art Deco façade, and small shops that have kept their decoration from the beginning of the century. Among these are the tobacconist's near Nicola with *azulejos* by Rafael Bordalo Pinheiro, and the corner shop which serves *ginginha*, the well-known cherry liqueur, off Largo de São Domingos, next to a milliner's dating from the late 19C.

The north side of the square is bordered by the **Teatro Nacional Dona Maria II**, built in 1840 on the site of the former Palace of the Inquisition. The façade is adorned with a statue of Gil Vicente, the father of Portuguese theatre. In the middle of the square, between the Baroque fountains, is the bronze statue of Dom Pedro IV, after whom the square is named (*see the box above*) and who was crowned Pedro I, Emperor of Brazil.

Parallel to the Rossio to the east is the **Praça da Figueira**, a square of classical buildings with an equestrian statue of Dom João I in the centre.

South of the square is the grid of Baixa streets, some pedestrianised, which forms Lisbon's main shopping district. The streets running south between the Rossio and Praça do Comércio are named after the guilds that originally practised there. Among them are Rua dos Correeiros (Saddlers' Street) and Rua dos Sapateiros (Cobblers' Street). The three main ones are Rua do Ouro (Goldsmiths' Street), **Rua Augusta**, at the end of which there is a huge arch with statues of some famous figures from Portugal's history, including Vasco da Gama and the Marquis de Pombal), and Rua da Prata (Silversmiths' Street).

Pedro IV or Maximilian of Austria?

The statue atop the column in the centre of the Rossio is believed to be that of Maximilian, Emperor of Mexico. The boat transporting the statue to Mexico had called at Lisbon, and whilst there news of the emperor's assassination was received. The captain decided to leave the statue in Lisbon and it was finally used to replace the existing one of Pedro IV which was rather rudimentary. It was also thought that the two men were so similar in looks that nobody would notice the difference!

Elevador de Santa Justa★
Open daily 7am–11pm. €1.50.
The lift was built in 1901 by Raúl Mesnier de Ponsard, a Portuguese engineer of French origin who was influenced by Gustave Eiffel. It gives direct access to Chiado. From the upper platform there is a good **view**★ of the Rossio and the Baixa, 32m/105ft above the street.

Rua do Ouro (or Rua Áurea)
In the 15C and 16C, this street was the gold trading area of Lisbon; today it is lined with banks, jewellers and gold-smiths and the streets have plenty of vendors selling bottled water, snacks and items like sunglasses. One very interesting diversion in the Baixa is a trip below the streets into the **Núcleo Arqueológico** (213 211 700; call in advance to reserve; guided tours on Wed and Sat, times vary – entry is via the Banco Comercial Portuguesa on Rua dos Correeiros) where you can see the remains of what was either a Roman spa or temple dating from the 1C together with other items from the same era.

View from Elevador de Santa Justa

Praça do Comércio★★
The finest square in Lisbon (also known as **Terreiro do Paço**) is the site where the Royal Palace once stood, facing the Straw Sea (*Mar da Palha*). The palace was destroyed by the earthquake. The square was designed as a whole and is an excellent example of the Pombaline style. It is 192m/630ft long by 177m/581ft wide

and lined on three sides by Classical buildings with tall arcades supporting two upper storeys with red façades.

A 19C Baroque triumphal arch forms a backdrop to the equestrian statue of King José I. This statue by the late 18C sculptor Machado de Castro is cast in bronze and is the reason for the square also being known as Black Horse Square.

On 1 February, 1908, King Carlos I and his heir, Prince Luís Felipe, were assassinated on the square.

South east of the square is Lisbon's South Station, the **Estação do Sul e Sueste** (*estação fluvial on plan*), which is decorated with *azulejo* panels of towns in the Alentejo and the Algarve.

Praça do Comércio

Passengers embark from here by ferry to the railway station on the opposite shore of the Tagus for destinations to the south and south east of Portugal, including the Algarve.

Chiado★
2hr 30min

The name Chiado applies not only to **Largo do Chiado** but also to a whole district of which the main streets, Rua Garrett and Rua do Carmo, link the Rossio to Praça Luís de Camões. The **Santa Justa** lift ascends to the area struck by fire on 25 August 1988. The four blocks of buildings damaged were mainly shops including the *Grandella* department store (since replaced by the *Printemps* store) and the famous *Ferrari* tearoom. Over 2 000 people lost their jobs at the time as a result of this tragedy, though no lives were lost. Immediately after the event, the mayor of Lisbon entrusted the rehabilitation of the area to the well-known Portuguese architect Álvaro Siza who put forward a resolutely classical plan to rebuild and safeguard the façades of the buildings, and to transform their interiors into pleasant patios, elegant shops and café terraces.

Igreja do Carmo and Museu Arqueológico★
🕐*Open Mon–Sat 10am–6pm (5pm in winter).* 🕐*Closed, 1 Jan, 1 May and 25 Dec.* 🎫*€2.50, free Sun until 2pm*
Once through the doorway of the Carmelite Church, which was almost totally destroyed during the 1755 earthquake, the visitor is struck by the atmospheric aura of the ruins and the silence.
Today, the ruins of the late 14C Gothic church, built by Constable Nuno Álvares Pereira, house an archaeological museum. Among the collections are Bronze Age pottery, marble low reliefs, an Egyptian and two Peruvian mummies, Romanesque and Gothic tombs (including the recumbent statue of Fernão Sanchez, illegitimate son of Dom Dinis) and Spanish Arabic *azulejos*.

Rua do Carmo and Rua Garrett★
These elegant streets with their old-fashioned shop fronts are renowned for their bookshops, patisseries and cafés. The most famous of the latter is the **Brasileira**, once frequented by the poet Fernando Pessoa whose centenary was celebrated in 1988. A bronze statue of the poet stands on the terrace.

Museu Nacional do Chiado★
R Serpa Pinto, 4. 🕐*Open Tue 2pm–6pm, Wed–Sun 10am–6pm.* 🎫*€3 (free Sun and public holidays until 2pm).* ☎*213 432 148. www.museudochiado-ipmuseus.pt.*
The building, originally a 13C abbey, was transformed into a contemporary arts museum in 1911. Following the 1988 fire, it was refurbished by the French architect, Jean-Michel Wilmotte. The museum, which is beautifully lit and laid out, displays an exhibition of predominantly Portuguese paintings, drawings and sculpture from the period between 1850 and 1950. The first floor is devoted to French sculpture, including Rodin's *Bronze Age* and Canto da Maia's *Adam and Eve*. Soares dos Reis' sculpture *O Desterrado (The Exile)* stands out among the works on the second floor. Various periods are represented: the **Romantic**, **Naturalist** (*A Charneca de Belas* by Silva Porto, *Concerto de Amadores* by Columbano, and *A Beira-Mar* by José Malhoa) and **Modernist** (*Tristezas* by Amadeo de Souza-Cardoso, *O Bailarico no Bairro* by Mário Eloy, *Nú* by Eduardo Viana, and the drawing *A Sesta* by Almada Negreiros), and a small collection of **Symbolist** and **neo-Realist** works.

Teatro Nacional de São Carlos
Rua Serpa Pinto, 9. ☎*213 25 30 45. www.saocarlos.pt.*
This lavish theatre, situated in a calm area overlooking the Tagus, was built in 1793 in Neoclassical style with a façade inspired by the San Carlo theatre in Naples. The interior décor is rich in gold and red velvet, making it well worth a visit. It is the venue for regular concerts, ballet and opera.

Praça Luís de Camões

Luís de Camões is regarded as Portugal's top poet, famed for his love sonnets and plays. He was well educated and attended the University in Coimbra, where he began his writing. After a few mishaps and a time in prison he was sent as an army officer to Goa (where his father had died many years before) and then to Macau, where, despite losing one eye, he wrote *The Lusiads*, his greatest poem. He also chronicled the voyages of his colleagues in this new part of the world, including his own shipwreck, in which his Chinese lover died. He returned to Portugal and died in Lisbon in 1580, aged 56.

The square, with a statue of the great poet at its centre, was one of the stages for the revolution on 25 April 1974. The square is the transition zone between the Chiado and the Bairro Alto. To the south, at the foot of Rua do Alecrim, the Tagus comes into view.

Rua da Misericórdia

The street is part of the Praça Camões and borders the Bairro Alto quarter to the west of Chiado.

Museu da Farmacia (Pharmacy Museum)

Rua Marechal Saldanha, 1. ○*Open 10am–6pm.* ◉€2. ☎*213 400 680.*
This museum, little known to tourists, is in a palace dating from 1870 and contains over 14 000 objects from all over the world; pharmacies dating from the 15C to 19C are represented including a Chinese pharmacy from Macao that was functioning there until 1996.

Bairro Alto★

3hr

This picturesque working-class quarter dating from the 16C has kept its character in spite of it becoming the centre for trendy fashion houses, designers, restaurants and *fado* houses over the past few years. It is also, these days, a very busy nightlife area. The main shopping streets are **Rua do Diário de Notícias** and **Rua de Atalaia**. Sunsets over the Tagus are wonderful when viewed from the **Alto de Santa Catarina**★ belvedere with its statue of Adamostor, the giant who was transformed into the Cape of Storms (Cape of Good Hope).

Igreja de São Roque★

○*Open 8.30am–5.30pm.*
The Church of St Rock was built in the late 16C by the Italian architect Filippo Terzi. The original façade collapsed in the great earthquake of 1755. The **interior**★ decoration is striking. The wooden ceiling, painted with scenes of the Apocalypse above the nave, is by artists of the Italian School. The third chapel on the right has 16C **azulejos** and a painting on wood of the Vision of St Rock by the 16C artist Gaspar Vaz.

Steep street of Bairro Alto

G. Bludzin/Michelin

The **Capela de São João Baptista**★★ *(4th on the left)*, a masterpiece of Italian Baroque, was built in Rome by Salvi and Vanvitelli with the help of 130 artists. After being blessed by the Pope, it was dismantled, transported to Lisbon in three ships and re-erected in this church in about 1750. The columns are of lapis lazuli, the altar front of amethyst, the steps of porphyry, the angels of white Carrara marble and ivory, the pilasters of alabaster; the flooring and the wall pictures are coloured mosaics, and the friezes, capitals and ceiling are high-lighted with gold, silver and bronze. The first chapel on the left contains two paintings attributed to the school of Zurbarán *(Nativity* and *Adoration of the Magi)*, and the **sacristy** has a 17C coffered ceiling and paintings of St Francis by Vieira Lusitano and André Gonçalves.

Museu de Arte Sacra de São Roque★

○*Open Tue–Sun 10am–5pm.*
The museum abuts on the church and contains 16C Portuguese paintings and part of the treasure from the Capela do São João Baptista. The furnishings and ecclesiastical plate by 18C Italian artists are outstanding for their Baroque decoration. There is also a collection of **vestments**★ in silk or lamé embroidered in gold.

Miradouro de São Pedro de Alcântara★

The belvedere takes the form of a pleasant garden suspended like a balcony over the lower town with a wide **view**★★ of the Baixa, the Tagus and Castelo de São Jorge on the hill opposite *(viewing table)*.

▶ *The Calçada da Gloria funicular descends to Praça dos Restauradores.*

Jardim Botânico (Botanical Gardens)

Entry via the old Faculty of Science, Rua Escola Politécnica, 56–58, or via Rua da Algeria ○ *Open May–Sept, Mon–Fri 9am–8pm, Sat, Sun and public holidays 10am–8pm; rest of the year* *9am–6pm, Sat, Sun and public holidays 10am–6pm.* ○*Closed 1 Jan, 25 Dec.* ⊕€3. ☎213 921 802.

This beautiful garden, established in 1873 to further the study of plants and part of the Academy of Sciences, is one of the most respected in Europe for its collection of subtropical flora, much of it brought from what were at the time Portugal's overseas territories. There are ideal spots for picnics and a majestic avenue of palms.

Alfama★★ 4hr

The most pleasant way to see the Alfama quarter, which may be approached from above, Largo das Portas do Sol, or from below, along-side the Tagus, is simply to spend time wandering through the district, prefer-ably in the morning when the market is open. Give yourself a half day in this neighbourhood.

The Alfama, a district demarcated by the castle to the north, Graça and Mouraria to the north east and the Tagus to the south, is a maze of narrow streets and alleys *(becos)*, steps and archways, and is one of the oldest in the city. It was largely spared in the earthquake, a sym-bol of hope to Lisbonites. Today it is a bustling, lively area, houses fronted by wrought-iron balconies bursting with flowers, and decorated with *azulejos* representing The Virgin and St Anthony (patron saint of Lisbon).

Sé (Cathedral)★★

○*Cathedral open 9am–7pm; cloisters open summer 10am–6pm; winter 10am–5pm.* ○*Closed public holidays.* ⊕*Cathedral free, Cloister €2.50.*
Lisbon's cathedral *(sé)*, like those of Oporto, Coimbra and Évora, was once a fortress, as can be observed from the two towers flanking the façade and its battlements. It was built in the Roman-esque style in the late 12C, shortly after Afonso Henriques had captured the town with the aid of the Crusaders. The architects, it is believed, were the Frenchmen Robert and Bernard who designed Coimbra Cathedral. Remod-elling followed the earthquake of 1755

View of Alfama with Sé in the background

when the chancel collapsed. Much of its former Romanesque appeal can be seen on the façade and in the nave, although Gothic features and the remodelling of the 17C and 18C are still apparent.

In the **interior**, the nave, supported by wide arches and graceful groined vaulting, is in plain Romanesque style. An elegant triforium runs above the aisles and the transept. The Bartolomeu Joanes Chapel, off the north aisle, containing a lovely terracotta crib by Machado de Castro, is Gothic in style.

The chancel, with its groined vaulting, was rebuilt in the 18C, but the ambulatory, pierced with lancet windows, kept the earlier Gothic style of the 14C when it was remodelled. The third chapel on the south side contains the 14C **Gothic tombs**★ of Lopo Fernandes Pacheco, companion in arms to King Afonso IV, and his wife. Note an elegant Romanesque wrought iron **grille**★ enclosing a chapel near the entrance to the cloisters.

The rather damaged **cloisters** are in the late 13C style of Cistercian Gothic: the lower gallery is supported alternately by massive buttresses and Gothic arches, above which are star-shaped oculi. The chapter-house contains the tomb of Lisbon's first bishop. Excavations in the garden of the cloisters have led to the discovery of vestiges from the Phoenician (8C BC) and Roman periods, as well as the ruins of a former mosque (9C and 10C).

Treasury★

Access to the treasury on the right, near the entrance to the cathedral. Open 10am–5pm. Closed Sun and public holidays. €2.50.

A staircase leads to a series of rooms displaying magnificent vestments, reliquaries and gold and silver plate. The impressive 18C chapter room contains the **King Dom José I monstrance**, richly decorated with 4 120 precious stones.

Not far from the cathedral stands the **Igreja de Santo António da Sé** which was built in 1812 on the site of the house in which St Anthony of Padua (1195–1231), known to the city's inhabitants as Saint Anthony of Lisbon, was born. He is Lisbon's patron saint and a small museum, the **Museu Antoniano**, (open Tue–Sun 10am–1pm, 2pm–6pm; closed public holidays; €1.25), testifies to his popularity.

Miradouro de Santa Luzia★

A small terrace near the Igreja de Santa Luzia has been laid out as a lookout point on the remains of the old Arab fortifications. It affords an excellent **view**★★ of the Tagus, the harbour and, just below, the Alfama quarter, a maze of alleys from which rise the belfries of São Miguel and São Estêvão. The outer walls of the Igreja de Santa Luzia are covered with small panels of *azulejos*, one of which shows Praça do Comércio and another Lisbon's capture by the Crusaders and the death of Martim Moniz in the Castelo de São Jorge. *Azulejos* covering a wall marking the south edge of the square show a general view of Lisbon.

Largo das Portas do Sol★

The Sun Gateway was one of the seven gates into the Arab city. The square, situated on the other side of the Church of Santa Luzia, has a pleasant small esplanade which offers a wonderful **view**★★ over the rooftops, São Vicente de Fora and the river.

Museu de Artes Decorativas – Fundação Ricardo Espírito Santo da Silva★★

Largo das Portas do Sol, 2. Open Tue– Sun 10am–5pm. Closed 1 Jan, Good Fri, 1 May and 25 Dec. €5. 218 814 651. The former palace of the Counts of Azurara (17C) and the wonderful collections it contains were bequeathed to the city of Lisbon by Ricardo Espírito Santo Silva. The museum brings to life the Lisbon of the 17C and 18C through a series of small, intimate rooms decorated with *azulejos* and frescoes on three floors. Level 4 (second floor) is quite elegant, while Level 3 displays interiors with a plainer, yet no less handsome, decorative touch. The Portuguese and Indo-Portuguese furniture is particularly interesting; there are also collections of silver, Chinese porcelain and several tapestries from the 16C and 18C.
Starting from Largo das Portas do Sol, take the steps down from **Rua Norberto de Araújo**, which are supported on one side by the Moorish town wall.

Igreja de São Miguel

Although the church is medieval in origin, it was rebuilt after the earthquake. It contains some fine Baroque woodwork.

Largo de São Rafael

On the west side of this small square, which is surrounded by 17C houses, there still stand the remains of a **tower**, which formed part of the Arab wall and later the defences of Christian Lisbon until the 14C when King Fernando had a new wall built.

Rua da Judiaria (Jewish Quarter)

In this street stands a 16C **house** with paired windows, above the fortification of the old Arab wall. It was customary, under Moorish occupation, for the Jewish community to live outside the city walls and here you can see the juxtaposition of the two.

Rua de São Pedro and Rua dos Remédios

These are the busiest trading streets in the Alfama, lined with small shops and taverns. Rua de São Pedro is at its liveliest in the morning when its fish market is held. At the top of Rua dos Remédios, note on the left-hand side the Manueline door on the Igreja do Santo Espírito. Farther along, at no 2 Calçadinha de Santo Estêvão, another doorway from the same period can be seen.

Escadinhas de Santo Estêvão★

The harmonious interplay of stairs, terrace and architecture make this one of the Alfama's most picturesque spots. As you head behind the Igreja de Santo Estêvão, note a balcony and a panel of *azulejos*. Climb the stairs which skirt the side of the church. At the top you have a fine **view**★ over the rooftops to the harbour and Tagus.

Beco de Carneiro

An extremely narrow street with very steep steps. At the bottom of the street to the right you will see a **public washing-place**. Look behind you for a fine view of the façade of the Igreja de Santo Estêvão.

Beco das Cruzes

At the corner of this street and Rua de Regueira stands an 18C house where the overhanging upper floors are supported by carved corbels. Above one of the doors a panel of *azulejos* shows the Virgin of Conception; from the same spot there is a view up the alley to where it is crossed by an arch surmounted by a cross.

▶ *Take Beco de Santa Helena back up to Largo das Portas do Sol.*

▶ *Take Travessa de Santa Luzia, which leads to the castle.*

Castelo de São Jorge★★

Ⓞ*Open 9am–9pm (Nov–Feb until 6pm).* ☞*€3.* ☏*218 800 620.*

The castle stands high above the city in a remarkable position. Built by the Visigoths in the 5C, enlarged by the Moors in the 9C and then modified during the reign of Afonso Henriques, it has since been turned into a shaded flower garden. After passing through the outer wall you reach the former parade ground from where there is a magnificent **view**★★★ of the Tagus.

The castle's ten towers are linked by huge battlemented walls. Once through the barbican at the castle entrance, steps lead to the parapet walk and the towers which provide **viewpoints** over the town. In the north wall there is a door where the Portuguese knight **Martim Moniz** lost his life as he prevented the Moors from shutting the gate while Afonso Henriques was making his attack.

The Royal Palace, **Paço Real**, built on the site of a former Arab palace, was used as the royal residence by the kings of Portugal from the 14 to 16C.

Near the castle is a modern multimedia exhibition (**Olisipónia** Ⓞ*open 10am– 1pm, 2pm–5.30pm;* ☞*€5*) with 33min commentary detailing Lisbon's history, though a little sanitised with the unsavoury bits left out.

Around the Alfama

The following sights can all be reached on tram no 28.

Mosteiro de São Vicente de Fora

Ⓞ*Open Tue–Sun 9am–6pm.* Ⓞ*Closed 1 Jan, Easter Sun and 25 Dec.*

This monastery church was built by the Italian architect Phillippe Terzi between 1582 and 1627. Its name Fora, meaning beyond the wall, derives from the fact that, when it was built, it was outside the city walls.

The interior, covered with a fine coffered vault, is outstanding for the simplicity of its lines. On the south side of the church, the **cloisters** have walls covered in 18C

azulejos★ illustrating the *Fables* of La Fontaine. Galleries lead to the former monks' refectory which, after the reign of Dom João IV, was transformed into a pantheon for the House of Bragança.

Campo de Santa Clara★

The attractive square between the churches of São Vicente and Santa Engrácia is the setting on Tuesdays and Saturdays for the **Feira da Ladra**, a colourful flea-market. On the northern side of the square stands the graceful 18C **Palácio Lavradio**. The small **Jardim Boto Machado** offers a haven of peace and tranquillity amid its exotic plants.

Igreja de Santa Engrácia★

Ⓞ*National pantheon open Tue–Sun 10am–5pm.* Ⓞ*Closed 1 Jan, Easter Sun, 1 May and 25 Dec.* ☞*€2 (free on Sun and public holidays until 2pm).* ☏*218 88 15 29.*

Begun in the 17C the church was never completed. In the form of a Greek cross, it is now surmounted by a cupola inaugurated in 1966 which completes the Baroque façade. The church houses the cenotaphs (though not necessarily the tombs) of several great Portuguese men and women: Luís de Camões, Prince Henry the Navigator, Pedro Álvares Cabral, Vasco da Gama, Afonso de Albuquerque, Amália (the famous *fadista*) and Nuno Álvares Pereira.

Graça

This popular residential district, where several villas from the 19C can still be seen, is situated on the hill to the north of the city, overlooking the Alfama. Although a separate area it is easily reachable from Alfama's top end.

Igreja and Convento de Nossa Senhora da Graça

This imposing religious complex on the Graça hill dominates the city. The church and convent were founded in the 13C, but have been rebuilt on a number of occasions, particularly after the earthquake in 1755. Note the bell-tower from 1738 next to the convent doorway. The interior is Baroque and contains fine 17C and 18C *azulejos*. Opposite the church

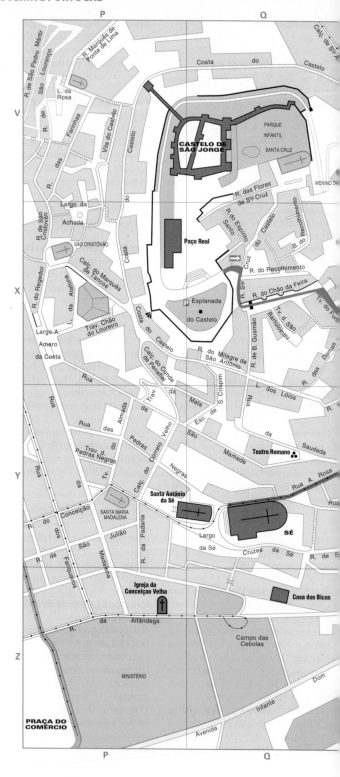

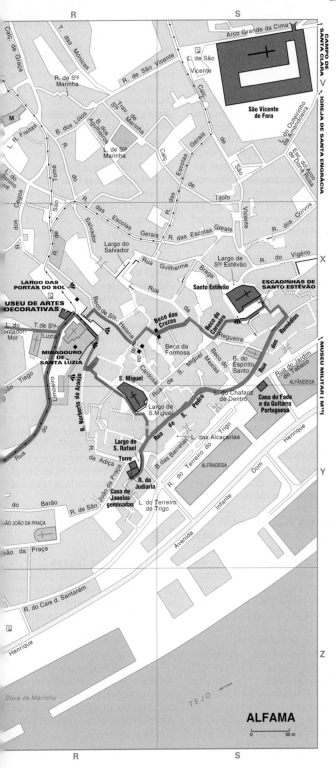

ALFAMA

0   50 m

there is a belvedere with an extensive **view**★ over the city.

Museu-Escola de Artes Decoratives

○*Open Wed–Mon 10am–5pm.* €5.
Set in a bright red building that is the 17th century former palace of the Count of Azurara. Portugal's most important furniture collection is housed here, with valuable wooden Portuguese, French and English furniture dating from the 16th to the 19th centuries. Bedrooms, dining rooms, function rooms, music rooms and dressing rooms from different eras have been reconstructed in their original forms. Wall hangings, silver, porcelain, ceramics and books complete the touch of authenticity.

Miradouro da Senhora do Monte

This vantage point offers an extensive **view**★★★ over Lisbon (the best, without doubt) and in particular over the Castelo de São Jorge and the Mouraria quarter. The chapel next to the belvedere dates from 1796, although its origins can be traced back to 1147, the year of Lisbon's reconquest.

Museu Nacional do Azulejo

○*Open Tue 2pm–6pm, Wed–Sun 10am–6pm.* €3, free on Sun. Take the 104 or 105 bus from Praça do Comércio; it is down near the river-front.
Despite its rather unattractive location near the waterfront and the old docks, this fascinating museum is housed in the **Madre de Deus Convent**, an absolutely magnificent building and arguably one of the best in Lisbon. It contains a wonderful collection of *azulejos*, those exotically painted Hispano-Moorish tiles dating back to the 15C. Wherever you go in Portugal you cannot escape *azulejos*, and this is a good opportunity to find out something about them. The galleries on the ground floor are arranged around the cloisters and contain *azulejos* brought in from Seville in the 15C. Particularly noteworthy is the altarpiece of Nossa Senhora da Vida (1580) depicting a Nativity scene. The highlight of the museum, in the cloisters, is a blue and white composition of 1300 tiles, 23m/75.4ft in length, of Lisbon's city-scape which was produced in 1738, prior to the earthquake.

Leaving the cloisters and entering the **church**★★ you come through the low choir, whose walls with their 16C Seville *azulejos* have been preserved. The 18C church and in particular the Baroque altar are resplendent with gilded woodwork. The nave has a coffered vault with panels depicting scenes from the life of the Virgin. Other paintings depict the lives of St Clare and St Francis.

In the **chapter-house**★ are ceiling panels painted with portraits from the16C and 17C of King João III and his Queen, Catherine of Austria, attributed to Cristóvão Lopes. The walls are adorned with scenes from the life of Christ.

Igreja da Conceição Velha

The **south side**★ of the transept, the only remains of the original church which collapsed in the earthquake of 1755, is a fine example of the Manueline style. The carving on the tympanum shows Our Lady of Compassion sheltering with her cloak Pope Leo X, Dom Manuel, Dona Leonor, bishops and others.

Casa dos Bicos

This **House of Facets**, faced with diamond-shaped bosses, once formed part of a 16C palace, damaged in the 1755 earthquake. It belonged to the son of Afonso de Albuquerque, the viceroy of India. It lost its entire top floor, but it was rebuilt in 1982.

The Tagus

Boat trips on the Tagus★

The trips give a good view of Lisbon and its surroundings and the harbour where, in addition to the commercial traffic, Venetian style barges with large triangular sails may sometimes be seen. The crossing of the estuary in one of the regular ferries makes a pleasant trip as well as giving fine **views**★★ of the city. Approaching Lisbon by boat at Terreiro do Paço (Praça do Comércio) is a wonderful experience, providing the visitor with the feeling of having entered the very heart of the city.

Ponte Vasco da Gama

Museu da Água★

Rua do Alviela 12 ◷Open 10am–6pm. ◷Closed Sun and public holidays. €3. ☎218 135 522. museudaagua.epal.pt/ museudaagua.

The museum traces the history of water supply to Lisbon and more particularly of the Águas Livres (Free Water) project drawn up by the engineer Manuel de Maia. Attempts to bring water to Lisbon from springs at the foot of the Serra de Sintra had begun in 1571, but it wasn't until 1732 that the aqueduct was started (completed in 1748). The water ran into the Mão d'Água des Amoreiras reservoir and was then channelled to the town's fountains and pipes. In 1880 the third link in the chain, the Barbadinhos pumping station, was built. The combined system supplied the town with water for almost 250 years until 1967.

Museu Nacional de Arte Antiga (MNAA)★★★

Rua das Janelas Verdes. ◷Open Wed–Sat 10am–6pm; Tue 2pm–6pm. ◷Closed 1 Jan, Good Fri, Easter Sun, 1 May and 25 Dec. €2.50 (no charge Sun before 2pm). ☎213 912 800. www.mnarteantiga-ip museus.pt.

The Museum of Ancient Art, housed in the 17C palace of the Counts of Alvor and in an annexe built in 1940, has an outstanding collection of paintings, sculptures and decorative arts from the 12C to the early 19C, reflecting the history of Portugal.

The main wealth of the museum lies in the Portuguese Primitives of which the major work is the famous **polyptych**★★★ of the Adoration of St Vincent painted between 1460 and 1470 by Nuno Gonçalves. The panels of this previously unknown work were discovered in an attic in the monastery of São Vicente da Fora in 1882.

The masterly **Annunciation**★ by Frei Carlos (1523), is a remarkable example of Luso-Flemish painting. Among other Portuguese works are the *Cook Triptych* by Grão Vasco and the *Martyrdom of the Eleven Thousand Virgins* from the Igreja da Madre de Deus. It is an unsigned work showing the arrival in Portugal of the relics of Santa Auta which were given by

---

Ponte Vasco da Gama★★

This magnificent road bridge was built across the Tagus between 1995 and 1998. It is 18km/11mi long, 10km/6.2mi of which passes over water. At its lowest point, the bridge has the illusion of balancing directly on the Tagus. This superb feat of engineering is made up of several sections supported on pillars, some of which rise to 150m/492ft and are buried to a depth of 95m/311.6ft. The height of the superstructure varies from 14m/46ft to 30m/98.4ft to enable shipping to pass beneath it.

1. St Vincent
2. King Afonso V
3. Prince João, future João II
4. Prince Henry the Navigator
5. Queen Isabel
6. Isabella of Aragon, her mother
7. Nuno Gonçalves
8. Prince Fernando
9. Knights
10. The Archbishop of Lisbon accompanied by two canons
11. The Chronicler, Gomes Eanes de Azurara
12. Cistercians from Alcobaça
13. Fishermen and navigators
14. Fernando, Second Duke of Bragança
15. Fernando, his oldest son
16. João, his youngest son
17. A Moorish knight
18. A cleric proffering St Vincent's skull
19. A Jew
20. A beggar before the saint's coffin

Museu Nacional de Arte Antiga – Adoration of Saint Vincent

the Holy Roman Emperor Maximilian I to his cousin Dona Leonor in 1509.

Notable among the paintings from other European schools is the extraordinary **Temptation of St Anthony**★★★ by Hieronymus Bosch. Mention should also be made of the *Virgin and Child* by Memling, *St Jerome* by Dürer, *Virgin, Child and Saints* by Hans Holbein the Elder and the **Twelve Apostles**★ by Zurbarán.

A panel of the polyptych of the Adoration of St Vincent (1460-70) by Nuno Gonçalves

One of the rooms contains precious **Nambans** or **Japanese screens**★★ showing the arrival of the Portuguese on the island of Tane-ga-Shima in 1543. The Japanese called the Portuguese *Namban-jin* meaning barbarians from the south (they had approached Japan from the south) and the art that ensued came to be known as Namban. There is also a rich collection of gold and silver plate, the finest of which is the **monstrance from the Mosteiro de Belém** (1506) attributed to Gil Vicente who, it is believed, made it from gold brought from the Indies by Vasco da Gama. The newer section of the museum houses the **chapel**★ from the former Carmelite Convent of Santa Alberto, outstanding for its gilded woodwork and its 16C–18C *azulejos*.

Parque das Nações

(Expo'98 site) *see Address Book for details of transport within the park.* The site, which hosted Expo'98, is spread out along the Tagus in front of the Doca dos Olivais to the east of the city, not far from the airport. It has plenty of bars, restaurants, gardens and shops, including the huge Vasco da Gama shopping centre. The Oceanário and a Science Centre are ideal for children, though adults will find them fascinating as well. There is also the Lisbon Casino. In the grounds there are twenty or so works by contemporary Portuguese and foreign artists including João Cutileiro in the Passeio das Tágides, an immense iron oxide-coated steel sculpture by Jorge Vieira; stone paving by Fernando Conduto, works by Pedro Cabrita Reis and Pedro Calapez, and stone-paving by Pedro Proença.

You could easily spend an entire day at the Park. The easiest way to arrive is by metro, at the modern Oriente station.

Estação do Oriente★

This intermodal complex houses a railway station, metro, suburban and a regional bus terminal. It was designed by the Spanish architect Santiago Calatrava and is covered by a strong yet delicate steel and glass structure which provides the building with an abundance of natural light.

Oceanário de Lisboa★★   Kids

🕐 Open Apr–Oct, daily 10am–7pm; Nov–Mar, daily 10am–6pm (afternoons only 25 Dec and 1 Jan). Guided tours available; call or see website for details. €11 (children under 12, €5.50). ☎218 917 002. www.oceanario.pt.

Designed by the American architect Peter Chermayeff, Europe's largest aquarium (and second largest in the world, after one in Japan) has five main tanks providing an introduction to the natural habitats of the Arctic, Indian, Pacific and Atlantic Oceans. In total over 15 000 marine animals and fish and 250 species of plants are exhibited here. Visitors are plunged deep into the marine world with its sounds and smells on a tour around the enormous 5 000cu m/176 570cu ft main tank, representing the high seas, as grouper, rays, different species of shark and shoals of mackerel glide past. On a journey both above and underwater, visitors are transported to the coastline of Antarctica to view the acrobatic feats of cormorants and penguins, to the temperate Pacific with its sea-otters, and to the waters of the Tropics, with its explosion of colours and superb coral reefs. A fabulous look at the world beneath the seas and ideal for all ages, including children.

Pavilhão do Conhecimento Ciência Viva (Understanding Science)   Kids

🕐 Open Tue–Fri, 10am–7pm, Sat–Sun 11am–7pm. €7 (children under 12 €4). www.pavconhecimento.pt.

Many interactive exhibits explaining science and its place in our life fill this ever-changing exhibition. Very interesting and a great place for children.

Torre Vasco da Gama

This tower, situated at the far end of the park, has great views of the Tagus and surrounding areas. Other facilities include a panoramic restaurant, bars, night-club and a huge shopping centre which stays open late, until 11pm.

The Kids Jardin da Água section of the park area is a fun and leisure area with a water-based theme. Many statues can be found among the fountains and jets of water – most enjoyable.

The attractive Jardim Garcia da Orta in front of the Olivais dock, alongside the Tagus, takes its name from the 16C doctor who studied and classified Asiatic plants. The vegetation contained within the gardens is from regions visited by the Portuguese during the period of the Great Discoveries. At night in summer, concerts are held on the Praça Sony, at the Palco da Doca, in the Pavilhão Atlântico and in the park's numerous bars and restaurants.

Museu Militar

🕐 Open Tue–Sun 10am–12.30pm, 2pm–5pm. 🕐 Closed public holidays. €2.50. ☎218 842 300.

This former 18C arsenal on the banks of the Tagus has preserved its outstanding woodwork as well as azulejos and interesting ceilings★ mainly illustrating battle scenes. Models, paintings and in particular numerous weapons from the 16C to the late 19C, some manufactured on the spot, recall Portugal's military past. It claims to have the largest collection of artillery in the world – for a museum at least!

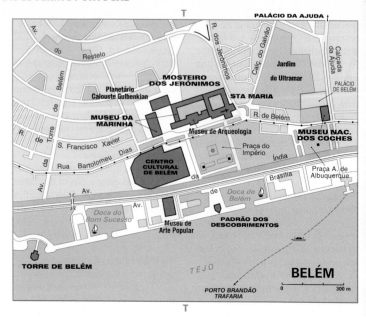

BELÉM

Museu das Marioneta – Puppet Museum `Kids`

Rua da Esperança, 146 (Convento das Bernardos). ⏰*Open Wed–Sun 10am–1pm, 2pm–6pm.* ≈*€2.50, children €1.50.* ☎ *213 942 810. museudamarioneta. egeac.pt.*

Located in a beautiful 18C Cistercian monastery this fascinating museum has traditional puppet shows at certain times by the São Lourenço company, as well as many older examples of puppets. On display are shadow puppets from Turkey, string puppets from Indonesia, Punch-and-Judy puppets and Plasticine Wallace & Gromit-style models, with an explanation of how they are moulded for film. The museum offers activities for children in Portuguese and English.

Docks

The docks area along the river was formerly occupied by warehouses, but has been transformed in recent years into a fashionable district with a multitude of bars, restaurants and discos. It is a pleasant place for a stroll in the late afternoon, or at night when activity is at its liveliest.

Belém★★

Allow one day, though check carefully for closing days: usually Mon.

It was from the harbour at Belém (Portuguese for Bethlehem) that sailing ships set forth on their brave journeys in search of hitherto unknown lands and continents.

▸ *Starting from Praça do Comércio, either drive alongside the Tagus or take tram number 15 to Belém.*

Mosteiro dos Jerónimos★★★

⏰*Open Apr–Oct, Tue–Sun 10am–6pm; Nov–Mar, Tue–Sun 10am–5pm. Last entry 30min before closing.* ⏰*Closed 1 Jan; Good Friday, Easter Day, 1 May, 25 Dec. Restricted access Sat mornings.* ☞*You are specifically asked to respect the religious services during which access may be denied.* ≈*€6. www.mosteiro jeronimos.pt.*

In 1502, on the site of a former hermitage founded by Prince Henry the Navigator, King Dom Manuel, undertook to build this magnificent Hieronymite monastery, considered to be the jewel of Manueline art. This style of art glorified the great discoveries; in this case that of Vasco da Gama who, on his return from the Indies, had moored his caravels in Restelo harbour near Belém. The architects of the monastery, benefiting from the riches then pouring into Lisbon from these overseas expeditions, were able to throw themselves into an ambitious, large-scale work. The Gothic style adopted by the Frenchman Boytac until his death in 1517 was modified by his successors who added ornamentation typical of the Manueline style with its diverse influences: João de Castilho, of Spanish origin, added a Plateresque form to the decoration, Nicolas Chanterene emphasised the Renaissance element, while Diogo de Torralva and Jérôme de Rouen, at the end of the 16C, brought in a Classical note.

The Monastery is now a UNESCO World Heritage Site.

Igreja de Santa Maria★★★

Same hours as the Monastery. €3.

The **south door**, the work of Boytac and João de Castilho, combines a mass of gables, pinnacles and niches filled with statues. Crowning all is a canopy surmounted by the Cross of the Order of the Knights of Christ.

The **west door**, sheltered beneath the 19C porch which leads to the cloisters, is by Nicolas Chanterene and is adorned with fine statues, particularly those of King Manuel and Queen Maria. Represented above the doorway are the Annunciation, the Nativity and the Adoration of the Magi.

The **interior** is outstanding for the intricate beauty of the stonework, carved throughout in great detail but never obscuring the architectural lines, as, for instance, in the network **vaulting**★★ of equal height over the nave and aisles. This vaulting withstood the 1755 earthquake. The decoration on the pillars and the vaulting over the transept crossing are by João de Castilho. The transepts are Baroque, designed by Jérôme de Rouen, and contain the tombs of several princes. In the chancel, reconstructed in the Classical period, are the tombs of Dom Manuel I and Dom João III, with their queens. Beneath the gallery of the *coro alto* at the entrance to the church are the neo-Manueline tombs of Vasco da Gama and the great poet and chronicler of the discoveries, Luís de Camões, whose recumbent figure wears a crown of laurel leaves.

Cloisters★★★

Same opening times as the Monastery. €4.50 (no charge Sun 10am–2pm).

This masterpiece of Manueline art is fantastically rich in sculpture. The stone is at its most beautiful when it takes on the golden tint of the late afternoon sun. The cloisters, forming a hollow square of which each side measures 55m/180.4ft, are two storeys high. The ground level galleries with groined vaulting by Boytac have wide arches with tracery resting upon slender columns, and Late Gothic and Renaissance decoration carved into the massive thickness of the walls. The chapter-house contains the tomb of the writer Alexandre Herculano.

Cloister, Mosteiro dos Jerónimos

©Uwe Blosfeld/Dreamstime.com

A staircase leads to the church's **coro alto** with another view of the vaulting. The graceful Renaissance stalls carved out of maple are by Diogo de Carça.

Museu da Marinha★★

Located opposite the Centro Cultural de Belém. Open Jun–Sept, Tue–Sun 10am–6pm (5pm the rest of the year). Closed public holidays. €3 (free Sun before 1pm). www.museumarinha.pt.

This museum, containing a remarkable collection of **models**★★★ of seafaring craft over the centuries, is located on both sides of the esplanade of the **Calouste Gulbenkian planetarium** in two separate buildings: the west wing of the Mosteiro dos Jerónimos and the modern Pavilhão das Galeotas.

▸ *Once through the entrance, take the stairs in front of the door on the right.*

The Sala da Marinha de Recreio, a room dedicated to pleasure craft on the upper floor, includes a small collection of models of 18C and 19C yachts. The Sala da Marinha Mercante (Merchant Navy Room) recalls the history of merchant shipping in Portugal, with exhibits such as the *Santa Maria* and the *Infante Dom Henrique*, which transported soldiers to the colonies, and the *Neiva* oil tanker. The Sala da Construção Naval at the far end takes an informative look at naval construction techniques.

▸ *Return to the main floor.*

Main building

Giant sandstone statues of historical figures (including Henry the Navigator) and ancient cannon can be seen in the entrance hall. On the ground floor there is an immense room devoted to the Discoveries and the Navy, from the 15C to the 18C, with maps and magnificent models of sailing ships, caravels and frigates, including the 18C vessel, the *Príncipe da Beira*. There are displays of figureheads and navigational instruments such as 15C astrolabes. Warships of the 19C and 20C can also be seen (small-scale models of gunboats, frigates and corvettes, and modern sub-

marines) as well as a fishing fleet (the Henrique Seixas Collection) with models of various boats which used to fish in the estuaries or along the coast: a *muleta* from Seixal with its many sails, a *calão* from the Algarve, a *galeão* from Nazaré. Models of boats used for river navigation include frigates of the Tagus and *rabelos* of the Douro. In the last room there is a reconstruction of the royal stateroom of the yacht *Amélia* (late 19C).

Planetário Calouste Gulbenkian (Planetarium) Kids

Praça Império, Belém. Open Sat–Sun 11am–3.30pm; special shows for children Sun 11am. €4. ☎213 620 002. www.planetario.online.pt.

A special show looking at Portugal's starry skies, an imaginary voyage through the planetary system, a trip to the moon, a journey across the polar region, various films, plus eclipses of the sun and the moon – these are just some of the audio-visual adventures on offer at the Planetarium.

Museu do Design★

Open 11am–7pm (last entry at 6.15pm). Closed 25 Dec. €3.50.

Housed in a wing of the cultural centre, this new museum has been created to display the collection of Francisco Capelo, who has assembled works here from the Museu de Arte Moderna in Sintra. The collection consists of works by some 230 designers of furniture and other objects representing trends in design from around the world from 1937 to the present day. The museum is divided into four main sections: Interior Design, Modernism, Pop and Cool.

Padrão dos Descobrimentos – Monument of Discoveries

Open May–Sept, Tue–Sun 10am–7pm; Oct–Apr, Tue–Sun 10am–6pm (last entry 30min before closing). Closed public holidays. €2.

The 52m/170.6ft Monument to the Discoveries by the sculptor Leopoldo de Almeida, erected in 1960 beside the Tagus on the 500th anniversary of the death of Prince Henry the Navigator, represents the prow of a ship with the prince pointing the way to a crowd of

View from inside Torre de Belém

F. Vidal/MICHELIN

important figures. Among them, on the right side, are King Dom Manuel carrying an armillary sphere, Camões holding verses from *The Lusiads* and the painter, Nuno Gonçalves.

Torre de Belém★★★

Open 10am–6pm (5pm in summer). Closed Mon, 1 Jan, Good Fri, Easter Sun, 1 May and 25 Dec. €3.

This elegant Manueline tower was built between 1515 and 1519 in the middle of the Tagus to defend the river mouth and the Mosteiro dos Jerónimos. Today, as the river altered course during the earthquake in 1755, and with further silting up since then, it stands on the north shore.

It is an architectural gem; the Romanesque-Gothic structure is adorned with loggias like those in Venice, and small domes like those in Morocco where the tower's architect, Francisco de Arruda, had travelled.

On the keep terrace, facing the sea, is a statue of Our Lady of Safe Homecoming. The tower is five storeys high ending in a terrace. On the ground floor are openings through which prisoners were thrown into the dungeons below. On the third floor paired windows with elegant balconies, a magnificent Renaissance loggia surmounted by the royal arms of Manuel I and two armillary spheres mellow the granite tower's original architectural severity. It looks particularly spectacular at night when fully floodlit. To be honest, it is possi-ble to see it all from off-site without paying the entrance fee. The best photos you will take will be by night.

Palácio da Ajuda★

Guided tours (1hr 30min) Mar–Jan, Thu–Tue 10am–5pm (last entrance at 4.30pm). Closed 1 Jan, Easter Sun, 1 May and 25 Dec. €4 (no charge Sun and public holidays 10am–2pm).

This former royal palace (18C–19C) to the north of Belém was built after the earthquake, yet never completed. It was the residence of the Portuguese monarchs, Dom Luís and Dona Maria Pia, from 1862 onwards. Its two floors offer a succession of rooms with painted ceilings and an interior richly filled with furniture, tapestries, statues and decorative objects from the 20C.

At the top of the Calçada da Ajuda is the **Jardim Botânico da Ajuda**, which is connected to the romantic **Jardim das Damas** (18C) (open Thu–Tue 9am–8pm; winter until 8pm; €1.75) with its waterfalls and ponds. It was here that the ladies of the Court would enjoy pleasant strolls.

Museu Nacional dos Coches
(National Coach Museum)

Praça Afonso de Albuquerque Open Tue–Sun 10am–6pm (last entry 30min before closing). €4.

In the former riding stables of the Royal Palace, this is a fascinating collection of coaches dating back to the 17C – the oldest being one used by Filipe II to tour Portugal in 1619; it has a mirrored ceiling. Each coach is magnificent, showing the lengths to which the major coach-makers of the day went to make their vehicles stand out from the others. One of the most outstanding examples has gilded figures on the tailgate. Another, used by Louis XIV, has cherubs, and yet another model was built in 1716 for Portugal's ambassador to Pope Clement XI. Other coaches had formerly belonged to several European royal families, including a 19th century coach built in London and used by Queen Elizabeth II on a state visit to Portugal.

Around Avenida da Liberdade

Allow at least a half day.

Avenida da Liberdade★
The Avenida da Liberdade is the most majestic of Lisbon's avenues. On either side late 19C buildings and more recent constructions house hotels and offices. The pavements are covered in black and white mosaics. To the north, the Avenida leads to the **Praça do Marquês de Pombal**, Lisbon's nerve centre, where several wide avenues converge. In the centre of this circular "square" stands a monument to the Marquis of Pombal.

▸ *Take Avenida Fontes Pereira de Melo then Avenida António Augusto de Aguiar on the left.*

Parque Eduardo VII★
This formal, elegant landscaped park, crowning Avenida da Liberdade, was named after King Edward VII of England on the occasion of his visit to Lisbon in 1902. There is a magnificent **vista**★ from the upper end of the park over the Baixa district and the Tagus, dominated on either side by the castle and the Bairro Alto hills.

Estufa fria★
◷*Open 9am–5.30pm (4.30pm 1 Oct to 21 Mar).* ◷*Closed 1 Jan, 25 Apr, 1 May and 25 Dec.* ☞€1.20.

Wooden shutters in the cold greenhouse provide protection from the extremes of summer heat and winter cold. The many exotic plants displayed grow beside fish-ponds or cooling waterfalls near small grottoes.

Gulbenkian Foundation

Just north of the Parque Eduardo VII
Calouste Gulbenkian, an Armenian oil magnate and patron of the arts born in Istanbul in 1869, was nicknamed "Mister 5%" on account of his five per cent share in the profits of the Iraq Petroleum Company. His keenness for collecting started at an early age with the acquisition of a few old coins, and was to lead to the creation of an outstanding collection of works of art over a period of forty years. On his death in 1955 he bequeathed his immense fortune (c. USD55 billion/c. €35.3 billion in today's money) to Portugal, where he had lived for many years. A year later the Calouste Gulbenkian Foundation was set up – a private institution which runs its own museums, an orchestra, a ballet company and a choir.

The foundation's headquarters, set in beautiful gardens, consist of a complex of modern buildings which house the Gulbenkian Museum, the Modern Art Centre, four multi-purpose lecture halls, of which one is open-air, a conference centre, two large galleries for art exhibitions and a library with 152 000 books.

Museu Calouste Gulbenkian★★★
◷*Open Tue–Sun 10am–6pm.* ◷*Closed holidays.* ☞€5 for the two museums in the Foundation. www.gulbenkian.pt.
The museum was especially designed for the Gulbenkian collections which consist of selected exhibits of great value and beauty. They are particularly rich in Oriental and European art. The lower floor displays contemporary art.

Ancient art
Ancient art section is represented by works from Egypt (an alabaster bowl about 2 700 years old; a stone statuette

of "Judge Bes"; a bronze sun-boat; and a silver-gilt mask for a mummy dating from the 30th Dynasty), the Graeco-Roman world (a superb 5C BC Attic crater; jewellery; the head of a woman attributed to Phidias; iridescent Roman vases; and a magnificent collection of gold and silver coins) and Mesopotamia (9C BC Assyrian stele and a Parthian urn).

Near Eastern art

The finest pieces in the vast Near Eastern art collection are the pottery and carpets. The sumptuous woollen and silk carpets, mainly Persian from the 16C and 17C and the shimmering Prusa velvets from Turkey are especially beautiful. The pottery (12C–18C), silk costumes and lamps from the mosque of Alep are as finely worked as Persian miniatures. There are also collections of poetry, Korans and Armenian manuscripts.

Far Eastern art

Far Eastern art, primarily Chinese, is represented by magnificent porcelain (a 14C Taoist bowl; a 17C vase of the hundred birds) and "rough stones" (an 18C green nephrite bowl); Japanese exhibits include prints and a selection of lacquerware from the 18C and 19C.

European art

The **European art** section begins with **medieval religious art**, some beautiful carved **ivories**, illuminated manuscripts and books of hours. A section

on **15C, 16C** and **17C painting** and **sculpture** follows: The *Presentation at the Temple* by the German artist **Stephan Lochner** was one of Gulbenkian's first acquisitions. The Flemish and Dutch schools are well represented with a *St Joseph* by **Van der Weyden**, an admirable *Annunciation* by **Dirk Bouts**, a magnificent *Old Man* by **Rembrandt** and a masterly *Portrait of Helen Fourment* by **Rubens**. From the Italian school there is a delightful *Portrait of a Young Woman* attributed to **Ghirlandaio**.

The 18C French school of painting, famous for its portraits and festive scenes, is represented here by **Lancret** *(Fête Galante)*, **Hubert Robert** *(Gardens of Versailles)*, **Quentin de la Tour** *(Portrait of Mademoiselle Sallé* and *Portrait of Duval de l'Epinoy)*, and **Nicolas de Largillière** *(Portrait of M. et Mme. Thomas-Germain)*. Among the sculptures note the proud **Diana** in white marble by Houdon.

18C English painting includes works by **Gainsborough** (a lovely *Portrait of Mrs. Lowndes-Stone*), **Romney** *(Portrait of Miss Constable)*, **Turner** *(Quilleboeuf)* and **Thomas Lawrence**.

A gallery on the Venetian apprentice of Canaletto, **Francesco Guardi**, is hung with some of his large and impressive scenes of Venice.

The 19C French school is represented by **Henri Fantin-Latour** *(La Lecture)* the Impressionists, including **Manet** *(Boy with Cherries* and *Blowing Bub-*

Gulbenkian Foundation

C. Bastin/MICHELIN

bles), **Degas** (Self-portrait), and **Renoir** (Portrait of Mme. Claude Monet), a number of canvases by **Corot** (Bridge at Mantes,Willows), as well as a fine collection of bronzes (Spring) and marble sculptures (Benedictions) by **Rodin**.

In the last room there is an extraordinary collection of works and jewels from the Art Nouveau period by the French decorative artist **René Lalique** (1860–1945).

Centro de Arte Moderna★

🕐Open Tue–Sun 10am–6pm. 🕐Closed public holidays. ☎217 823 474 www.cam jap.gulbenkian.pt. ☞€4 – or included in the €5 combined entry ticket (free Sun).

The centre, which was built by the British architect Sir Leslie Martin in 1983, has a roomy design in which plants have been incorporated, giving the impression of a screen of greenery. It houses modern works by Portuguese artists from 1910 to the present.

Among the artists represented are Vieira da Silva, Amadeo Souza-Cardoso, Almada Negreiros and Julio Pomar. Several sculptures, including the Reclining Woman by **Henry Moore**, are exhibited in the gardens surrounding the centre.

Close to the Gulbenkian

Igreja de Nossa Senhora de Fátima

This modern church is adorned with beautiful **stained-glass windows**★ by Almada Negreiros.

Biblioteca Municipal

The library is housed in the 16C Galveias Palace opposite the neo-Moorish **bullring** at Campo Pequeno.

Amorairas

This district, to the west of Parque Eduardo VII, and bordering on the Parque Florestal de Monsanto, Lisbon's answer the Parisian Bois de Boulogne, is dominated by the Torres das Amoreiras and the Aqueduto das Águas Livres. The name recalls the mulberry trees which existed here to produce silkworms used in the manufacture of silk.

Torres das Amoreiras

The famous pink, grey and black postmodern towers designed by the architect Tomás Taveira were completed in 1983. They are situated close to one of the entrances to the city and can be seen from afar. They comprise three floors, and contain offices, luxury apartments, restaurants and a large shopping centre.

Fundação Arpad Szenes – Vieira da Silva★

🕐Open Wed–Sat and Mon noon–8pm. 🕐Closed public holidays. ☞€2.50. www. fasvs.pt.

This foundation is located on one side of the leafy Praça das Amoreiras, next to the Águas Livres aqueduct. It is a fine 18C workshop which has been remodelled in a sober, elegant manner. Maria Helena Vieira da Silva (1908–92), who lived a great part of her life in Paris with the artist Arpad Szenes, is one of Portugal's most famous 20C artists. The museum displays a small collection of exhibits by the artists, as well as works donated by collectors and institutions.

Aqueduto das Águas Livres★

🕐Open Mar–Nov, Mon–Sat 10am–6pm. 🕐Closed public holidays.

The aqueduct built between 1732 and 1748 (👈see Museu da Água) measures a total of 58km/36mi, including all its ramifications. Thirty-four of its arches stride across the Alcântara valley. The tallest is 65m/213ft high with a span of 29m/95ft. The best view of the aqueduct is from Avenida de Ceuta, north of the N 7 motorway bridge.

Parque Florestal de Monsanto★

Kids 🕐Open 24hr. ☞€2. ☎217 71 09 91. www.cm-lisboa.pt/pmonsanto.

This hilly, wooded park of 900ha/2 224 acres is dissected by roads giving panoramic **views**★ of Lisbon, particularly from the Monsanto belvederes. The park contains several small parks that are ideal for children – the Parqu Alvito has plenty of games and two swimming pools for children 3–14yrs (🕐open Jul–Sept); and the Parque dos Índios, for children aged 4–12yrs, one of the most popular places in Lisbon for youngsters.

Additional Sights

Casa-Museu Dr Anastácio Gonçalves

Open Tue–Sun 10am–6pm (Tue 2pm–6pm). *Closed 1 Jan, Easter Sun, 1 May and 25 Dec.* *€2 (free Sun until 2pm).* *213 540 823 www.cmag-ipmuseus.pt.*
This museum is housed in two villas formerly owned by the artist José Malhoa, and more recently by Dr Anastácio Gonçalves, a great patron of the arts and a friend of Gulbenkian. The first part of the museum is used to display temporary exhibitions predominantly devoted to early 20C Portuguese artists (modernists such as Columbano, Eduardo Viana, Amadeo de Souza Cardoso, Vieira da Silva and Mário Eloy, and naturalists including Silva Porto and Sousa Pinto). The permanent collection comprises ancient Chinese porcelain, furniture, textiles and jewellery, as well as an interesting set of drawings by Almada Negreiros.

Palácio dos Marqueses de Fronteira★★

Take the metro to Sete Rios, followed by a 20min walk along Rua das Furnas and Rua São Domingo de Benfica. *Guided tours (45min), Jun–Sept, Mon–Sat 10.30am, 11am, 11.30am, noon; Oct–May, Mon–Sat 11am, noon. Gardens open Mon–Fri 2pm–6.30pm.* *Closed public holidays.* *€7.50 (gardens only €3).* *217 782 023.*
The palace, to the north of the Parque de Monsanto near Benfica, was built as a hunting lodge by João Mascarenhas, the first Marquis of Fronteira, in 1670.
While a strong Italian Renaissance influence is apparent, particularly in the layout of the gardens, the palace is one of the most beautiful Portuguese creations with its **azulejos**★★ of outstanding quality and variety. Inside the palace, the *azulejos* in the Victory Room depict the main events in the War of Restoration in which the first Marquis of Fronteira distinguished himself. The dining room is adorned with 17C Delft tiles, the first to be imported into Portugal. Outside, on the terraces and in the gardens, every conceivable flat surface has been decorated with small ceramic tiles.

H. Champollion/MICHELIN

Palácio dos Marqueses de Fronteira

Some depict country scenes of the seasons and work in the fields, others more stately, solemn subjects like the twelve horsemen in the Kings' Gallery which are reflected in a pool.

Jardim Zoológico★★   Kids

Metro: Sete Rios. *Open Apr–Sept 10am–8pm (6pm Oct–Mar); last entry 1hr before closing.* *€12 (children €9) www.zoo.pt.*
The park, which is both a lovely garden and a zoo as well as a great place for children to play, is laid out in the 26ha/64 acres of the Parque das Laranjeiras, which includes the rose-coloured palace of the Counts of Farrobo, to the right of the entrance. The lower part includes the rose garden, a variety of other flowers and enclosures for the 2 500 animals, many of which are exotic species.
Just inside the entrance there is a little amusement park with rides called **Animax** (11am–8pm) – yet another reason to spend money!
Also make sure you see the Kids **Museu das Crianças** (Children's Museum), established in 2006, with interactive exhibits for children from 4–13yrs. *Near the main entrance.* *Open Mon–Fri 10am–5pm, Sat–Sun 10am–6pm.* *€2.*

Museu da Música★

Open Tue–Sat 10am–6pm. *€2.* *217 71 09 91.*

Jardim da Estrela

The small museum, located inside the Alto dos Moinhos metro station, contains a wide variety of musical instruments and publications from the 16C–20C, including a set of Baroque harpsichords and a large collection of string and wind instruments.

Basílica da Estrela★

Tram number 28. ⏰*Open 8am–12.30pm, 3pm–7.30pm.*
The white Baroque edifice was built at the end of the 18C. Inside, the transept crossing is covered by a fine **cupola** topped by a lantern tower. Note also a Christmas crib with life-size figures carved by Machado de Castro.
The **Jardim da Estrela**★ opposite the basilica is one of the most beautiful gardens in Lisbon with its varied display of exotic plants and trees.

Casa Fernando Pessoa

Rua Coelho da Rocha, 16–18. ⏰*Open Mon –Fri 10am–6pm (Thu 11am–8pm).* ☎*213 968 190; www.casafernandopessoa.com.*
This house, where the poet Fernando Pessoa spent the last 15 years of his life, has been refurbished and now serves as a cultural centre specialising in Portuguese poetry as well as an exhibition centre for painting and sculpture.
The works of Pessoa and his archives are also assembled here. He is regarded as Portugal's greatest 20C poet, a true Modernist in his thinking and writing.

Museu da Cidade

Campo Grande, 345. Metro: Campo Grande. ⏰*Open 10am–1pm, 2pm–6pm.* ⏰*Closed public holidays.* ☙€2. ☎217 591 617.
The municipal museum stands above Campo Grande – unfortunately a bit too close to the motorway interchange – in the graceful 18C Palácio Pimenta built during Dom João V's luxurious reign. The different stages in the history of Lisbon may be traced through Roman, Visigothic, Arab and medieval remains. The emblem of the city, a caravel transporting the body of St Vincent guided by ravens, can be seen on the many coats of arms displayed.
A model of Lisbon in the early 18C gives an idea of the city before the earthquake as do the *azulejos* of Terreiro do Paço square showing the Royal Palace still in place. The palace kitchens are adorned with *azulejos* of country scenes. The first floor is devoted to ceramics and engravings of Lisbon. Note the famous *Fado* canvas by Malhoa.

Museu Rafael Bordalo Pinheiro

Campo Grande, 382. Metro: Campo Grande. ⏰*Open Tue–Sun 10am–6pm.* ☙€2 (no charge Sun).
The museum, which stands across the Campo Grande from the Museu da Cidade, contains collections of drawings, caricatures and particularly **ceramics**★ by Rafael Bordalo Pinheiro (1846–1905). He was a prolific artist and together with

his brother and sister had some influence on social life in Lisbon at the end of the 19C.

Museu Nacional do Traje★

Open Tue–Sun 10.am–6pm. Closed 1 Jan, Good Fri, Easter Sun, 1 May and 25 Dec. €3, including entrance to Museu Nacional do Teatro; no charge Sun 10am–2pm. 217 590 318.

The graceful palace of the Marquis of Angeja now holds outstanding costume exhibitions. The beautifully presented collections bring a whole era, or a town or profession, to life, through the art of dress.

Museu Nacional do Teatro

Open Wed–Sun 10am–6pm, Tue 2pm–6pm. Closed 1 Jan, Easter day, 1 May and 25 Dec. €3, including entrance to Museu Nacional do Traje; free Sun 10am–2pm. 217 56 74 10).

Housed in the palace of Monteiro-Mor, which was rebuilt after a fire, this small museum holds temporary exhibitions on drama-related themes.

Below the palace, the attractive botanical gardens, **Jardim Botânico do Monteiro-Mor** (*open Tue–Sun 10am–5.30pm (7pm Apr–Sept); closed 1 Jan, Easter Sun, 1 May and 25 Dec; €1.50, free Sun and public holidays 10am–2pm*), with their pools and a rich variety of plants, lie in a wild, hilly setting.

Excursion

Cristo Rei

See COSTA DA CAPARICA. Leave Lisbon by ② on the map. 3.5km/2mi from the south toll gate of the 25 de Abril suspension bridge, turn left at motorway exit 1 towards Almada. Then follow the signs and leave the car in the car park near the monument. Open 9.30am–8pm. €4. 212 751 000.

This enormous statue (28m/92ft high) of Christ in Majesty, which can be seen from the Lisbon side of the river but is on the opposite shore, was erected in 1959 to thank God for having spared Portugal during World War II. Although the country was officially neutral there was always a threat that it might become involved. Thankfully it did not, though Allied aircraft used the Azores for refuelling on their way across the Atlantic. It is a slightly smaller replica of the statue of Christ the Redeemer in Rio de Janeiro. From the pedestal *(access by lift; plus 74 steps)* which is 85m/279ft above ground level and 113m/371ft over the Tagus, there is a **panoramic view★★** of the Tagus estuary, Lisbon and the plain to the south as far as Setúbal.

Turismo de Lisboa

Looking across the Tagus with a view of Cristo Rei

PALÁCIO AND CONVENTO DE MAFRA★★

LISBOA

MICHELIN MAP 733 – MICHELIN ATLAS SPAIN & PORTUGAL P 58 (P 2)

Mafra monastery stands some 40km/25mi northwest of Lisbon. Its impressive size and mix of Baroque and Italian Renaissance style, in which marble proliferates, testify to the rich reign of King João V who, having no children after three years of marriage, vowed to build a monastery if God would grant him an heir. A daughter, Barbara, was born, later to become Queen of Spain. Work began in 1717 with 50 000 workers and artisans under a German architect, though the plans were drawn up by a group of Roman artists under the direction of the Marquis de Fontes, Portugal's ambassador to the Holy See. Originally planned for just 13 monks it ended up housing 300, together with the entire royal family (and their considerable staff). It has often been compared to the Escorial in Spain. Part of the Palace is used as a military academy so you can only visit as part of a guided tour, in various languages.

- **Information:** In the Palace itself. ☎261 817 170. www.cm-mafra.pt.
- ▶ **Orient Yourself:** 40km/25mi northwest of Lisbon: take the A 8 then N 116.
- **Don't Miss:** The Basilica and the library in the Palace.
- **Organizing Your Time:** Spend a full morning in the palace, then have lunch in the gardens or on the coast at nearby Ereiceira.
- **Also See:** SINTRA.

A School of Sculpture

The Mafra School

While the monastery was under construction, João V took advantage of the presence of so many foreign artists at Mafra to found a school of sculpture. The first principal was the Italian, Alessandro Giusti, and among the teachers were such men as José Almeida, Giovanni Antonio of Padua, who carved the main statues in the cathedral at Évora and, particularly, **Joaquim Machado de Castro** (1731–1822). The total number of students who attended this school is unknown but certainly their work spread far and wide and a great many works of sacred art from this renowned school can be found throughout Europe.

Visit

The visit to Mafra includes the **Palace**, the **monastery** and the **basilica**. The Palace and Monastery are visited as part of a guided tour – the English versions of these are normally at 11am

and 2.30pm, though check carefully on arrival or through the website. There are also extensive gardens ⚇ see **Tapada Nacional de Mafra**. (⚇Palace/Convent open Wed–Mon 10am–5pm; ⚊guided tour (1hr 15min) Wed–Mon 10am–5pm; last entry 1hr before closing time; ⚇Closed Good Fri, 1 May and 25 Dec; ⚎€4, free Sun and public holidays 10am–2pm). The 220m/722ft long façade is flanked at either end by Germanic-style wings surmounted by bulbous domes. The basilica stands in the centre of the façade.

Basílica★★

The basilica, with its flanking wings, is built of mock marble, its façade breaking the monotony of the main face by its whiteness and Baroque decoration. The towers (68m/223ft tall) are joined by a double row of columns; niches high up contain Carrara marble statues of St Dominic and St Francis and below of St Clare and St Elizabeth of Hungary. The church **interior** is strikingly elegant in its proportions and in the marble ornamentation. The rounded vaulting

Palácio and Convento de Mafra

rests upon fluted pilasters which divide the lateral chapels, each of which contains statues and an altarpiece in white marble with a low-relief carved by sculptors from the Mafra School. The jasper and marble altarpieces in the transept chapels and the chancel pediment are also by the Mafra School. Note especially the fine marble altarpiece of the Virgin and Child in the chapel off the north aisle and the sacristy and lavabo where marble of every description may be seen.

Four delicately worked arches at the transept crossing support a magnificent rose and white marble **cupola**★ which rises to a height of 70m/229.6ft. The bronze candelabra and six fine organs dating from 1807 are also remarkable. The bell towers contain no less than 92 bells ordered from a Flemish bell-maker. The initial order was for 50 but when this was queried Dom João doubled the order and paid in advance!

Palace and Monastery

The guided tour proceeds through a museum of comparative sculpture, the monks' infirmary (with its beds on wheels so that sick monks could still be wheeled into Mass), the pharmacy, the kitchens and a museum of sacred art.

The Palace reached the height of its opulence at the start of the 19C and on the second floor, you are guided through the extensive royal apartments which form a long succession of galleries, with the Queen's Pavilion at one end and the King's at the other.

The ceilings are painted and the rooms have been refurnished with reproductions of the originals, most of which were taken to Brazil by Dom João VI in 1807 when he fled into exile.

The grandiose and harmoniously proportioned **Audience Room** (Sala da Bênção) gives onto the basilica. It was from this gallery with its columns and mouldings faced with coloured marble, that the royal family attended mass. The bust of Dom João V is by the Italian master, Alessandro Giusti.

The **Sala dos Troféus** (Trophy Room), is almost shocking to modern eyes and sensibilities with its furniture made from boars' heads, antlers and upholstered in deerskin.

The highlight (as in the Escorial) is the impressive Rococo **library**★ (biblioteca), 83.6m/274ft long, beautifully illuminated and containing over 35 000 bound books in many languages. They are kept in mint condition by a colony of small bats which, each night, fly about devouring any insects that might fancy nibbling a book!

Tapada Nacional de Mafra

◔Open 10am–6pm, though entry is only possible to the walking/cycling trails between 10am and 11am, then from 2pm–3pm. ☞€4.50 or €6 depending which trail you take, or €10 for cyclists. ☏261 814 240. www.tapadademafra.pt. There is a road-train that takes you round if you do not wish to walk ☞€10 (€6 children), though weekdays it is normally reserved for groups of visiting school children. The gardens, about 7km/4.3mi north of the Palace, were originally designed as hunting grounds for the royal family and you are likely to see deer and wild boar roaming around (some people still do hunt here) and are totally enclosed by walls. The beautiful trails, either for walking or cycling, do cover some beautiful landscape. There is also a carriage museum, a wildlife museum and plenty of space for picnics.

Câmara Municipal Mafra

Wild boars in Tapada Nacional de Mafra

SERRA DO MARÃO ★
PORTO AND VILA REAL
MICHELIN MAP 733 AND 441 – LOCAL MAP SEE VALE DO DOURO

The Serra do Marão is a block of granite and shale bounded to the east by the Corgo, to the west by the Tâmega and to the south by the Douro. The dislocations caused by the range's upheaval in the Tertiary Era are the reason for its variation of altitude; the wildness and desolation are due to intense erosion.

▶ **Orient Yourself:** This is the Douro Valley area, inland from Porto.
🕃 **Don't Miss:** A diversion on the train ride from Livração to Amarante.
🕐 **Organizing Your Time:** The Driving Tours outlined here take a couple of hours, though along the way you can stop as many times as you choose.
🕃 **Also See:** VALE DO DOURO.

Driving Tours

From Vila Real to Amarante

70km/43.5mi – about 1hr 30min – Itinerary ③ on the VALE DO DOURO map.

Vila Real – 🕃 *See VILA REAL.*

▶ *Leave Vila Real by the Porto road (IP 4/ E 82), heading west.*

As soon as the road reaches the slopes maize, pine and chestnut trees replace the vineyards and olive groves. At Parada de Cunhos there are fine views of the serra's foothills and of Vila Real.

▶ *After Torgueda leave the N 304, the Mondim de Basto road on your right.*

The road continues to climb and shortly, to the left the view of the summit of the **Marão**, the highest of the serra's peaks.

▶ *At the Alto do Espinho pass leave IP 4 and take the road south towards Pico do Marão. You pass the Pousada de São Gonçalo. Continue for a short while then bear left. The road rises through a landscape of crystalline rocks and ends on a ledge near the summit of Nossa Senhora da Serra.*

Pico do Marão ★★
Alt 1415m/4642ft. The summit, topped by an obelisk, commands a magnificent **panorama** of the serra's bare peaks.

▶ *Return to the road and continue westwards to Amarante via Candemil.*

Amarante ★ – 🕃 *See AMARANTE.*

From Vila Real to Mondim de Basto

61km/38mi – about 1hr 30min – Itinerary ④ on the VALE DO DOURO map. Leave Vila Real westwards on IP 4 described above, then bear right after Torgueda onto N 304.

The road climbs to the Alto de Velão pass from where there is a **view** to the left of the upper basin of the Olo river. You cross the western end of the beautiful **Parque Natural do Alvão** dotted with jumbled granite rock formations, then begin the **descent ★** to Mondim de Basto in the Tâmega valley.

▶ *Leave Mondim de Basto on N 312 to the north and then bear right on a forest road which climbs between rocks and pine trees.*

Capela de Nossa Senhora da Graça ★

▶ *Leave the car at the bottom of the majestic staircase (68 steps) which leads to the chapel.*

From the top of the steeple (reached by 54 steps and rungs, so take great care) there is a vast **panorama** of the Tâmega valley, Mondim de Basto and the Serra do Marão.

MARVÃO★★
PORTALEGRE

POPULATION 3 739 (159 IN VILLAGE) – MICHELIN MAP 733
LOCAL MAP SEE SERRA DE SÃO MAMEDE

Marvão is a fortified medieval village on the Serra de São Mamede near the Spanish border. This outstanding **site**★★ played a major part in the Portuguese Civil War in 1833.

- **Information:** Largo de Sta Maria. ☏245 993 886. www.turismarvao.pt.
- ▶ **Orient Yourself:** On the Spanish border 21km/13mi northeast of Portalegre.
- **Don't Miss:** The castle and particularly the views from the ramparts.
- **Organizing Your Time:** Half a day is sufficient to stroll round this charming little village.
- **Also See:** PORTALEGRE.

Sights

Igreja de Santa Maria★
⏱Open 9am–12.30pm, 2pm–5.30pm. ✆€1. ☏245 90 91 32/30.
The 13C church at the foot of the castle now houses the **Museu Municipal**, which displays Roman stelae, old maps of Marvão and other artefacts.

Castle★
The late 13C castle was remodelled in the 17C. It consists of a series of perimeter walls dominated by a square keep. Go through the first fortified gate and immediately to the right take the stairs which lead down to a **cistern**★. Ten wide arches are reflected in the water. A second fortified gate leads into the first courtyard where the parapet has fine **views**★ of the village stretching out below. In the second courtyard take the stairs to the right up to the parapet walk and follow it round to the keep. Impressive **views**★★ give a good idea of the various walls and particularly of the crenellated towers built on the overhanging rocks. The vast **panorama**★★ extends to the jagged mountain ranges of Spain in the east, the Castelo Branco region and Serra da Estrela and the Serra de São Mamede.

Village of Marvão

F. Fouché/MICHELIN

MÉRTOLA
BEJA
POPULATION 8 712 – MICHELIN MAP 733

The town of Mértola emerges from the middle of the lonely Alentejo countryside, rising in a tiered amphitheatre up a hillside overlooking the confluence of the Guadiana and Oeiras rivers. Dominating the town are the restored keep and ruined walls of its 13C fortified castle. The former mosque, now converted into a church, testifies to Mértola's Moorish past.

- **Information:** Largo Vasco da Gama. ☎286 610 109. www.cm-mertola.pt.
- ▶ **Orient Yourself:** Almost in the Algarve but close to the Spanish border.
- **Don't Miss:** A close look at the church – which used to be a mosque.
- **Organizing Your Time:** Ideally a couple of hours, plus time for a coffee.

Sight

Igreja-Mesquita

Open Wed–Sun 10am–1pm, 3pm–7pm. The square plan and forest of pillars reveal the church's origin; look at the ancient *mihrab* behind the altar, the niche from which the Imam conducted prayers, and outside at the doorway leading to the sacristy.

Museums

You will find several museums throughout the old town, each catering for a different style or era. They include exhibitions on Roman and Islamic periods, a Sacred Art museum and a museum showing traditional weaving skills, as well as an ancient forge.

MIRANDA DO DOURO ★
BRAGANÇA
POPULATION 7 707– MICHELIN MAP 733 OR 441

Miranda is an old town perched on a spur above the Douro valley. It has its own dialect, somewhat similar to Low Latin, known as *mirandês*. Guarding the entrance to the village from a hillock are the ruins of a medieval castle which was destroyed by an explosion in the 19C.

- **Information:** Largo do Menino Jesus da Cartolinha. ☎273 431 132.
- ▶ **Orient Yourself:** In the extreme northeast of the country, close to the border with Spain – only the river Douro separates them.
- **Don't Miss:** The upper Douro Valley from Miranda do Douro to Barca de Alva.
- **Organizing Your Time:** Allow a couple of hours for the town but a half day to see the landscapes in the Douro Valley.

The Town

Miranda do Douro

This place has had an interesting history, having been vital to the rise of Afonso Henriques, the first King of Portugal as he fought off his Spanish masters at the start of the 12C. The Independence, Spanish Succession and Seven Year wars were all fought out across the region and the explosion in 1762 left the town a desolate mass of ruins. Yet that desolation allowed the local dialect, Mirandês, to flourish and even today road signs are to be found in that dialect as well as in Portuguese. A market is held on the first weekday of each month and is worth a visit.

Cathedral

🕙*Open Tue–Sun 10am–12.30pm, 2pm–6pm.* 🕙*Closed 1 Jan, Easter Day, 1 May and 25 Dec.*

It seems odd to have a cathedral in such a small village, but Miranda was once a major city. The former cathedral *(sé)* has an austere granite façade with two quadrangular bell-towers. The three-nave interior, with its ribbed vaulting, a 16C edifice of granite, contains a series of gilded and carved wood **altar-pieces**★: the one in the chancel by the Spaniards Gregório Hernandez and Francisco Velázquez, depicts the Assumption, round which are scenes from the Life of the Virgin, the Evangelists and several bishops. The whole is crowned with a calvary. On either side of the chancel, the 18C gilded wood stalls are embellished with painted landscapes.

An amusing statuette of the Child Jesus in a top hat stands in a glass display case in the south transept. He is much loved and venerated by the people of Miranda. On the Day of the Kings (Dia dos Reis), four boys carry the statue in a wooden frame during the procession. Opposite the cathedral, the ruins of the episcopal palace cloisters can be seen.

Museu da Terra de Miranda★

🕙*Open Wed–Sun 9.30am–12.30pm, 2pm–5.30pm (6.30pm Jun–Sept); Tue 2pm–5.30pm.* 🕙*Closed 1 Jan, 1 May and 25 Dec.* ⊚€1.50. ☎273 431 164.

This museum, located in a 17C building that has served as the town hall and a prison, has a multitude of local items from the past, showing life through the ages and, as such, is very interesting.

MIRANDELA
BRAGANÇA
POPULATION 10 700 – MICHELIN MAP 733

Although Mirandela is Roman in origin, the town visible today was founded by Dom Afonso II. It looks down upon the Tua, which is spanned by a long Romanesque bridge, rebuilt in the 16C, which is 230m/754.6ft long and has 20 different arches. It is an elegant, flower-decked town with many gardens and lawns and various options for visitors, such as a boat trip on the Tua river, a journey by train along the old railway line connecting Mirandela with Carvalhais, or a visit around the city by mini-train.

- **Information:** Praça do Cocheira. ☎278 200 272. www.cm-mirandela. espigueiro.pt.
- **Orient Yourself:** Halfway between Vila Real and Bragança.
- **Don't Miss:** The Roman bridge – the most beautiful in Portugal.
- **Organizing Your Time:** Normally the place you'd drive past, but worth a half day to walk through the town and along the river bank.

Sights

Palácio dos Távoras

This beautiful 18C palace, now occupied by the town hall, stands at the top of a hill. Its three-part granite façade (with the middle part the highest) is topped with curved pediments and crowned by spiral pinnacles.

A statue of Pope John Paul II sits in the middle of the square, with a more recent church to one side.

Museu Municipal Armindo Teixeira Lopes★

🕙*Open Mon–Fri 10am–12.30pm, Sat 2pm–6pm.* ☎278 265 768.

This interesting museum, housed in the town's cultural centre, is devoted to sculpture and painting. It has been created from donations from the children of Armindo Teixeira Lopes, and contains more than 400 works by 200 predominantly Portuguese artists from the beginning of the century to the present day. These include Vieira da Silva, Tapiès, Cargaleiro, Nadir Afonso, Graça Morais, José Guimarães, Júlio Pomar and Teixeira Lopes.

Tua Railway

The narrow-gauge Tua Railway from Mirandela is beautifully scenic and well worth a detour, taking 90 minutes to reach Tua (€4.80 one way).

Excursion

Jerusalém do Romeu
Population 478. 11km/6.8mi to the north-east of Mirandela.

In the heart of the Trás-os-Montes, Romeu, together with **Vila Verdinho** and **Vale do Couço**, form a group of colourful villages bedecked with flowers, in a landscape of valleys wooded with cork oaks and chestnuts. Recent restoration work has given them a new lease of life.

Museu das Curiosidades do Romeu
🕑*Open Apr–Sept, Tue–Sun noon–6pm (4pm Oct–Mar).* €1.50. ☎278 93 91 33. The museum contains the personal collection of Manuel Meneres, the benefactor of all three villages. In one room are early machines such as typewriters, sewing machines, stereoscopes and a phenakistoscope (predecessor to the cinema); in another room are objects of all kinds, including a music box, chairs, dolls and clocks. There are also some old and interesting cars and motorbikes.

MONSANTO★★
CASTELO BRANCO
POPULATION 4 672 – MICHELIN MAP 733

Monsanto clings to the foot of a granite hill in the middle of a plain. It is visible from afar in a chaotic mass of rocks which blends in with its castle. The origins of the village date from prehistory, when it was linked with pagan rituals; it was subsequently occupied by the Romans, and in 1165 was handed over by Dom Afonso Henriques to Gualdim Pais, master of the Knights Templar, who built the impregnable citadel. Every year in May (🕯*see Calendar of Events*), young girls throw pitchers of flowers from the ramparts to commemorate the defiant throwing out of a calf when the castle was once besieged and those inside wished to convince the assailants that they would never be starved into capitulation.

- **Information:** Rua Marquês da Graçiosa. ☎277 314 642.
- ▶ **Orient Yourself:** In central Portugal but close to the Spanish frontier – almost directly inland from Coimbra on the map.
- **Don't Miss:** The views from the top of the keep – they're worth the climb!
- 🕑 **Organizing Your Time:** It's the sort of place you pass through, pausing for an hour or two to take in the view, but it is worth the drive to get there.
- **Also See:** CASTELO BRANCO, GUARDA.

Sights

Village
Steep and rough alleys cut across the village. The façades of the houses, many of them built with rough boulders from the surrounding countryside, are pierced by paired windows and, in some cases, Manueline-style doorways. In 1938 (some time ago it must be said) the village was voted as the "most Portuguese" in the country.

Village of Monsanto

Castle★

An alley and a steep path lead to the castle, where it is not unusual to find hens or rabbits in openings formed in the rocks, and the odd pig or sheep sheltering within a Roman ruin. Although it was rebuilt by Dom Dinis, countless sieges have since reduced it to a romantic ruin. From the top of the keep, an immense **panorama**★★ spreads northwest over the wooded hills of the Serra da Estrela and southwest over the lake formed by the Idanha dam, the Ponsul Valley and, in the far distance, the town of Castelo Branco.

Capela de São Miguel

This Romanesque chapel next to the castle is now in ruins, yet it has preserved its four archivolts and historiated capitals.

MONSARAZ★★
ÉVORA
POPULATION 1 290 – MICHELIN MAP 733

The old fortified village of Monsaraz occupies a strategic position in an outstanding site★★ on a height near the Guadiana Valley on the border between Portugal and Spain. When it lost its military role, Monsaraz also lost its importance in favour of Reguengos de Monsaraz. As a result, the town has retained much of its historic character.

- **Information:** Praça D. Nuno Álvares Pereira, 5. ☎266 557 136.
- ▶ **Orient Yourself:** About 53km/40mi southeast of Évora.
- 🅿 **Parking:** Just by the entry to the castle – cars are not allowed inside.
- 🚫 **Don't Miss:** The views from the ramparts of the castle.
- 🕐 **Organizing Your Time:** Two hours should be enough to see all you need.
- ◔ **Also See:** The many Neolithic megaliths in the countryside around Monsaraz.

Sights

Leave the car in front of the main gate to the town as vehicles are not allowed inside the village itself. It's a short walk through the Porta da Vila, the village's main entrance, which leads into Rua São Tiago, one of the two main streets in the village. Parallel to it is Rua Direita, which leads to the castle.

Rua Direita★

The street retains all its original charm as it is still lined with 16C and 17C white-washed houses, many flanked by outside staircases and balconies with wrought-iron grilles. All the village monuments may be seen in this street.

Igreja Matriz – Parish Church

🕐Open 10am–1pm, 2pm–6pm.

Rebuilt after the 1755 earthquake, the church still contains an impressive 14C marble tomb carved with 14 Saints. Outside you can see an 18C stone pillory topped with a Manueline globe.

Tribunal do Antigua

🕐Open 9am–7pm.⊛€2.
☎266 55 71 36.

The former court building, on the left of Rua Direita, can be distinguished by the pointed arches above its doors and windows. Inside an interesting fresco depicts

Igreja Matriz

true and false Justice with, above, Christ in Majesty with arms held aloft.

Castle

The castle was rebuilt by King Dom Dinis in the 13C and given a second perimeter wall with massive bastions in the 17C. Look especially for the Torre das Geiticei-ras (Witches' Tower). The parapet walk commands a magnificent **panorama** of the Alentejo.

MONTEMOR-O-VELHO
COIMBRA
POPULATION 25 084 – MICHELIN MAP 733 L 3 OR 441

The town of Montemor-o-Velho in the fertile Mondego Valley is dominated by the ruins of the citadel built in the 11C to defend Coimbra against the Moors.

🛈 **Information:** Praça da República. ☎239 689 114. www.cm-montemorvelho.pt.

▶ **Orient Yourself:** Roughly in between Coimbra and Figueira da Foz.

🅐 **Don't Miss:** The ancient castle and the views from the keep; some of the lovely parts of the nearby River Mondego.

🕐 **Organizing Your Time:** An hour or so to see the castle.

Kids **Especially for Kids:** Close to the town the Europaradise Zoo.

Sights

Castle

🕐Open Sept–May, Tue–Sun 10am–7pm, Jun–Aug, 9am–8pm. 🕐Closed 1 Jan, Good Fri, Easter Sun and 25 Dec.

Of the original castle, originally built by the Romans then re-fortified by the Moors, there remains little – a double perimeter wall, oval in shape, battle-mented and flanked by many towers; the north corner is occupied by the church and the keep. From the top of the ramparts there is a **panorama**★ of the Mondego Valley.

Igreja de Santa Maria de Alcáçova

This Manueline church, designed by Diogo do Boitaca (who designed the Mosteiro dos Jerónimos at Belém), is extremely beautiful with its wooden ceilings, twisted columns and some very good Moorish azulejos.

Outside there are vast lawns, which are kept very neat and tidy. Once a month (the date varies between the second and fourth Wednesday) the town has a huge market which completely fills its otherwise neat but tiny streets. There are plenty of restaurants and cafés.

MOURA
BEJA
POPULATION 17 600 – MICHELIN MAP 733

Moura, the Town of the Moorish Maiden (she is said to have opened the gates to the Christians in 1223), stands grouped round the ruins of a 13C castle. It was a small spa whose mineral waters were regarded for their healing properties but is no longer in use.

- **Information:** Largo da Sta Clara. ☎285 251 375. www.cm-moura.pt.
- **Orient Yourself:** In the Alentejo about 40km/25mi from the Spanish frontier.
- **Don't Miss:** Mouraria, the Moorish part of the village and the oil press.
- **Organizing Your Time:** A morning here should suffice.

Sights

Igreja de São João Baptista★
The Gothic Church of St John the Baptist is entered through an interesting Manueline **doorway**. Inside an elegant twisted white marble column supports the pulpit; the chancel, with network vaulting, contains a beautiful Baroque crucifixion group and the south chapel is adorned with 17C azulejos representing the Cardinal Virtues.

Mouraria
The former Moorish quarter with the vestiges of that occupation, which only finally came to an end in 1496.

Lagar de Varras do Fojo
Open Tue–Sun 9.30am–12.30pm, 2.30pm–5.30pm.
An old olive pressing factory with giant stone-wheel presses that is well worth a quick visit.

NAZARÉ★
LEIRIA
POPULATION 15 500 – MICHELIN MAP 733

Nazaré lies in an exceptional **site**★★ with its long beach dominated to the north by a steep cliff. The town has three distinct quarters: **Praia** (the beach), the largest, which runs alongside the seafront, **Sítio**, built on the clifftop and **Pederneira**, on a hill. The name Nazaré comes from a statue of the Virgin brought back from the town of Nazareth in Palestine by a monk in the 4C.

- **Information:** Av. da República. ☎262 561 194.
- **Orient Yourself:** 100km/62mi north of Lisbon on the A 8.
- **Don't Miss:** The Sitio quarter of the town, or the beaches.
- **Organizing Your Time:** Ideally, take a day – swim in the sea, explore Sitio, then relax with a glass of wine in the evening in the fishermen's area.
- **Especially for Kids:** The beach of São Martinho do Porto.
- **Also See:** The monasteries at Alcobaça; the fortified town of Óbidos.

Praia

Praia is the name of the lower town with its geometrically laid out streets giving onto the beach of fine sand. There are many hotels, restaurants and souvenir shops.

Nazaré has long promoted itself as the best resort on this coast and obviously that has brought with it a lot of housing development, primarily apartment blocks which now line most of the seafront, as in many seaside towns throughout Europe and, in the height of summer, throngs of mainly Portuguese tourists. This popularity is obviously a double-edged sword but outside the main summer months it is a fairly pleasing place, with plenty to do in and around the town.

Bairro dos Pescadores

The fishermen's quarter stretches from Praça Manuel de Arriaga to Avenida Vieira Guimarães. Small whitewashed cottages line the alleys leading to the quayside though these days they are more likely to be used as B&Bs .

Harbour

South of the beach a harbour shelters the fishing boats. The catch normally comprises sole, whiting, perch, coalfish, hake, skate, mackerel and sardines.

Sítio

The Sítio quarter may be reached by car or on foot (up a flight of steps) although most enjoyable way is by the **funicular** *Funicular operates daily, 7am–midnight (2am in summer).* €0.85. 262 56 11 53.

Miradouro

The belvedere, built on the edge of the cliff overlooking the sea from a height of 110m/361ft, affords a fine **view**★ of the lower town and the beach.

Ermida da Memória

Open Apr–Sept, 9am–7pm; Oct–Mar, 9am–6pm. 262 56 18 78.

This tiny chapel near the belvedere commemorates the miracle which saved the life of the local lord, Fuas Roupinho. One morning in 1182 Roupinho on horseback was giving chase to a deer which suddenly somersaulted into the air off the top of the cliff. Just as the horse was about to do the same, Dom Fuas implored Our Lady of Nazaré for help and the horse stopped. The façade, roof and the two floors inside the chapel are covered with *azulejos*: those of the façade on the side facing the sea evoke the knight's jump; those of the crypt, the miracle of the Marian intercession. In the staircase leading to the crypt a recess still has the footprint which the horse is said to have left on the rock face. It is also the place where the long-lost statue of the Virgin, brought back from Nazareth in the 4C was found in the 18C.

Igreja de Nossa Senhora da Nazaré

This imposing 17C church is on the main square and has a façade with a forepart forming a gallery, and a Baroque doorway opening at the top of a semicircular flight of steps. The interior has a profusion of Dutch *azulejos* depicting Biblical scenes.

©Tommy Devoye/Fotolia.com

Beach of Nazaré

Festivals

Nazaré is proud of its festivals. Each year, on 8 September and through the following weekend, is the **Nossa Senhora da Nazaré** pilgrimage and festival, with sombre processions to the chapel in Sitio (&see main text), followed by more temporal celebrations including fireworks, folk dancing and a bullfight (though in Portugal the bulls are not killed in the ring). The most interesting festival, though, is Carnaval, at the start of Lent (February, normally) with wildy extravagant costumes and dancers in the long procession through the streets. See www.carnavaldanazare.com.

Lighthouse

800m/875yd west of the church.

The lighthouse *(farol)* is built on a small fort at the farthermost promontory of a cliff. Behind, and lower down, a path with steps and a parapet wall and then an iron staircase leads to a point *(15min return)* overlooking a magnificent **seascape**★★; jagged rocks through which the sea swirls furiously. Go round the headland a little, to the left, where there is a beautiful view over the bay of Nazaré.

Excursion

São Martinho do Porto

13km/8mi south.
Leave Nazaré by the N 242.

This seaside resort lies north of a saltwater lake linked to the sea by a narrow channel edged with tall cliffs. Its **Kids beach** is one of the safest in the region for children.

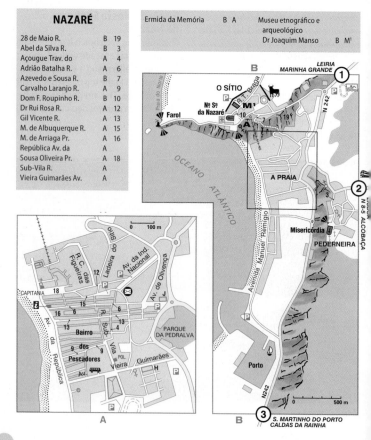

ÓBIDOS★★
LEIRIA
POPULATION 11 300 – MICHELIN MAP 733

Óbidos, which commands a vast sweep of countryside consisting of green valleys and heights topped by the occasional windmill, has managed to keep its proud medieval character through the ages. The fortified city, protected by its perimeter wall, flanked by small round towers and massive square bastions, once commanded this part of the coastline. The silting-up of its bay created a lagoon (Lagoa da Óbidos) which deprived the town of its coastal position and today Óbidos stands 10km/6.2mi inland. Óbidos is also known as the "Wedding City" having regularly been "given" throughout the ages as a wedding gift by the King to his new Queen.

- **Information:** Rua Direita. ☎262 959 231. www.cm-obidos.pt.
- ▶ **Orient Yourself:** In Estremadura, about 100km/62mi north of Lisbon.
- **Don't Miss:** A walking tour of the ramparts.
- **Organizing Your Time:** Spend the morning here, then have lunch.
- **Also See:** ALCOBAÇA.

The Medieval City★★

1hr 30min

Park the car outside the ramparts.

Porta da Vila
The inside walls of this double-zig-zag gateway are covered with 18C *azulejos*.

Rua Direita★
A paved channel runs through the centre of this narrow main street bordered with white houses bright with flowers, shops, restaurants and art galleries.

Praça de Santa Maria★
The church square stands below the main street and forms an attractive scene.

Igreja de Santa Maria
Open Nov–Mar, 9.30am–12.30pm, 2.30pm–5pm (until 7pm Apr–Oct).
It was here that the ten-year-old King Afonso V married his eight-year-old cousin, Isabella, in 1444. The **interior**★ is noteworthy for its painted ceilings, and its walls, entirely covered with blue-and-white 17C *azulejos*. In the chancel, in a bay on the left, a Renaissance (16C)

View of Óbidos village with ramparts

A. Cassaigne/MICHELIN

Address Book

For coin ranges, see the Legend on the cover flap.

WHERE TO STAY

Casa d'Óbidos –*Quinta de São José (1km/0.6mi south of town, nr Senhor da Pedra church).* 262 950 924. *6 rooms min 2 night stay* . Charming guest house in a 19C manor house with lovely gardens, a pool and tennis court.

Casa do Religio – *R. do Graca.* 262 959 282. *8 rooms* . Just outside the walls, this lovely little hotel in an 18C house has small but cleanly furnished rooms and bathrooms. Not large, but friendly nonetheless.

Casa d São Thiago – *Largo de São Thiago.* 262 950 587. *9 rooms* . Lovely old family-run house full of flowers inside and out. Breakfast is served in a little courtyard overlooking the castle walls and although the rooms are not ultra-modern they are comfortable.

Estalagem do Convento – *Rua D. João d'Ornelas.* 262 95 92 16. *31 rooms* . An attractive inn set in an old convent. A rustic atmosphere, with pleasant and spacious rooms.

Casa das Senhoras Rainhas –*R. Padré Nunes Tavares, 6.* 262 955 360. www.senhorasrainhas. com. *10 rooms* . An old house set at the foot of the ramparts it has a simple though pleasing style, marble floored bathrooms and soothing colours. There might not be a grand view, although the rooms all open onto the terrace, but it has charm. It also has a very good restaurant that is open to non-guests.

Pousada do Castelo – *Paço Real, 2510 Óbidos.* 262 955 080. www.pousadas.pt. *9 rooms.* The former convent of Óbidos, set within the castle, today houses one of the best *pousadas* in Portugal. Book ahead.

WHERE TO EAT

Petarum Domus Bar – *R. Direita* 262 95 96 20. Old beams, leather armchairs, stone tables and soft lighting go to make this wine bar a place to relax and be comfortable. *Celta*, a local speciality, will delight you.

Senhor da Pedra – *Largo do Santuário do Senhor da Pedra (near the church of the same name)* 262 959 315. Very inexpensive, simple, good.

Alcaide – *R. Direita.* 262 959 220. www.restalcaide.com. Its central location, beautiful views and simple traditional cooking make this a very popular restaurant.

A Ilustre Casa de Ramiro – *R. Porta do Vale.* 262 95 91 94. *Closed Thu and Jan.* Fine traditional cuisine served in an old country house outside the walls.

Adega do Ramada – *Trav Josefa d'óbidos.* 262 959 462. *Closed Mon.* Specialises in steaks, chops, pork and salmon, all cooked on an outside grill.

---

tomb★ is surmounted by a *Pietà*. This outstanding work is attributed to the studio of the French sculptor Nicolas Chanterene. The retable at the high altar is adorned with paintings by João da Costa and there are also some paintings by the renowned Josefa de Óbidos, who learnt here skills here.

Museu Municipal

Open 10am–1pm, 2pm–6pm. Closed 1 Jan, 11 Jan (local holiday), Easter day and 25 Dec. € 1.50. 262 955 557.
The small municipal museum next to the church houses a statue of St Sebastian dating from the 15C or 16C and also a 17C polychrome *Pietà*. The "Josefa de Óbidos" room, in the first basement, contains various works by this artist, including the remarkable *Faustino das Neves* (1670) while exhibits in another room include mementoes of the war against Napoléon.

▶ *Go to the end of the main street to the ramparts. Follow the signs to the Pousada.*

City walls★★

The best access points are near the Porta da Vila or the Castelo.

The walls (*muralhas*) date from the Moorish occupation but were restored in the 12C, 13C and 16C. Along the north side, the highest, are the keep and the castle towers. The sentry path commands pleasant **views**★ over the fortified city and the surrounding countryside.

Castle

The castle, built in the 13C by Dom Dinis, is now a *pousada*, and had been converted into a royal palace in the 16C. Its façade has paired Manueline windows with twisted columns and a Manueline doorway surmounted by two armillary spheres.

Additional Sight

Santuário do Senhor da Pedra

🕒 *Open Tue–Fri 9.30am–12.30pm, 2.30pm–5pm (until 7pm Apr–Oct).* ☎262 95 96 33.

In a glass case above the altar is a primitive stone cross dating from the 2C. The nave contains Baroque statues of the Apostles. A coach, kept in the sanctuary, was used to transport the statue of the Virgin from the church of Santa Maria in Óbidos to the church of Nossa Senhora in Nazaré during the festival on 8 September.

OLHÃO
FARO
POPULATION 40 800 – MICHELIN MAP 733
LOCAL MAP SEE ALGARVE

Olhão, despite its very Moorish appearance in the old town, is a fairly modern development, having only been founded by fishermen in the 18C. It quickly became the busiest fishing port on the Algarve – sardines and tunny in particular – but has now been fairly extensively developed as a tourist resort with its beaches, in particular, being of major importance. Like many places in the eastern Algarve they are on *ilhas* – little reef-type islands offshore and reachable only by boat. Many visitors from nearby Faro use these beaches, which are excellent.

▪ **Information:** Largo Sebastião Martins Mestre. ☎289 713 936. www.cm-olhao.pt.
▸ **Orient Yourself:** 11km/6.8mi east of Faro on the Algarve.
🏛 **Don't Miss:** The bell-tower of the parish church; the Saturday market.
🕒 **Organizing Your Time:** As long as you like on the beach, but the town itself is only worth a couple of hours.
Kids Especially for Kids: The beaches and safe swimming.
🚹 **Also See:** TAVIRA.

Viewpoints

An unusual **panorama**★ of the whole town may be had from the belfry of the 17C **parish church** (🕒*open Tue–Sun 9am–noon, 3pm–6pm;* ☜€1 for belfry, church free; standing in the main street (access through the first door on the right as you enter the church). At the back of the church, outside, is an iron grille protecting the chapel of the **Nossa Senhora dos Aflitos** where, traditionally (but still today) the town's womenfolk pray for the safe return of their men from sea. There is also a small museum, Museu da Cidade (🕒*open 10am–12.30pm, 2pm–5.30pm Tue–Fri, free*) with archaeological remains from Roman times to the present.

The beaches, reachable by ferries, are impressive: the best is **Praia de Farol**. Olhão is also the gateway fro the **Parque Natural da Ria Formosa**, a 60km/37mi stretch of marshy coastline that is a protected area containing extensive birdlife and fauna.

OLIVEIRA DO HOSPITAL
COIMBRA
POPULATION 5 222 – MICHELIN MAP 733

Hills clad with vines, olive groves and pine trees form the setting of Oliveira do Hospital, the name of which recalls the 12C Order of the Hospitallers of St John of Jerusalem, now the Knights Templar of Malta. You will find it about 60km/37mi northeast of Coimbra along the N17. The countryside is beautiful. *(see LEÇA DO BAILIO)*.

- **Information:** Rua do Colégio (Casa da Cultura de Oliveira). ☎238 659 119. www.oliveiradohospital.com/ingles.
- ▶ **Orient Yourself:** 60km/37mi northeast of Coimbra.
- **Parking:** Very few problems.
- **Organizing Your Time:** The town is small but the countryside around is very nice and deserves a gentle drive with several stops along the river.
- **Also See:** COIMBRA.

Visit

Parish church
🕐*Open 9am–7pm.* ☎*238 60 27 89.*
The church, originally Romanesque, was reconstructed in the Baroque period. The interior, covered by a fine ceiling painted in false relief, contains the late 13C tombs of Domingos Joanes and his wife. An equestrian **statue**★ of a 14C medieval knight has been fixed to the wall above the tombs. Also noteworthy is a beautiful 14C stone **altarpiece**★ of the Virgin.

OURÉM
SANTARÉM
POPULATION 4 498 – MICHELIN MAP 733

The fortified city of Ourém was built round the top of a hillock, the summit of which is occupied by the remains of a castle. The town lived through a period of sumptuous richness in the 15C when the Count of Ourém, Dom Afonso, built several grand monuments and changed the castle into a palace. Napoléon's troops destroyed it but it has since been rebuilt.

- ▶ **Orient Yourself:** About 7km/4.3mi northeast of Fátima. The fortified town is 2km/1.2mi south of the new town.
- **Don't Miss:** The castle and the church, as detailed below.
- **Organizing Your Time:** Give yourself a couple of hours at most.
- **Also See:** FÁTIMA.

Sights

Castle
Two advanced towers appear on either side of the road; note the unusual brick machicolations crowning the walls all round the castle.

▶ *Go through the porch of the right tower. A path leads to a point where a former tunnel comes into view. Steps go up to a square tower commanding the entrance to an older triangular castle; in the courtyard is a Moorish underground cistern from the 9C. A path leads to the village and the collegiate church.*

Collegiate church

Enter through the south transept. A door immediately to the right opens onto a stairway down to the crypt with its six monolithic columns. The Gothic and highly ornate white limestone **tomb** of Count Dom Afonso in the crypt has a recumbent figure attributed to the sculptor Diogo Pires the Elder. Two lifting mechanisms are engraved on the tomb.

PAÇO DE SOUSA
PORTO

POPULATION 3 536 – MICHELIN MAP 733 OR 441

Paço de Sousa was the headquarters of the Benedictines in Portugal and has retained its monastery, founded early in the 11C, a vast Romanesque church (restored) in which lies the tomb of Egas Moniz, the companion in arms of Prince Afonso Henriques.

▶ **Orient Yourself:** Inland from Porto on the A 4, halfway to Vila Real.

🕐 **Organizing Your Time:** It's no more than a brief stopping place along the road to or from Vila Real, but the church is worth a visit.

🅿 **Parking:** No problems parking here.

👁 **Don't Miss:** The figures supporting the tympanum of the monastery.

Visit

Igreja do Mosteiro de São Salvador

The 10C church is fairly dark inside but its façade has a tiers-point doorway with recessed orders ornamented with motifs, repeated on the surround of the rose window. The tympanum is supported on the left by a bull's head and on the right by an unusual head of a man. On the tympanum on the left is a man carrying the moon, on the right one carrying the sun. Inside, the three aisles with pointed arches shelter, on the left, a naive statue of St Peter and, on the right near the entrance, the 12C tomb of Egas Moniz.

Low-relief sculptures carved somewhat crudely on the tomb depict the scene at Toledo and the funeral of this loyal preceptor. A battlemented tower stands to the left.

PALMELA★
SETÚBAL

POPULATION 14 444 – MICHELIN MAP 733 – LOCAL MAP SEE SERRA DA ARRÁBIDA

This pretty white town is built in tiers on the northern slope of the Serra da Arrábida at the foot of a mound crowned by a large castle which became the seat of the Order of St James in 1423. Palmela lies at the heart of one of Portugal's richest wine growing regions, growing the Periquita variety of grape.

🛈 **Information:** Castelo de Palmela. ☎212 332 122.

▶ **Orient Yourself:** Just a couple of miles inland from Setúbal, close to Lisbon.

👁 **Don't Miss:** The castle and the church, but also soak up the local ambiance.

🕐 **Organizing Your Time:** Why not stay overnight in the *pousada*? A real treat!

👣 **Also See:** SÉTUBAL (Peninsula de Tróia).

Sights

Castle★

Follow the signs to the pousada. Leave your car in the outer yard. ○*Open daily with the exception of one part of the castle, which opens from 9am–6pm (8pm in summer).* ☎212 33 15 80.

The castle, now partly converted into a *pousada* (and with a wonderful restaurant open to non-residents), was originally Moorish. Part of it is occupied by the Church and Monastery of St James, erected in the 15C by the Knights of St James. The views are magnificent, looking out over the Sado estuary and even as far as Lisbon. The Bishop of Évora died a painful death in the dungeon here, punishment for his part in a conspiracy against King João II.

Igreja de São Pedro

○*Open Thu–Tue 10am–1pm, 2pm–7pm, Sun 10am–1pm.* ○*Closed public holidays.* ☎212 35 00 25 (early evening only).

The church dates from the 18C. The interior is entirely lined with **azulejos**★ depicting scenes from the life of St Peter; outstanding are those in the south aisle illustrating the miraculous catch of fish, Christ walking on the waters as well as the crucifixion of St Peter.

PARQUE NACIONAL DA PENEDA-GERÊS★★

BRAGA, VIANA DO CASTELO AND VILA REAL

MICHELIN MAP 733

Peneda-Gerês, Portugal's only **national park**, was established in 1971 and covers 72 000ha/178 000 acres in the northern districts of Braga, Viana do Castelo and Vila Real. The valleys of the Lima, Homem and Cávado rivers divide the region into *serras* – da Peneda, do Soajo, da Amarela and do Gerês. The park is designed to protect the natural sites, archaeological remains, and the outstanding flora and fauna – many of which cannot be seen elsewhere.

- ⓘ **Information:** Largo da Misericórdia, Ponte da Barca. ☎258 452 250. www.geira.pt/pnpg/index.html.
- ▶ **Orient Yourself:** Northern Portugal, on the border with Spain. Nearest large town is Braga.
- ⊚ **Don't Miss:** The wonderful journey from Mezio to Lamas de Mouro.
- ⓒ **Organizing Your Time:** Each driving tour has approximate times.
- **Kids Especially for Kids:** Get them looking for wildlife – otters, badgers, boar, deer and ponies.

Driving Tours

From Rio Cávado to Portela do Homem★★

1 Northwards from the N 103

20km/12.4mi – about 3hr

The N 304 branches north from the N 103 between Braga and Chaves and winds downhill through a landscape of rocks and heather. After 2km/1.2mi you pass the beautifully situated São Bento *pousada* with its panoramic view of the Caniçada reservoir (have the camera handy). Two bridges cross, successively, the Cávado and its tributary, the Caldo, turned into reservoir-lakes by the Caniçada dam. The first bridge crosses a submerged village which appears

H. Champollion/MICHELIN

Parque Nacional da Peneda-Gerês

when the water level drops.Here you are close to the **Rio Caldo** water sports activity centre.

▶ *From the first bridge onto the peninsula between the two lakes, take N 308 on the right at the intersection, and then cross the second bridge. Head for Caldas do Gerês (also called Vila do Gerês or just Gerês).*

Caldas do Gerês, as its name implies, is a pleasant little spa at the bottom of a wooded gorge. Its waters, rich in fluorine, are used in the treatment of liver and digestive disorders. After Gerês, the road is lined first with hydrangeas, then winds up through woods of pines and oaks. Some 8km/5mi from Gerês you reach the nature reserve. The road climbs gently and crosses the Homem river, which races through a rocky course.

▶ *Turn back and take the track on the right towards Campo do Gerês. The track crosses the remains of a Roman road at two points: after 1.3km/0.8mi and 2km/1.2mi.*

Remains of the Roman Way (Geira)★
The milestones on the side of the road are the remains of the Roman Way (Via Romana) which stretched some 320km/198.8mi between Braga and Astorga in Spain via the Homem Pass. The track continues, affording lovely views of, and then skirting, the **Represa de Vilarinho das Fumas**, a blue-water reservoir set in a wild, rocky landscape, before you reach the mountain pass and customs post at **Portela do Homen**.

Serra do Gerrês★★

② From Gerês to the Vilarinho das Furnas reservoir
15km/9.3mi – allow 2hr

From Gerês take the N 308 south then turn right to **Campo do Gerês**★★ where there is an interesting little local museum, picnic area and adventure sports centre. This road with tight hairpin bends offers good views of the Caniçada reservoir and of the superb rock falls. When the road stops climbing turn right towards the **Miradouro de Junceda**★ which offers a bird's-eye view of Gerês and its valley. Return to the main road and continue on to Campo do Gerês. In the centre of a crossroads, note an ancient Roman milestone bearing a sculpture of Christ. Continue along the road to the right to reach the Vilarinho das Furnas reservoir.

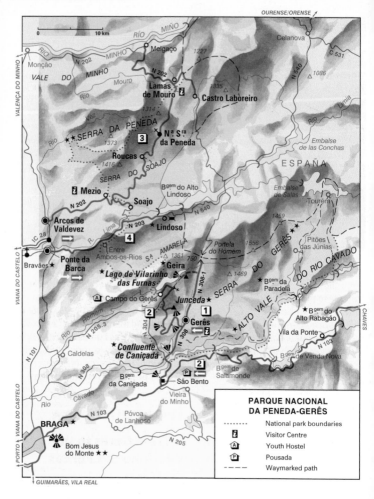

Serra de Peneda★★

③ From Arcos de Valdevez to Melgaço

70km/43.5mi – allow half a day

This itinerary takes you through the north, the wildest part of the park. From **Arcos de Valdevez**, where the towers of two churches dominate this little town on the banks of the Vez, you reach **Mezio**: a village at the entrance to the national park. The road to Peneda begins 2.5km/1.5mi further on, but continue towards **Soajo**, an isolated village with a group of 18C granaries or **espigueiros**★ (see LINDOSO) and some good accommodation options.

▸ *Return to the junction and take the Peneda road.*

The **Mosteiro de Nossa Senhora da Peneda** stands in a magnificent **setting**★ preceded by 300 steps climbed by pilgrims in early September each year. Continue past Castro Laboreiro, a village which has preserved several traditional stone houses and the ruins of a castle

▸ *Return to Lamas de Mouro and take the Melgaço road.*

④ From Ponte da Barca to Lindoso

31km/19mi – See LINDOSO.

PENICHE
LEIRIA
POPULATION 27 312 – MICHELIN MAP 733

Peniche, built to command access to the mile-long promontory, is today Portugal's second most important fishing port (crayfish, sardines, tunny). The remains of ramparts and the citadel recall the former military role played by the city. A pleasant public garden planted with palm trees surrounds the Tourist Information Centre (Posto de Turismo) on Rua Alexandre Herculano.

- **Information:** Rua Alexandre Herculano. ☎262 789 571. www.cm-peniche.pt.
- **Orient Yourself:** 100km/62mi north of Lisbon, on the coast.
- **Parking:** Anywhere in the town at pay-and-display sites.
- **Organizing Your Time:** To see the island of Berlenga you need a morning, then have lunch and wander round Peniche for a few hours.
- **Especially for Kids:** Take them cycling along the coast.
- **Also See:** ÓBIDOS, NAZARÉ, ILHA DA BERLENGA.

The Town

The revival of handmade lace

Peniche has been trying to revive its former speciality of bobbin lace. An apprentice school has been set up at the town's Industrial and Business School (avenida 25 de Abril). On the first floor there is an exhibit of samples from past and present production. Lacemakers can also be seen working at the Casa de Trabalho das Filhas de Pescadores (rua do Calvário), and handmade lace can still be bought in the town (avenida do Mar).

Sights

Citadel

Open Tue 2pm–5.30pm, Wed–Fri 9am–12.30pm, 2pm–5.30pm, Sat–Sun 10.30am–12.30pm, 2pm–5.30pm. €1.40 for museum.

A 16C fortress, converted in the 17C into a Vauban-style citadel, stands proudly with its high walls and sharp edged astions topped with watchtowers. Until 1974 it was a state prison, then it became an emergency city for refugees from Angola. There is a little museum inside with a mix of history, archaeology and local crafts and the top floor houses the old solitary confinement cells. It dominates both the harbour to the east and the sea to the south with excellent views.

Harbour

The harbour is situated to the south east of the town. The esplanade (Largo da Ribeira) is always the scene of a highly colourful spectacle with the **return of the fishing fleet**★, when the catch of sardines, tunny fish or crayfish is unloaded. Hundreds of squealing seagulls hover overhead in the hope of finding some left-overs and it is a colourful scene.

Igreja de São Pedro

The 17C chancel was embellished in the 18C with gilded woodwork into which were incorporated four huge canvases from the 16C attributed to the father of Josefa de Óbidos.

Ilha da Berlenga

Peniche harbour is a departure point for trips to the island of Berlenga. See ILHA DA BERLENGA.

The Beaches

Peniche is famed for its wide, spacious beaches where a wide variety of water sports activities can be found. It is the main centre of surfing in Portugal and World Championships have been held here. There are several surf schools and camps, particularly around the island-village of Baleal just to the north (4km/2.5mi) of Peniche. Enthusiasts of kite-surfing and diving are also very well catered for here.

PINHEL
GUARDA
POPULATION 3 237 – MICHELIN MAP 733

Pinhel, an old village and former fortified outpost on a mountainous shelf near to Spain, has many houses decorated with coats of arms and beautiful wrought-iron balconies. The road approaching Pinhel from the southwest (N 221) crosses a countryside covered with olive trees and vines; towards the end, near the town, there is a large group of wine vats, with very prominent white pointed domes.

- ▶ **Orient Yourself:** 29km/18mi northeast of Guarda
- 🕐 **Organizing Your Time:** The village is small so you won't need much time here, though spend a day travelling around the countryside close by.
- 👤 **Also See:** GUARDA (Almeida).

Sight

Museu Municipal
🕐 *Open Mon–Fri 9am–12.30pm, 2pm–5.30pm.* ☎*271 41 00 00.*
This small municipal museum contains prehistoric and Roman remains, religious works of art, weapons and Portuguese pewterware. Upstairs, there is a collection of naive folk art and other paintings.

Driving Tour

Serra da Marofa
20km/12.4mi – about 1hr 30min. Leave Pinhel on N 221 going north.
The road linking Pinhel and Figueira de Castelo Rodrigo was known locally as the **Excomungada** (Accursed Road) because of the danger presented by its countless bends when crossing the **Serra da Marofa**, after which you reach the Figueira de Castelo Rodrigo plateau which is planted with fruit trees. To the left, the *serra's* highest peak, with an altitude of 976m/3 202ft commands an interesting view of the ruins of the fortified village of **Castelo Rodrigo**, an important city since the Middle Ages.

Castelo Rodrigo
Castelo Rodrigo is a fortified village set high on a hill with magnificent views across into Spain. Its history dates back to 500 BC and it has recently undergone some much appreciated renovation. Now, its cobblestoned streets and alleys have been restored, many shops have opened (yes, many selling souvenirs) but it is a pleasant enough place to stop for an hour or two. There is also the remains of a castle and fortifications, from where you have magnificent views.

Barca de Alva
20km/12.4mi to the north of Figueira.
The blossoming of the almond trees between late February and mid-May, provides a delightful spectacle with its sea of pink flowers.

Estrada de Almeida★
25km/15.5mi to the southeast.
This route provides a picturesque link between Pinhel and Almeida.

- ▶ *Take N 324 south east of Pinhel.*

The road then comes to a desolate plateau strewn with enormous blocks of granite forming a lunar **landscape**★. After Vale Verde you cross a tributary of the Côa river by a narrow old humpback bridge.

- ▶ *At a crossroads 2.5km/1.5mi further on, turn left onto N 340: the road then crosses a bridge over the Côa river and rejoins N 332; take the road to the left towards Almeida.*

Almeida★ – 👤 *See GUARDA.*

POMBAL
LEIRIA
POPULATION 12 469 – MICHELIN MAP 733

The town of Pombal at the foot of its medieval castle evokes the memory of the Marquis of Pombal. Born in 1699 as Sebastião de Carvalho e Melo he began his career as a diplomat in London and Venice. In 1750 he became a minister and oversaw the rebuilding of Lisbon after the 1755 earthquake and improved the country's finances. In 1769 he was given the title of Marquis of Pombal.

🛈 **Information:** Largo do Cardal. ☎236 21 32 30.

▶ **Orient Yourself:** About 49.6km/31mi south of Coimbra on the main A 1 highway, on the western edge of the Serra da Lousã.

🕐 **Organizing Your Time:** Stop for an hour as you are passing through.

Castle

Take the Ansião road on the right at the corner of the Palácio de Justiça; upon reaching a cross, bear sharp right into a narrow surfaced road which rises steeply. Leave the car at the foot of the castle. 🕐*Open 8.30am–12.30pm, 2.30pm–5pm.*

The castle, built originally in 1161 by Gualdim Pais, Grand Master of the Order of the Knights Templar, was modified in the 16C and restored in 1940. From the top of the ramparts, overlooked by the battlemented keep, there is a view of Pombal to the west and the foothills of the Serra da Lousã to the east.

PONTE DE LIMA
VIANA DO CASTELO
POPULATION 2 800 – MICHELIN MAP 733

The charming town of Ponte de Lima is in the far north of Portugal, close to the Spanish border. Its Roman bridge was part of the main road north to what is now Spain. In the early 12C, Queen Tareja (Teresa) came to live in Ponte de Lima and granted it local privileges. Its streets are lined with Romanesque, Gothic, Manueline, Baroque and Neoclassical constructions while its environs are particularly rich in manor houses *(solares)* and seigneurial country estates *(quintas)*.

🛈 **Information:** Paço do Marquês. ☎258 942 335.

▶ **Orient Yourself:** About 42km/26mi north of Braga, midway between Viana do Castelo and the Peneda-Gerês National Park.

👁 **Don't Miss:** The **Ponte Medieval**★, the Roman bridge with 16 rounded arches, five of which remain: the Igreja-Museu dos Terceiros; the fountain.

🕐 **Organizing Your Time:** One day will be ideal though worth a stop-over.

👁 **Also See:** BRAGA, PARQUE NACIONAL DE PENEDA-GERÊS.

A Brief Look

The town is beautiful and well worth a couple of days looking around the area. The Roman bridge, several arches of which are still standing, is a focal point but there are many beautiful manor houses around dating from the 16–18C, adorned with coats-of-arms, may with covered galleries. The town is also a major centre in the production of *vinho verde*.

PORTALEGRE
PORTALEGRE

POPULATION 26 800 – MICHELIN MAP 733
LOCAL MAP SEE SERRA DE SÃO MAMEDE

Portalegre is an important town close to the Spanish frontier. The ruins of the town's fortified castle, built by King Dinis I in 1290, are still visible and the bustling town makes an ideal stop-over place. It has a history of tapestry making and cork manufacture. Portalegre is the starting point for the excursion in the Serra de São Mamede (💰 see SERRA DE SÃO MAMEDE).

- ℹ️ **Information:** R. Guilhermo Gomes Fernandes. ☏245 307 445.
- ▶ **Orient Yourself:** About 105km/65mi northeast of Évora in Alentejo.
- 🅿 **Parking:** In the Praça de República (fee).
- 🐦 **Don't Miss:** Summer evening spectacles in the Praça de República.
- 🕐 **Organizing Your Time:** A good half day though worth an overnight stop.
- 💰 **Also See:** MARVÃO, ESTREMOZ, ÉVIRA.

Sights

Museu José Régio

🕐 *Open Tue–Sun 9.30am–12.30pm.* 🚫 *Closed public holidays.* 💶€2.
The collection of art assembled by the poet José Régio (1901–69) is the most interesting part of the museum, which is in the house where he lived: there are around 400 crucifes dating from the 16C to 19C and naive statuettes of St Anthony. There are also lots of ceramics from Coimbra.

Museu da Tapeçaria Guy Fino

🕐 *Open Tue–Sun 9.30am–12.30pm, 2.30pm–6pm.* 💶€2. ☏245 307 980.
A lovely little museum housed in the former San Sebastian College in the lower town, with fascinating creations of tapestry from the last century, including a selection of the 5 000 different colours of wool used in copying major works of art.

Museu da Fábrica Robinson

🕐 *Open Mon–Fri 9.30am–12.30pm, 2pm–5.30pm. Slightly out of town, but you'll recognise it by its two large chimneys.*
Originally started by the Robinson family from Yorkshire (England) this factory made corks for wine and olive bottles and today you can see the history of cork-making; there's also a gift shop where everything is made of cork!

Museu Municipal

🔒 *Currently closed for renovation.*
Installed in the former diocesan seminary, the museum contains a rich collection of sacred art: a Spanish *Pietà* in gilded wood dating from the end of the 15C, a 16C altarpiece in polychrome terracotta, a magnificent 17C tabernacle in ebony, four ivory high reliefs (18C Italian School), an 18C ivory crucifix and 16C gold and silver plate.

Cathedral (Sé)

The 18C façade has distinctive marble columns. The interior (16C) the second chapel on the right has a beautiful retable illustrated with the life of the Virgin. The sacristry walls are covered in azulejos.

Walking round the town itself you should take time to look particularly at the **Rua 19 de Junho**, which is lined with late Renaissance and Baroque mansions, and take time to have a coffeee on one of the pavement cafés in the **Rossio**, the main square with its lovely fountain – the heart of Portalegre.

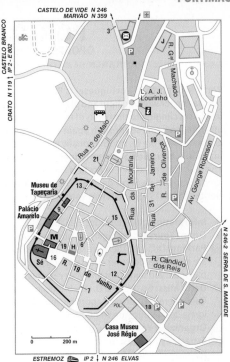

PORTIMÃO

FARO

POPULATION 44 391 – MICHELIN MAP 733

LOCAL MAP SEE ALGARVE

Portimão is the second-largest town on the Algarve and is a fishing port nestled at the back of a bay. The best view★ is at high tide from the bridge across the Rio Arade at the end of the bay. The town specialises the canning of tunny and sardines, but is also a major tourist resort – though that is more based on Praia da Rocha, very close by, which contains the town's famous beach.

- **Information:** Avda Zeca Afonso 282 470 732. www.cm-portimao.pt.
- ▶ **Orient Yourself:** In the western part of the Algarve coast.
- **Don't Miss:** The *azulejos* on benches in the Largo 1° de Dezembro.
- **Especially for Kids:** The beaches; boat cruises to exciting sea-caves.
- **Also See:** ALBUFEIRA, LAGOS, SILVES.

The town and beach

Portimão itself is a large working town that has also succumbed to mass tourism. In summer it is mainly block-booked by holiday companies. But having said that it still has its charm particularly in tha back streets near the **Largo da**

Barca and it does have its "own" resort in nearby Praia da Rocha, where the glorious beaches stretch out, there are plenty of restaurants and bars and you can take cruises out either for the day (big game fishing is very popular) or for a couple of hours to nearby sea-caves. There is good golf nearby.

PORTO★★
OPORTO – PORTO
POPULATION 1.6 MILLION – MICHELIN MAP 733

Porto (or Oporto in Portuguese) is Portugal's second-largest city, and has a reputation for working hard and playing hard. It occupies a magnificent **site**★★, its houses clinging to the banks of the Douro: the legendary river that ends here after its long course through Spain and Portugal. Not least among the city's claims to fame are its internationally celebrated port wines which are matured in the **Vila Nova de Gaia** wine lodges across the river.

The best **general view**★ of Porto is from the terrace of the former Convento de Nossa Senhora da Serra do Pilar. The historical city centre is a UNESCO World Heritage Site (1996) and it was voted *European Capital of Culture* in 2001.

- 🛈 **Information:** Rua Clube dos Fenianos. ☎223 393 472.
- ▶ **Orient Yourself:** Portugal's second city, Porto is in the north, on the coast.
- 🅿 **Parking:** Difficult. There are several large underground car-parks and these are recommended over street parking. Beware people who offer "private" parking... you might not find your car when you get back!
- 🚫 **Don't Miss:** Go over the D. Luís bridge (on metro or by foot) to Vila Nova de Gaia where you can enjoy port-tasting. The views from the belltower of the Igreja dos Clérigos are wonderful, looking out over the city.
- 🕐 **Organizing Your Time:** Give yourself three days to get to know the city.
- 🧒 **Especially for Kids:** Get the latest information from the tourist office with their *Famílias Nos Museus* (Families in Museums) brochure.
- ♿ **Also See:** VALE DO DOURO.

An Overview

The City

The city centre spreads across a network of shopping streets around Praça da Liberdade and São Bento station. The main street is **Avenida dos Aliados** (just known as Aliodos). This is very lively during the day with its crowds of people, pavement cafés and restaurants; old-fashioned shop fronts can be found in Rua Miguel Bombarda (upmarket with lots of art galleries), Formosa, Sá da Bandeira and Fernandes Tomás.

The working districts of **Ribeira** and **Miragaia** near the Douro have been restored and renovated over the last few years. Porto's **nightlife** is now centred in Ribeira (along the riverfront) with its many fashionable restaurants and bars, which are lively on summer evenings, particularly Fridays. The quarter also provides a good selection of moderately priced restaurants and bars.

Porto's business centre has been moving gradually westwards around **Avenida da Boavista** between Porto and Foz.

Major banks, businesses and shopping centres are springing up in modern tower blocks. If you are staying in the city for a couple of days the best way to get around is on public transport with a good metro, bus and tram service. Make sure you buy a **Porto Card** (tourist office) which also gives free or reduced price entry to museums.

You will also probably want to go on a river cruise; these depart from either Ribeira or Vila Nova de Gaia.

The Bridges

The river banks are linked by several outstanding bridges.

The **Ponte Ferroviária Maria**★, a railway bridge which is the furthest upstream and the most graceful, was designed by the French engineer Gustav Eiffel in 1877.

The **Ponte Rodoviária D. Luís I**★★ is the most spectacular of Porto's bridges with two superimposed road tracks, serving both upper and lower levels of the town on both banks. It is a World

View of Ponte Rodoviária D. Luís I from the south bank of the Douro

Heritage Site with a span of 172m/564ft and was built in 1886.

The **Ponte Rodoviária Arrábida**, opened in 1963 and used by the IC 1 road which runs through Porto, is a particularly bold structure. It crosses the Douro in a single reinforced concrete span of nearly 270m/886ft.

The **Ponte do Freixo**, which is used by the IP 1, is situated to the east of Porto, providing motorists with an alternative route avoiding the city centre.

The Centre

Praça da Liberdade and Praça do General Humberto Delgado

These two squares in the city centre form a vast open space dominated by the Town Hall. Nearby is the pedestrian **Rua de Santa Catarina**, with the city's smartest shops and the famous Café Majestic. The **Mercado Muncipal de Bolhão**, the municipal market, located between Rua de Fernandes and Rua Formosa, is colourful.

Igreja dos Clérigos

A Baroque church built by the architect Nasoni between 1735–48. The oval plan of the nave bears out the Italian influence. Dominating the church is the 75.60m/248ft high **Torre dos Clérigos**★ (◷*Tower and belfry open 8.45am–12.30pm, 3.30pm–7pm; ☞€2*),

Porto's most characteristic monument, which in the past served as a seamark to ships. The extensive **panorama**★ from the top takes in the city, the cathedral, the Douro and the wine lodges across the river. There are 225 steps to climb though!

Igreja do Carmo and Igreja das Carmelitas

The two Baroque churches stand side by side. The Igreja do Carmo is decorated on the outside with a large panel of *azulejos* showing Carmelites taking the veil. The older and rather less ostentatious Igreja das Carmelitas, is more sombre but just as interesting. An ancient law stated that two churches could not share the same wall (in this case to keep the monks from one and the nuns from the other apart to thwart any amorous liaisons) so they are divided by the narrowest house in Portugal, no wider than a letter-box. Incredibly it was inhabited until the 1980s.

Museu Nacional Soares dos Reis

◷*Open Wed–Sun 10am–6pm; Tue 2pm–6pm.* ◷*Closed 1 Jan, Easter Sun, 25 Apr, 1 May and 25 Dec.* ☞€3.www.mnsr-ipmuseus.pt.

This museum, one of the best in Porto, is housed in the 18C Palácio dos Carrancos, exhibits permanent collections of Portuguese paintings and sculpture from the 17C to 20C. Most interesting

Address Book

For coin ranges, see the Legend on the cover flap.

USEFUL INFORMATION

Passe Porto – Tourist pass valid for one day (€7.50), two days (€11.50) or three days (€15.50) with free or reduced entry to 18 museums and monuments; free travel on all public transport; rebates in 28 shops, on cruises, visits to wine cellars or bus tours. Available at ticket machines on the metro or at Tourist Information Centres.

Pass Transport – Two passes that give free public transport in the city. One-day €4; three-day €9. On sale at the three Tourist Information Centres.

TRANSPORT

Airport – The Dr Francisco Sá Carneiro airport, recently rebuilt, is on the EN 107 about 14km/8.7mi northwest of the town. A metro line runs direct into the city centre €1.90. There are also regular buses to Av. dos Aliados from 6.45am–7.15pm.

Railways – Two main stations:

Campanhá, *R. da Estação* - both national and international services;

São Bento – *Praça Almeida Garret* – serves the north of Portugal and local destinations.
Train information on ☎808 208 208 or at *www.cp.pt.*

Metro – There are four lines serving the entire city and its outskirts. For more information obtain maps from any metro station or Tourist Information Centres or visit *www.metro-porto.pt.*

Buses (STCP) – Porto has 78 different lines covering the entire city with an efficient service. Single tickets are available for €1.30; day tickets for €2.10 cover the city centre. If you're a night-owl there are 13 lines that run all night. *www.stcp.pt.*

CITY TOURS

You can book all city tours, including cruises, at **Porto Tours** *(Torre Medieval, near the Cathedral;* ☎222 000 073; *www.portotours.com)* or at the main tourist office.

Porto Vintage – A good way to get to know the city quickly is by hop-on-hop-off bus, every hour during the day. ☎808 200 166. €10 (P5 children).

Wine Cellar visits – The port wine cellars are all at Vila Nova de Gaia and you can visit and taste. There is normally a nominal entrance fee for the tour and tasting (about €5 – refundable against purchases). They are easily identifiable once across the river by huge signs .

River Cruises – A dozen or more companies operate river cruises on the Douro, each taking about one hour. Departures are from the Quai Ribeira or Quai Amarelo every day from 10am. €10. You can also take a full-day cruise upriver into the port wine country, normally returning by bus. Price, including lunch, is about €60–85 depending on time of year.

Metro do Porto

© Oleg Kozlov - Fotolia.com

WHERE TO STAY

Castelo Santa Catarina – *R. de Santa Catarina 1347, (metro: Marquês, line D).* ☎*225 095 599. www.castelosanta catarina.com.pt. 26 rooms* ⊟ **P**. This astonishing fairy-tale villa complete with a crenellated tower, extensive terraced gardens and massive reproduction furniture provides reasonably priced, comfortable accommodation only 10min-walk from Porto's centre.

América – *R. Santa Catarina, 1018* ☎*223 392 930. www.hotel-america. net.* &. **P** *30 rooms* ⊡. This hotel has wood floors and lovely furniture. 15min walk from the city centre.

Da Bolsa – *R. Ferreira Borges, 101. www.hoteldabolsa.com.* ☎*222 026 768. 36 rooms* &.⊡.
An interesting address in the lively Ribeira riverside district. Beautiful 19C façade, although the interior has been completely refurbished in a rather dull modern style. The top-floor rooms are more expensive but have good views.

Residencial Vera Cruz – *R. Ramalho Ortigão, 14.* ☎*222 323 396. www. residencialveracruz.com. 30 rooms* ⊡.
Very nice little hotel with beautifully styled bedrooms and, from the 8th floor, where breakfast is served, a lovely view over the city. A very central location, ideal for touring the city.

Grande Hotel do Porto – *R. de Santa Catarina 197.* ☎*222 076 690. www.grandehotelporto.com. 100 rooms* &.⊡. Although this landmark hotel has lost much of its former splendour, its public areas still retain an old fashioned charm. The rooms are appointed in a basic modern style. Its location on a bustling pedestrian shopping street in the centre is a plus for those visiting the city on foot.

Infante de Sagres – *Praça D. Filipa de Lencastre 62.* ☎*222 398 500. www.hotelinfantasagres.pt. 72 rooms* ⊡. The centrally located Infante de Sagres, close to the Praça da Liberdade, is the most prestigious hotel in Porto with a charm all of its own. Its interior contains wood-panelling, period furniture and stained glass.

Plaça de Ribeira

Residencial dos Aliados – *Avda dos Aliados 27.* ☎*222 004 853. www.residencialaliados.com.* **P** *38 rooms.* A beautiful beaux-arts building in the centre of town with polished wood floors, newly furnished rooms though the rooms at the front can be a bit noisy at night. Some rooms have a/c.

WHERE TO EAT

D. Luis – *Av. Ramos Pinto 264–266.* ☎*223 751 251. Closed Mon.* Beautiful décor makes this little restaurant in Vila Nova de Gaia a cosy place to spend the evening, with room for only 20 guests. Fish plays a big part on the menu. Reservations essential at weekends.

Don Tonho - *Cais da Ribeira.* ☎*222 004 307.* Owned by a Portuguese pop star, this riverside restaurant serves wonderful seafood and traditional Portuguese meals with a modern twist.

O Chanquinhas – *R. de Santana 243.* ☎*229 951 884. Closed Sun.* A converted ancient mansion, this elegant family restaurant has high-quality cuisine.

A Mesa Com Bacchus – *R. de Miragaia, 127 (tram no. 1, Alfândega stop) 222 000 896, closed Sun, reservations essential for evenings* ⊟. At the heart of the old town and not far from the river, this is a restaurant not to miss if you enjoy fine food and great service. It is a wine-lover's paradise with wines chosen by the *patron* and a suggestion for every dish. You will enjoy excellent food in an intimate and friendly atmosphere.

H. Chamollion/MICHELIN

View of the cathedral over the roofs of Porto

dos Reis (1847–89). Portuguese painting between 1850 and 1950 is represented by canvases by Silva Porto, Henrique Pousão, who was influenced by the Impressionists and Symbolists, José Malhoa, João Vaz and Columbano.

Older paintings on display include Portuguese works by Frei Carlos, Gaspar Vaz, Vasco Fernandes and Cristóvão de Figueiredo, and foreign works by Francis Clouet (portraits of *Marguerite de Valois* and *Henri II of France*), Quillard, Pillement, Teniers, Troni and Simpson. Particularly worthy of note are two 17C Namban screens illustrating the arrival of the Portuguese in Japan.

The decorative and applied art section is just amazing, perhaps the best things on display with a collection of old ceramics, gold articles and sacred art.

Old Porto★★

Cathedral★

🕐 *Open Apr–Oct 8.45am–12.30pm, 2.30pm–7pm; rest of year until 6pm. Free, though entrance to cloisters is ⊜€3.*

The cathedral *(sé),* begun as a fortress-church in the 12C, was considerably modified in the 17C and 18C. The main façade, still austere in appearance, is flanked by two square, domed towers; there is a 13C Romanesque rose window and a Baroque doorway. Inside, the narrow central nave is flanked by aisles on a lower level.

The transept and chancel were modified in the Baroque period. The Chapel of the Holy Sacrament, which opens off the left arm of the transept, contains a very fine **altar★** with a chased silver altarpiece worked by Portuguese silversmiths in the 17C.

PORTO
STREET INDEX

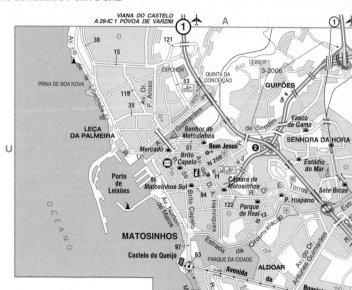

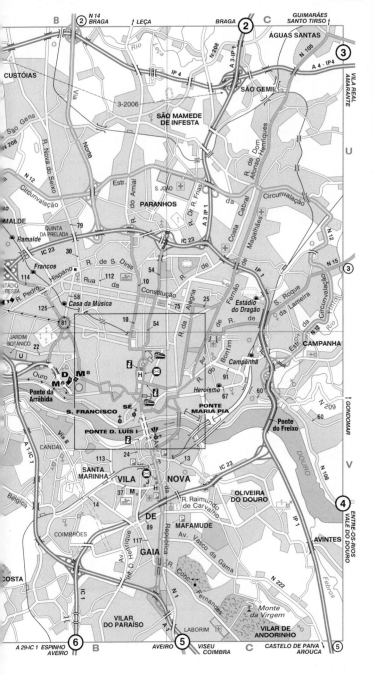

Biblioteca Almeida Garrett	BV	M[7]	Galeria do Palácio	BV	M[7]
Casa Tait	BV	D	Igreja da Imaculada Conceição	BU	F
Fundação António de Almeida	BU	M[1]	Museu Romântico	BV	M[6]

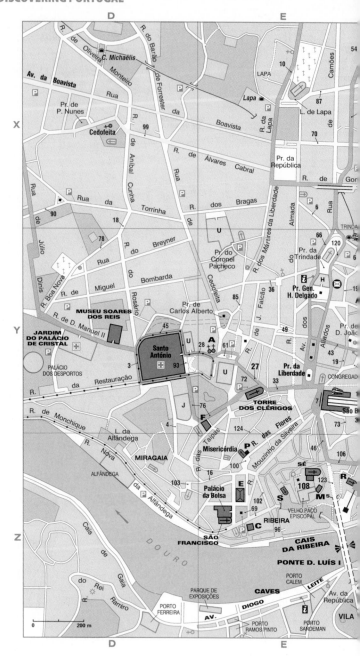

Cloisters

The 14C cloisters are decorated with **azulejos★** panels, illustrating the Life of the Virgin, and Ovid's *Metamorphoses*, made by Valentim de Almeida between 1729 and 1731. The original Romanesque cloisters containing several sarcophagi can be seen from these cloisters. A fine granite staircase designed by Nicolau Nasoni in the 18C leads to the chapter-house which has a coffered ceiling painted by Pachini in 1737.

Behind the cathedral is the delightful **Museu Guerra Junqueiro**.

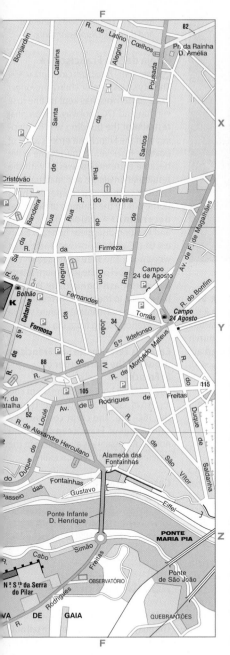

Tree of Jesse, Igreja de São Francisco

The Mannerist-style **Igreja de São Lourenço dos Grilos**, built by the Jesuits in the 17C, is now the headquarters of the Grand Seminary. The church also houses a **museum of sacred art** (🕐*open 10am–noon, 2pm–5pm;* ⊶€1).

▶ *On reaching Rua Mouzinho da Silveira, cross over to Largo de São Domingos. Leading off from it is Rua das Flores.*

Rua das Flores
This narrow street leading to São Bento railway station is bordered by traditional shops and 18C houses with coats-of-arms adorning the façades. It was once the main street for jewellers as well as gold and silversmiths.

The **Santa Casa da Misericórdia** (🕐*open Mon–Fri 9.30am–noon, 2pm–5.30pm;* ⊶€1.50; ☎222 074 710). Beside the Baroque Igreja da Misericórdia, this museum contains an outstanding painting from the Flemish School called **Fons Vitae**★ or the Fountain of Mercy, with Dom Manuel and his family kneeling before the crucified Christ. It has been attributed to different people including Holbein, Van der Weyden and Van Orley: perhaps it was the work of a Portuguese artist who drew his inspiration from Flemish painters...

▶ *Return to Largo de São Domingos and then take Rua Belomonte.*

Igreja de São Francisco★★
🕐*Open 9am–7pm (5pm Oct–Apr).* ⊶€3.
The city's most Gothic church *(no longer in use for services)* has kept its fine rose window and 17C doorway. The original restraint of the building was in keeping with the Franciscan order's ideal of poverty. However, in the 17C the order became extremely powerful with the result that privileges and material possessions were bestowed upon it. This is borne out by the triumph of **Baroque decoration**★★ inside: altars, walls and vaulting disappear beneath a forest of 17C and 18C carved and gilded woodwork. The **Tree of Jesse**★ in the second chapel on the left is particularly noteworthy, as is the high altar. Beneath the gallery, to the right on entering the church, is a polychrome granite statue of St Francis dating from the 13C.

Casa dos Terceiros de São Francisco (House of the Third Order of St Francis)
The building houses a permanent collection of sacred art with objects from the 16C–20C. The crypt contains the sarcophagi of Franciscan friars and nobles. An ossuary is also visible in the basement through an iron railing.

Casa do Infante
Rua da Alfândega.
This is where Prince Henry the Navigator is believed to have been born. It was the city's Customs House from the 14C to the 19C.

Additional Sights

Cais da Ribeira★
The quayside dominated by the tall outline of the D. Luís I bridge is the most picturesque spot in Porto. Ancient houses look down from a great height on the waterfront with its fish and vegetable market and lively nightlife. Several old boats lie moored at the water's edge. This section of the old city is a World Heritage site and has undergone major restoration work over the past few

years. Cross the Douro by the D. Luís I bridge to reach the wine lodges *(5min on foot – see Wine Lodges opposite)*.

Jardim do Palácio de Cristal (Crystal Palace Gardens) [Kids]

Open Oct–Mar, 8am–7pm; Apr–Sept, 8am–9pm.

This garden provides a haven of peace in its tree-lined paths, its beautiful flowers, lagoons, grottos and fountains. Animals roam freely and it is the ideal place for a picnic whilst watching the children play. There are some spots with lovely views over Vila Nova da Gaia, the Douro and the coast. A crystal palace was built here similar to that used for the great Exhibition of 1865 in London, but it has since been demolished and replaced by a rather uninspiring sports pavilion, to the chagrin of many locals. At one part of the garden you will find the Galeria do Palácio, which has regular exhibitions and also houses the **Biblioteca Almeida Garrett**. Nearby is the Quinta da Macierinha, a small house where the King of Sardinia spent his final days in exile. Part of the house has been turned into the charming **Museu Romântico** (*open Tue–Sat 10am–12.30pm, 2pm–5.30pm, Sun 2pm–5.30pm; €2*), which contains his belongings and furniture. The lower floor is now the *Solar do Vinho do Porto* (*see below*).

Solar do Vinho do Porto

R de São Pedro de Alcântara.
Open Mon–Sat 11am–midnight.
Closed public holidays.

This is the headquarters of the Port Wine Institute. Hundreds of different types of port may be tasted in very pleasant surroundings with prices varying from €4 to €25 per glass.

Museu do Carro Eléctrico

R de São Pedro de Alcântara. Open Tue–Fri 9.30am–12.30pm, 2.30pm–6pm, Sat, Sun and public holidays 3pm–7pm. www. museu-carro-electrico.stcp.pt.

This interesting museum, close to the Palácio de Cristal, west of the old town, charts the story of Porto's electric trams and has the oldest tram in Iberia, dating from 1872.

Port wine celler

Wine Lodges★

The city's wine lodges cover several acres (a couple of hectares) on the south bank of the Douro in the lower quarter of **Vila Nova da Gaia**. More than 58 port companies are established in the area. In bygone days, boats known as *barcos rebelos* would transport the wines of the Upper Douro some 150km/90mi along the river to the lodges where they would be transformed into port. Several wine lodges have tours with tastings. There is normally an entrance fee of up to €5 though this is credited against the price of any bottle you might buy to take away.

Igreja de Santa Clara★

Open Mon–Fri 9.30am–11.30am, 3pm–6pm.

The church, which dates from the Renaissance, has kept its original granite doorway with figures in medallions. The rather austere exterior contrasts with the profuse decoration of 17C **carved and gilded woodwork**★ inside. The ceiling is Mudéjar in style.

Antigo Convento de Nossa Senhora da Serra do Pilar

Across Luís I bridge in Vila Nova de Gaia.

The old convent has one of the finest views of Porto including the remains of the 14C walls to the right of D. Luís I bridge. It is a curious building erected in the 16C and 17C in the form of a rotunda designed by Filippo Terzi.

Fundação de Serralves (Museu de Arte Contemporânea)★

🕐Open Apr–Sept, Tue–Sun 10am–7pm (and later at certain times – see local notices). ☎226 156 500. www.serralves.pt. ◉Museum and park €5; museum only €2.50; park only €2.50; free Sun 10am–2pm.

The Casa de Serralves complex, which stands in a magnificent **park**★, is an outstanding example of 1930s architecture with an Art Nouveau interior. Inside, note the architecture, decoration, graceful **forged iron grilles**★ designed by Lalique and the luxurious inlaid parquet floors on the first floor.

Igreja da Cedofeita

🕐Open 10am–12.30pm, 3pm–7pm.

This is the city's oldest church (12C) and is a fine example of early Romanesque architecture despite changes made in the 17C. The original Romanesque portal adorned with a Lamb of God and the barrel vaulting in the nave are intact.

Fundação Eng° António de Almeida

👁‍🗨Guided tours (30min) Sept–Jul, Tue–Sat 2.30pm– 5.30pm. 🕐Closed public holidays. ◉€2. ☎226 067 418. www.feaa.pt.

Throughout his lifetime, the rich industrialist António de Almeida put together a fine **collection of gold coins**★ (Greek, Roman, Byzantine, French and Portuguese) which is exhibited in the house where he lived. The interior decoration includes some fine antique furniture and porcelain from various countries.

PÓVOA DE VARZIM
PORTO
POPULATION 23 846 – MICHELIN MAP 733

Póvoa de Varzim is an old fishing port and also an elegant seaside resort. It is also the birthplace of the great novelist Eça de Queirós (1845–1900).

▶ **Orient Yourself:** About 35km/25mi north of Porto, on the coast, the last stop on the local train along the coast from Porto, about an hour's ride.

🖼 **Don't Miss:** The Fishermen's quarter, south of the main beach.

🕐 **Organizing Your Time:** Soak up some sun but see the two churches nearby.

Kids **Especially for Kids:** The beach is the place they will want to see!

👣 **Also See:** Foz do Douro and also nearby Vila do Conde 👣see Vila do Conde.

Excursion

Romanesque Churches of Rio Mau and Rates

15km/9.3mi – about 1hr.

▶ Leave Póvoa de Varzim by the Porto road (N 13) going south; after 2km/1.2mi turn left onto the N 206 towards Guimarães.

Rio Mau

Turn right opposite the post office onto an unsurfaced road.

The small Romanesque **Igreja de São Cristóvão** is built of granite; the rough decoration of the capitals contrast with the more detailed ornamentation on the **capitals**★ in the triumphal arch and in the chancel which is later in date.

▶ 2km/1.2mi beyond Rio Mau, take a turning to the left to Rates (1km/0.6mi).

Rates

The granite Igreja de São Pedro was built in the 12C and 13C by Benedictine monks from Cluny. The façade is pierced by a rose window and a door with five arches, and capitals decorated with animals; on the tympanum a low-relief sculpture presents a Transfiguration.

The **beaches** around Póvoa de Varzim are excellent, being just after the Rio Mau empties into the Atlantic. There are about 8km/5mi of open beaches.

PALÁCIO NACIONAL DE QUELUZ★★
LISBOA
MICHELIN MAP 733 – MICHELIN ATLAS SPAIN & PORTUGAL P 58 (P 2)

The **Royal Palace of Queluz**, between Sintra and Lisbon, takes the visitor right back into the heart of the 18C. In the formal gardens adorned with pools and statues, overlooked by pastel-coloured Rococo façades with their many windows, one almost expects to come upon a romantic scene from a painting by Watteau. Although inspired by Versailles, the Queluz Palace is smaller in proportion, making it more intimate.

- **Information:** ☎219 343 860.
- ▶ **Orient Yourself:** 21km/13mi west of Lisbon and 16km/10mi east of Sintra.
- **Parking:** Not difficult except at very busy times (summer weekends).
- **Don't Miss:** Pedro IV's bedroom and the gardens (included in ticket price).
- ○ **Organizing Your Time:** A full morning, or afternoon, but have lunch as well.
- **Especially for Kids:** They'll enjoy eating in the original kitchens, now a restaurant ☎214 356 158 Wed–Mon, lunch and dinner.
- **Also See:** SINTRA, LISBON.

A Bit of History

At the end of the 16C, the land belonged to the Marquis of Castelo Rodrigo, who had a hunting lodge here. After the restoration of the monarchy and Dom João IV's accession to the throne, the property was confiscated and several years later, in 1654, became the residence of the *Infantes*. Dom Pedro (1717–86), son of Dom João V and the future Dom Pedro III, was the first *infante* to show a real interest in the estate and decided to build a palace. From 1747 to 1758, the Portuguese architect Mateus Vicente de Oliveira built the main façade in a washed-pink stone as well as the wing that would later contain the Throne Room. While the overall style of the palace is Rococo, architectural differences between the three periods are apparent.

Visit

○ *Open Wed–Mon 9.30am–5pm.* ○ *Closed 1 Jan, Good Fri, Easter Sun, 1 May, 29 Jun and 25 Dec.* ⊗€4.

The sumptuous **Sala do Trono**★ (Throne Room), recalls the Hall of Mirrors in Versailles. Magnificent Venetian crystal chandeliers hang from the ceiling decorated with allegorical illustrations and supported on caryatids.

Just beyond this you come to the Music Chamber with a portrait of Queen Maria above the grand piano.

The **Sala dos Azulejos** is so called on account of the wonderful multi-coloured 18C *azulejos* depicting landscapes of China and Brazil. The Sala da Guarda Real (Royal Guard Room) contains a fine 18C Arraiolos carpet. The **Sala dos Embaixadores** (Ambassadors' Hall), where visiting diplomats and statesmen were received during the 19C, decorated

Palácio Nacional de Queluz

with marble and mirrors, has a painted ceiling of a concert at the court of King Dom José and diverse mythological motifs.

Beyond the Queen's Boudoir and sitting room, French Rococo in style, is the Sculpture Room though the only item on display is an earthenware bust of Maria. Then comes the **Sala Don Quixote** which was used as Pedro IV's bedroom and where eight columns support a circular ceiling with paintings of Cervantes' hero decorating the walls. In the **Sala das Merendas** (Tea Room), embellished with gilded woodwork, are several 18C paintings of royal picnics.

The original kitchens (**Cozinha Velha**) of the Palace have been reopened as a restaurant where you can have lunch or dinner *(12.30pm–3pm, 7.30pm–10pm).*

Gardens

The sumptuous gardens were designed by the French architect JBRobillon in the style of the 17C French landscape gardener, Le Nôtre. Individual attractions include the Amphitrite basin. The walls of the **Grand Canal** are covered in 18C *azulejos* of between which flows the Jamor river. In the past the royal family went boating along the canal. Note the façade of the Robillon wing, fronted by a magnificent **Lion Staircase**★ (Escadaria dos Leões) which is extended by a beautiful colonnade.

If, after having seen how the Kings lived, you want to live like a King, part of the Palace has been converted into a *pousada.* Not cheap for the night but luxurious. ☎214 356 158. www.pousadas.pt.

A Victim of the Revolution

This palace, built as a place of celebration, was also the setting for the dramatic life of **Maria I**. Maria was pious almost to the point of superstition and considered the death of her uncle and husband Pedro III in 1786 to be a warning of the misfortune that was to afflict her family and people. The loss in 1788 of two of her children, Crown Prince Josef, who died at the age of 27, and the Infanta Maria-Anna, who was married to the son of the Spanish king, in less than two months, merely confirmed her premonitions. Her feelings of melancholy were increased by the death of her confessor soon after. She became so disturbed by the outbreak of the French Revolution that by 1791 she was already showing the first signs of dementia. Her second son, João, governed in her name and took the title of Regent in 1799. When French troops invaded Portugal, João took his mother to Brazil, where she died, still Portugal's reigning sovereign, in 1816.

PONTA DE **SAGRES** AND CABO DE **SÃO VICENTE**★★★

FARO

MICHELIN MAP 733
LOCAL MAP SEE ALGARVE

The windswept headland falling steeply to the sea is the southwest extremity of mainland Europe. It was here, facing the Atlantic Ocean, the great unknown, that Prince Henry the Navigator retired in the 15C to found the Sagres School of Navigation, which would prepare the way for the Great Discoveries.

- **Information:** Praça da República, Sagres. ☎282 620 003.
- **Orient Yourself:** The most southwesterly tip of mainland Europe.
- **Parking:** No problems in Sagres or at Cabo de São Vicente.
- **Don't Miss:** The views from the Cape – hopefully near sunset.
- **Organizing Your Time:** An afternoon excursion – Sagres first then the Cape.
- **Especially for Kids:** Children will love the view from the clifftop.

A Man of Wisdom

Prince Henry the Navigator, third son of King John I of Portugal and his wife Philippa (sister to Henry IV of England) was born in Porto in 1394. Softly spoken, devout, kind and gentle, he was sent by his father on several overseas voyages, falling in love with the oceans and coming to realise how important the sea could be to Portugal's trading interests. In 1415 he relocated to Sagres where he founded a School of Navigation, using the best Arab cartographers he could find. Theories were tested and put to practical use in expeditions which set out on several voyages down the coast of West Africa. Improvements in the astrolabe and the sextant, enabling calculations to be made far out to sea, led to the prince's introduction of navigation by the stars: mariners learned to

Cabo de São Vicente

B. Brillion/MICHELIN

The Caravel

One of Portugal's most significant contributions to maritime history is the **caravel**. This type of light sailing ship, developed by Portuguese fishermen, was widely used in the 15C–17C in Europe, particularly for exploring uncharted seas. Caravels were rigged with lanteen (triangular) sails, which enabled them to sail to windward (taking advantage of a wind from the side of the ship). These elegant craft, which superseded the oared galley, generally measured about 23m/75ft in length, with two or three masts (later versions added a fourth with square rigging for running before the wind). The caravel was capable of remarkable speed, and was well-adapted to long voyages. Two of the three ships under the command of Christopher Columbus in 1492, the *Niña* and the *Pinta*, were caravels.

calculate their latitude from the height of the stars above the horizon and chart their positions with greater accuracy. The demands of the voyages also compelled the Portuguese to design a new type of ship which revolutionised navigation – the **caravel**. Henry died in Sagres in 1460.

Sights

Ponta de Sagres★★★

The headland is partially occupied by the remains of a 16C **fortress** (♥open 10am–8.30pm (6.30pm Nov–Apr); ♥closed 1 May and 25 Dec; ◉◉€3;

☎282 62 01 40). The entrance tunnel leads into a vast courtyard with an immense wind compass.

Cabo de São Vicente★★★

Cape St Vincent, the most southwesterly point of continental Europe, towers above the ocean at a height of 75m/246ft. ⚡There is a wonderful walk along the top of the cliffs from Sagres, 6km/3.7mi each way, wild and windy but it's worth it (there are cafés along the way). To be honest there is not much at the Cape as most of the buildings were destroyed by Sir Francis Drake in 1587. A tall lighthouse (still in use) guides hundreds of vessels a night as they pass this point.

SANTA MARIA DA FEIRA
AVEIRO

POPULATION 28 644 – MICHELIN MAP 733

North of the town of Aveiro, and about halfway to Porto (which is only another 30mins away), the castle of Santa Maria da Feira stands on a wooded height facing the town which lies scattered over the opposite hillside. Feira itself is now becoming built up with commuters who travel by train each day to Porto but its castle in the old section is one of the most spectacular in Portugal. It has been lovingly restored and is a wonderful example of how to build an impregnable defence. At the foot of the hill is a shaded, wooded picnic area.

- ℹ **Information:** Praça da República. ☎256 37 08 00.
- ▶ **Orient Yourself:** 30km/18.6mi south of Porto, just off the main A 1 highway.
- 🅿 **Parking:** Not difficult. Parking near the castle is advisable.
- 👀 **Don't Miss:** The castle is perhaps one of the best in Portugal.
- 🕐 **Organizing Your Time:** A "passing-through" town – no more than an hour.
- 🧒 **Especially for Kids:** A great view from the castle's walls but probably more important are the secret passages and concealed entrances.
- 👁 **Also See:** AVEIRA.

Visit

Castle★

🕐Open Mon–Fri 9.30am–12.30pm (from 10.30am Sat–Sun), 1.30pm–6pm. ⊜€3.
The 11C castle was reconstructed in the 15C. A keep flanked by four tall towers with pepperpot roofs overlooks a fortified perimeter wall whose entrance is defended on its eastern side by a barbican. Follow the wall walk; latrines can still be seen. Stairs lead to the first floor of the keep where there is a vast Gothic hall; the upper platform (60 steps) affords a panorama of the castle's fortifications, the town, the surrounding wooded hills and the coastline, where one can make out the Ria de Aveiro in the distance.

Igreja da Misericórdia

The chancel, under a coffered ceiling, has a lovely gilded altarpiece. In a south chapel there are some unusual statues, one of which is a Saint Christopher, 3m/9.8ft high.

SANTARÉM
SANTARÉM
POPULATION 64 124 – MICHELIN MAP 733

At some point in distant history Irene, a young nun in a convent near Tomar, was murdered by a monk whose advances she refused. Her body was thrown in the Tagus and washed up in the former Roman town of Scalabis. The town was renamed Saint Irene – Santarém – in her honour. On a hill on the north bank of the Tagus, it overlooks the vast Ribatejo plain. It was an important Roman town, was recaptured from the Moors in 1147 by Alfonso I and later became a royal residence and seat of the Cortes. From this rich past, Santarém retains several monuments, mostly Gothic, dotted about the town's attractive old quarter.

- **Information:** Rua Capelo e Ivens, 63. ☎243 304 437. www.cm-santarem.pt.
- ▶ **Orient Yourself:** About 80km/50mi northeast of Lisbon, on the Tagus.
- ⊚ **Don't Miss:** The views over the surrounding countryside and the Tagus.
- 🕐 **Organizing Your Time:** An afternoon is best to enjoy the atmosphere.

Old Town

The historical centre, with its mainly pedestrianised alleyways and steps, is a pleasant area for a stroll.

Igreja do Seminário

The late 18C Baroque façade of this former Jesuit college has as its main feature the superimposition of several storeys outlined by cornices and pierced by windows and niches, which gives the church more the appearance of a palace than a church.

The **interior** remains austere in spite of the marble incrustations decorating the altar and the pilasters. The single nave is covered with a ceiling painted to represent the Immaculate Conception and Jesuit evangelical activities overseas.

Igreja de Marvila

This church was founded in the 12C following the reconquest of Santarém from the Moors in 1147. 16C additions included the graceful Manueline doorway. The interior is lined with 17C *azulejos*, the most interesting being those known as carpet or *tapete azulejos*, painted in many colours with plant motifs, which date from 1620 and 1635. Note the Manueline features in the three chapels and the Baroque gilded wood altar. The pulpit, made of 11 miniature Corinthian columns, is also interesting.

Igreja da Graça★

🕐 Open Tue–Sun 9.30am–12.30pm, 2pm–5.30pm. 🕐Closed public holidays.
This Gothic church of 1380 has a fine Flamboyant façade with a spectacular rose window carved from a single block

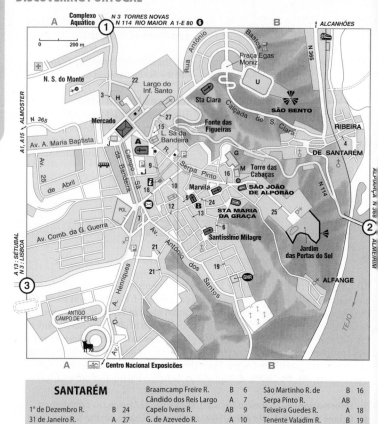

SANTARÉM			Braamcamp Freire R.	B	6	São Martinho R. de	B	16
			Cândido dos Reis Largo	A	7	Serpa Pinto R.	AB	
1° de Dezembro R.	B	24	Capelo Ivens R.	AB	9	Teixeira Guedes R.	A	18
31 de Janeiro R.	A	27	G. de Azevedo R.	A	10	Tenente Valadim R.	B	19
5 de Outubro Av.	B	25	João Afonso R.	A	12	Vasco da Gama R.	A	21
Alex Herculano R.	A	3	Miguel Bombarda R.	B	13	Zeferino Brandão R.	A	22
Alf. de Santarém R.	B	4	Piedade Largo da	A	15			

Igreja da Misericórdia	B	B		Igreja do Seminário	A	A

of stone. The **nave** has been restored to its original lines. The church contains several tombs including, in the south transept, that of Dom Pedro de Meneses, first Governor of Ceuta. The 15C tomb, resting on eight lions, is carved with leaf motifs and coats of arms. On the pavement of the south apsidal chapel can be seen the funerary stone of the navigator Pedro Álvares Cabral who discovered Brazil in 1500.

Igreja do Santíssimo Milagre

Built in the 14C and subsequently modified on several occasions, this small church is well worth a visit. The sacristy contains the host that is said to have been transformed into the blood of Christ in 1247.

Igreja da Misericórdia

This 16C church had a Baroque façade added following the earthquake of 1755. The interior is noteworthy for its elegant ribbed vault supported by Tuscan columns.

Igreja de São João de Alporão (Museu Arqueológico)★

⏰ Open Tue–Wed 9.30am–12.30pm, 2pm–5.30pm, Thu–Sun 10am–12.30pm, 2pm–5.30pm. ⏰Closed public holidays. €1. ☎243 39 15 17.

To the left of the entrance of this Romanesque and Gothic church, built by the Knights Templar in 12–13C, is the **tomb** of Duarte de Meneses, Count of Viana, which was erected by his wife in the 15C to contain a tooth, the only recoverable remains of her husband who had been killed by the Moors in North Africa. The stone balcony was carved by Mateus Fernandes.

Torre das Cabaças
⏱*Open 9am–12.30pm, 2pm–5.30pm.*
⏱*Closed Mon.* ⬭€1.
There is a good overall **view** of Santarém from the top of Calabash Tower, a vestige of the old medieval wall, which faces the church of São João de Alporão. The tower also houses an innovative Museum of Time with a collection of time-pieces from ancient sundials to ornate 19C clocks.

Additional Sights

Igreja de Santa Clara
⏱*Open Tue–Sun 9am–12.30pm, 2pm–5.30pm.* ⏱*Closed public holidays.*
This vast Gothic church was once part of a 13C convent. The lack of a doorway on the façade intensifies the bare appearance of the church's exterior.
Inside, the narrow nave ends with a beautiful rose window above the 17C tomb of Dona Leonor, founder of the convent. The church also contains the original 14C tomb of Dona Leonor. On either side of it are Franciscan monks and Poor Clares, at the foot St Francis receiving the stigmata, and at the head the Annunciation.

Miradouro de São Bento★
The belvedere affords a vast **panorama**★ of the Tagus plain and Santarém where the main buildings can easily be distinguished.

Capela de Nossa Senhora do Monte
The 16C chapel stands in the middle of a horseshoe-shaped square. The façade is bordered on both sides by an arcaded gallery with capitals adorned with leaf motifs and heads of cherubim. At the east end stands 16C statue of Our Lady.

SÃO JOÃO DE TAROUCA
VISEU
POPULATION 8 303 – MICHELIN MAP 733

The former monastery of Tarouca, overlooked by the heights of the Serra de Leomil, lies in a hollow in the Barossa valley. The church erected in the 12C by Cistercian monks, was remodelled in the 17C. A full description appears below.

▶ **Orient Yourself:** South of Lamego, easily accessible from the Douro Valley.
🅿 **Parking:** Not a problem.
◉ **Don't Miss:** The church is the main thing to see.
⏱ **Organizing Your Time:** Really only a couple of hours are needed.
⬡ **Also See:** LAMEGO.

The Church

⏱*Open May–Sept, Wed–Sun 10am–12.30pm, 2pm–6pm; Tue 2.30pm–6pm (closes 5.30pm Oct–Apr).*
Built in 1169 this Romanesque church remains pretty much intact. Of particular interest are the choir and the Baroque organ, dating from 1766 and whose central figure beats time during Mass. *Azulejos* in the transept depict the life of St Bernard, one showing him standing in a barrel of wine! A side chapel contains paintings attributed to Gaspar Vaz and there is a superb rendition of St Peter in one of the side chapels. The monumental 14C granite tomb contains he remains of Dom Pedro, Count of Barcelos, illegitimate son of King Dimis. Pedro was the author of the Great Chronicle of 1344, and was considered one of the greatest Portuguese writers of the Middle Ages.

SERRA DE SÃO MAMEDE★
PORTALEGRE
MICHELIN MAP 733

The Serra de São Mamede is a small island of greenery in an arid and stony region; its altitude (at its highest point: 1 025m/3 363ft) and the impermeable soil combine to provide sufficient humidity for a dense and varied vegetation. The triangular-shaped massif is composed of hard rock that has resisted erosion.

- **Information:** (Portalegre) Rua General Jorge Conde de Avilez. ☎245 203 631.
- ▶ **Orient Yourself:** Near Portalegre, close to the Spanish frontier, directly inland from Óbidos.
- ⏱ **Organizing Your Time:** You could spend a night in Portalegre and travel this area for a couple of days, no more.
- ♿ **Also See:** PORTALEGRE.

Driving Tour
73km/45mi – about 2hr 30min

▶ *Leave Portalegre to the east; then turn northwards.*

After leaving Portalegre the road rises through woods, with views back over Portalegre. On the entire route there are ample opportunities to stop and walk and the tourist office in Portalegre has a series of pamphlets and maps that will assist you.

▶ *Go to São Mamede.*

São Mamede
São Mamede is the highest point here, rising to 1 025m/3 363ft and from the top there is a vast **panorama**★, extending south over the Alentejo, west and north over the Serra de São Mamede and east over the Spanish *sierras*.

▶ *Return to the main road and continue on to Marvão.*

Marvão★★
– ♿*See MARVÃO.*

The hilltop village is still totally enclosed by its defensive walls and makes a great place to stop for a couple of hours.

Castelo de Vide; Monte da Penha – ♿*See CASTELO DE VIDE.*

Castelo de Vide has a lovely little village square and the ruins of an old castle. Close by is the Monte da Penha, another high mountain (700m/2 297ft) with glorious views over the surrounding countryside, stony, ochre but fascinating to look at. Take the camera.

▶ *Return to Portalegre on the Carreiras corniche road★.*

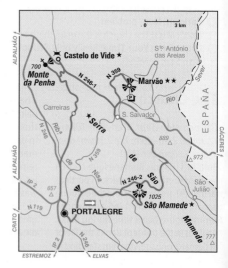

SERNANCELHE
VISEU
POPULATION 1 060 – MICHELIN MAP 733

The old town of Sernancelhe, off the beaten track about 50km/31mi northeast of Viseu, occupies a rocky height in the Beira Alta. It was once a commandery of the Order of Malta, which built the castle that now lies in ruins. It had a sizeable Jewish quarter and still has some magnificent 16 and 17C mansions, one of which is reputedly the birthplace of the Marquis de Pombal.

▶ **Orient Yourself:** The north of Portugal, well inland and just north of Viseu.
🅿 **Parking:** Near the outskirts of the village you'll find plenty of space.
🚫 **Don't Miss:** The old Jewish quarter with the houses of the "converted" marked with a cross.
🕐 **Organizing Your Time:** Worth a few hours to look around and have lunch.
♿ **Also See:** VISEU, ALMEIDA.

The Village

Church
The façade of this 13C Romanesque church flanked by a vast square belfry, is pierced by a beautiful rounded doorway in which one of the arches is adorned with an unusual frieze of archangels. The tympanum is carved with plant motifs. Two niches on either side of the door shelter six granite statues of the Evangelists Sts Peter and Paul. They are the only free-standing Romanesque statues in Portugal.

SERPA
BEJA
POPULATION 9 200 – MICHELIN MAP 733

Serpa, a market town in the Lower Alentejo east of the Guadiana river, crowns a hilltop overlooking vast plains of wheat fields interspersed with rows of olive trees. The town has kept its ramparts which partially surround the town and there are the remains of an ancient **aqueduct**, with a chain-pump at one end.

🛈 **Information:** Largo D. Jorge de Melo, 2. ☎284 544 727.
▶ **Orient Yourself:** South east of Beja in the lower Alentejo.
🅿 **Parking:** Only outside the walls, but plenty available.
🚫 **Don't Miss:** The entire village is just a lovely walk.
🕐 **Organizing Your Time:** You could spend the best part of a day here.
♿ **Also See:** BEJA.

Visit *2hr*

The fortified gate, the **Porta de Beja**, leads through the ramparts into the narrow streets of this whitewashed town. The main square, the **Praça da República**, is delightful with its palm and cypress and a couple of restaurants. The Igreja de Santa Maria has an interesting 13C altarpiece surrounded by 17C *aluzejos*. A street on the right leads to the **castle**. The entrance looks like a romantic 19C engraving with its crumbling tower which now forms a porch. The aqueduct is closed to the public but at one end you can see an interesting chain-pump. At nearby **Capela de Guadalupe** (*Follow signs to the Pousada*) you have excellent views over the surrounding countryside.

SESIMBRA
SETÚBAL

POPULATION 37 570 – MICHELIN MAP 733
LOCAL MAP SEE SERRA DA ARRÁBIDA

Sesimbra occupies a pleasant site in an inlet at the foot of the southern slope of the Serra da Arrábida. Its beach is popular with Lisbonites. Sesimbra is a centre for deep-sea fishing for swordfish. These sports provide a counterpoint to the more traditional fishing activities which remain the town's main industry.

- **Information:** Largo da Marinha. ☎212 288 540.
- ▶ **Orient Yourself:** Cross the 25 de Abril bridge from Lisbon along the A 2 and turn onto the N378 and just keep going. It's on the coast.
- P **Parking:** No major problems apart from the tiny village centre at night.
- **Don't Miss:** The old town on a warm evening with the smell of fish cooking.
- **Organizing Your Time:** Mid-afternoon is the time to arrive and stay for dinner in one of the restaurants along the seashore.
- **Also See:** Drive along the coast road to Setúbal – there are some lovely bays and a couple of restaurants on the beach.

Visit

The small fishing harbour has grown into an important seaside resort but has nonetheless preserved its atmosphere, seen best in its steep streets leading down to the sea. Along these picturesque alleyways you'll see washing hanging out to dry. The many restaurants along the shore serve grilled fish and seafood. The **beach** is alive with holidaymakers at weekends and in summer. The rest of the time it reverts to fishermen who may be seen mending their lines and nets on either side of **Fortim de Santiago** (fort). The fishing boats bring in sardines, eel, bream and shellfish every morning and evening and several boats take visitors out deep-sea fishing. The **castle**, on the crest of a bare ridge, occupies a first-class defensive position which the first King of Portugal, Afonso Henriques, captured from the Moors in 1165. From its crenellated walls surrounding the cemetery there are fine **views**★ of Sesimbra and its harbour.

Sesimbra harbour with colourfully decorated boats

Manuel Maria Barbosa du Bocage

Manuel Maria Barbosa du Bocage was born in Setúbal in 1765. A prodigy, he began writing verse as a child and at age 14 left school and decamped for Lisbon where he joined the Navy, though spent most of his time chasing girls. Postings to Brazil, Goa, India and China followed, though he deserted and took to writing satire. His return to Lisbon brought him into contact with other "radicals" and into conflict with the authorities and he spent some time incarcerated in various prisons, though often recanted to gain his liberty. Unable to make much money he lived a mainly bohemian life, though his work was, and still is, highly popular in Portugal. In 1805 he died from syphilis. A monument was erected to him in Setúbal in 1871.

Castelo São Filipe★

▶ Take Avenida Luísa Todi to the west then follow the signs to the Pousada.

The fortress overlooking the town has been partially converted into one of Portugal's most beautiful *pousadas*. It was built in 1590 on the orders of King Philip II of Spain to prevent the English from establishing themselves in Tróia. Cross a covered passage to a chapel with 18C *azulejos* attributed to Policarpo de Oliveira Bernardes which illustrate the life of St Philip. There is a wide **panorama**★ from the top of the ramparts looking out over the Sado estuary, the Troia peninsula, and on a clear day you can see as far as Lisbon. It is possible to stay at the *pousada* (www.pousadas.pt) and the restaurant is open each evening for non-residents.

Península de Tróia

▶ Cross the Sado by the ancient ferry (10min – departures every 30min, and just continue along the 4km/2.5mi from the pier, 2.5km/1.5mi along a sandy though the road off N 253-1.)

The Tróia peninsula, an immense strip of fine sand across the Sado estuary, lined with dunes and pine, was intended to be developed as a major resort but apart from a magnificent golf course nothing much happened as early developments sank in the sand. You reach the **Roman ruins at Cetóbriga**. Some of the remains of an important Roman town destroyed by the sea in the early 5C have been excavated in a pleasant site beside the Sado lagoon. They include an installation for salting fish, a sepulchral vault, the remains of a temple decorated with frescoes, and some baths.

Address Book

⌖For coin ranges, see cover flap.

WHERE TO STAY

⊖⊖ **Residencial Bocage** – *R. de São Cristóvão.* ☎*265 543 080. 34 rooms* ☲. This is a nice guest house in the old town with well furnished clean rooms. Good value.

⊖⊖ **Residencial Setúbalense** – *R. Major Afonso Pala.* ☎*265 525 790. 24 rooms* ☲. This quietly located little guest house provides a good welcome at budget rates.

⊖⊖ **Albergaria Solaris** – *Praça Marquis de Pombal*– ☎*265 541 770* ⊞ *36 rooms* ☲. This hotel has good views overlooking the square. Some rooms have balconies.

WHERE TO EAT

⊖⊖ **Solar do Lago** – *Parque das Escolas.* ☎*265 238 847.* A lovely restaurant with high ceilings and wooden tables; excellent seafood. Some outside tables.

⊖⊖ **Antoóniu's** – *R Trabalhadores do Mar.* ☎*265 523 706* . Long established and long popular, one of the best places for seafood in town.

⊖⊖⊖ **Pousada de São Filipe** – ☎*218 442 001.* One of the top restaurants in the area with views outside to match. Reservation recommended.

SILVES ★
FARO
POPULATION 10 860 – MICHELIN MAP 733
LOCAL MAP SEE ALGARVE

Of the ancient city of Xelb with its many mosques, the Moorish capital of the Algarve, the magnificence of which was said to eclipse even that of Lisbon, there remain the red sandstone walls of a castle standing above the white-walled town which rises in tiers up the hillside. Thanks to its protected position inland, in the foothills of the Serra de Monchique, Silves has managed to preserve its character with its steep, cobbled streets.

- **Information:** Rua 25 de Abril. ☎282 44 22 55.
- ▶ **Orient Yourself:** 18km/13mi inland from the coast road midway between Albufeira and Lagos.
- **Don't Miss:** The cathedral and the castle.
- **Organizing Your Time:** To see it all you need almost a full day, including time for lunch.
- **Especially for Kids:** Fabrica do Inglês
- **Also See:** ALBUFEIRA, LAGOS, PORTIMÃO.

Visit

Castle★
There is no parking by the castle. ◷Open summer: 9am–6pm; winter until 5pm. €1.50. ☎282 44 56 24.

The castle was built in the 11C though on the site of a former Roman fortress and was occupied by the Moors. Attacked by the Crusaders they agreed a truce and the gates were opened to let in the investing forces. Sadly the Crusaders did not hold to their word and slaughtered the Moors and their families.

The gardens were spectacular at the time, and moves are afoot to restore them. You can see the giant cistern from which water was fed to the town, and there are superb views from the walls.

Cathedral★
◷Open 8.30am–6.30pm.

The cathedral was built on the site of a former mosque. The 13C Gothic nave and aisles have a beautiful and striking simplicity; the chancel and transept are of the later Flamboyant Gothic style. The numerous tombs are said to include those of some of the Crusaders who helped to capture the town in 1242. Note the **Manueline door** opposite the cathedral's entrance.

Fábrica do Inglês
Rua Gregório Mascarenhas. ☎282 44 04 80. www.fabrica-do-ingles.pt.

This old factory (acquired by English investors – hence the name) has been transformed into a vast pleasure park. Games for youngsters, boutiques, cafés, several restaurants. In the summer there are evening performances including the highly-acclaimed Aquavision and street theatre.

Museu Arqueológico
◷Open Mon–Sat 9am–6pm. ◷Closed 1 Jan, 25 Dec. €1.50. ☎282 44 08 38.

The archaeological museum is housed in a modern building beside the town walls, built around a large 12C–13C cistern. The collections retrace the history of the region beginning with the Palaeolithic Age. Note the menhirs and the funerary stelae from the Iron Age. The Moorish period with its ceramics and architectural displays is particularly well presented although only in Portuguese!

Cruz de Portugal (The Portuguese Cross)
At the eastern exit of the town, N 124, the São Bartolomeu de Messines road.

On one side of this 16C Calvary is Christ crucified, on the other, a *Pietà*.

SINTRA★★★
LISBOA

POPULATION 26 400 – MICHELIN MAP 733
PLAN IN THE MICHELIN GUIDE SPAIN & PORTUGAL

Less than an hour from Lisbon, Sintra, up against the north slope of the *serra*, is a haven of peace and greenery. For six centuries the town was the favourite summer residence of the kings of Portugal. In the 19C several English Romantic poets, including Lord Byron, stayed here.

Three different areas make up the town of Sintra: the old town (Vila Velha), grouped round the royal palace, the modern town (Estefânia), and the former village of São Pedro, famous for its market of secondhand goods held on the second and fourth Sundays of each month. Sintra's popularity, particularly during weekends, is reflected in the old town's many antique and craft shops, smart boutiques, restaurants and tea-rooms where one may sample the local gastronomic speciality: delicious small tarts known as *queijadas*.

- **Information:** Praça da República. ☎219 23 11 57.
- ▶ **Orient Yourself:** 25km/15.5mi northeast of Lisbon.
- **Parking:** Difficult in the centre, especially at weekends.
- **Don't Miss:** The royal palace; the Palaces at Mafra and Queluz, as well as the Cabo da Roca, the westernmost point of mainland Europe.
- **Organizing Your Time:** Ideally a couple of days to explore the region.
- **Especially for Kids:** The toy museum (Museu do Brinquedo).

Sintra is a popular tourist town as well as housing a good sized population of its own. Reachable by train from Lisbon in about 45 minutes it makes for an ideal day out from the capital, though many people choose to stay in one of its charming hotels for a few nights. It is a UNESCO World Heritage Site.

Palácio Real★★

Open Thu–Tue 10am–5.30pm. Closed days of official ceremonies, 1 Jan, Good Fri, Easter Sun, 1 May, 29 Jul and 25 Dec. €4 (no charge Sun 10am–2pm). ☎219 10 68 40.

The palace's irregular structure is due to the additions made during different periods; the central part was erected by Dom João I at the end of the 14C and the wings by Dom Manuel I early in the 16C. Apart from the two tall conical chimneys, the paired Moorish-style *(ajimeces)* and Manueline windows are the most striking features of the exterior.

The interior is interesting for its remarkable decoration of 16C and 17C **azulejos★★**. The finest embellish the dining room or Arabic Hall (Sala dos Árabes), the chapel and the Sirens' Hall (Sala

das Sereias). The **Sala dos Brasões** (Armoury), which is square, is covered with a **ceiling★★** in the form of a dome on squinches, the dome itself consisting of coffers painted with the coats of arms of Portuguese nobles of the early 16C – the missing blazon is that of the Coelho family who conspired against Dom João II.

The **Sala das Pegas** (Magpie or Reading Room) has a ceiling painted in the 17C with magpies holding in their beaks a rose inscribed with the words: *por bem* – for good – words pronounced by Dom João I when his queen caught him about to kiss one of her ladies-in-waiting. To put an end to the gossip the king had as many magpies painted on the ceiling as there were ladies at court. Don't miss the kitchens with their chimneys rising to the sky.

Museu do Brinquedo★ (Toy Museum)

Rua Visconde de Monserrate. Open Tue–Sun 10am–6pm. Closed 1 May and 25 Dec. €3, children €1.50. ☎219 24 21 71. www.museu-do-brinquedo.pt.

Address Book

For coin ranges, see the Legend on the cover flap.

GETTING THERE

The easiest, fastest and most environmentally friendly way of getting to Sintra is by train from Lisboa-Rossio. From Sintra station there is a bus to the centre of the old town. Trains run every 10–15min and the journey takes 35min With the **Lisboa Card** the train is free.

WHERE TO STAY

⬭⬭🍴 **Pensão Residencial Sintra** – *Traversa dos Avelares. 12 219 230 738.* 🔲📇 *15 rooms* 🛏. This 19C building in the centre of town has a certain elegance. Large bathrooms and a beautiful garden.

⬭⬭🍴🍴 **Palácio de Seteais** – *R. Barbosa do Bocage 8.* ☎*219 233 200* 🔲📇 *29 rooms* 🛏. This elegant 18C palace was the site where the Convention of Sintra was signed in 1808. Nowadays the hotel, with its magnificent park, is considered one of Portugal's finest.

⬭⬭🍴🍴 **Quinta da Capela** – *On the Colares road, 4.5km/3mi from Sintra.*

☎*219 290 170. Closed mid-Oct–Feb.* 🔲📇 *7 rooms* 🛏. This former homestead in the heart of the Serra de Sintra, offers guests a level of comfort and charm in keeping with its setting. A delightful garden (with a small pool) and fine views over the surrounding area.

WHERE TO EAT

Casa de Chá Raposa – *Rua Conde Ferreira, 29.* ☎*219 244 482.* Enjoy a pot of tea in cosy surroundings, decorated with old furniture, tea sets, silverware, paintings and plants. There is also a reading area for moments of quiet contemplation. Tea is served with toast, scones and home-made jams.

Fábrica das Queijadas da Sapa – *Volta do Duche, 12.* ☎*219 230 493.* Queijadas are the traditional pastries from Sintra made with eggs, *fromage frais* and cinnamon. This particular pastry company, founded in 1786, has a small tea-room with a fine view overlooking the royal palace where these famous local delicacies can be enjoyed accompanied by a pot of tea.

This toy museum has been put together by a single collector, João Arbués Moreira, who has brought together a vast collection of toys from around the world, ranging from small, 3 000-year-old bronze figures to modern robots. The very first toy motor car, wooden horses, miniature trains, lead soldiers and typical Portuguese toys from the past are just some of the exhibits which will provide visitors with nostalgic memories of their childhood years.

Museu de Arte Moderna (Colecção Berardo)★

🕐*Open Tue–Sun 10am–6pm.* 💰*€3, free Sun 10am–2pm.* ☎*219 24 81 70.*
This museum, housed in the town's former casino near the train station, holds the valuable private collection of the benefactor, J Berardo. It features works from the second half of the 20C, and represents the avant-garde artistic trends which developed after 1945. The exhibits, which are shown on a rotating

basis, include works by Dubuffet (the oldest on display), Gilbert & George, David Hockney, Jeff Koons, Joan Mitchele, Richter, Rosenquist, Stella, Tom Wesselmann and Andy Warhol.
The museum also has a cafeteria, a bookshop and a gift shop.

Quinta da Regaleira★★

Rua Barbosa da Bocage – on the road to Steais, 800m/875yd from the village centre. 🕐*Open Jun–Sept, 10am–6pm; Mar–May and Oct–Nov 10am–4pm; Dec–Feb, 11am–3.30pm.* 🕐*Closed 1 Jan, 25 Dec.* 💰*€5.* 🔦*Guided tours (reservation essential) €10* ☎*219 10 66 50.*
On the site of a 17C quinta *(farmhouse)* just five minutes' walk from the town, Carvalho Monteiro (1848–1920), a successful businessman adopted an esoteric lifestyle and had this eclectic mix of buildings put up, notably in Gothic, Manueline or Renaissance style. You enter by a revolving stone door and

then go through a tunnel that comes out by a lake.

There are beautiful gardens here full of unexpected treasures – various styles of monument, chapels, statues (many of which have religious or mythological overtones, or refer to freemasonry). Notable are the **gruta de Leda** (grotto of Leda), the **Capela da Santíssima Trinidade** and the **tour da Realeira**.

SERRA DE SINTRA★★
LISBOA
MICHELIN MAP 733

The Serra de Sintra is a lovely natural area to the west of Sintra, with several convents, palaces, castles and parks. Rugged in parts it is very inviting for visitors and the beach resorts on the coast are very good, one being the location for the World Bodysurfing Championships. The restored Sintra Tram now runs down to the coast from Sintra, making a lovely way to travel, though you could drive.

- **Information:** Parque Natural de Sintra-Cascais, R Gago Coutinho, Sintra. ☎219 247 200.
- **Orient Yourself:** Runs to the west of Sintra as far as the coast.
- **Parking:** Parking is available at most tourist sites.
- **Don't Miss:** Moors castle; Pena Palace; Capuchin Convent; Cabo da Roca.
- **Organizing Your Time:** A day at least to include lunch at one of the beaches.
- **Especially for Kids:** Cabo da Roca; the Sintra tram makes for a great ride.
- **Also See:** PALÁCIO, CONVENTO DE MAFRA.

Driving Tours

Parque da Pena★★

Open mid-Jun–end Oct, 9am–8pm; Nov–Apr, 9.30am–6pm; May–mid Jun, 9am–7pm. Closed 1 Jan and 25 Dec. €3.50, though buy the combination tIcket to include both the palace and the gardens €6. ☎219 079 955. Minibus service in the park. €2.

South of Sintra the beautiful **Parque da Pena**★★ covers 200ha/500 acres on the granite slopes of the Serra de Sintra; the park is planted with rare species of trees, and there are several lakes and fountains. It is best visited on foot to fully appreciate its great charm, but the motorist can gently drive along the small roads which cross it, or at least go to the top of the two culminating points; the Palácio da Pena stands on one, and the Cruz Alta (High Cross) on the other.

- *Leave Sintra to the south, on the road to Pena.*

After skirting the Estalagem dos Cavaleiros, where Lord Byron planned *Childe Harold*, the road rises in a series of hairpin bends.

- *At the crossroads with the N 247-3, turn left to Pena.*

Castelo dos Mouros★

30min round trip on foot from the car park. Open 9am–8pm (6pm or 7pm at other times). €3.50. ☎219 107 970. The Moorish Castle, built in the 8C or 9C, still has a battlemented perimeter wall guarded by four towers and a ruined Romanesque chapel. From the tower, which is climbed by a series of staircases, there is a wonderful **view**★ of Sintra and its palace, the Atlantic coast and the Castelo da Pena.

- *Go through the wrought-iron gate at the entrance to the Parque da Pena and leave the car in the car park.*

Palácio Nacional da Pena★★

Open Jul–mid-Sept, Tue–Sun 10am–6.30pm; mid-Sept–Jun 30, 10am–5.30pm.

Castelo dos Mouros

⊙*Closed 1 Jan, Good Fri, Easter Sun, 1 May, 29 Jun, 25 Dec.* ⊛€6 *(no charge on Sun and holidays until 2pm).* ☎*219 10 53 40.*
The palace, perched on one of the highest peaks of the range, was built by Ferdinand (&*see box opposite*) in the middle of the 19C around a former Hieronymite monastery dating from the 16C. Its eccentric architecture evokes some of Ludwig II of Bavaria's castles – with domes, towers, ramparts and a drawbridge that was never designed to draw – although it predates them by 30 years. It is a pastiche in which several styles merge with varying degrees of success: Moorish, Gothic, Manueline, Renaissance and Baroque. A drawbridge leads through a Moorish doorway to the palace courtyard where the remains of the monastery, the Manueline cloisters and the chapel – with an alabaster altar by Nicolas Chanterene – are decorated with *azulejos*. From the terraces there are fine **views**★★ over the Atlantic coast to the Tagus. The gardens are very calming with follies and ponds.

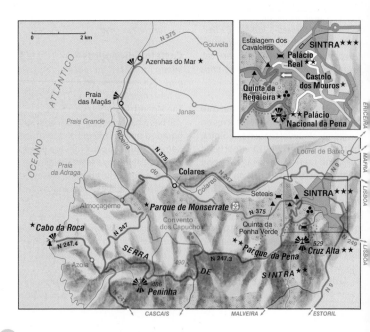

Around the Serra★
30km/18.6mi – about 3hr

▶ *Leave Sintra on the road towards Pena then turn onto the N 247-3 towards Cabo da Roca.*

After several kilometres (a few miles) a 16C **Capuchin monastery** appears amid a striking landscape of jumbled rocks. The monks' cells were cut out of the living rock and the walls lined with cork: the best insulator against cold at the time.

▶ *Head towards Peninha along the narrow road opposite the one leading to the monastery. This road passes through a landscape dotted with enormous rocks.*

Peninha
The panoramic **view**★★ from the chapel terrace includes the vast beach of Praia do Guincho in the foreground.

▶ *You can go directly to Cabo da Roca by heading towards Azóia.*

Cabo da Roca★
The Serra da Sintra ends in a sheer cliff, the Cabo da Roca or Cape Rock, nearly 140m/459ft above the sea. This cliff is mainland Europe's most westerly point.

▶ *Return to N 247: continue to Colares.*

Colares
Colares is an attractive town known for its red and white table wines.
From here continue northwards to **Azenhas do Mar**★ *(6km/3.7mi)* via the resort of **Praia das Maçãs**. The approach to Azenhas do Mar gives a good general view of the town's **setting**★, with its houses rising in tiers up a jagged cliff above the Atlantic.

▶ *From Colares return to Sintra on the N 375. This narrow road offers some superb views of the surrounding hills as it winds its way through the lush landscape.*

Parque de Monserrate★
🕐Open May–Sept, 9am–7pm; Oct–Apr, 9am–6pm. 🕐Closed 1 Jan, 1 May, 25 Dec. ⊜€3.50. ☛Guided tours 10am, 3pm (€7) booking essential. ☎219 237 300.
The landscape **park**★ surrounding the neo-Oriental palace built by Sir Francis Cook (based on the design of Brighton Pavilion, though the dome is modelled on the Duomo in Florence) in the 19C contains many different species of trees and plants including cedars, arbutus, bamboos and bracken, which stand beside pools and waterfalls.

The Artist King

Prince **Ferdinand of Saxe-Coburg-Gotha** (1816–85), nephew of the Belgian king, Léopold I, married Queen Maria II, widow of Duke Auguste of Beauharnais-Leuchtenberg, the grandson of the Empress Josephine, in 1836. Upon the birth of Crown Prince Pedro in 1837, he received the honorary title of Ferdinand II of Portugal. Intelligent and diplomatic, modern and liberal, Ferdinand was Regent of Portugal from 1853 to 1855 and was offered the Spanish throne in 1870. He was a highly cultured man, gifted with a rare artistic sensitivity, who devoted himself to etching, ceramics and watercolours. President of the Royal Academy of Science and Fine Arts and a patron of Coimbra University, he purchased the ruined monastery of Nossa Senhora da Pena in 1838 and built around it a palace which was in keeping with his philosophical tastes.

Ferdinand was also a Grand Master of the Order of the Rosy Cross and his château is rich in alchemical symbols. Here, Ferdinand and his second wife, Elisa Hensler, a singer of Swiss origin, received the greatest artists of the day. Richard Strauss said of the palace, where he stayed and which prefigured the castles of Ludwig II of Bavaria: "The gardens... are the gardens of Klingsor, and above them is the castle of the Holy Grail".

TAVIRA
FARO

POPULATION 24 317 – MICHELIN MAP 733
LOCAL MAP SEE ALGARVE

Tavira is a charming fishing town with whitewashed houses and numerous churches, pleasantly situated on an estuary of the Gilão river at the foot of a hill girded by the remains of ramparts built by King Dinis. The Roman bridge and Moorish walls testify to the town's long history.

- **Information:** Rua da Galeria. ☎281 322 51.
- ▶ **Orient Yourself:** Near the Spanish frontier in the south, 37km/23mi east of Faro.
- **Don't Miss:** The Roman bridge and the fish restaurants.
- **Organizing Your Time:** Try to spend a day here.
- **Especially for Kids:** The beach on the Ilha da Tavira.

Sights

The well-preserved centre of Tavira is attractive with its narrow streets, river banks lined with gardens, and a lively covered market. From Praça da República you can see the **Roman bridge**. The town is full of lovely old churches including the **Igreja da Misericórdia** and the **Igreja de Santa Maria do Castelo**, built over an old mosque. The choir still contains the tomb of seven knights from the Order of St James. The 17C **Igreja de São Paulo** contains seven chapels with impressive Baroque gilded wood decoration dating from the 18C. Also see the 18C Baroque-style **Igreja do Carmo** in the Largo do Carmo with its fine gilded wood altarpiece.

TOMAR
SANTARÉM

POPULATION 20 000 – MICHELIN MAP 733

Tomar stretches along the banks of the Nabão at the foot of a wooded hill crowned by a fortified castle built in 1160 by Gualdim Pais, Grand Master of the Order of the Knights Templar. Within the castle grounds stands the Convento de Cristo which is a UNESCO World Heritage Site.

- **Information:** Av. Dr Cândido Madureira. ☎249 32 24 27.
- ▶ **Orient Yourself:** Inland from Nazaré, close to Óbidos.
- **Parking:** There are several large car parks in the town centre.
- **Don't Miss:** The Convent of Christ (Convento de Christo).
- **Organizing Your Time:** Visit the convent early before the groups of tourists, then have lunch in Tomar and wander round before calling it a day.
- **Also See:** BATALHA, FÁTIMA, LEIRIA, SANTARÉM.

A Bit of History

From Knights Templar to Knights of Christ

In the early 12C, at the height of the **Reconquest**, the border between Christian and Moorish territories passed through Tomar. The Order of the Knights Templar, founded in Jerusalem in 1119, built a convent-fortress in Tomar in 1160 which became the headquarters for the Order throughout Portugal. In 1314 Pope Clement V ordered the suppression of the Templars. A new Order, the Knights

PARQUE ARQUEOLÓGICO DO VALE DO CÔA★★
GUARDA
MICHELIN MAP 733

The **Parque Arqueológico do Vale do Côa** is situated in the northeast of the country near the border with Spain. The archaeological park was created to preserve one of the world's most important open-air sites for Palaeolithic rock art alongside the Côa river, close to its confluence with the Douro.

- **Information:** The Park headquarters are in Vila Nova de Foz Côa, Avda Gago Coutinho, ☎279 768 260. You must pre-book your visit and it is a guided tour.
- **Orient Yourself:** On the Douro inland from Porto, near the Spanish border.
- **Parking:** There is ample parking at each site.
- **Don't Miss:** If you only have time for one site visit the Penascosa site.
- **Organizing Your Time:** You are limited by the guided tour which must be pre-booked– you cannot go in alone.
- **Especially for Kids:** An introduction to the wonders of archaeology and ancient art.

A Bit of History

The landscape in this area has hardly changed since the age when Cro-Magnon man made rock engravings of animals living in nature. As a result of the area's isolation, the rock art in the Côa valley has been preserved to the present day; one could even say that it has been perpetuated over the course of history with every age leaving its mark engraved in stone as travellers passed through the region.

In 1992, during the construction of a dam at Canada do Inferno, rocks with engravings from the Palaeolithic period (between 30 000 and 10 000 years ago) were discovered. Work on the dam was suspended and, to date, about 150 rocks with engravings have been found, of which 18 can be visited. Other sites containing ornamented rocks have also been discovered (some of which are under water); as a result, and because archaeological work continues, the park is in a state of continual flux as more discoveries are being made by current excavations.

Palaeolithic rock art

The Palaeolithic Age was the oldest, and longest (2.5 million years), era in the history of humanity and corresponds to the Stone Age. The oldest engravings in the Vale do Côa, identifiable by the species of animals represented, come from the Upper Palaeolithic, or Solutrean, Age and are 20 000 years old. Rock engravings can also be seen at Siega Verde in the Duero (Douro) valley in Spain, just 60km/37mi from the Vale do Côa site, although discoveries on this site date from a later era.

Engraving techniques used in the Côa valley (where paintings may have been made as well) are of three main types: **abrasion**, which consisted of creating a deep groove through the repeated use of an instrument (a fragment of stone) along a marking; **pecking**, a succession of points hammered into the rock using a stone, occasionally finished off using the abrasion technique; and **fine line incision**, which resulted in finer markings that are more difficult to distinguish. The animals most frequently represented were the horse, aurochs and mountain goat. In general, the same rock was used to depict various animals, with one drawing added on top of another. What is particularly special about art in the Côa valley is the exceptional beauty of the engravings, the representation of the shape and movement of the animals through the simple, firm lines.

Palaeolithic rock art, Penascosa

Visit

Penascosa

Visit: 1hr 40min, including 40min round trip by jeep. ⊘*Closed Mon.*

The Reception Centre at **Castelo Melhor** (♿*see GUARDA*) is located in an old schist house which is typical of the region. The jeep ride provides beautiful views of the surrounding hills planted with vines used for Port, particularly the famous Quinta da Ervamoira. Penascosa is the most accessible of the three sites and contains engravings which are the most legible in the park. These include a fish (one of only a handful of depictions of fish to be found worldwide) and some superimposed animals, the reason for which is not fully understood. It is located alongside the river, which has created a beach in this part of its course, and jeeps can park just a few metres from the rocks. The site is best visited in the afternoon, when the light is at its best for viewing the engravings. The movement of animals has been reproduced to an extraordinary degree here, particularly in a mating scene, in which a mare is mounted by a horse with three heads to interpret the downward movement of its neck. Seven rocks can be visited here at present.

The village of Penascosa has a couple of little restaurants and a very attractive ruined castle which makes it an ideal place to see and have lunch before your afternoon visit to the cave paintings.

View of Ribeira de Piscos site

😊 A Bit of Advice 😊

ACCESS

The only sensible way of getting to the Vale do Côa is by car.
From Lisbon: 387km/240.5mi via Albergaria-a-Velha, allow 5hr.
From Oporto: 214km/133mi via Mirandela, allow 3hr 30min.

ORGANISING YOUR VISIT

Visits must be reserved at least a week (more in summer) in advance by calling the **Tourism Office** for the Park: *Avenida Gago Coutinho, Foz Côa; ☎279 76 82 60/61; www.ipa.min-cultura .pt/parc.* The Reception Centre for **Castelo Melhor** is on ☎279 71 33 44. The Reception centre for **Muxagata** is on ☎279 76 42 98. Transport to the sites is by 8-seater **jeep**. *Closed Mon, 1 Jan, 1 May and 25 Dec. Admission fee: ☞€5 per visit* (children are counted as an adult in the vehicles).

Visits are led by specially trained young from the region and last two hours. The Park reserves the right to temporarily cancel visits during bad weather. Exact times for visits will be advised when reservations are made.

Two days should be allowed for those wishing to see all three sites. If you only have time to visit one site we would suggest that Penascosa is the one to choose. The park can also organise walks and mountain-bike excursions (bikes not provided) for groups of up to 15 people.

The visit to the Ribeira de Piscos site can also be arranged in conjunction with a Port tasting or lunch at the Quinta da Ervamoira (*☎279 75 93 13 or 935 26 34 90*) where there is a museum devoted to the environment of the Côa valley.

DON'T FORGET...

Suitable footwear, boots in winter, a hat in summer, a bottle of water; keep your hands free (use a backpack) to make walking easier, particularly in Canada do Inferno and Ribeira de Piscos, where the uneven terrain and slopes mean you might need both hands to cling onto something. Visitors who are sensitive to heat should avoid the summer months, when temperatures can reach 40°C (104°F). 😊The visits are not suitable for people with walking difficulties.

Ribeira de Piscos

Visit: 2hr 30min, including 1hr round trip by jeep.

The visit in itself is an extremely pleasant stroll along the river bank. The engravings, particularly fine line incisions, are dispersed over the hills and are not easily discernible. The main one is an engraving of two horses apparently "kissing" and you can also see some examples of the auroch bison, a species now extinct as well as a rare engraving of a fellow man from the Palaeolithic period. The grace and purity of the engravings are moving in their beauty. Five engraved panels are currently on display.

Canada do Inferno

Visit: 1hr 40min, including 20min round trip journey by jeep and 20min return on foot.

This was the first site to be found during construction work on the dam. Jeeps depart from the park headquarters *(sede do parque)* in Vila Nova de Foz Côa. This site is situated in the steepest part of the valley, where a canyon has formed, 130m/426ft deep, making access a little more difficult. From here the suspended work on the dam 400m/437yd downstream can be seen. The best time of day to see the engravings, the majority of which are fine line incisions, is in the morning. Although Canado do Inferno is the most interesting of the three sites, many rocks are under water, and only six are currently visible. These include engravings of several animals including horses and bison.

Near the Ribeira de Piscos site is a private site owned by the Ramos Pinto port producers, at Quinta da Ervamoira (*☎279 759 229; www.ramospinto.pt*) which has vineyard tours with port tasting. The visit often includes a look at the engravings on their land though times vary and the best place to enquire is at the tourist office in Vila Nova de Foz Côa as they will have the latest information.

VALENÇA DO MINHO ★
VIANA DO CASTELO
POPULATION 14 324 – MICHELIN MAP 733

Valença, on a hillock overlooking the south bank of the Minho, has stood guard for centuries over Portugal's northern border. The town is situated on the main highway linking Santiago de Compostela with Oporto, as well as on the northerly and westerly pilgrims' route to the shrine of St James. The road crosses the river by a metal **bridge** built by Gustave Eiffel in 1884. The old town is an unusual double city, consisting of two fortresses and a single bridge spanning a wide ditch and continuing through a long vaulted passage.

- ▪ **Information:** Avda de Espanha. ☎251 823 374.
- ▸ **Orient Yourself:** The very north of Portugal on the border with Spain.
- ⬮ **Don't Miss:** The fortified town and the Minho Valley.
- ◔ **Organizing Your Time:** Two hours or so are needed to visit.
- 🄺🄸🄳🅂 **Especially for Kids:** The town's huge gates.
- ♿ **Also See:** CAMINHA, PONTE DE LIMA.

Sight

Fortified Town (Vila Fortificada)★
Access by car from the south on a shaded road off N 13.
Each of the two fortresses in this double town, unchanged since the 17C, is in the shape of an irregular polygon with six bastions and watchtowers, in front of which are the defensive outworks and two monumental doorways. Old cannon are still in position on the battlements. From the north side of the ramparts there is a fine **view**★ over the Minho valley, Tui and the Galician mountains. Each stronghold is a self-sufficient quarter with its own churches, narrow cobbled streets, fountains, shops, and houses.

Excursions

Monte do Faro★★
7km/4mi. Leave Valença on N 101 going towards Monção; bear right towards Cerdal and shortly afterwards left to Monte do Faro.
Leave the car at the last roundabout and walk up the path to the summit 565m/1854ft which lies to the left of the road. From the summit, the **panorama**★★ is extensive: to the north and west lies the Minho valley, scattered with white houses grouped in villages, and dominated in the distance by the

Galician mountains; to the east is the Serra do Soajo and south west the wooded hills of the coastal area and the Atlantic.

Vale do Minho
From Valença to São Gregório 52km/32mi; leave Valença on N 101, to the east.
The Portuguese bank of the Minho on the east side of Valença is the most interesting. The river, which at the beginning is majestically spread out, becomes hemmed in until it is practically invisible between the steep green slopes. The road winds through trees and climbing vines which produce the well-known *vinho verde*.

Monção
This attractive little town overlooking the Minho is also a natural spa whose waters are used in the treatment of rheumatism. The **parish church**, which has preserved some of its Romanesque features, the **belvedere**★ over the Minho and surrounding countryside, and the well-known local Alvarinho wine make Monção a pleasant place to stop for a while.

3km/1.8mi south on the road towards Arcos de Valdevez, the early-19C **Palácio da Brejoeira** can be seen. Below the road vines, fields of maize and pumpkins grow on terraces facing the verdant slopes of the Spanish side, dotted with villages.

VIANA DO ALENTEJO
ÉVORA
POPULATION 5 581– MICHELIN MAP 733

This sleepy agricultural town in the vast Alentejo plain, away from the main roads, hides an interesting church behind its castle walls. The castle's ramparts have fortified walls flanked at each corner by a tower with a pepperpot roof surrounding the pentagonal edifice. The entrance porch is adorned with worn capitals decorated with animals, including tortoises and lions.

- **Information:** Câmara Municipal. ☎266 95 31 06.
- **Orient Yourself:** South of Évora by about 25km/17mi.
- **Parking:** There are no problems parking.
- **Don't Miss:** The beautiful parish church with its carved doors.
- **Organizing Your Time:** The place to stop for a coffee break while passing through.

Church

The church façade has a fine Manueline doorway: a slender twisted column serves as the supporting pier for twin arches framed by two candlestick shaped pilasters; it also supports the tympanum which is decorated with stylised flowers and the cross of the Order of Christ in a medallion surmounted by the Portuguese coat of arms: a gable formed by a twisted cable ends in a type of pinnacle flanked by two armillary spheres. The interior, which is Romanesque is outstanding for its size. The walls are decorated at their base with 17C azulejos. A particularly fine Crucifix can also be seen in the chancel.

VIANA DO CASTELO★★
VIANA DO CASTELO
POPULATION 91 238 – MICHELIN MAP 733

Viana do Castelo, lying on the north bank of the Lima estuary at the foot of the sunny hillside slope of Santa Luzia, is perhaps the nicest holiday resort on the Costa Verde. Until the 16C Viana was a humble fishermen's village but it attained prosperity when, following the Great Discoveries, its fishermen set sail to fish for cod off Newfoundland. It was during this period that the Manueline and Renaissance houses were built which today make the old town so attractive.

- **Information:** Rua do Hospital Velho. ☎258 822 620.
- **Orient Yourself:** On the coast midway between Porto (80km/50mi) and the northern border of Portugal.
- **Don't Miss:** The old quarter and the views from Santa Luzia.
- **Organizing Your Time:** A half day is plenty, unless you're here for the *Festa*.
- **Especially for Kids:** Take them to the beach at Cabadelo, south of the town.

The Old Quarter★
(Bairro Antigo)

Praça da República★

Everything in this charming town revolves around the beautiful Praça da República. Its 16C buildings, including **Casa dos Sá Sottomayores**, surrounding the vast square, make up a graceful, picturesque ensemble. There is a **Fountain** built by João Lopes the Elder in 1554, crowning its several basins

with sculptured decoration supporting an armillary sphere and a cross of the Order of Christ.

Only the façade of the former **town hall** has retained its original 16C appearance. It bristles with merlons above, has pointed arches at ground level, and on the first storey has windows crowned with the coat of arms of Dom João III, the armillary sphere or emblem of Dom Manuel I and the town's coat of arms which features a caravel, as many sailors from Viana do Castelo took part in the Great Discoveries.

Hospital da Misericórdia★

This 1589 Renaissance hospice, with Venetian and Flemish influence in its style, was designed by João Lopes the Younger. Its noble façade, to the left of the monumental doorway, rises from a massive colonnade with Ionic capitals as two tiers of loggias supported on atlantes and caryatids. The adjoining **Igreja da Misericórdia** (◐ open Mon–Fri

10am–12.30pm, 2pm–5pm) was rebuilt in 1714. It is decorated with *azulejos* by the master craftsman António de Oliveira Bernardes and gilded woodwork dating from the same period.

Parish church

The church dates from the 14C and 15C, but the two crenellated towers flanking the façade are Romanesque. The Gothic doorway has a series of three historiated archivolts which rest on statue columns of St Andrew, St Peter and the Evangelists; the outer archivolt shows Christ surrounded by cherubim holding the emblems of the Passion. In the baptistry, a carved polychrome wooden panel (17C) represents the Baptism of the Infant Jesus.

Museu Municipal★

◐Open Jun–Sept, Tue–Sun 9am–1pm; 3pm–7pm; Oct–May, Tue–Sun 10am–1pm; 3pm–6pm. ◐Closed public holidays. ✎€2. ☎258 82 03 77.

Região de Turismo do Alto Minho

Basílica de Santa Luzia with a view of the Lima estuary

The museum is housed in a former 18C palace and bears testament to Viana's rich and opulent past. The interior walls are covered with lovely **azulejos**★★ depicting distant continents, hunting and fishing scenes and receptions painted by Policarpo de Oliveira Bernardes in 1721. These *azulejos* together with some fine wooden ceilings decorate the rooms on the first floor which contain an outstanding collection of **Portuguese glazed earthenware**★ said to be the largest in Portugal.

The rooms on the ground floor, with coffered ceilings of varnished wood, contain some fine pieces of 17C Indo-

Address Book

&For coin ranges, see the Legend on the cover flap.

WHERE TO STAY

⊖⊖🗑 **Casa da Torre das Neves** – Lugar de Neves, Vile de Punhe (10km/6.2mi southeast of Viana do Castelo)⇥🅿🌫 ☎258 771 300. www.casatorredasneves.com. 5 rooms. In a 16C family mansion this comfortable hotel reflects the Minho region perfectly with its charm.

⊖⊖🗑🗑 **Estalagem Casa Melo Alvim** – Ac Conde da Carreira, ☎28 258 808 200 - www.meloalvimhouse. com🅿& 17 rooms ⌷. An old country mansion house has been converted into a beautiful hotel with contrasting and artistic styles. The rooms have every comfort and particularly beautiful bathrooms.

WHERE TO EAT

⊖⊖🗑 **Cozinha das Malheiras** – Rua Gago Coutinho, 19. ☎258 823 680. Closed Tue and Dec 22–28. This restaurant has been created inside a former chapel. The menu focuses on local dishes, as well as fish and seafood specialities.

⊖⊖🗑 **Os 3 Potes** – Beco dos Fornos (near the Praça da República). ☎258 829 928. A typical restaurant with live music and *fado* on summer Saturdays.

⊖⊖🗑🗑 **Casa d'Armas** – Largo 5 de Outubro, 30. ☎268 824 999. Closed Wed. The Casa d'Armas serves tasty, regional cuisine within the walls of an old mansion. House specialities include fish, seafood and grilled meats.

RIVER CRUISES

A river cruise is particularly good here and can be taken from the beach at Cabedelo. ☎258 842 290.

INTERNET ACCESS

The municipal library is the best place – it's free. 9.30am–12.30pm, 2pm–7pm, Sat 9.30am–12.30pm. Closed Sun.

Portuguese furniture, carved or inlaid, including a sumptuous cabinet made of ivory and tortoiseshell, ceramics, antique Portuguese, Italian and Dutch earthenware, and a small *Virgin and Child* in ivory.

Rua Cândido dos Reis

Some of the houses fronting this street have Manueline façades. Particularly noteworthy is **Palácio de Carreira** which houses the present Town Hall. Its beautiful Manueline front is strikingly symmetrical. The **Casa das Lunas**, Italian Renaissance in style, also has some Manueline features.

Monte de Santa Luzia★★

4km/2.5mi on the road from Santa Luzia.

This belvedere is on the hill of Santa Luzia, north of the town and topped by a modern basilica which has developed into a place of pilgrimage. By car the approach is via a cobbled road with a series of hairpin bends, which climbs through pines, eucalyptus and mimosas. There are plans to reopen the funicular which used to make this an easier journey but it makes for a good walk and there are places where you can picnic at the top, as well as a very nice *pousada*.

Praia do Cabedelo

The main beach for Viana is across the river, reachable by a little baot that crosses about every hour between 9am and dusk (about €1 each way) or you can take a circuitous bus ride. The beach is wide and very good, ideal for swimming and also for water sports – there are several outlets which hire out surfboards, and kitesurfs. Lessons are also available for the less experienced or those wishing to learn.

VILA DO CONDE
PORTO
POPULATION 25 731 – MICHELIN MAP 733

Vila do Conde at the mouth of the Ave, birthplace of the poet José Régio, is a seaside resort, fishing harbour and industrial centre (shipbuilding, textiles and chocolate). The town is also well known for its pillow-lace and for its festivals. The Feast of St John *(see Calendar of Events)* **is the occasion for picturesque processions by the** *mordomas* **adorned with magnificent gold jewellery and by the** *rendilheras,* **the town's lacemakers in regional costumes.**

- **Information:** Rua 25 de Abril, 103. ☎252 248 473.
- ▶ **Orient Yourself:** Just about 36km/22mi north of Porto, on the coast.
- **Don't Miss:** The lace museum.
- **Organizing Your Time:** On a normal day a couple of hours to stroll around and buy some lace; but if arriving at festival time, plan to spend longer.
- **Kids Especially for Kids:** Watch lace being made – then play on the beach!

Sights

Museu-Escola das Rendas de Bilros

Open Mon–Fri 9am–noon, 2pm–7pm, Sat–Sun 2.30pm–6pm. ☎252 643 070.
Pilllow-lace has been manufactured in Vila do Conde since the 16C. This **lace museum-school** has been created to revitalise this manual activity, which requires great skill on the part of the lace-makers who use a cylindrical cushion to produce the designs for the models. Onto these they then insert pins, between which they pass the spindles containing the threads of cotton, linen or silk. The museum provides visitors with an introduction to the different aspects of this activity through an exhibition of old and modern lace, photos, and the presence of the lace-makers.

Convento de Santa Clara★

The Convent rises above the Ave river. Behind the 18C façade are 14C buildings. Today the convent is a reformatory and only the church is open to the public. The **church**, founded in 1318 and designed as a fortress, has retained its original Gothic style. In the west face is a beautiful rose window. The interior, with a single aisle, has a coffered ceiling carved in the 18C. The Capelada Conceição *(first chapel on the left)*, built in the 16C, contains the Renaissance **tombs**★ of the founders and their children. The low-relief sculptures on the sides of the tomb of **Dom Afonso Sanches** represent scenes from the Life of Christ. The reclining figure on the tomb of **Dona Teresa Martins** is dressed in the habit of a nun of the Franciscan Tertiaries. Scenes of the Passion are depicted on the sides and St Francis receiving the stigmata is shown at the head. The children's tombs have the Doctors of the Church *(left tomb)* and the Evangelists *(right tomb)* carved upon them. A fine grille divides the nave from the nun's chancel. The arches of the 18C cloisters can still be seen to the south of the church; the fountain in the centre of the close is the terminal for the 18C aqueduct from Póvoa de Varzim.

Museu da Construão Naval

Rua do Cais da Alfândega (©open 10am–6pm Tue–Sun).

Housed in the imposing former Customs House this neat little museum details the history of the construction of ships here in Viano. It also has information on cartography, navigations and details of life on board ship during the 17 and 18C. Close by you will see the imposing white dome of the **Capela do Socorro**, where Moorish tradesmen were "converted" to Catholicism in order to keep working.

VILA FRANCA DE XIRA
LISBOA
POPULATION 23 512 – MICHELIN MAP 733

This industrial town on the west bank of the Tagus, inland from Lisbon, is known for its festivals and bullfights. The city comes alive, particularly in July, at the time of the Festival of the **Colete Encarnado**, the *campinos'* "red waistcoat" festival, with its picturesque processions of *campinos* and bulls running loose through the streets. Folk dancing, bullfights, open-air feasts and the occasional regatta on the Tagus complete the festivities.

- **Information:** Rua Almirante Cândido dos Reis 147–149. ☎263 27 60 53.
- ▶ **Orient Yourself:** Follow the Tagus (and A1) inland from Lisbon until it narrows about 35km/21.7mi northeast.
- **Don't Miss:** The belvedere at Monte.
- **Organizing Your Time:** No more than half a day will allow you to see all you need.
- **Also See:** MAFRA.

Visit

Museu Etnográfico

South side of town on Lisbon Rd (N 10). Guided tours, Tue–Sun 10am–12.30pm, 2pm–6pm. ©Closed public holidays. ☎263 27 30 57.

This small museum, housed in the bullring, displays paintings, sketches, photos and sculptures relating to the region and its traditions. Aspects covered include bullfighting, the raising and training of horses for which the town is famous, fishing on the Tagus, and a collection of 19C traditional costumes (fishermen, peasants, cattle breeders) and 18C and 19C *campinos*.

The Lusitanian horse and Portuguese equestrian art

The Lusitanian thoroughbred was already known to humans during the Upper Palaeolithic period, as shown by engravings on rocks in the Côa valley. It has been ridden for almost 5 000 years and is the world's oldest saddle horse. Its spirited, yet docile temperament, its agility, strength and courage have made this particular breed the battle horse par excellence. Since the Middle Ages in Portugal, the nobility used the Lusitanian horse during times of war, preparing it for battle by pitting it against Iberian bulls. Although the Portuguese School of Equestrian Art was created in the 18C, Portuguese riders of today still wear the same ceremonial dress and the horses the same equipment as in the past. These features combine to create an equestrian show of rare beauty, in which the rider and horse execute highly complex manoeuvres in perfect harmony, with a lightness and agility that do justice to the "son of the wind" nickname which has been given to this magnificent breed.

Miradouro de Monte Gordo

3km/1.8mi to the north on the Rua António Lucio Baptista, passing under the motorway, and then onto a surfaced road which climbs steeply.

From the belvedere between two windmills at the top of the hill there is a **panoramic view** to the west and north over the hills covered with woods, vineyards and *quintas*; to the east over the Ribatejo plain to the Ponte de Vila Franca over the Tagus; to the south over the first two islands in the river's estuary.

Excursion

Alverca do Ribatejo

8km/5mi southwest on N 1, then follow signs to the **Museu do Ar**. A hangar at the military aerodrome has been converted into an aviation museum, the **Museu do Ar** (*open Tue–Sun 10am–5pm (6pm Jul– Sept); closed 1 Jan, Easter Sun, 24, 25 Dec; €1.50 (no charge Sun 10am–12.30pm); 219 58 27 82; www.emfa.pt*).

The history of Portuguese aviation is retraced through a collection of photographs, archives and genuine old planes and replicas such as the Blériot XI, the 1908 Demoiselle XX, which was piloted by the Brazilian Santos-Dumont, and the 1920 Santa Cruz flying boat which was the first to cross the South Atlantic.

Address Book

EQUESTRIAN CENTRES

Centro Equestre da Lezíria Grande – *3km/1.8mi from the centre of Vila Franca on the N 1 towards Carregado.* 263 28 51 60. *Restaurant. Function rooms available for receptions and special events. Closed Mon.* The centre, which is situated in a rural setting, is devoted to the native Lusitanian horse. It was established by the great equestrian master Luís Valença, who taught Portuguese equestrian art to riders from around the world. The names of the centre's most famous horses are engraved on *azulejos* above their individual stables.

A high level of horsemanship is required to be taught here, although ordinary visitors to the centre can eat at the pleasant restaurant *(open lunchtime)*, from where they can enjoy the centre's special atmosphere.

Centro Equestre do Morgado Lusitano – *Quinta de Santo António de Bolonha. From the bullring, follow the N 10 towards Lisbon – 2665 Póvoa de Santa Iria –* 263 56 35 43 / 219 53 54 00 *– Function rooms available for receptions and special events – Shop selling riding equipment – Closed Mon.* This centre breeds Lusitanian horses and trains experienced riders. It also presents a magnificent show of Portuguese equestrian art using 18C traditional costumes and harnesses.

VILA REAL
VILA REAL
POPULATION 24 181 – MICHELIN MAP 733
LOCAL MAP SEE VALE DO DOURO

Vila Real is a lively small town enhanced by numerous houses dating from the 16C and 18C. It stands on a plateau among vineyards and orchards at the foot of the Serra do Marão. Fine black pottery is made in the surrounding countryside and can be bought in the town, particularly on 28–29 June at St Peter's Fair (*Feira de Sâo Pedro*).

- ▌ **Information:** Av. Carvalho Araújo 94. ☎259 322 819.
- ▶ **Orient Yourself:** 120km/74.5mi east of Porto along the A4.
- ☒ **Don't Miss:** The Manor-house at Mateus; and the train to Peso da Regúa.
- ◔ **Organizing Your Time:** A morning in the Mateus mansion and park, lunch in the town.
- ◔ **Also See:** VALE DO DOURO, AMARANTE.

Walking Tour

The main sights are to be found in the vicinity of Avenida Carvalho Araújo.

▶ *From the central crossroads by the cathedral, walk down the avenue on the right.*

Cathedral
The cathedral, a former conventual church built at the end of the Gothic period, has preserved certain of its Romanesque details, particularly noticeable in the treatment of the capitals in the nave.

Casa de Diogo Cão
At no 19 (door-plate).
So-called because, according to tradition, the well-known navigator, Diogo Cão, was born here. The façade was remodelled in the 16C in Italian Renaissance style.

Town Hall
Built early in the 19C, the town hall has a lantern pillory in front, and a remarkable monumental stone staircase with balusters in the Italian Renaissance style.

▶ *Continue along towards the cemetery which you skirt round on the right.*

Esplanada do Cemitério
This shaded walk along the cemetery esplanade, on the site of the old castle, overlooks the junction of the Corgo and Cabril rivers. In direct line with the cemetery and behind it there is a **view** looking steeply down into the Gorges of the Corgo and its tributary. Further to the left, there is an extensive view over the Corgo ravine and the houses which overhang it.

▶ *Return to Avenida Carvalho Araújo, turn right and climb upwards.*

Tourist Information Centre
At no 94. The Tourist Information Centre (*Poste de Turismo*) occupies a 16C house which has a lovely Manueline façade.

▶ *From here take the first road on the right (by the law courts) to the Igreja de São Pedro.*

Igreja de São Pedro
St Peter's Church is decorated in the chancel with 17C multicoloured *azulejos* and a fine coffered **ceiling**★ of carved and gilded wood.

Palácio de Mateus

Mateus
3.5km/2mi to the east on N 322 towards Sabrosa.

Palácio de Mateus

Chestnut trees, vines and orchards herald the approach to the village of Mateus, famous for the manor belonging to the Counts of Vila Real and the renowned rosé wine made on the estate.

Palácio de Mateus★★

🕐*Open Jun–Sept, 9am–7.30pm; Oct and Mar–May, 9am–1pm; 2pm–6pm; Nov–Feb 10am–1pm; 2pm–5pm.* 🕐*Closed 25 Dec.* ✆€*6.50 (gardens only, €3.25)* ☎*259 32 31 21.*

Dating from the first half of the 18C, this manor by Nicolau Nasoni is a perfect example of Portuguese Baroque architecture. Behind lawns planted with cedars, followed by a garden laid out with clumps of boxwood and a tree-covered walk, appears the **façade**★★ of the manor, preceded by a mirror of water. The central section of the manor is set back, and has a beautiful balustraded

stairway and a high emblazoned pediment, surrounded by allegorical statues. The main courtyard is protected by an ornamental stone balustrade. The windows upstairs are topped with moulded gables. Beautiful pinnacles top the roof cornices. To the left of the façade there is a tall elegant Baroque chapel built in 1750, also by Nasoni.

Inside the palace there are magnificent carved wooden ceilings in the main hall and the salon, a rich library, furniture from Portugal, Spane, China and 18C France, and in two rooms which have been made into a museum **copperplate engravings** by Fragonard and Baron Gerard, precious fans, liturgical objects and vestments, a 17C altar and religious sculptures, one of which is a 16C ivory crucifix.

😊If you drive, park outside the walls as it is free; inside you pay.

VILA REAL DE SANTO ANTÓNIO
FARO

POPULATION 17 956 – MICHELIN MAP 733
LOCAL MAP SEE ALGARVE

The border town was founded by the Marquis of Pombal in 1774 as a counterpoint to the Andalusian city of Ayamonte on the opposite bank of the Guadiana. The new town, which was built in five months, is a fine example of the town planning of the day with its grid plan streets and whitewashed houses with distinctive roofs. Vila Real de Santa António has become one of the largest fishing and commercial ports on the Algarve and is also a considerable fish canning centre. Yachts for export are also built here. Vila Real de Santo António is very popular with the Spanish who cross the border to buy cotton goods (table linen, sheets, towels etc.).

- **Information:** Rua Teófilo Braga. ☎281 542 100.
- **Orient Yourself:** Right on the Spanish border in the far southeast of Portugal.
- **Don't Miss:** The bustling port area, full of life and colour.
- **Organizing Your Time:** A half day is enough; have lunch and then head for the beach in the afternoon.
- **Also See:** TAVIRA.

Sight

Praça do Marquês de Pombal
This is the main square in the centre of the Pombaline quarter, surrounded by orange trees and paved with a black and white mosaics. The pedestrianised streets around the square are lined with shops selling cotton goods. There are some good restaurants.

VILA VIÇOSA ★
ÉVORA

POPULATION 9 100 – MICHELIN MAP 733

Vila Viçosa, on a hillside where orange and lemon groves abound, is a town of shade (viçosa) and bright flowers. Vale Viçosa, as this village was first called, was granted a charter in 1270 by Alfonso III under its new name, Vila Viçosa (the charter was renewed in 1512). It was at one time the seat of the Dukes of Bragança and also the residence of several kings of Portugal.

Nowadays Vila Viçosa is a quiet little town making a living from various crafts such as pottery and wrought iron as well as the marble quarries nearby. While the centre around Praça da República is fairly lively, the atmosphere in the town near the ducal palace and the old quarter is more like that of a museum-city, evoking the sumptuous past of the Bragança family.

North of the town is a huge park of 2 000ha/4 950 acres which was formerly the Bragança hunt. Just a few miles away, on 17 June 1665, the Battle of Montes Claros was fought, which confirmed Portugal's independence from Spain.

- **Information:** Praça da República. ☎268 881 101.
- **Orient Yourself:** Vila Viçosa lies east of Évora, almost on the border with Spain, and 20km/12.4mi southeast of Estremoz.
- **Don't Miss:** The old town and the Ducal Palace.
- **Organizing Your Time:** Give yourself half a day here, and have lunch too.
- **Also See:** ÉVORA, MONSARAZ, ELVAS.

A Bit of History

The Ducal Court

It was as early as the 15C that the second Duke of Bragança, Dom Fernando, chose Vila Viçosa as the residence of his court. The execution of the third duke, Dom Fernando (*see below*), however, annihilated the ducal power, and it was only in the following century that court life became really sumptuous. In the palace, built by Duke Jaime, great seignorial festivals followed one after the other, as did gargantuan banquets and theatrical performances, with bullfights in the grounds outside..

This golden age ended in 1640 when the eighth Duke of Bragança acceded to the throne of Portugal as Dom João IV.

The execution of the Duke of Bragança

On his succession to the throne in 1481, King João II instituted stern measures to abolish the privileges granted by his father, King Alfonso V, to the nobles who had taken part in the Reconquest. The first to be brought low was the Duke of Brangança, brother-in-law of the king, the richest and most powerful nobleman in the land, and a man already guilty of plotting against the monarchy. After a summary trial, the duke was executed in Évora in 1483.

Paço Ducal

H. Champollion/MICHELIN

Terreiro Do Paço★

Paço Ducal★

🕐 *Open Tue 2pm–5.30pm; Wed–Sun 10am–1pm, 2.30pm–5.30pm; (times vary in winter slightly)* 🕐 *Closed public holidays.* ⬤€5. ☎268 980 659. ☛*You can* **only** *see the Palace on a 1hr guided tour. As this is normally in Portuguese or at best broken English, unless you speak Portuguese you will miss much of the detail, but you can buy an English guide book (⬤€5).*

The **Ducal Palace** overlooks the Terreiro do Paço, in the centre of which is a bronze statue of Dom João IV. Tired of the discomfort of the old castle which dated from the time of King Dom Dinis, the fourth duke, Dom Jaime I, began the construction of the present palace in 1501.

The interior is now a museum. The well of the staircase to the first floor is adorned with wall paintings depicting the 15C Battle of Ceuta and the 16C Siege of Azamor. Much of the original furniture went to Lisbon when Dom João IV ascendedthe throne, and on to Brazil when the royal family went into exile but there are still some very good items to see, especially the toiletries and clothes of Dom Carlos and his wife Marie-Amélie – they are left out as if they were due back any minute.

A superb 16C Persian rug lies in the Dukes' Hall.

The Main wing is decorated with 17C *azulejos*, Brussels and Aubusson tapestries and Arraiolos carpets.

The rooms are embellished with finely painted ceilings representing a variety of subjects including David and Goliath, the adventures of Perseus and the Seven Virtues. There are also portraits of the Braganças by the late 19C Portuguese painters Columbano, Malhoa and Sousa Pinto, and paintings by the 18C French artist Quillard in the Sala dos Tudescos (Teutonic Hall). The west face looks over a boxwood topiary. **The Transverse wing** comprises the apartments of King Carlos I (1863–1908), who was a talented painter and draughtsman, and Queen Amelia. In the chapel there is an interesting 16C triptych, attributed to Cristóvão de Figueiredo, illustrating scenes from the Calvary. The 16C Manueline style cloisters are beautifully cool.

Museu dos Coches★ Kids

⏱*Open same hours as the Ducal Palace (see above) €1.50.*

More than 70 coaches, four-wheelers and carriages dating from the 18C to the 20C are displayed in four buildings including the **Royal Stables★**, built at the request of King José I in 1752. The stables, with room for hundreds of horses, are 70m/230ft long with a vaulted roof resting on marble pillars. Among the carriages, note number 29, the landau in which Dom Carlos I and his son were assassinated on 1 February 1908. The condition and the variety of exhibits are outstanding; there are mail coaches, charabancs, phaetons, landaus, four-wheelers and state carriages.

On leaving the museum the "Knot Gate" stands beside the Lisbon road.

Porta dos Nós★

The so-called Knot Gate is one of the last remains of the 16C perimeter wall. The House of Bragança, whose motto was *Despois vós, nós* (After you, us), chose knots as emblems on account of the two meanings of the word *nós* (us or we and knots).

▸ *Return to the Terreiro do Paço.*

Convento dos Agostinhos

The **church**, rebuilt in the 17C by the future Dom João IV, stands at the east end of the Terreiro do Paço and is now the mausoleum of the Dukes of Bragança. Bays in the chancel and the transept contain the veined white marble ducal tombs.

Antigo Convento das Chagas

The building on the south side of the Terreiro do Paço was founded by Joana de Mendonça, the second wife of Duke Dom Jaime I. The walls of the church, which serves as the mausoleum for the Duchesses of Bragança, are covered in *azulejos* dating from 1626.

Old Town

🅿*Leave the car outside the ramparts.*

The castle and ramparts built at the end of the 13C on the order of King Dinis were reinforced with bastions in the 17C. The crenellated walls flanked with towers still gird the old town. Enter through a gateway cut into the ramparts. The alleys are lined with whitewashed houses, their lower sections painted with bright colours. A narrow street leads to the western glacis on which stands the **Igreja de Nossa Senhora de Conceição**, without doubt the best of the town's 22 churches (if it is open) with a very good collection of 18C azulejos and a 16C **pillory** *(pelourinho)*. Some of the other churches are worth a brief look but only if you are passing.

Castle

🔊 *Guided tour (1hr 30min) Apr–Sept, Tue 2pm–5.30pm; Wed–Fri 10am–1pm, 2.30pm–5.30pm; Sat–Sun 9am–1pm, 2.30pm–6pm; Oct–Mar, Thu–Tue 9.30am–1pm; 2pm–5pm (Wed, from 10am).* ⏱*Closed public holidays.* €3.

The castle, which has been modified since the earliest parts were built in the 13C, is surrounded by a deep moat. The tour includes the original building's dungeons. An archaeological museum, **Museu de Caça e Arqueológico** *(Archaeology and Hunting Museum;* ⏱*same opening times as Paço Ducal;* €3; ☎*268 98 01 28)* on the first floor displays a collection of Greek vases as well as items from the sport of hunting in the nearby grounds. There are the skins and trophies that show you how many animals the Dukes and their honoured managed to shoot.

Although you pay to enter the castle you can climb its walls free of charge and from the top you have some magnificent views around and over the surrounding countryside.

Beyond the castle is the old hunting grounds (**Tapada Real**) used by the Dukes. Enclosed by an 18km/11mi circuit of walls this is a delightful place though sadly not open to visitors.

VILAMOURA
FARO
MICHELIN MAP 733
LOCAL MAP SEE ALGARVE

The resort of Vilamoura and its southeast neighbour **Quarteira** are modern tourist resorts, with Vilamoura being one of the best golf destinations on the Algarve. Quarteira's high-rise blocks line a wide avenue beside Vilamoura's holiday villages, hotels, casino, seven golf courses and a vast marina which can accommodate several hundred yachts. The ruins of a Roman city come as a surprise among all these modern constructions.

🛈 **Information:** Town Hall. ☎289 389 209 or www.vilamoura.net.

▶ **Orient Yourself:** On the Algarve coast, 23.6km/14.6mi west of Faro airport.

🅿 **Parking:** No problems other than around the marina at night-time.

👁 **Don't Miss:** The Marina at night with its lively atmosphere. Any of the golf courses, if you are a golfer.

🕐 **Organizing Your Time:** The sort of place you might want to be based in for a few days.

👁 **Also See:** FARO.

Visit
Vilamoura Golf
The prime reason for a visit to Vilamoura would be to play golf. The original town of Quarteria hardly exists nowadays, apart from a church, some Roman ruins and couple of old farms. The modern town of Vilamoura is a completely man-made resort but quite lovely with careful thought having gone into the planning. High (but not too high) rise apartments and hotels dominate the scene but the main feature in the town itself is the vast marina, lined with dozens of shops, bars and restaurants. A little pricey, perhaps, but not too much.

Yet the main reason for coming to Vilamoura is golf and there are now seven golf courses, including two recently designed by Nick Faldo and Christy O'Connor Jnr. All of the courses are magnificent, the Old Course and the Victoria (designed by Arnold Palmer and host club to the 2006 World Cup of Golf) being the best among them.

Address Book

NIGHTLIFE

Along with Albufeira, Vilamoura has some of the Algarve's liveliest night-life. The promenade along the **marina** has a huge number of bars and restaurants to get your evening underway. Another possibility is the dinner-show at the **casino** in Vilamoura *(dinner: 8.30pm; show: 10.30pm; ☎289 30 29 99)*. The **Black Jack** disco in the same building is also one of the Algarve's most popular clubs *(daily)*. If the Black Jack is too crowded, you might want to try its twin, the **Black Jack Beach Club**, just a few kilometres (couple of miles) down the road in Vale do Lobo, with its pool, three dance floors and views overlooking the ocean. The **Kadok**, on the old road between Vilamoura and Albufeira, is one of the biggest and liveliest clubs on the Algarve with three dance floors and music for all tastes (house, pop/rock and techno), seven bars and spacious outdoor areas *(closes around 6am)*. In Quinta do Lago, the same venue is home to both the **T Clube** (popular with the Portuguese jet set) and the **Trigonometria** on the first floor (for their children), both of which attract a mix of party-goers and styles.

VISEU ★
VISEU
POPULATION 98 753– MICHELIN MAP 733

The town of Viseu has developed in the region of the famous Dão vineyards in a wooded and somewhat hilly area on the south bank of the Pavia, a tributary of the Mondego. It is an important centre of agriculture (rye, maize, cattle and fruit) and crafts (lace, carpets, basket-making and black clay pottery). Its egg sweetmeats *(bolos de amor, papos de anjo, travesseiros de ovos moles, castanhas de ovos)* **are a speciality.**

- **Information:** Av. Gulbenkian. ☎232 420 950.
- ▶ **Orient Yourself:** Northeast of Coimbra; southeast of Porto, almost midway.
- **Don't Miss:** The Grão Vasco museum with its wonderful paintings; the Serra Caramulo.
- 🕐 **Organizing Your Time:** Between two and four hours will be enough.
- **Also See:** AVEIRO, COIMBRA, GUARDA.

A City of Art

Viseu School of Painting

Viseu had a flourishing school of painting in the 16C, led by two masters, Vasco Fernandes and Gaspar Vaz who, in their turn, were greatly influenced by Flemish artists such as Van Eyck and Quentin Metsys.

Gaspar Vaz, who died about 1568, developed his style at the Lisbon School. He was gifted with a brilliant imagination and could give great intensity of expression to forms and draped figures. The landscapes he painted kept their regional flavour.

His principal works, still showing considerable Gothic influence, hang in the Igreja de São João de Tarouca.

The early works of **Vasco Fernandes** (1480–c.1543), to whom legend has given the name of Grão Vasco (Great Vasco), reveal Flemish influence (altarpieces at Lamego and at Freixo de Espada-à-Cinta). His later work showed more originality, a distinct sense of the dramatic and of composition, a richness of colour and a violent realism inspired by popular and local subjects particularly in his portraits and landscapes. His principal works are in the Viseu museum.

The two masters probably collaborated in the creation of the polyptych in Viseu cathedral, which would explain its hybrid character.

Old Town ★ *(Cidade Velha)*
2hr

Old Viseu is an ancient town with narrow alleys paved with granite sets and Renaissance and classical corbelled houses emblazoned with coats of arms.

▶ *Follow the route marked on the plan starting at Praça da República.*

Praça da República (or Rossio)

Facing the town hall, this pleasant tree-planted square is the town's lively centre. From here you can climb up the Rua Soar de Cima to the Porta do Soar.

Porta do Soar

Go through this interesting, plain but impressive gateway built in the town wall by King Dom Afonso in the 15C to enter the old town which is a jumble of little alleyways and streets lined with an eclectic mix of modern boutiques and craftsmen's shops – printers, shoe-menders, key-cutters, florists, undertakers and grocers.

Adro da Sé★

The peaceful cathedral square in the heart of the old town is lined with noble granite buildings: the Museu de Grão Vasco, the cathedral and the Igreja da Misericórdia.

Museu Grão Vasco★★

⏲ *Open Tue 2pm–6pm; Wed–Sun 10am–6pm.* ⏲ *Closed 1 Jan, Good Fri, Easter Sun, 1 May and 25 Dec.*⊜ *€3 (no charge Sun until 2pm).* ☎*232 42 20 49.*

The museum is the former Palácio dos Três Escalões, which was built in the 16C and remodelled in the 18C as originally designed by Vasco Fernandes (known as The Great Vasco). The ground floor is devoted to 13C–18C sculpture. Outstanding are the 14C **Throne of Grace**★, of which only a representation of God the Father remains, and the 13C *Pietà*; some 16C Spanish-Arabic *azulejos* and Portuguese porcelain (17C and 18C) are also interesting.

On the **First floor** are several works by Portuguese painters of the 19C and early 20C. The **Second floor**, with the exception of one room which contains paintings by **Columbano** (1857–1929) including a self-portrait, the second floor is devoted to the **Primitives**★★ of the Viseu School. Particularly noteworthy is the painting of **St Peter on his Throne**, one of Vasco Fernandes's masterpieces. While it is a copy of the one in São João de Tarouca attributed to Gaspar Vaz, it shows great original-ity. Another major work by Grão Vasco is the **Calvary**, in which the figures are depicted with forceful violence. The fourteen paintings, which comprise the altarpiece which stood formerly in the cathedral, are by a group of artists from the Viseu School: the *Descent from the Cross* and the *Kiss of Judas* are among the best. In the *Adoration of the Magi*, the Black King has been replaced by an Indian from Brazil, as the country had just been discovered by Pedro Álvares Cabral in 1500. Also from the Viseu School are *The Last Supper* and *Christ in the House of Martha*.

Cathedral★

This Romanesque cathedral was considerably remodelled between the 16C and 18C. The façade was rebuilt in the 17C, the central statue among the six which ornament the façade is of São Teotónio, patron saint of Viseu.

The roof, which rests on Gothic pillars, is supported by twisted **liernes**★ which form knots at regular intervals; the keystones are decorated with the arms of the founder bishop and the royal mottos of Afonso V and João II (the latter's symbol is a pelican). The chancel is 17C; the

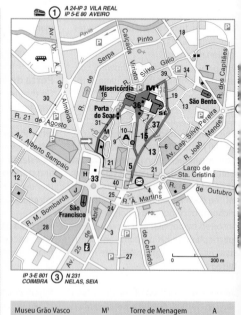

©José Luis Gutiérrez/iStockphoto.com

Cathedral

barrel vaulting shelters a monumental Baroque **altarpiece**★ of gilded wood; above the high altar is a 14C Virgin carved in Ança stone. The north chapel is decorated with *azulejos* dating from the 18C.

Stairs lead from the north transept to the gallery *(coro alto)* where there is a wooden lectern brought from Brazil in the 16C. Go to the first floor of the cloisters where the chapter-house contains a **treasury of sacred art** (◯ *open Tue–Fri 9am–noon, 2pm–5pm, Sat–Sun and public holidays 2pm–5pm; ∞ €2.50; ✆232 42 88 18 (Tesouro de Arte Sacra))* including two 13C Limoges enamel reliquary caskets, a 12C Gospel in a 14C binding and a crib by Machado de Castro.

The **cloisters** are Renaissance. The ground-level gallery, where the arches rest on Ionic columns, is decorated with 18C *azulejos*. In the Chapel of Our Lady of Mercy there is a fine 16C low relief of the Descent from the Cross which is said to be by the Coimbra School. A beautiful doorway in the transitional Gothic style leads from the cloisters back into the cathedral.

Igreja da Misericórdia

This Baroque building has an attractive rhythmic façade in contrast to its white walls and grey granite pilasters. The central section, focused beneath an elegant pediment, is pierced by a pretty Baroque doorway surmounted by a balcony.

Casas Antigas

The following old houses are worthy of note: in the **Rua Dom Duarte** a keep *(Torre de Menagem)*, embellished with a lovely Manueline window; in the picturesque narrow, bustling **Rua Direita**, 18C houses with balconies supported on wrought-iron brackets and a very good place to buy souvenirs and many more items; in the **Rua dos Andrades** (south of the Rua Direita), corbelled houses; and in the **Rua da Senhora da Piedade**, houses built in the 16C.

▸ *Take the Rua Direita before returning to Praça da Sé via Rua Escura.*

Viseu has an interesting street-market every day but a huge one on Tuesdays near Largo Castanheiro dos Amores (near the ring road). You might also want to take a look at the crafts market in **Casa da Ribeira** (◯ *open Tue–Sat 9am–12.30pm, 2pm–5.30pm).* Just a short walk from the town centre across the river and set in an old manor house, you'll often find potters at their wheels.

View on the Pico Ruivo from the Pico Arieiro, Madeira
©Vera Bogaerts/iStockphoto.com

THE MADEIRA ARCHIPELAGO

The Madeira Archipelago consists of the main island which has the greatest area (740sq km/286sq mi) and the largest population (254 880), the island of Porto Santo (42sq km/16sq mi), lying 40km/25mi to the north east, and two groups of uninhabited islands, the Ilhas Desertas or Empty Isles, 20km/12.4mi from Funchal and the Ihlas Selvagens or Wild Isles, situated near the Canaries, 240km/150mi away.

Address Book

GETTING THERE

ACCESS BY AIR

There are daily direct flights from London and from several other UK cities via Lisbon (*see Planning Your Trip for connections between the UK and Lisbon and the USA and Lisbon*) to Funchal Airport, Madeira.

WHEN TO GO

The temperature is mild throughout the year with an average of 16°C/61°F in January and 22°C/72°F in July. Rain usually falls in March, April, October and November.

To choose a hotel or restaurant in Madeira, consult the red *Michelin Guide Spain & Portugal*. Funchal has most of Madeira's hotels, although the island of Porto Santo, beautiful and calm, has some mid-range accommodation.

GETTING AROUND

MADEIRA BY CAR

Madeira has spectacular landscapes that can be explored by following the routes we have outlined for you. Taxis may be used for short distances and cars hired for longer ones. There are also many regular **bus services** *For information on bus itineraries ask at the Direcção Regional de Turismo, Avenida Arriaga, 18. 9004 519 Funchal.* ☎*291 22 90 57.*

MADEIRA ON FOOT

Madeira offers a wide choice of walks. Some paths follow the *levada* network, while others take mountain routes around Pico Ruivo (not for those with respiratory problems). The paths are rated according to difficulty. Some of the walks including Pico Ruivo, Balcões, Levada do Norte to Estreito do Lobos, and Rabaçal are described in this guide.

BEACHES

Madeira island itself has practically no beaches. The island of Porto Santo, however, has a long stretch of beach –8km/5mi of white sand, with an ideal temperature for most of the year.

SPORTS

Sports on Madeira include golf at Serra da Santo and Palheiro, and on Porto Santo, angling and deep-sea fishing. Diving, surfing, paragliding and mountain biking are also becoming increasingly popular.

MADEIRA★★★
FUNCHAL
POPULATION 254 880 – MICHELIN MAP 733 FOLD 43

Madeira rises from the Atlantic Ocean, a volcanic island mass climbing high above the ocean swell. The "pearl of the Atlantic", 900km/559mi from Lisbon, offers visitors a climate that is mild, as well as vegetation that is subtropical and transforms the island into a blossoming garden all year round. The landscape, beautiful and varied, opens out into vast panoramas.

▶ **Orient Yourself:** 900km/559mi south west of Lisbon, on the same latitude as Casablanca in Morocco.

🅿 **Parking:** Parking in Funchal can be a problem, but elsewhere in the island you will encounter no major difficulties.

🐾 **Don't Miss:** The Botanical Gardens; Funchal, or the Monte sled; Porto Santo if you have the chance – if not, go out on a cruise from Funchal.

🕓 **Organizing Your Time:** Stay a week to really enjoy Madeira; be sure to take a few day trips, including one to Porto Santo.

🧒 **Especially for Kids:** The Aquarium at the Museu Municipal, the Toy Museum and the Madeira Story in Funchal. A boat trip out to sea on the "*Santa Maria*".

A Bit of History

Discovery and colonisation
In 1419, **João Gonçalves Zarco** (1390–1467)and Tristão Vaz Teixeira, leaders of an expedition dispatched by Prince Henry the Navigator, landed first on the island of Porto Santo, and later on Madeira itself. The island appeared to be uninhabited and entirely covered in woodland and they therefore named it the wooded island, *a ilha da madeira*.

Aerial view of Funchal

Marcial Fernandes/DRT Madeira

The navigators reported their discovery to Prince Henry, who commanded them to return the following year. He also divided the territory into three *captaincies*: Zarco received the land centred on Funchal and extending south of an imaginary line drawn from Ponta do Oliveira to Ponta do Tristão; Tristão Vaz Teixeira received Machico and all the rest of the island, and **Bartolomeu Perestrelo** the island of Porto Santo. The islands are volcanic having been thrust up from the Atlantic during a period of volcanic eruption in the Tertiary Era, and climb to over 1 200m/3 937ft culminating in high peaks such as Pico Ruivo (1 862m/6 109ft).

Madeira, which is almost at the same latitude as Casablanca, enjoys a temperate climate. Mild with no extremes, the average temperature only varies from 16°C/61°F to 24°C/75°F from winter to summer. The rainy season is short though in the mountains mist and some drizzle are possible on many days, even in summer.

Flowers

The entire island of Madeira is a mass of flowers; every hillside, every garden and roadside verge is covered with hydrangeas, geraniums, hibiscus, agapanthus, bougainvilleas, fuchsias and euphorbias. Certain species such as orchids, anthuriums and strelitzias (or Birds of Paradise) are grown in large quantities for export. There are also several species of flowering trees – mimosas, magnolias, sumaumás and jacarandas. Bananas are the island's major export crop.

Madeira wine

Vines were introduced to Madeira in the 15C from Crete and planted in the rich and sunny volcanic soil along the south coast. In 1660 a commercial treaty between England and Portugal encouraged the export of the wine and increased production. Overseas buyers, for the most part English (Blandy, Leacock and Cossart Gordon), were drawn to Madeira by the prosperous trade, which reached its height in the 18C and 19C.

There are three principal wines. **Sercial**, made from grapes whose vines originally came from the Rhine valley, is a dry wine with a good bouquet; it is amber in colour and is served chilled and drunk as an aperitif. **Boal** originates from Burgundy; the rich, full-bodied flavour of this red-brown wine makes it primarily a dessert wine. **Malmsey**, the most famous, is rare today; again a dessert wine, honeyed in flavour with a deep-red, almost purple colour. A medium sweet all-purpose wine, **Verdelho**, a Muscatel and *Tinto* or red wine are also produced.

At one time, barrels of Madeira were used as ballast in ships making the long journey to India or America; the trip there and back gave the wine ample time to heat.

Florist in Funchal

Vintage Madeira made from the best wines in exceptionally good years may be consumed up to and over 150 years later.

Madeira embroidery

Embroidery is one of the mainstays of the island's economy. Madeira embroidery owes its origin to an Englishwoman. In 1856 **Miss Phelps**, the daughter of a wine importer, started a workroom where women embroidered designs after the manner of *broderie anglaise*. The work was sold for charity. Samples of the embroidery reached London and were received with such enthusiasm that Miss Phelps decided to sell the work abroad. In less than a century, embroidery became one of Madeira's major resources; today 30 000 women are employed. The embroidery on linen, lawn or organdie is very fine and varied in design.

Funchal★★

🄸*Av. Arriaga 18. ☎291 21 19 02.*
The island's capital rises in tiers up the slopes of a natural amphitheatre around the bay. When the early settlers arrived they found the heights covered in wild fennel, hence the name Funchal. The luxuriant vegetation, the *quintas*, hotels, shopping, night-life and sports facilities combine to form a popular city resort, attracting visitors from many countries year round. The harbour faces central Funchal. East of this stretch the lively alleyways of the old town, bustling with locals in the mornings and early evenings.

In February each year Funchal comes alive with its fantastic **Carnaval**, a lively procession of brightly-coloured dancers and musicians who parade through the streets on a Sunday evening. Not quite as spectacular as Rio de Janeiro's in Brazil, but great fun. Also well worth seeing is the Flower Festival each April when the entire town is covered in the rich aroma of fresh flowers. A flower-bedecked Wall of Hope is decorated by children.

Walking Tour

The Centre
Follow the itinerary on the town plan.

Avenida das Comunidades Madeirenses or Avenida do Mar

This wide promenade bordered with flowers runs parallel to the marina. Along the quayside are restaurants and cafés, all very popular especially on warm evenings. There is a fine **view**★ of the town from the end of the jetty.

Avenida Arriaga

This is Funchal's main street. The jacaranda trees along it are covered in purple flowers throughout the spring. The **Jardim Público de São Francisco** is an interesting botanical garden with a wide variety of plants. Between the garden and the tourist information centre (Turismo) are the **Blandy Wine Cellars**★ (☛*guided tours (1hr 30min including wine-tasting), Mon–Sat 10.30am–3.30pm (from 11am Sat); ⊙closed public holidays; ☞€4.20).* They are housed in a former 16C Franciscan monastery. Opposite the cellars is **Forte de São Lourenço**, which still serves as residence to the Commandant of Madeira.

Cathedral (Sé)★

Enter by the main altar or at the back of the church. ⊙Open Mon–Fri 10am–noon, 1pm–5pm; Sat 10am–noon. ⊙Closed for visits Sun and public holidays. ☎291 22 81 55.
The first Portuguese cathedral to be constructed out of the mainland dating from 1514. The apse, decorated with openwork balustrades and twisted pinnacles, is flanked by a crenellated square belfry, the roof of which is tiled with *azulejos*. In the nave, slender columns support arcades of painted lava rock while above, and also over the transept, extends a remarkable *artesonado* **ceiling**★ in which ivory inlays in the cedar have been used to emphasise the stylistic motifs. The floor is made of wood.

Praça do Município

The square is bordered to the south by the former episcopal palace, now the Museu de Arte Sacra (Sacred Art

Praça do Município

Museum – *see below*) and to the east by the town hall.

Town Hall

The town hall, formerly the 18C palace of Count Carvalhal, is surmounted by a tower that dominates the area. The inner courtyard is decorated with *azulejos*. There is also a small museum inside the town hall with items relating the history of Funchal.

Museu de Arte Sacra

Open Tue–Sat, 10am–12.30pm, 2.30pm–6pm; Sun 10am–1pm. Closed public holidays. €3. 291 22 89 00. www.museuartesacrafunchal.org.
In the 15C and 16C much of the Madeiran economy was based on the production and export of sugar, much of it to the Netherlands. Some of the profits were used to commission and purchase Flemish art and most of this is now in the Museum of Sacred Art, housed in the former episcopal palace. It contains fine religious items and liturgical ornaments but its main interest lies in a collection of **paintings**★ on wood from the 15C and 16C Portuguese and Flemish Schools. From the Portuguese School, see particularly the triptych depicting *St James and St Philip*. From the Flemish School are a *Descent from the Cross*

attributed to Gérard David; a full-length portrait of *St James the Less*; a triptych attributed to Quentin Metys of *St Peter*; an *Annunciation*, a portrait of *Bishop St Nicholas*, a *Meeting between St Anne and St Joachim*, a *Crucifixion*, and an *Adoration of the Magi*.

Igreja do Colégio

Open Mon–Fri 3pm–6pm, Sat 4pm–6pm, Sun 9am–1pm, 6pm–9pm. 291 723 35 34.
The Jesuit Church of St John the Evangelist was built early in the 17C, extended and changed over the years and has just undergone a major renovation (which lasted 70 years). The austere white façade has also been hollowed out to form four statuary niches. These contain marble figures on the upper level of St Ignatius and St Francis Xavier, and on the lower of St Francis Borgia and St Stanislas. Carved birds, vines, barley-twist columns and *azulejos* make for a fascinating sight. Well worth a visit.

Museu Municipal　Kids

Open Tue–Fri 10am–6pm; Sat–Sun and holidays, noon–6pm. Closed 1 Jan, Easter Sun and 25 Dec. €3 (no charge Sun). 291 22 97 61.
The former mansion of Count Carvalhal now houses an aquarium and a natural

history museum. The aquarium contains various sea creatures from the waters around Madeira, including red scorpion fish, mantis shrimps and morays. Among many stuffed and mounted animals are sharks, horned rays and white-bellied seals.

Museu Frederico de Freitas★

◷ *Open 10am–12.30pm, 2pm–6pm.* ◷*Closed Sun afternoon, Mon and holidays.* ◉€2.50 *(no charge Sun).* ☏*291 22 05 78.*

The former mansion of Dr Frederico de Freitas contains engravings, drawings and water-colours illustrating Madeira through the centuries. The more intimate first floor shows the interior of a 19C middle-class home. Its English furniture has been preserved as have its 'sugar chest' cupboards, musical instruments and cabinets adorned with ivory and whalebone.

Convento de Santa Clara

 Guided tours (20min), Mon–Sat 10am–noon, 3pm–5pm. ◷*Closed public holidays.* ◉€2. ☏*291 74 26 02.*

The convent was built in the 17C on the site of a church founded in the 15C by Zarco. His Gothic tomb, supported by lions, is at the far end, and his two granddaughters who founded the original convent of the Order of St Clare are buried here. The Sisters still in residence

Reid's Palace Hotel

The most famous hotel on Madeira, Reid's Palace has about the best location on the island, on a promontory jutting out overlooking the bay. It is a beautiful place easily identifiable by its red-ochre roofs and whitewashed walls.

Non-residents can enjoy the tradition of afternoon tea on the terrace overlooking the sea (€26). Winston Churchill wrote much of his war memoirs here and also painted. Bernard Shaw learnt to tango in its ballroom.

are always happy to show you round. Take a look at the stunning gardens.

Quinta das Cruzes★★

◷*Open Tue–Sat 10am–12.30pm, 2pm–5.30pm; Sun, 10am–1pm.* ◷ *Closed public holidays.* ◉€2.50. ☏*291 74 13 82/84/88.*

Zarco's former mansion has been converted into a museum of decorative arts (Museu de Artes Decorativas). The ground floor contains 16C Portuguese furniture. There are many 17C cabinets and chests known as *caixa de açucar* or sugar chests made with wood taken from boxes in which Brazilian sugar was transported. At the back of one room

Mercado dos Lavradores

DRT Madeira

stands a 15C Flemish altarpiece of the Nativity. The rooms on the first floor contain a rich collection of 18C and 19C English furniture in the Hepplewhite and Chippendale style.

Additional Sights

Mercado dos Lavradores

The town's main market, which is now housed in a modern building, is particularly lively in the morning when you can buy (or just look at) all types of fresh fish, fruit and vegetables. At the entrance are the flower sellers who stay all day.

Vila Velha (Old Town)

This is the site where the original town was founded in the 15C. Today, the narrow streets are a multitude of boutiques, taverns, bars and restaurants. It has a wonderful atmosphere, especially in the early evenings when everyone seems to be out on the streets.

Madeira Story Centre

Rua D Carlos 1. 27/29. ○*Open 9am–8pm.* *€9; children €4.50.* *291 00 07 70;* *www.storycentre.com.*
Located in the old part of Funchal, near the cable cars that go from Funchal to Monte. The centre gives an overview of 14 million years of the history of Madeira in a visit lasting 1½ hours.
There are recreations of Madeira's history, exhibits of authentic historical

objects and an interactive, multimedia experience. Volcanic Origins, the Discovery of Madeira, Turmoil and Trade, The Development of Madeira, and Explore Madeira.

Forte de São Tiago

○ *Open Mon–Fri 10am–12.30pm,* *2pm–5.30pm.* *Guided tour (30min).* *€2.50,* *291 21 33 40.*
The fort was built in 1614. Its yellow walls rise above the shore where fishing boats lie moored beside small blue and white striped huts. It also houses the exciting **Museum of Contemporary Art** with a rich collection of European art from the 60s, 70s and 80s.

Núcleo Museológico A Cidade do Açucar – Sugar Museum

Praca Colombo, ○*Open Mon–Fri 10am–* *12.30pm, 2pm–6pm.* ○ *Closed public* *holidays.* *€2.* *291 236 910.*
Sugar was an important commodity in 16C and 17C Madeira. This interesting museum traces the history of that trade with maps and items from the sugar fields and traders.

Toy Museum

Rua da Levada dos Barreiros, 48. ○*Open* *Tue–Sat 10am–8pm, Sun 10am–2pm.* *291 922 2722.* *€4.*
This museum houses José Manuel Borges Pereira's collection of old toys together with some contributions from other private collections.

Botanical Garden with a view of Funchal harbour

Instituto do Bordado

🕒*Open Mon–Fri 10am–12.30pm, 2pm–5.30pm.* 🕒*Closed public holidays.*≈€2. ☎291 22 31 41.

Several rooms in the embroidery institute have been converted into a museum where magnificent examples of Madeiran workmanship are displayed.

Western Funchal

Jardins do Casino

Funchal casino was built in 1979 by the Brazilian architect Óscar Niemeyer, and stands in a park of beautiful exotic trees.

Botanical Gardens★

🕒*Open 9am–6pm.* 🕒*Closed 25 Dec.* ≈€3. ☎291 21 12 00. *Accesible by bus, no. 29, 30 or 31.*

Many outstanding examples of Madeiran flora can be viewed. The elegant white house with green shutters contains a small museum showing botanical, geological and zoological collections; note the vulcanised wood.

There is a fine **view**★ of Funchal harbour.

Excursions

Quinta da Palmeira

Take Rua da Carne Azeda north. Bear left on Rua da Levada de Santa Luzia. The Quinta entrance is just before a left bend; its name is in white shingle inlaid in the roadway. Although it is private property, visitors may walk in the gardens Leave the car near the entrance gate.

The terraces of this well-kept park overlook Funchal. There are fine *azulejo* benches and a Gothic stone window which, it is claimed, was formerly in the house in which Christopher Columbus stayed when he lived in Funchal.

Quinta do Palheiro Ferreiro★★

Leave Funchal on Rua Dr Manuel Pestana towards the airport. Take the first road towards Camacha. After several bends, turn right on a narrow cobbled road signposted Quinta do Palheiro Ferreiro. 🕒*Open Mon–Fri 9am–4.30pm.* 🕒*Closed 25 Dec.* ≈€9. ☎291 79 30 40.

The vast mansion is set in a well-maintained **park** approached by paths lined with camellias. Over 3 000 plant species include exotic trees and rare flowers. There is also a golf course here.

Monte★

7km/4.3mi. About 1hr.

Monte, at an altitude of 600m/1 970ft, is an area developed as an escape from the heat and bustle of Funchal for its well-off traders. The Quinta do Monte, which lies below the former Belmonte Hotel, became the house of the last Emperor of Austria when he was exiled to the island in 1921. Karl I died in the house the following year. You can reach Monte by cable-car from the old town of Funchal *(10min trip;* 🕒*open 9am–6pm* 🕒*closed 25 Dec;* ≈€10 *one-way;* €14.50 *round trip, children* €5; €7.25). The Palace (with a permanent exhibition of 1950s and 60s Zimbabwean sculpture) and Tropical Gardens are well worth seeing if you adore beautiful flowers and plants. 🕒*Open 9.30am–6pm* ≈€10. ☎291 74 26 50; www.montepalace.com.

For your return journey to Funchal try the "**Monte sled**" *(*≈€12*)*– a huge wicker basket on runners steered by two drivers in traditional dress and boaters. It's fun but bumpy.

Igreja de Nossa Senhora do Monte

The church was built on the site of a chapel erected in 1470 by Adam Gonçalves Ferreira. He and his twin sister Eva were the first children to be born on the island. The Baroque façade is highly decorative. In a chapel to the left is the iron tomb of Karl I of Austria. A tabernacle worked in silver above the high altar shelters a small cloaked statue of Our Lady of the Mountain, the patron saint of Madeira. The figure, discovered in the 15C at Terreiro da Luta at the spot where the Virgin appeared to a young shepherdess, is the goal of a popular pilgrimage held on 14 and 15 August each year.

▶ *Walk down Largo dos Barbosas to the left of the staircase.*

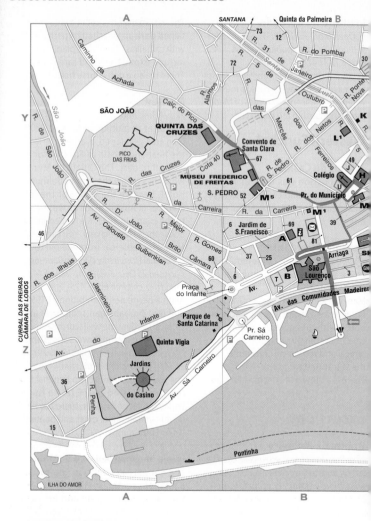

The Lovers of Machico

There is a legend that in 1346 an English ship sank in a tempest at the mouth of the river. Robert Machim and Ana d'Arfet, who had fled from Bristol to get married in spite of their parents' opposition, survived the shipwreck but died a few days later. Their companions took to sea again on a raft, were captured by Arab pirates and taken to Morocco. The story of their adventure was told by a Castilian to the King of Portugal who decided to equip an expedition to find the island. When Zarco landed at Machico he found the lovers' tomb at the base of a cedar tree and named the village after the young Englishman, Machim.

Santa Cruz

Santa Cruz, a fishing village, possesses several Manueline monuments. The **Igreja São Salvador**★ borders the main square. Built in 1533 it is the oldest on the island. The interior, divided into three aisles, is covered with a painted ceiling. The chancel contains a metal memorial plaque to João de Freitas. The tomb of the Spínolas is in the north aisle. The former **Domus Municipalis**, with beautiful Manueline windows, stands on the other side of the square. The small street on the east side of the square leads to the present **town hall** *(Câmara Municipal)*, a fine 16C building.

Miradouro Francisco Álvares Nóbrega★

A road to the left leads to this belvedere named after a Portuguese poet, known also as the Lesser Camões (1772–1806), who sang Madeira's praises. From the belvedere there is a view of Machico and the Ponta de São Lourenço.

Machico

The town of Machico, situated at the mouth of the Ribeira de Machico valley, is divided by a river: the fishermen's quarter, the Banda d'Além, lies on the east side, the old town on the west. It was at Machico that Zarco and his companions landed.

Parish church

The 15C Manueline parish church stands in a square shaded by plane trees. The façade is pierced by a lovely rose window and a doorway adorned with capitals carved with the heads of animals. The side doorway, a gift from King Manuel I, consists of paired arches supported on white marble columns. A Manueline arch in the north wall leads to the Capela de São João Baptista.

Capela dos Milagres

As ruler, Tristão Vaz Teixeira had a chapel constructed in 1420 on the east bank of the river. This Chapel of Miracles was

Machico

destroyed by floods in 1803. The original Manueline doorway was reinstalled when it was rebuilt.

▶ *Take the Caniçal road.*

There are views, as the road rises, of the valley of Machico dominated by mountain summits. The road leaves the valley through a tunnel under Monte Facho.

Caniçal
After whaling was banned in 1981, Caniçal stagnated for a few years before regaining its status as a major port, this time for tunny fishing which has become an important activity as the port facilities and canning factory testify.

▶ *Continue to Ponta de São Lourenço.*

Ponta de São Lourenço★
The headland of red, black and ochre-coloured volcanic rocks stretches far out into the sea and is the only place on the island with a sand beach, **Praínha**. This lies sheltered at the foot of a hillock upon which stands the hermitage of **Nossa Senhora da Piedade**. The road continues to a parking area near Abra bay. A footpath leads to a viewpoint overlooking some extraordinary rocks. There are impressive **views★★** from here of the sheer cliffs on the island's northern coast, in particular from the **Miradouro Ponta do Resto** viewpoint *(narrow road to the left before the chapel)*.

▶ *Return to Machico and take the road to Portela.*

As you climb, the banana and cane sugar plantations of the valley floor give way to pine and eucalyptus trees.

Boca da Portela
At the Portela Pass (alt 662m/2 172ft) crossroads, go up to look at the view from the belvedere overlooking the green Machico valley.

Santo da Serra
Santo da Serra, built on a forest-covered plateau (pines and eucalyptus) at an altitude of 800m/2 500ft, has become

popular with the residents of Funchal as a country resort with a cool climate in a restful setting. From the main square by the church, go into the Quinta da Junta park. At the end of the main drive lined with azaleas, magnolias and camellias, a belvedere provides a view of the Machico valley; in the distance can be seen the Ponta de São Lourenço and in clear weather, Porto Santo.

Camacha
Camacha is a village in the woods at 700m/2 296ft. It is famous for its basketwork and for its group of folk dancers and musicians. The dances are accompanied by chords from a *braguinha*, a four string guitar, while the rhythm is accentuated by an amusing looking stick caparisoned with a pyramid of dolls and castanets, known as a *brinquinho*.

▶ *Follow the signs back to Funchal.*

Driving Tour of the Island★★

Itineraries 2 , 3 *and* 4 *on the Island map. Starting from Funchal – 220km/137mi. Allow two days.*

The following tour of the island covers Madeira's main sights. It can be done in a day but if you wish to go on some of the walks we suggest you allow at least two days with a stopover in Santana.

2 From Funchal to Santana via Pico do Arieiro

This section of the itinerary describes the journey north from Funchal up to the island's highest peaks and then the descent to the north coast.

▶ *Leave Funchal by Rua do Til.*

Beyond Terreiro da Luta the road, lined with flowering hedges, rises in hairpin bends through pine and acacia wood becoming more barren.

Marcial Fernandes/DRT Madeira

Walking trail on the Pico do Arieiro

▶ *At the Poiso Pass (Boca do Poiso), take the road on the left to the Pico Aceiro.*

The road follows the crest of the mountains with good views of both Funchal, and the southern and northern coasts. The road ends near the Pousada do Pico do Arieiro.

Miradouro do Pico do Arieiro★★

There is a magnificent view from the Arieiro belvedere on the very summit of the mountain at 1 818m/5 965ft. The landmarks include the Curral das Freiras crater, the distinctive outline of the crest of the Pico das Torrinhas (turrets) and, standing one before the other, the Pico das Torres and Pico Ruivo. To the north east are the Ribeira da Metade, the Penha d'Águia (Eagle's Rock) and the Ponta de São Lourenço.

▶ *A path has been constructed from Pico do Arieiro to Pico Ruivo.*

Miradouro do Juncal★

A path goes round the summit of Pico do Juncal – 1 800m/5906ft – to the belvedere *(15min round trip on foot)* from which there is an attractive view along the full length of the Ribeira da Metade valley to the sea below Faial.

▶ *Return to Poiso and take the road on the left going to Faial. The road descends in a series of hairpin bends through pines and tree laurels.*

Ribeiro Frio★

Near a little bridge over the Ribeiro Frio (meaning cold river) stands a restaurant, settled in a pleasant site amid the greenery at an altitude of 860m/2 822ft.

The **Levada do Furado**, which irrigates these slopes as far as Porto da Cruz and Machico, passes through Ribeiro Frio. It is possible to walk along it eastwards to the Portela Pass *(3hr 30min)* or westwards as far as Balcões.

Balcões★★

40min round trip on foot. Take the path to the left of the bend below Ribeiro Frio.

The path runs alongside the Levada do Furado through passages hewn out of the basalt rock to the Balcões belvedere. The view extends from the upper valley, which begins among jagged peaks (Pico do Arieiro, Pico das Torres and Pico Ruivo), to the open valley with its richly cultivated slopes which runs down to the coast.

▶ *Return to the road and head for Faial.*

Continuing along the valley you will come to **São Roque do Faial**, a village perched on a long crest between two

Triangular house in Santana

B. Brillion/MICHELIN

valleys. The houses with roofs covered in vines are surrounded by small, terraced gardens, willow plantations and orchards scattered with straw-thatched byres *(palheiros)*.

▶ *Turn right towards Portela.*

From the bridge over the Ribeira de São Roque there is an attractive view of the Faial valley and the village perched on the clifftop. Bananas, sugar cane and vines are grown on the sunny slopes.

▶ *Head for Porto da Cruz.*

A belvedere built on the left of the road has one of the island's most interesting **views**★★, that of Porto da Cruz, a village nestled at the foot of a cliff.

▶ *At Porto da Cruz turn round and make for Faial.*

4km/2.5mi from Faial, two belvederes on the right provide an overall **view**★ of Faial, the Penha d'Águia, the village of São Roque at the confluence of the Metade and São Roque valleys and, on the horizon, the Ponta de São Lourenço.

Santana★

Santana, situated on a coastal plateau at an altitude of 436m/1 430ft, is one of the prettiest villages on the island.

Parque das Queimadas

Bear left off the main road onto Caminho das Queimadas.

The road leads to some thatched cottages, at 883m/2 897ft. In a peaceful **setting**★ at the foot of the Pico Ruivo slopes is a beautiful park where the trees stand reflected in a small pool. Some rather difficult paths, which are not advisable in the wet, lead off from here to Pico Ruivo and the Caldeirão Verde crater *(1hr 30min walk)*.

Pico das Pedras and Achada do Teixeira

10km/6.2mi.

The road from Santana runs to Pico das Pedras and then continues to Achada do Teixeira. A path leads from here to Pico Ruivo. A short distance along the path there is a fine **view**★★ of the Pico Ruivo massif. From the viewpoint near the car park you can see Faial and, in the foreground, a basalt formation known as **Homem em Pé** (the Man Standing).

③ From Santana to Santa 70km/44mi

As you leave Santana there is a splendid panorama to your left of the mountains. The road, lined with hydrangeas, arum and cana lilies, crosses coastal valleys where a variety of crops are grown.

São Jorge

São Jorge's 17C **church** is unusually rich in its Baroque ornament, recalling the sumptuous period of King João V. The decoration includes a ceiling painted in false relief, *azulejos*, a gilded wooden altarpiece, paintings, twisted columns and, in the sacristy, an elegant vestment cupboard. Before beginning the descent to **Arco de São Jorge**, a belvedere to the right of the road affords a wide **vista**★ of the coast as it curves to form São Vicente bay. Many vines grow on trellises on the more sheltered slopes, for this is a region which produces Sercial wine.

Boa Ventura

This small village lies among vineyards in a pretty setting on a hill dividing two valleys. About 3km/1.8mi on there is a beautiful **view**★ to the right over the

Driving Tours

See São Miguel map.

1 Sete Cidades and the West of the Island★★★

80km/50mi – allow half a day.

▶ *Take the airport road from Ponta Delgada and then the fork marked Sete Cidades.*

Pico do Carvão★

A lookout point at this spot dominates a large area of the island affording views of the centre, the northern coast and Ponta Delgada. The road runs past a moss-covered aqueduct and then some small lakes, including **Lagoa do Canário**, which is surrounded by botanical gardens.

Sete Cidades★★★

Sete Cidades, the natural wonder of the Azores, is a volcanic crater with a circumference of 12km/7.4mi. It is best seen from the **Vista do Rei★★★** belvedere to the south. The view takes in the twin lakes, one green, the other blue, and the village of Sete Cidades at the bottom of the crater. The caldeira is believed to have been formed in 1440 when an eruption completely changed the lie of the land in this part of the island.

▶ *A road (marked Cumeeiras) leads from Vista do Rei along the edge of the crater (allow 2hr to walk). There are views of both sides of the crater, inside and out. The road crosses another one leading down to Sete Cidades. Beyond that are the lakes.*

The road runs across a bridge built between the two lakes. On the other side of the bridge a path to the left leads to a picnic area beside the blue lake, Lagoa Azul.

Miradouro da Vista do Rei★★★

The King's lookout might be the best translation of this and when you stand here, on the side of the southern (green) lake and look at the surrounding sea,

land and sky, you'll understand why. A view fit for a king, indeed.

The route back to Ponta Delgada depends upon the amount of time you have:

⟲ If you have about 1hr, take the road round **Lagoa de Santiago**, and back up to Vista do Rei, then the road which begins near Monte Palace. This descends between banks of glorious flowering hydrangeas to join the road to Ponta Delgada.

⟲ If you have at least 3hr, head north west to **Miradouro do Escalvado★** on the coast which has a fine view of the village of Mosteiros and its rocks, then continue along a winding road to Capelas where you head south to Ponta Delgada via Fajã de Cima.

Centre of the Island★★

2 From Ponta Delgada to Furnas

71km/44mi – 4hr

▶ *Take the Lagoa road east of Ponta Delgada. Beyond Lagoa head north towards Remédios and Pico Barrosa.*

Lagoa do Fogo★★

An eruption in the 16C formed a crater lake that was given the name Fire Lake. Today this is a peaceful, beautiful spot with the clear water of the lake covering the crater floor. A white sand beach (an ideal place for a picnic) borders the lake on one side, a sheer cliff face on the other.

▶ *The road continues uphill towards Ribeira Grande.*

Ribeira Grande

Ribeira Grande, the second-largest town on the island, is an ideal place to stop for lunch with several good, inexpensive restaurants, and has some fine 16C–18C mansions, including **Solar de São Vicente**, which houses the arts centre.

The vast garden square in the middle of town, alongside which flows the Ribeira Grande, is surrounded by interesting buildings including the 16C **Town Hall** with its double staircase and square tower, and the **Igreja do Espírito Santo** with its elaborate Baroque façade. The church is also known as the Dos Passos Church as it contains the statue of Christ (Senhor dos Passos) which is carried in traditional processions on Saints' Days and at the great church festivals throughout the year.

The large 18C **Igreja de Nossa Senhora da Estrela** stands at the top of a wide flight of steps. Inside, the walls and ceilings are painted and, as elsewhere on the island, the gilt altarpieces are richly decorated.

▶ *Head south from Ribeira Grande following signs to Caldeiras.*

Caldeiras

This is an active volcanic area heralded by a group of small fumaroles. There is a natural spa centre and some springs that produce a well-known mineral water that is bottled and sold throughout Portugal.

▶ *Return to the coast road and head east.*

The coast is a series of capes and bays within which nestle small beaches like that of **Porto Formoso**.

▶ *Take the Furnas road.*

Miradouro de Pico do Ferro★★

The view stretches across the whole Furnas valley, taking in the village, Terra Nostra park and the lake.

Achada das Furnas★★

The **Achada valley** is an idyllic site set in a crown of hills and mountains. The best views of it are from the Pico do Ferro and Salto do Cavalo belvederes. The name Furnas derives from the hollows in the ground from which spurt hot springs and sulphurous, bubbling mud geysers that can be seen from a distance by their jets of steam. The vegetation surrounding the charming, whitewashed town of Furnas is exceptionally luxuriant thanks to the area's warm, moist soil and the humidity.

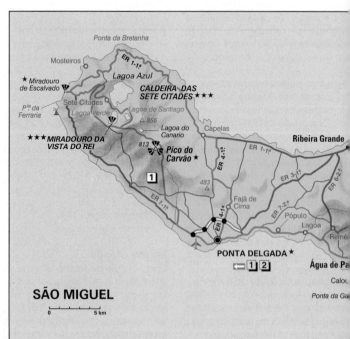

SÃO MIGUEL

Furnas

Furnas is very popular for its waters, which are used in the treatment of respiratory ailments, rheumatism and depression. You can book a treatment here, ideal also for easing aches and pains and an overall detox.

Caldeiras★★

The sulphurous waters in the area with their volcanic eruptions and vapours boil at temperatures of around 100°C/212°F. Known as *caldeiras*, the geysers punctuate the landscape with their boiling water from deep in the earth.

Parque Terra Nostra★★

🕐 *Open 9am–5.30pm.* ⊜€4. ☎296 58 47 06.

The park contains a diverse range of plant species with hibiscus, azaleas, hydrangeas and tropical plants and flowers thriving in the shade beneath Japanese larches. The avenues are bordered by magnificent royal palms.

Excursions from Furnas

Ribeira Quente

8km/5mi from Furnas.

The road between Furnas and Ribeira Quente is one of the most attractive on the island. At a point between two tunnels an impressive waterfall cascades down to the right. The village of Ribeira Quente (Hot River) is mainly known for its beach warmed by the hot springs after which the place is named.

Lagoa das Furnas

3.5km/2mi along the Ponta Delgada road.

Clouds of steam rising up from the northwest shores of the lake at the foot of steep slopes mark the presence of geysers. The warm earth has been hollowed out and cemented to form underground ovens with large wooden lids. Traditionally the villagers would cook their food in this way, burying the pots for hours on end while the meat and fish gently simmered in the hot earth.

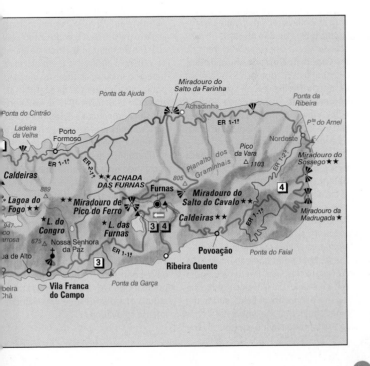

③ From Furnas to Ponta Delgada

52km/32mi – 3hr

▶ *Leave Furnas on the Ponta Delgada road. After 16km/10mi turn right and 3km/1.8mi further on turn left. After 300m/330yd you reach a fork; turn right and continue for another 457m/550yd.*

Lagoa do Congro★

To reach Lagoa do Congro, which is an emerald green lake at the bottom of a large crater, you leave the pastureland with its hydrangea hedges and follow a footpath *(40min round trip)* that leads rapidly down the crater slopes through thick vegetation and magnificent trees. ☺Wear good walking shoes.

▶ *Return to the road and travel west for a few kilometres (couple of miles).*

Vila Franca do Campo

The town, the island's early capital, was partly destroyed by an earthquake in 1522. Facing the town is a volcanic **islet** which appeared when a crater subsided. In the town centre is a beautiful square with a public garden dominated by the Gothic **Igreja de São Miguel**.
Standing on a rise above Vila Franca is the **Capela de Nossa Senhora da Paz**, a chapel that is approached by a flight of steps rather like a small-scale version of that of Bom Jesus at Braga. There is a fine **view**★ of the coast, Vila Franca and the sea of white hothouses in which pineapples are ripened.
Once past the long **Água do Alto beach** turn south to the headland, **Ponta da Galera**, with the delightful little harbour of Caloura and attractive holiday homes.

Água de Pau

Follow the signs to Ermita and Miradouro (20min round trip on foot).
The lookout point gives an interesting **view**★, to one side, Ponta da Caloura and a volcanic cone covered right to the top in a patchwork of fields, and to the other, the hermitage which stands out against a mountain background. The road continues along the coast past a series of beaches including those of Lagoa and Pópulo to Ponta Delgada.

④ The East of the Island from Furnas

85km/53mi – about 4hr

The road climbs from Furnas eastwards onto the Graminhais plateau. There is a beautiful view of the Furnas valley from **Miradouro de Salto do Cavalo**★★. The road continues to the **Salto da Farinha** belvedere beyond Salga, which affords a good view of the north coast.

The East Coast★★

The eastern part of the island has a strikingly beautiful coastline. In most parts it's rocky with some wonderful places to stop and look out over the sea though none of the other islands is visible from this side of the island – Santa Maria is too far south. The most spectacular views are from viewing points on the cliffs south of the village of Nordeste: **Miradouro do Sossego**★★ and **Miradouro da Madrugada**★. Along much of this coast cliffs drop sheer to the sea. Beyond Miradouro da Madrugada a narrow winding road 2km/1.2mi long leads to the beach at Lombo Gordo. This coast is dominated by **Pico da Vara**: at 1 100m/3 600ft, it is the high point here and makes a wonderful viewing point. It is also the site of a terrible air crash. On 27 October 1949 an Air France Constellation aircraft flying from New York to Paris was attempting to land at Ponta Delgada to refuel, but on its third attempt to land in bad weather, it crashed into the mountain, killing everyone on board. Among them was Marcel Cerdan, the world middleweight boxing champion who was the lover of Edith Piaf.

Povoação

This is the first place on the island to have been settled (*povoação* means population). The village stands at the mouth of a picturesque valley under intense cultivation.

TERCEIRA★★
ANGRA DO HEROÍSMO
POPULATION 68 706
MICHELIN ATLAS SPAIN & PORTUGAL P 96

Terceira, the Portuguese word for third, was the third island in the archipelago to be discovered. It is also the third largest island, after São Miguel and Pico. While its landscape is less striking than those of the other islands, Terceira is more interesting in terms of architecture, traditions and festivals.

Terceira is a tableland overlooked in the east by the Serra do Cume, the remains of Cinco Picos, the island's oldest volcano. The central area is demarcated by a vast crater known as Caldeira de Guilherme Moniz, which is surrounded by other volcanic formations. To the west is the Serra da Santa Bárbara, the island's most recent and highest (1 021m/3 350ft) volcanic cone with a wide crater. The islanders live essentially from farming, cultivating maize and vines, as well as stock rearing. Terceira is the granary of the Azores.

- **Information:** Rua Direita, 74. ☎295 213 393.
- ▶ **Orient Yourself:** The eastern-most of the five islands grouped together in the Azores – about 161km/100mi north west of São Miguel
- P **Parking:** Not too bad, even in the main town. Elsewhere, no problems.
- ⊙ **Don't Miss:** Make a special effort to seek out some of the "Impérios" – the little chapels dedicated to the Holy Spirit. You'll find them in every village.
- ⊙ **Organizing Your Time:** You'll find it beneficial to stay here a couple of nights to enjoy all this lovely island has to offer.

A Bit of History

Impérios
The Azorean tradition of the worship of the Holy Ghost is particularly strong in Terceira. Every quarter in each village has its little chapel known as an *império* or "empire" of the Holy Ghost. The chapels look like salons, their picture windows adorned with net curtains; they are maintained by brotherhoods whose chief task is to organise festivals. The festivals follow a ritual that dates back to the early days of colonisation when the islanders would call upon the Holy Ghost in times of natural disaster. They were originally intended to be charitable events and one of their main functions was to provide meals for the poor.

During today's festival an "emperor" is still elected by the people. He is presented with a sceptre and crown on a silver platter and is crowned by a priest. He is then accompanied to the *Império do Santo Espírito* where he receives the gifts to be distributed to the poor and then invites the whole village to take part in the feast which is followed by a traditional *tourada da corda* (⊙ *see below*).

The Island of Bulls
Terceira is known for its **touradas à corda** which take place during village festivals. A bull with a long rope about its neck is allowed to rush at crowds of men who jump out of the way leaving

Address Book

GETTING THERE

There are regular flights between Terceira and Lisbon, and the other islands in the archipelago.
In summer, the boat connecting the central group of islands calls at Terceira several times a week.

TOURING THE ISLAND

Allow two days to tour the island and spend some time in Angra do Heroísmo.

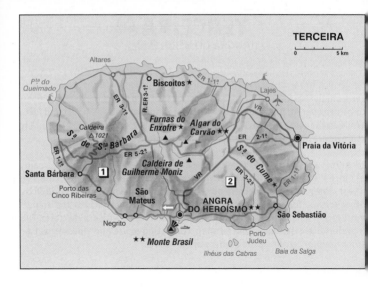

the bravest to taunt the bull by opening a large umbrella beneath its muzzle.

Angra de Heroísmo★★

The town, set in the curve of a wide bay or *angra* and dominated by Monte Brasil on a little promotory, is without doubt the most beautiful harbour in the archipelago and is home to the Minister of the Republic and to a branch of the University of the Azores.

The architecture is fascinating with a mix of Portuguese, Brazilian, English and American.

On 1 January, 1980, a violent **earthquake** shook the town and demolished a large part of it without taking any lives. In 1983 Angra do Heroísmo was given World Heritage status by UNESCO and the outstanding work carried out has since restored its former beauty.

Historical quarter

Beyond the Bahía de Angra lies the geometric street plan that follows the original layout. The houses within the square

Angra de Heroísmo

ANGRA DO HEROÍSMO		Conceição R.	10	M. Terras R. das	22
		Cons. José Silvestre Ribeiro R.	12	Miragaia R. da	24
		Covas Alto das	13	Oliveira R. da	25
Alfândega Pátio da	3	Dr Anibal Bettencourt R.	15	Palácio R. do	27
Barreiro Can. do	4	Faleiro R. do	16	San Francisco Ladeira de	29
Canos Verdes R. dos	6	Gançalo Velho Cabral R.	19	Santo Espírito R. do	30
Carreira dos Cavalos R.	7	Gaspar Corte Real Estrada	18	Velha Pr.	32
Ciprião Figueiredo R.	9	Jacome de Bruges Av.	21		

Museu de Angra	M	Palácio dos Bettencourts	P¹
Paços do Concelho	H	Palácio dos Capitães-Generais	P²

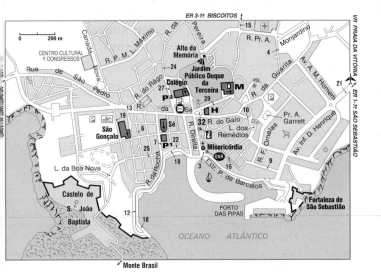

of streets bordered by the harbour, Rua Direita, Rua da Sé and Rua Gonçalo Velho, are adorned with wrought-iron balconies and window and door frames made of stone that set off the pastel colours of the façades.

Cathedral

The cathedral *(Sé)* is the Episcopal See of the Azores. Building began in 1570 on the site of a 15C church and was completed in 1618. The austere design is in keeping with the architecture prevalent during Philip II's reign. The cathedral was badly damaged by the 1980 earthquake. Inside, there is some fine carved wooden vaulting and a beautiful silver altarpiece in the chancel. The collection of 17C sculptures by Masters of the Cathedral of Angra show a Spanish and Oriental influence, a sure sign of the voyages undertaken by the Portuguese.

Palácio dos Bettencourt

Open Jul–Sept, Mon–Fri 9am–5pm; Oct–Jun, Mon–Sat 9am–7pm (noon Sat). Closed public holidays. ☎295 21 26 90/7.

The 17C Baroque mansion houses the public library and the city archives. *Azulejos* inside illustrate episodes from the history of Terceira.

Praça da Restauração or Praça Velha

The 19C **Town Hall** or Paços do Concelho looks onto the square.

Igreja do Colégio

The collegiate church was built by the Jesuits in the middle of the 17C. Of particular interest are the carved cedarwood ceiling, the delft earthenware in the sacristy and the many altarpieces and Indo-Portuguese ivory statues.

357

Palácio dos Capitães-Generais

The former Jesuit college was converted into the Palace of the Captain-Generals after the expulsion of the Society of Jesus by the Marquis of Pombal. The palace was largely rebuilt in 1980 and painted white and yellow. Today it houses the offices of the Regional Government of the Azores. It was in this palace that President Pompidou of France held a meeting with President Nixon in 1971.

Convento de São Francisco: Museu de Angra

◷Open Tue–Fri, 9.30am–noon, 2pm–5pm; Sat–Sun 2pm–5pm. ◷Closed public holidays. ✎€2 (no charge on Sun or for children under 14). ☎295 21 31 47/8.

The museum houses collections of weapons, musical instruments, ceramics, porcelain, furniture and paintings, including some 16C panels of St Catherine. The gardens are of particular interest.

Igreja de Nossa Senhora de Guia

This vast church with painted pillars forms part of the São Francisco Monastery. It was built in the 18C on the site of a chapel where Vasco da Gama buried his brother Paulo who died on his return from a voyage to the Indies.

Alto da Memória

The obelisk was erected on the site of the castle to honour Dom Pedro IV.

Castelo de São João Baptista

The fortress stands at the foot of Monte Brasil and commands the entrance to the harbour. Built during the Spanish domination of Portugal, it was first called the St Philip Fortress and is one of the largest examples of military architecture from 16C and 17C Europe. The Igreja de São Baptista inside the fortress was built by the Portuguese to celebrate the departure of the Spanish.

Monte Brasil★★

It is worth climbing to the Pico das Cruzinhas, passing the fortress of São João Baptista. There is a view of the Monte Brasil crater and an outstanding **pano-**rama★★ of Angra from the commemorative monument or *padrão*.

Fortaleza de São Sebastião

This fortress was built during the reign of King Sebastião and dominates the harbour.

Driving Tours

1 Tour of the Island: From Angra do Heroísmo

85km/53mi – Allow one day

The coast road between Angra do Heroísmo and the village of São Mateus is lined by country estates with fine houses *(quintas)*.
From the road there is a beautiful view of São Mateus.

São Mateus

The picturesque fishing village is dominated by its church, the tallest on the island. The west of the island is dotted with charming little villages such as the summer resorts of **Porto Negrito** and **Cinco Ribeiras**. There are views of the islands of Graciosa, São Jorge and Pico.

Santa Bárbara

The 15C village **church** contains a statue of St Barbara in Ançã stone (which comes from mainland Portugal).

Serra da Santa Bárbara Road

Head towards Esplanada then bear left onto a forest road which climbs to the summit.
The road affords wonderful panoramas of the island. From the top there is a view of the vast crater of the **Caldeira de Santa Bárbara**.

▶ *Return to the road, bear left, continue to the junction with the road between Angra do Heroísmo and Altares. Turn left.*

Biscoitos★

The name *biscoitos* has been given to the strangely shaped layers of lava which flowed up from the earth during volcanic eruptions and formed a lunar landscape.

Biscoitos is famous for its vines or *curraletas*, protected by stone walls beneath which they grow. A wine museum, **Museu do Vinho** (◷*open Tue–Fri 10am–noon, 1.30pm–5.30pm (4pm Oct–Mar);* ◷*closed third week of Sept;* ☏*295 90 84 04*), displays the equipment in which generations of wine-growers have made *verdelho*, a sweet aperitif wine, produced and bottled by the museum itself.

▸ *Take the Angra road from Biscoitos and bear left towards Lajes.*

The terrain in the centre of the island has suffered from volcanic upheaval which has left craters like the vast Caldeira de Guilherme Moniz.

▸ *Follow signs to Furnas do Enxofre.*

Furnas do Enxofre★ 🏃

Follow the path to the left (after taking the Estrada do Cabrito at the Pico da Bragacina crossroads) until you reach a small car park ℗. 10min round trip on foot.

You soon reach a wild landscape where fumaroles rise up from sulphur wells in the ground. The air is hot and smelly. The sulphur crystallises into beautiful bright yellow flowers; in some places a red colour dominates, spreading over the ground and rocks.

Caldeira de Guilherme Moniz

As the road descends between Furnas do Enxofre and Algar do Carvão you catch glimpses of the immense crater with its 15km/9.3mi perimeter.

Algar do Carvão★★

◷*Open Apr, May and Oct, 3pm–5.30pm; Jun and Sept, 2.30pm–5.45pm; July–Aug, 2pm–6pm.* ◉€3.50. *Contact "Os Montanheiros", Rua da Rocha 6/8 – 9700 169 Angra do Heroísmo.* ☏*295 21 29 92.*

A tunnel some 45m/50yd long leads to the base of a volcanic chimney, a sort of moss-covered well of light 45m/148ft high. You continue down into an enormous cave which was formed by escaping gases when the lava cooled. Above is a series of majestic overlapping arches of different colours: beige, obsidian black and ochre. Several siliceous concretions have formed milky-white umbrella shapes on the cave walls. The arches can be seen reflected in a pool.

▸ *The road connects with the Via Rápida which leads back to Angra do Heroísmo. One can also follow itinerary ② in the opposite direction to return to Angra.*

②From Angra do Heroísmo to Praia da Vitória

35km/22mi – 2hr

The strange rocks, Ilhéus Cabras, a short distance beyond Angra, look as though they have been sawn through the middle.

São Sebastião

The village was the first site to be settled on the island and has preserved some old monuments.

Igreja de São Sebastião★

The Gothic church built in 1455 has a graceful doorway and chapels with Manueline and Renaissance vaulting. The nave has some interesting 16C frescoes, illustrating on the left, the Last Judgement, and on the right, St Martin, St Mary Magdalene and St Sebastian set in a medieval castle.

Opposite the church is the **Império do Espírito Santo** decorated with romantic paintings.

▸ *Beyond São Sebastião take ER 3.2 left to Serra do Cume, then a road right which climbs to the top.*

Serra do Cume★

The gentle slopes of this eroded volcano form a patchwork of fields divided by low stone walls where Dutch cows can be seen grazing. At certain times of the day, particularly in the evening, the countryside takes on a lush bucolic air.

Praia da Vitória

The "Praia" in the name derives from the beautiful white sand **beach** which stretches the full length of the bay, and the "da Vitória" commemorates the battle in 1829 between Liberals and supporters of Dom Miguel. The Lajes air base nearby, which was established by the British in 1943 and enlarged by the Americans in 1944, was used extensively during and after World War II as a refuelling stop on the transatlantic routes. Praia da Vitória is a lively place when the weather is fine and the beach and the surrounding cafés fill with people. The town centre has been preserved and has a 16C **Town Hall** and an old church.

Parish church

This large church was founded by Jacomo de Bruges, the island's first donee-captain. Its main doorway, a gift from the King, Dom Manuel, is Gothic in style, while another portal, a side entrance, is Manueline. The rich interior decoration includes *azulejos* and gilt altarpieces.

GRACIOSA★
ANGRA DO HEROÍSMO
POPULATION 6 966 – MICHELIN ATLAS SPAIN & PORTUGAL P 96

Graciosa – the "graceful" island – is the second-smallest island after Corvo and has the lowest altitude (the highest point, Pico Timão, rises to just 398m/1 306ft). The whole of the eastern part of the island is occupied by a vast crater. Graciosa or "gracious" island owes its name to its attractive main town, Santa Cruz, its countryside of well-tended vineyards and fields of maize, and its villages bright with flowers set at the foot of gently rolling hills dotted with windmills. These Dutch-style windmills with their red, pointed, onion-shaped tops that pivot in the direction of the wind are a rather surprising feature of the island's landscape. There are not so many as there once were but they are still an interesting feature and would make a good subject for a painting.

🅸 **Information:** Praça Fontes Pereira de Melo, Santa Cruz. ☎295 71 25 09.
▶ **Orient Yourself:** A small island just north of São Jorge and Pico.
🅶 **Don't Miss:** The caves at Furna de Enxofre.
🕐 **Organizing Your Time:** Being such a small island, a day tour will suffice.

Windmill in Graciosa

Azores Convention and Visitors Bureau

Santa Cruz da Graciosa★ *Population 2 000*

Santa Cruz is a delightful small town with its bright white house façades set off by volcanic stone and several older fishermen's cottages. There are also two small reservoirs in the town, originally intended to provide drinking water for cattle, though today they just reflect some lovely views and provide a nice change of colour.

Churches

Built in the 16C and reconstructed two centuries later the **Igreja de Santa Cruz** has some **panels**★ at the high altar illustrate the Holy Cross. A chapel has Flemish statues of St Peter and St

Anthony. See also the **Santo Cristo** church, and the **Nossa Senhora da Ajuda** (Our Lady of Charity), **São João** and **São Salvador** Chapels along with the **Cruz da Barra** (Iron Cross).

Museu Etnográfico

Guided tours, summer: Tue–Fri 9.30am–12.30pm, 2pm–5pm; winter: Tue–Fri 10am–noon, 2pm–5.30pm. €1 (no charge for senior citizens or students). ☎295 71 24 29.

The collections housed in a former mansion show traditional island life through various displays including tools, clothes and pottery as well as items from the cultivation of wine.

Ermidas do Monte da Ajuda

The three hermitages devoted to São João, São Salvador and **Nossa Senhora da Ajuda** dominate the town. There is a beautiful **view**★ of Santa Cruz.

Excursions

Farol da Ponta da Barca★

4.5km/3mi west of Santa Cruz.
There is a view from the lighthouse of the headland of red rocks plunging to a bright blue sea.

Praia

The old village stretches along its harbour and the beach after which it is named.

Furna do Enxofre★★

Guided tours, Tue–Sun 11am–4pm. €0.50. ☎295 71 21 25 or 295 73 00 40. *The best time to visit is from 11am to 2pm when the sun shines into the cave.*
Furna de Enxofre is in the middle of a vast caldeira or crater. A tunnel has been dug through one of the sides of the crater giving access by car. Once inside the crater the road zigzags down to the entrance of the chasm. From here a path and then a spiral staircase lead down to

the chasm. The cave itself is immense and contains a lake of hot sulphurous water.

Furna Maria Encantada

Leave the caldeira. Once through the tunnel take the first road left. About 91.4m/100yd further on there is a sign on the right to Furna de Maria Encantada. A path reinforced by logs leads up to a rock above the road (5min).
A natural tunnel in the rock about ten yards long opens onto the crater with a good overall view.
The road continues around the crater. There are views over Graciosa island with Terceira in the distance.

Carapacho

Carapacho is a small spa as well as a seaside resort. The hot springs that rise from the sea-bed are used for therapeutic purposes, particularly in the treatment of rheumatism.

Address Book

GETTING THERE

There are regular flights between Terceira and Graciosa and boat connections (3hr) between the two islands several times a week.

TOURING THE ISLAND

You can tour the island in a few hours although it is pleasant to spend time strolling through Santa Cruz or driving along narrow country roads.

FAIAL★★★
HORTA
POPULATION 14 920, MICHELIN ATLAS SPAIN & PORTUGAL P 96

The blue island, as Faial is also known, owes its name to the mass of hydrangeas that flower there in season. There is a magnificent view from Faial of Pico's volcano, while Faial itself has some interesting volcanic features such as the Caldeira crater and the Capelinhos volcano. The island's particular charm derives from Horta, the main town and harbour, its attractive villages, windmills and beaches (Porto Pim, Praia do Almoxarife and Praia do Fajã).

🅸 **Information:** Rua Vasco da Gama, Horta. ☎292 292 237.
▶ **Orient Yourself:** Just west of Pico, on the edge of the main group of islands.
😊 **Don't Miss:** The volcano – it's spectacular!
🕐 **Organizing Your Time:** Stay a night and get to know this peaceful island.

A Bit of History

Capelinhos, the birth of a volcano
The headland on the west of the island is covered in ashes from Capelinhos, the volcano that rose up from the depths of the ocean in 1957. On 27 September, there was a huge eruption under the sea accompanied by gaseous emissions and clouds of steam that reached a height of 4 000m/13 123ft. A first islet surfaced only to disappear a short time afterwards. Then a second islet-volcano formed and was joined to Faial by an isthmus of lava and ash. For thirteen months, until 24 October 1958, volcanic

activity continued in the form of underwater explosions, lava flows, eruptions and showers of ash that covered the village of Capelo and the lighthouse. As Capelinhos volcano rose, so the water level of the lake inside Faial's crater or caldeira, fell. By the end of the eruption the volcano had increased the size of Faial by 2.4sq km/0.9sq mi, although marine erosion has since reduced this to 1sq km/0.38sq mi.

Horta★

Horta stretches out alongside a bay that forms one of the rare sheltered anchor-

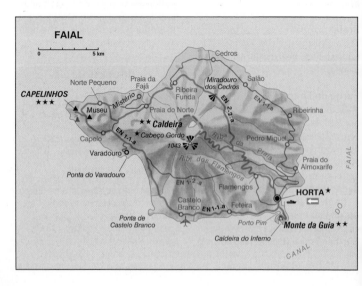

ages in the archipelago. Anglo-Saxon influence is apparent in Horta's architecture. This heritage comes down from the **Dabneys**, a family of wealthy American traders in the 19C. When they left, American presence in Faial continued through transatlantic cable companies. In the 1930s, Faial was a port of call and a refuelling station for sea-planes and it was not uncommon to see one or more of these in Horta harbour.

Marina da Horta★

The marina is where yachtsmen on their journeys across the Atlantic congregate. It has become a kind of open-air art gallery since each crew leaves a visual trace of its stay, otherwise, as the superstition goes, some mishap will befall it.

Historic quarter

The quarter is dominated by the imposing façades of its churches which face the sea. It comprises the area around **Rua Conselheiro Medeiros**, **Rua W. Bensaúde** and **Rua Serpa Pinto** which are lined with 18C and 19C shops and houses surmounted with unusual wooden upper storeys. This main thoroughfare leads to **Praça da República**, a charming square. The striking façade of the **Sociedade Amor da Pátria** building, dating from 1930 and decorated with a frieze of blue hydrangeas, can be seen in the northeast corner of the square on Rua Ernesto Rebelo.

Igreja Matriz de São Salvador

This vast 18C church, which formerly belonged to the Jesuit College, has some fine *azulejos* and interesting Baroque furniture. The **Nossa Senhora das Angústias** (Our Lady of Anguish), the **Nossa Senhora do Carmo** (Our Lady of Carmo), and the Church of St.Francis which is presently integrated with the **Museu Arte Sacra** Museum and the Horta Museum (*see below*) are also worth a visit as you wander round this peaceful town.

Museu da Horta

Guided tours 10am–12.30pm, 2pm–5.30pm. €2. 292 29 33 48.
The museum housed in the former Jesuit College, traces the history of the town, in

Address Book

GETTING THERE

There are direct flights from Lisbon to Horta and regular flights between Faial and the other islands. Boats connect Faial and the port of Madalena on Pico island (30min) several times a day, and Faial, São Jorge and Terceira several times a week in summer.

TOURING THE ISLAND

Allow at least two days to fully explore Horta and enjoy a relaxing tour of the island.

particular the laying of the underwater cables. There is also a collection of **miniatures made of fig-tree pith**★ carved by Euclíades Rosa between 1940 and 1960.

Forte de Santa Cruz

The fort was begun in the 16C, enlarged at a later date and now houses an inn.

"Chez Peter" Café

The café, a popular meeting place for visiting yachtsmen, contains the **Museu do Scrimshaw** (*guided tours, 9am–noon, 2pm–5pm; closed 1 Jan and 25 Dec; €1.50; 292 29 23 27*). Among the items on display are sperm-whale teeth engraved by whalers and newer portraits of well-known yachtsmen such as Sir Francis Chichester and the Frenchman Eric Tabarly.

Marina da Horta

Azores Convention and Visitors Bureau

Monte da Guia

A road leads up to the summit of Monte da Guia.

Horta bay is sheltered by two volcanoes linked to the mainland by isthmuses. The first volcano, Monte Queimado, dominates the harbour and is linked by an isthmus to the second, Monte da Guia. From the top of Monte da Guia, beside the **Ermida de Nossa Senhora da Guia**, there is a view of **Caldeira do Inferno**, a former crater that has been filled in by the sea.

As you return to Horta there is a good **view**★ of the town and the beach at Porto Pim inlet which was originally protected by fortifications – **Portão fortificado do Porto Paim** (large iron gate of Porto Paim); and the **Muralhas de São Sebastião** (walls of St.Sebastian).

It is also worth taking a little detour to climb to the top of Mount Carneiro from where you have some wonderful views over the Flamengos valley and, in the opposite direction, of the island of Pico, its volcano standing proudly against the blue sky.

Driving Tour

Tour of the Island

80km/50mi from Horta – allow 5hr.

▶ *Take the airport road from Horta and drive along the southwest coast.*

The road leads past **Castelo Branco** headland, named on account of its white cliffs, and continues to **Varadouro**, a small spa.

▶ *Follow signs to Capelinhos.*

Cross Capelo village with the ruins of houses destroyed by Capelinhos in 1957.

Capelinhos★★★

The best way to explore the volcano is to see it on foot. Park below the lighthouse and then allow for a walk of at least 1hr.

The landscape of the volcano, so recent it is still devoid of vegetation, is fascinating. The volcano's structure, with its ash, bombs (solidified lava) and scoria, is gradually being eroded by the sea, and the different mineral colours of ochre, red and black stand out.

Before reaching the lighthouse, you arrive at a house that has been rebuilt and now contains a **museum** (*open summer: Mon–Fri 10am–12.30pm, 2.30pm–5.30pm, Sat–Sun 2.30pm–5.30pm; winter: 10am–noon, 2pm–5pm, Sat–Sun 2.30pm–5.30pm; closed public*

Capelinhos volcano

After a 3hr climb you reach the crater, which is 30m/98ft deep. It is impressive – a bare landscape forming a circle with a 700m/2 297ft perimeter. **Pico Pequeno** (70m/230ft) rises at the far end to form the mountain summit. The fumaroles and smell of sulphur at the top act as a reminder that a volcano is never completely dormant. On a clear day the **panorama**★★★ takes in São Jorge island and Faial island with its volcano, Capelinhos. In the far distance are Graciosa and Terceira.

On the way back to Madalena, the cave at **Furnas de Frei Matias** *(5min walk)* has a series of long underground galleries stretching out between mossy wells of light.

Driving Tour of the Island

1 From Madalena to São Roque *28km/17mi – 2hr*

Madalena

The harbour is protected by two rocks, Em Pé (meaning upright) and Deitado (meaning recumbent), which are home

😊 A Bit of Advice 😊

Access: There is a boat shuttle service between Horta on Faial and Madalena on Pico several times a day. In summer, boats call in at Cais do Pico from Terceira and São Jorge several times a week. There are also flights to Pico.

Length of stay: It is possible to tour Pico island in a day from Faial. However, if you wish to climb the volcano, allow at least one night on the island.

to colonies of sea birds. Madalena is a pleasant little town centred around the **Igreja de Santa Maria Madalena**.

Cachorro★

After Bandeiras bear left off the main road and follow the signs.

The small village built of lava stretches out behind the airport landing strips beside black rocks and cliffs. These have been eroded into caves into which the sea rushes and roars.

The road continues through the villages of **Santa Luzia** and **Santo António**, where the plain-looking church contains a naïve Baroque altarpiece.

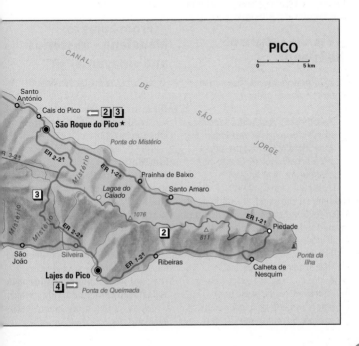

Convento and Igreja de São Pedro de Alcântara

The Baroque building has an interesting façade and, inside, the chancel is adorned with *azulejos* and an abundantly decorated altarpiece.

Igreja de São Roque

The church is a large 18C building decorated inside with statues, jacaranda wood furniture inlaid with ivory, and a silver lamp donated by Dom João V.

From São Roque to Lajes do Pico

There are two possible itineraries:

②Via the Coast

50km/31mi, allow 2hr 30min.

This itinerary is for those who have the time and who don't mind winding roads.

The villages along this route include **Prainha**, which is well-known for its *mistério*, **Santo Amaro** with its shipbuilding yard, and **Piedade** and the attractive countryside at the end of the island. The itinerary continues along the southeast coast and the fishing villages of **Calheta de Nesquim** and **Ribeiras**.

③Via the Centre of the Island

32km/20mi including an excursion to Lagoa do Caiado – allow 1hr.

▶ *Take the Lajes road which soon rises to cross the centre of the island. After 10km/6.2mi take the road left marked Lagoa do Caiado and continue for 5km/3mi.*

The centre of the island, at an altitude of 800m–1 000m/2 625ft–3 280ft, is often covered in cloud. There are a good many small crater lakes and the vegetation consists of strange low plants, some of which are indigenous species.

▶ *A road crosses the island from east to west affording good views of beautiful countryside (if one is*

lucky enough to be travelling on a clear day). After visiting Lagoa do Caiado, return to the main road and continue towards Lajes.

Lajes do Pico

This was the first settlement on the island. The main activity from the 19C, up until 1981, was whaling. Lajes, a small, quiet, white town in the middle of maize fields, extends into a lava plateau known as a Fajã (see SÃO JORGE).

Museu dos Baleeiros ★

Open Tue–Fri 9.30am–12.30pm, 2pm–5.30pm (5pm Oct–Apr), Sat–Sun 2pm–5.30pm (5pm Oct–Apr). Closed public holidays. 292 67 22 76.

The whaling museum is housed in a former boat shelter in the harbour. The fine **scrimshaw collection** contains engraved sperm-whale teeth and ivory walrus tusks.

Ermida de São Pedro

By continuing along the quayside you arrive at a white chapel, the oldest on the island, with an attractive altarpiece. Beside the chapel stands the **Padrão** monument, which commemorates the five-hundredth anniversary of the settlement of the island.

④From Lajes to Madalena – Mistérios and vineyards★★

35km/22mi – allow 1hr 30min.

The road crosses the *misterios* on either side of **São João** which date from an eruption in 1718.

São Mateus

The village is dominated by its impressive church.

The road passes through vineyards closed off by low lava walls. The countryside is striking with the black of the lava walls contrasting sharply with the soft green of the abandoned vines and the deep blue of the sea beyond.

The road passes through **Candelaria** and **Criação Velha**, the village in which *verdelho* wine originated, before reaching Madalena.

SÃO JORGE ★★
HORTA
POPULATION 10 219 – MICHELIN ATLAS SPAIN & PORTUGAL P 96

The cigar-shaped island stretches out parallel to Pico. Its wild, grandiose landscapes make a splendid environment for walking.

- **Information:** Rua Conselheiro Dr. José Pereira – 9800-530, Velas. ☎295 41 24 40.
- ▶ **Orient Yourself:** Almost at the centre of the main group of islands.
- ⏰ **Organizing Your Time:** One day is fine to see everything.
- **Don't Miss:** The Pico da Esperança, the centre of the island.
- ⏰ **Organizing Your Time:** Allow a full day to tour the island by car. .

Velas

Velas has preserved several old buildings including the 18C **Paços do Concelho** (Town Hall), of Azorean Baroque style with twisted columns on either side of its doorway, and the 18C **Portas do Mar**, a gateway remaining from the old ramparts. The 16C church of São Jorge has an interesting façade.

From Velas to Ponta dos Rosais
14km/9mi west.
The road runs alongside Baía de Entre-Morros, crosses the village of Rosais and continues to **Sete Fontes**, an attractive forest. You can continue to Ponta da Rosais by car although it is better to walk (*2hr 30min round trip*). There are fine views of both sides of the island. At the headland there is a lighthouse.

Driving Tour of the Island ★★

83km/52mi – 4hr

The North Coast

▶ *Take the Santo António road out of Velas.*

Fajã do Ouvidor ★★
The *fajã* with its hamlet is the largest on the north coast with a bird's eye view of a flat stretch of land covered in cultivated fields and houses, dominated by a sheer cliff.

Address Book

GETTING THERE
There are flights between São Jorge and the other islands throughout the year. In summer, the boat that serves the islands in the central group of the archipelago calls at São Jorge several times a week.

Miradouro da Fajã dos Cubres ★★
The landscape viewed from this lookout point, on the road beyond Norte Pequeno, is highly characteristic of São Jorge. The most impressive, **Fajã da Caldeira do Santo Cristo**, is occupied by a lagoon that has been made into a nature reserve to protect its clams, a particular type of scallop-shell only found here.

View from the Miradouro da Fajã dos Cubres

B. Brillon/MICHELIN

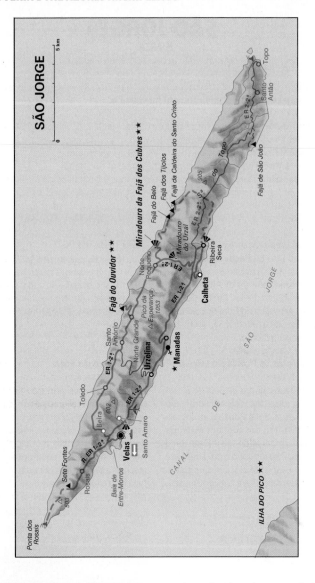

The road from the north coast to Ribeira Seca village on the south, crosses beautiful woodland criss-crossed by hedges of hydrangeas. The **view**★★ from the **Miradouro de Urzal** is good.

Manadas

The picturesque hamlet is known for its **Igreja de Santa Bárbara**★ (guided tours, Mon–Fri 9am–12.30pm, 2pm–5pm). It dates from the 18C and is one of the prettiest churches in the Azores. The finely worked **cedarwood ceiling**★ is adorned with sculptures including St George slaying the dragon. The *azulejos* tell the story of St Barbara.

Urzelina

The village, rebuilt after the volcanic eruption in 1808, was named after the island's brown lichen or orchil *(urzela)*. A tower emerges out of the lava beneath which the church lies buried. Small windmills still functioning beside the shore stand out against Pico island in the background.

FLORES★★
HORTA
POPULATION 4 329 – MICHELIN ATLAS SPAIN & PORTUGAL P 96

The island of flowers is the most westerly of the Azorean islands and the west-ernmost point in Europe. Along with its sister Corvo, Flores lies at quite some distance from the other islands in the archipelago. It is 236km/147mi from Faial. Flores is thinly populated, very rugged and its wild landscapes are among the most majestic in the Azores. Its luxuriant vegetation is explained by the very high rainfall; it rains on average nearly 300 days a year.

- 🗊 **Information:** Câmara Municipal, Santa Cruz das Flores. ☎292 592 369.
- ▶ **Orient Yourself:** This really is the western-most tip of Europe.
- 🕙 **Don't Miss:** The Convent and the Church of Christ (Igreja do Senhor Santo Cristo).
- 🕙 **Organizing Your Time:** This island can be seen in one day though if you are also planning to see Corvo you will need to book a couple of nights' accom-modation and take the boat to Corvo, which is a day trip.

Santa Cruz das Flores

Santa Cruz is a quiet, pleasant town with a small harbour.

Museu Etnográfico
🕙*Open Mon–Fri 9am–noon, 2pm–5pm.* 🕙*Closed public holidays. Call for admis-sion prices.* ☎*292 59 21 59.*
The museum, set up in an old house, dis-plays several reconstituted interiors of traditional homes as well as a collection of items illustrating the inhabitants' way of life on the island. This was centred around fishing and whaling – there are some scrimshaw pieces – and work in the fields.

Convento de São Boaventura
The 17C building, once a Franciscan monastery, has been restored to house part of the museum. The Baroque chan-cel in the church shows a Hispano-Mexi-can influence.

Driving Tour of the Island★★

68km/42mi – about 4hr

- ▶ *Take the Lajes road out of Santa Cruz.*

The road twists and turns with the relief, dipping into deep ravines and running alongside mountain ridges with superb views above the banks of bright red and yellow cannas and blue hydrangeas that line it.

Fazenda das Lajes
The **Igreja do Senhor Santo Cristo**, with its *azulejo* decoration on the façade, is one of the most representative exam-ples of Azorean religious architecture.

Lajes
The island's second-largest town thrives on its harbour activities and a major radio station.

- ▶ *Once past Lajes, take the road south. Turn right towards Lagoa Funda.*

Lagoa Funda★★
Lagoa Funda, meaning deep lake, is a crater lake that stretches for several kilo-

---

Address Book

GETTING THERE
Flores is only accessible by air from the other islands.

TOURING THE ISLAND
It is possible to tour the island in a day although it is well worth taking the time to explore Flores on foot. An extra day is required for an excursion to the island of Corvo.

Take the Mosteiro road.

The road passes **Mosteiro**, set in enchanting countryside with the sea in the background.

A little farther on, take the road to Fajãzinha and Fajã Grande.

Fajãzinha
As the road approaches Fajãzinha there is a beautiful **view**★★ of the village. The **Igreja de Nossa Senhora dos Remédios** dates from the 18C. The 300m/984ft Ribeira Grande waterfall is in the vicinity.

metres below the road. After 3km/1.8mi you reach an area where, to the right, and at a great depth, you can see the end of Lagoa Funda and, to the left, at road level, **Lagoa Rasa**.

Return to the road; 600m/660yd beyond the 25km marker, look up to admire the Rocha dos Bordões rock formation.

Rocha dos Bordões★★
Masses of flowers can be seen bursting from basalt organ pipes. These high, vertical stria were formed when the basalt solidified.

Waterfall
Turn right towards Ponta da Fajã. Continue for 400m/440yd and stop at the first bridge. Take the track on the left of the bridge as you stand looking towards the cliff. 🚶20min round trip on foot.
The track follows the stream and passes three water-mills. The waterfall plunges from the top of the cliff onto a ledge where it divides into a multitude of smaller cascades.

Return to the main road and head for Santa Cruz. Turn left towards the lakes.

Fajãzinha

CORVO ★
HORTA
POPULATION 393 – MICHELIN ATLAS SPAIN & PORTUGAL P 96

A large, black, sea-battered rock rises out of the water 15 nautical miles north-east of Flores. This is Crow Island, the visible part of Monte Gordo (718m/2 356ft), a marine volcano. As there is no protected bay, access is difficult. In 1452, Corvo was the last of the islands in the archipelago to display the Portuguese flag and settlement began only in the middle of the 16C. A remote community of farmers and herders began to develop. In winter, for weeks on end, it was impossible for boats to dock so communication with Flores was made through lighting fires on a hill.

- **Information:** Enquire on Flores as there is no information office on Corvo.
- ▶ **Orient Yourself:** The most northwesterly island, just above Flores.
- **Don't Miss:** The Caldeirão.
- **Organizing Your Time:** Plan no more than half a day to see the Caldeirão. The only practicable way to see the island is to take a day trip by boat from Flores, taking you back the same afternoon.

Sights

Vila Nova do Corvo
The **Igreja de Nossa Senhora dos Milagres** has preserved a 16C Flemish statue. Vila Nova do Corvo may well be the smallest and least populated district in Portugal, yet it possesses an airport. Walk alongside the landing strip and you reach some disused windmills and a restaurant.

Caldeirão★
6km/3.7mi from Vila Nova. The volcanic crater may be visited any time, free of charge.
You might be able to hitch a lift (ask at the town's restaurant, the only one on the island) with one of the locals to the Caldeirão, which is also accessible on foot along the road. *(3hr round trip).* There is a difference in altitude of 550m/1 804ft. Bring warm clothes as the uplands are often covered in cloud and can be cool. The road crosses beautiful countryside brightened by hedges of hydrangeas. The crater has a perimeter of 3.4km/2mi and is 300m/984ft deep, in the bottom of which are two blue lakes with two islets at the bottom. Tradition has it that these islets have the same lay-out as the islands in the Azores (without Flores and Corvo). The slopes of the crater were once cultivated.

Address Book

GETTING THERE
The only way of visiting Corvo is on a day trip from Flores as there is no accommodation on the island for visitors. The boat leaves Santa Cruz harbour at 10am, arrives at Corvo at noon and returns between 4pm–6pm depending on sea conditions. It is advisable to book in advance once you arrive in Flores as the boat only holds 20 passengers. Make sure you return by the same boat you came on. Cost is €20 return.

Countryside with hydragea hedges

Azores Convention and Visitors Bureau

INDEX

INDEX

MAPS AND PLANS

LIST OF MAPS

COMPANION PUBLICATIONS

MAP OF PORTUGAL NO 733

◆ a 1:400 000 scale map of Portugal showing the Portuguese road network, the sites and monuments described in this guide, in addition to a detailed index of place names

MAP OF NORTH WEST SPAIN NO 571 (GALICIA, ASTURIAS-LEÓN)

◆ a 1:400 000 scale map of northwest Spain and the northern half of Portugal

SPAIN/PORTUGAL ROAD ATLAS

◆ a useful 1:400 000 scale, spiral-bound atlas with a full index of place names and numerous town plans

SPAIN/PORTUGAL MAP NO 734

◆ a 1:1 000 000 scale map of the Iberian Peninsula

WWW.VIAMICHELIN.COM

◆ Michelin offers motorists a complete route planning service (fastest, shortest etc) on its comprehensive web site

Abbreviations

G   District government office
(Governo civil)

H   Town Hall (Câmara municipal)

J   Law courts
(Palácio de justiça)

M   Museum (Museu)

POL.   Police (Polícia)

T   Theatre (Teatro)

U   University (Universidade)

Selected monuments and sights

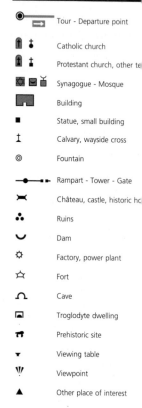

Tour - Departure point

Catholic church

Protestant church, other te[...]

Synagogue - Mosque

Building

Statue, small building

Calvary, wayside cross

Fountain

Rampart - Tower - Gate

Château, castle, historic ho[...]

Ruins

Dam

Factory, power plant

Fort

Cave

Troglodyte dwelling

Prehistoric site

Viewing table

Viewpoint

Other place of interest

Special symbols

Portuguese National Police
(Guarda Nacional Republicana)

Pousada
(Hotel managed by the State)

LEGEND

	Sight	Seaside resort	Winter sports resort	Spa
Highly recommended ★★★	☆☆☆	✳✳✳	‡‡‡
Recommended ★★	☆☆	✳✳	‡‡
Interesting ★	☆	✳	‡

Additional symbols

🄸	Tourist information
═══ ═══	Motorway or other primary route
❶ ❶	Junction: complete, limited
⊏══⊐ ═══	Pedestrian street
ɪ════ɪ	Unsuitable for traffic, street subject to restrictions
▭▭▭ ----	Steps – Footpath
🚆 🚉	Train station – Auto-train station
🚌 🚌	Coach (bus) station
•—•—•	Tram
Ⓜ	Metro, underground
P R	Park-and-Ride
♿	Access for the disabled
✉	Post office
☎	Telephone
▱	Covered market
⋅✗⋅	Barracks
△	Drawbridge
℧	Quarry
✗	Mine
B F	Car ferry (river or lake)
⛴	Ferry service: cars and passengers
⛴	Foot passengers only
③	Access route number common to Michelin maps and town plans
Bert (R.)...	Main shopping street
AZ B	Map co-ordinates

Sports and recreation

🏇	Racecourse
⛸	Skating rink
≋ ▱	Outdoor, indoor swimming pool
🎥	Multiplex Cinema
⛵	Marina, sailing centre
⌂	Trail refuge hut
▫–■–■–▫	Cable cars, gondolas
▫—+—+—▫	Funicular, rack railway
🚂	Tourist train
♦	Recreation area, park
⛷	Theme, amusement park
⚲	Wildlife park, zoo
❀	Gardens, park, arboretum
◉	Bird sanctuary, aviary
🚶	Walking tour, footpath
☺	Of special interest to children

Michelin Apa Publications Ltd

A joint venture between Michelin and Langenscheidt

Suite 6, Tulip House, 70 Borough High Street, London SE1 1XF, United Kingdom

No part of this publication may be reproduced in any form
without the prior permission of the publisher.

© 2009 Michelin Apa Publications Ltd
ISBN 978-1-906261-40-5
Printed: September2008
Printed and bound: Himmer, Germany